EDUCATIONAL MEDIA AND TECHNOLOGY YEARBOOK

BRENDA BRANYAN-BROADBENT and R. KENT WOOD,
Editors

EDUCATIONAL MEDIA AND TECHNOLOGY YEARBOOK

1991

VOLUME 17

Published in Cooperation with the
Association for Educational Communications
and Technology

1991

Libraries Unlimited, Inc. • Englewood, Colorado

LIBRARIES UNLIMITED, INC.
P.O. Box 3988
Englewood, CO 80155-3988

ISBN 0-87287-933-X

ISSN 8755-2094

Contents

Part Two
REPORTS FROM THE STATES

Part Three
LEADERSHIP PROFILES IN EDUCATIONAL
MEDIA AND TECHNOLOGY

Part Four
ORGANIZATIONS AND ASSOCIATIONS
IN NORTH AMERICA

Part Five
GRADUATE PROGRAMS

Part Six
MEDIAGRAPHY
Print and Nonprint Resources

Preface

The year 1990 was one of landmark events for AECT and the educational media and technology professions. AECT membership is growing, and a number of state legislatures have passed or are presently considering technology initiatives in education. As planned and mentioned in *EMTY 1990*, most of *EMTY 1991* is devoted to information about state activities and examples of state legislation.

The new decade began with a number of major changes, most notably in the areas of computer and video: educational technologists and leaders are recognizing the merging of video and computers into a unified communication and instructional system. People associated with the MIT Media Lab suggest we will soon stop making distinctions between computers and video. Desktop video (DVT) is being redefined to go far beyond producing videotapes with computer graphics; it may some day produce "virtual realities."

Perhaps one of the more anticipated events of early 1991 was the AMIGACOMM associated with the AECT/ICIA INFOCOMM™. Of great interest were the new Video Toaster associated with this event, soon-to-be-released, low-cost time-based correction computer boards, and the Interactive Video and Multimedia Conference and Showcase. The Amiga combined with the Toaster for desktop video may be a giant step toward lower-cost special effects, including titling. A 1989 Desktop Video Workshop for AECT revealed that most members view all computers as equally capable of performing the same tasks and believe that it will be only a matter of time before devices such as the Video Toaster are available for all computers. The more than five years of research and development that went into the Toaster indicate otherwise. The Amiga's compatibility with the NTSC (National Television Standard Code) makes it a unique computer video tool that will likely provide video special effects generation at a lower cost than any computer and will not require the expensive boards presently necessary for the IBM and the Mac to become color-video compatible. In looking ahead at these pending developments, it was suggested at the 1990 AECT national convention that perhaps the Toaster with the Amiga might be for Desktop Video and Presentation (DTVP) what the Mac was to desktop publishing. We will have to wait and see whether the projects are more reality than "vaporware."

During the past year new terms have been coined for recent combined video and computer technology. The **low-cost** "LC" color Mac and the remarkable Intel DVI (Digital Video Interactive) real-time video running from an IBM 750-megabyte hard disc were unveiled at COMDEX in mid-November 1990. The video camera records through the proprietary Intel Chips directly to computer **hard-disk** drive. CDTV and CDI also combine computers with video. Maybe the views of Seymour Papert and his MIT colleagues are correct about the integrated future of computers and video. The 1992 AECT theme, Capture the Vision, seems apropos as we continue into the 1990s.

Part One

Educational Media and Technology
The Year in Review

Introduction

The purpose of *EMTY*'s "The Year in Review" is to present broad overviews of the field that help provide a perspective of trends and issues concerning educational technology.

In this edition, Wood and Smellie reanalyze the position that computers should have in public education. Ely's analysis of the status of computers in schools follows. Complementing these two articles, Williams and Brown provide an agenda of research that must be undertaken if a clearer picture of the role of computers in education is to emerge.

Two articles update other technologies in the field. First, Allen provides an overview of the latest computer technology, virtualities. Wilson's analysis of the use of video technology in teacher training follows.

"The Year in Review" continues with Sayers and Miller's month-by-month time line of events and noteworthy developments in educational technology and concludes with Ainsley's review of AECT activities for 1990, a very busy year for that organization.

Educational Technology
Initiative for Change

R. Kent Wood*
*Professor of Instructional Technology and
Coordinator of Laboratory for Experimental Study of Instruction
Utah State University*

Don C. Smellie**
*Professor and Head of Instructional Technology
Utah State University*

"Knowledge will forever govern ignorance: And a people who mean to be their own governors, must arm themselves with the power which knowledge gives. A popular government without popular information, or the means of acquiring it, is but a prologue to a farce or a tragedy; or perhaps both."[1] As educators have learned, knowledge is, indeed, power. How freely and how equally citizens have access to knowledge determines the power they are able to exercise. As our need for knowledge grows, our dependence on complex sets of institutions and mechanisms to supply it becomes greater. The printed page, the television screen, and the computer terminal all supply needed information. All of these media are now major parts of the information society. Ease of access to information has already become a pressing need, and electronic access to information and knowledge is likely to become the most pressing need of the 1990s. It is within this context that educational leaders in some states have begun planning for improving access to information and knowledge through educational technology initiatives, which appear to be promising thrusts toward restructuring schools with optimized instructional design and technology.

The effectiveness of computers and related information technologies in changing educational environments is largely determined by the presence of three conditions: (1) good advance planning, (2) appropriate and extensive in-service training, and (3) easily accessible high quality courseware/software.[2] Utah is an example of a state that has implemented an educational technology act that provides the means to accomplish these three conditions with unified efforts of public and higher education agencies, as well as business and industrial corporations. With the cooperation of business and industry, this act provides some $200 million for public and higher education during the first half of the 1990s. This act appears to be the first and most extensive legislation passed by any state to upgrade education through technological applications.

*Dr. Wood is president of UCCE (Utah Council for Computers in Education, an affiliate of the International Society for Technology in Education).

**Dr. Smellie was 1988-89 president of AECT (Association for Educational Communications and Technology).

Educators generally have been slow to accept technology to improve the learning process. In 1977, the first U.S. secretary of education, Dr. Terrel H. Bell, highlighted the exceptionally slow educational changes related to technology:

> The education system is having a slow and difficult time adopting technological advances which could multiply the efficiency of instruction. Much of the task of storing and retrieving information and presenting it to students will be done by the computer. Progress toward that time is being impeded by those who warn that technology will dehumanize education. It is my view that technology will give teachers more time to meet personal and individual needs of students by taking over the information-giving function. We must somehow learn to persuade the decision makers to shake up and change our approach to teaching and learning. The potential of technology must be used to provide the nation a more effective and productive education enterprise. American Education is wobbling down electronic avenue in an oxcart![3]

It has been 13 years since Dr. Bell made that statement in a speech in Minneapolis, and in his opinion we are still wobbling as we enter the 1990s. Does anyone really believe that technology is dehumanizing? Our personal beliefs are that technology has the potential to make the learning process more humane than ever before in the history of public education! If teachers are freed from reinventing instruction, freed from always being the content person and the dispenser of information, they will have time for more one-on-one contact with learners. If we truly want to make educators more humane, then we must provide teachers with tools and resources that will deliver content more effectively so teachers can deal with learners more personally.

TECHNOLOGY IN CORPORATE AND PUBLIC EDUCATION

As education in the information society proceeds into an uncertain future, changes will continue. Educational technology provides an initiative for change. New roles for educators emerge in the application of instructional design and technology. Educators are having to rethink their traditional roles and how new technology will be utilized in the teaching/learning process. Even business leaders are discovering the necessity for employing educators who have instructional technology backgrounds. In his book *Education America: Lessons Learned in the Nation's Corporations*, Jack Bowsher, former director of education for IBM, called instructional design technologists the "Educational Architects of the Future."[4] He suggested that in the future there will be new career paths for educators. He describes, in some detail, instructional design and technology applications at IBM and suggests that professional educators who have built the existing courses and programs in most organizations probably constitute too small a group to deal with the explosive growth that will occur in the 1990s and beyond. He states that there are real needs to develop outstanding educators who will have long careers both as instructors and course developers in industry. Because education plays a critical role in helping a business meet strategic and tactical objectives, the education department in corporations is challenged to maintain a high level of staff competency and vitality as the pace of change quickens and the organization's dynamics become more complex. In 1986, IBM discovered it was spending $900 million a year on employee education without any central management. It was Jack Bowsher, director of education for external programs, whose two-year study revealed these facts. That discovery led to a major restructuring of IBM education, tied training directly to jobs, and streamlined delivery with big doses of instructional design and advanced technology.

Education at IBM is on the move. It has jumped to the top of the company management hierarchy, joining other key business functions, such as manufacturing and finance, that report directly to the top-ranking management committee. It is also heading rapidly out of the classroom into the world of advanced technology. Those two changes—a central role for education at a high corporate level and more technology for delivering it—are good predictors of what could happen in other large companies interested in a high-quality return from their big-ticket training expenses. The yearly education budget of $900 million includes the costs of the people, equipment, and facilities needed to deliver the training but does not include salaries of the trainees.[5]

Colleges of education, as well as the public schools, have been confronted with tremendous challenges in the past decade, including eroding economic factors, declining public support, and quality faculty leaving the teaching profession for higher-paying careers. Some individuals are questioning the need for teacher certification and whether colleges of education should even exist in the future. We believe colleges of education should exist but must broaden their base and begin immediately to prepare a new type of teacher. This teacher should be more a facilitator of the learning process than a dispenser of information. Teachers must be provided with and taught to manage well-validated interactive learning materials to help slow down the amount of instruction that is reinvented.

REINVENTING INSTRUCTION: NEW TOOLS NEEDED FOR TEACHING

For nearly 200 years, teachers in America have been reinventing instruction. Dr. Robert Heinich, in his article "The Proper Study of Instructional Technology," said that "the economy of American education is based on the reinventing of instruction each year."[6] Educators and the taxpayers can no longer afford this false economy. The idea of putting 35 young people in a room, only giving the teacher a textbook and piece of chalk, and expecting positive results is ludicrous. Dr. William Ridley, former vice president of Control Data Corporation, said, "We tell teachers to deal with individuals and then we put them into an environment that makes it impossible."[7]

Some instruction simply does not need to be reinvented by hundreds of teachers all over America staying up all night cutting paper plates and string trying to figure out a way to explain fractions each time they are taught. There are now storage and delivery tools that in combination with well-designed and validated courseware have the capability of presenting instruction to students that results in more learning in less time, with greater retention. We have personally witnessed laser-based videodisc math and science programs that combine the best teaching methods with outstanding content generated by the best minds in America and result in student mastery of the material at levels significantly higher than most teachers can achieve using traditional techniques.

These tools change the role of the teacher from dispenser of information to facilitator of the learning process. Our teachers deserve these tools, and yet we are slow to provide them. Educational administrators must get used to paying more for quality courseware. They must also invest more of the school's financial resources in well-designed learning materials rather than in salaries. These are tough decisions that are sometimes perceived as extremely threatening to faculty who fear being replaced by technology. There is a saying that "if people think they can be replaced by technology, they should be." However, good teachers have no fear of being replaced by technology. We do not think anyone really believes that technology can or should replace teachers. Nor does the National School Board, whose policy position about technology follows:

> Technologies will never replace classroom teachers, but are as essential to this profession's growth as they have been for law, medicine, and accounting. Teachers as managers of information will be more effective and capable of greater student individualization in their approach to classroom learning. Indeed real choice in education can come through the unlimited information and instructional development available for students.

What is wrong with admitting that new tools are needed by teachers and that they have a legitimate place in American education? It was Henry Ward Beecher who, in the nineteenth century, said that with tools a man has more power, more variety in his skills, and more efficiency in his job. Tools alone are not enough, however. A technology of instruction must be behind the use of tools, imbedding proper instructional design principles into the learning materials delivered by the tools. We believe that we are beginning to appreciate the potential of technology, but many educators still do not understand or define technology properly. Some educators and business people equate the term *technology* with computers and computers only. They have a hardware definition of technology and do not see it as a systematic process for designing instruction.

TECHNOLOGY DEFINED

John Kenneth Galbraith, the noted American scholar and economist, does not define technology as hardware but said that technology is "the systematic application of scientific or other organized knowledge to practical tasks."[8] This is how much of the world defines technology as it is applied to areas other than education. But what about technology as applied to education? Robert Heinich, Michael Molenda, and James Russell define a technology of instruction as "A teaching/learning pattern designed to provide reliable, effective instruction to each learner through application of scientific principles of human learning."[9] General characteristics of technology that should apply to instruction include replication, reliability, and improved cost-effectiveness through increased economy of scale. To these we would add a more humane education by increased one-on-one contact between teacher and learner, plus improved quality of instruction.

The sciences that have contributed to instructional technology include the behavioral, managerial, physical, and cognitive sciences. From the behavioral sciences, we concern ourselves with learning theory, perception, and communication. From managerial sciences come cybernetics, systems theory, and task analysis. From the physical sciences have come optics and electronics, and from cognitive science we are learning how individuals mentally process information. Technology does have a place in education, and the sooner we as educators begin to apply it to help solve critical problems, the better. There are two recent monographs that discuss in more detail the current needs of U.S. colleges of education, as well as present a worldwide view of needed changes in educational content.[10]

The 1970 presidential Commission on Instructional Technology defined instructional technology as "a systematic way of designing, carrying out, and evaluating the total process of learning and teaching in terms of specific objectives, based on research in human learning and communication, and [then employing a combination of both] human and nonhuman resources to bring about more effective instruction."[11] The nonhuman resources mentioned in this definition are the well-designed and validated curriculum materials delivered by sophisticated tools. The human resources are teachers who have been prepared to facilitate learning through the creative use of technology.

It has been said that schools are a technology of education in the same way that cars are a technology of transportation. Schools today include some 125,000 buildings, nearly three million teachers, 50 statewide systems of education, and some 15,000 local educational jurisdictions. This technology has touched the lives of every living American. Our forebears applied America's best information technologies to the then-unprecedented task of offering educational services to the masses of learners through the public schools. Somehow invention did not endure once the system was in place—schools today reflect their nineteenth-century technological roots more than do most other institutions.[12]

Public school decisionmakers (board members and administrators) will demand better-prepared teachers capable of using technology to manage student progress and facilitate the delivery of instruction. At the same time, they will demand validated learning materials that are delivered by highly sophisticated tools. Students entering colleges of education should have a choice of preparing for a career in the classroom or for employment with companies that design, develop, and validate quality learning materials. We need educators working in other sectors of society who understand the learning process and are capable of creating the resources that teachers need to be effective in their work with young people. Colleges of education should be concerned with learning wherever it occurs, in any environment, at any age. If schools of education limit themselves to K-12 and to preparing individuals only for classroom careers, they will be in serious trouble in the future. We need to look at broad solutions to the problems facing education and prepare professionals not only for careers in the schools but also for the corporate world, to prepare them to design, develop, evaluate, and validate the learning resources and processes needed in the schools.

THIRD WAVE EDUCATION

Charles Reigeluth made a comparison between our educational system and our transportation system.[13] Our transportation system consisted primarily of the horse for a very long time. Like the one-room schoolhouse, the horse was very flexible for meeting the needs of the individual; you could go almost anywhere you wanted to. Yet there were problems with the horse. It wasn't very fast or very comfortable, especially in bad weather. Some people spent a lot of time trying to reform the prevailing structure by breeding faster horses and building better trails and bridges to improve the horse's speed or making more comfortable saddles and creating carriages for the horse to pull to improve comfort. However, the gains to be made were small compared with the development of an alternative structure, the railroad.

The railroad was far faster, more comfortable, more reliable, and more efficient than the horse. It could transport many more people much greater distances far more cost-effectively. Somewhat like our current educational system, it was much less flexible; users were greatly restricted as to where the tracks took them and when. As society has continued to change, our transportation needs have also changed. We must travel even greater distances in less time, and people need to have much more flexibility as to when and where they will go. Many people have spent a great deal of time fine-tuning the railroad. But the quantum leap, again, came from an alternative structure, in this case one that entails the use of a variety of transportation modes, primarily the airplane and the automobile. As the one-room schoolhouse, a "first-wave" educational system, was appropriate for what Alvin

Toffler calls a "first-wave agrarian society,"[14] so our present second-wave educational system has a structure and philosophy that was appropriate for a second-wave industrial society. As John Goodlad points out, there are problems with the industrial production model of schooling.[15] One cannot help but note some structural similarities to an assembly line, whereby students move from one specialist teacher to another at the ring of a bell in an attempt to add the same new "component of education" to each learner. A third-wave educational system is needed to provide a quantum leap for meeting the changing needs of our third-wave information society, and like our current transportation system, it is probable that it will make use of a variety of means of facilitating learning. Charles Reigeluth concluded his analogy by saying that "each structural change that has occurred in our transportation system has become possible only by the advance of technology, and in fact technological advances have made the rise of alternative structures inevitable. But the change is never revolutionary; it is evolutionary. Horses are still used for transportation in some places. Many trains are still in use today. And, there are still some one-room school houses."

It is very easy to develop "hardening of the categories" and refuse to face up to the realities of a changing society. John Wedman, professor at the University of Missouri at Columbia, once told of an elderly professor who took his granddaughter to the airport to watch the airplanes take off and land. As a very large plane took off, the elderly professor said, "Isn't that fantastic!" His little granddaughter replied, "What's that grandfather?" And he said, "Isn't it fantastic that those big things can actually fly!" She looked up at him and said, "But grandfather, that's what they are supposed to do!" Young people just assume airplanes fly and computers compute, and they are not the least bit impressed or nervous about why. When it comes to thinking about technology and its place in education, many of us are looking at the situation from a perspective not unlike the elderly professor's. As educators, it is important for us to be open to the ways technology can be applied to the teaching/learning process and to not be so quick to find justification for our own insecurities. This is especially true of the computer, a universal and powerful technological tool for teaching with desktop multimedia presentations to full classes, as well as for individualized instruction. The potential of computer technology for teaching remains isolated from most teachers because of the limited access to computer laboratories secluded from the typical classroom. The personal computer is now at least equal in importance to paper and pencil in public schools and colleges of education.

A recent NEA Special Committee Report stated, as a major policy position, that "all schools should develop and implement a plan to install a computer with adequate software on the desk of each teacher by 1991."[16] It is seldom that such a sweeping pronouncement by the nation's largest educational association takes place. The NEA special report, released July 5, 1989, and other technology-related events are triggering a number of state educational and computer technology initiatives corresponding to Utah's *Educational Technology Programs* (Part 7 of Title 53A, State System of Public Education, Utah Code Annotated 1990 Cumulative Supplement, provided in full as Appendix A).

CONCLUSIONS

The several states that are passing legislation calling for the implementation of technology in the schools must be careful not to fall into the trap of the 1960s, which was a hardware-based approach. The majority of funds should be spent on courseware and in-service and preservice training of teachers. Obviously funds for hardware will be needed, but only after the critical curriculum decisions have been made. It is also important to understand that the word *technology* is not synonymous with *computers*. Many educators use the word *technology* when they should say *computers*.

Technology initiatives must be curriculum driven, or educators all over America will have egg on their face surrounded by millions of dollars of worthless hardware. Technology is not just equipment but instead a systematic process for designing effective learning experiences. The products of technology may be equipment, but the process of technology can help educators solve many of the current problems that plague education. The simple but powerful concepts of defining educational problems, developing technologically based solutions, and evaluating these over time (formative and summative) can help resolve the continuing education crisis in public and higher education and within corporate settings.

Two recently released videotape reports produced for the U.S. Congress Office of Technology Assessment electronically visit public schools in America that are beginning to utilize the educational technologies, equipment, materials, and processes. The first deals directly with the new tools for teaching and learning, and the second with electronic distance education.[17] Both deal with the potential of beginning electronic learning innovations in education and the promise of new educational technology.

It has been said that it takes 19 years for an innovation to be accepted in education. We hope that is no longer true. A window is now open to test the link between teaching and technology. It is a critical link, and we believe technology, both as a process and product, is at the core of a third-wave educational system. Educational technology, understood in this way, will likely become the most important initiative for change to transpire in American education.

APPENDIX A

TITLE 53A
STATE SYSTEM OF PUBLIC EDUCATION
UTAH CODE ANNOTATED 1990 CUMULATIVE SUPPLEMENT

Part 7
Educational Technology Programs

53A-1-701. Legislative declaration and authorization.*

(1) The Legislature recognizes that the quality of public education can be enhanced in the state by providing for educational technology programs that:

(a) support and encourage the use of educational technology in the state's public schools;

(b) train teachers and prospective teachers in the state's colleges of education to effectively use educational technology in the classroom;

(c) promote a strong technology partnership between public education and private enterprise;

---

*History: C. 1953, 53A-1-601, enacted by L. 1990, ch. 235, § 1; recompiled as 53A-1-701.

Compiler's Notes. — Sections 53A-1-701 to 53A-1-706 were enacted as §§ 53A-1-601 to 53A-1-606, but have been renumbered as these sections by the Office of Legislative Research and General Counsel because of the enactment at the 1990 session of other sections numbered 53A-1-601 et seq.

Effective Dates. — Laws 1990, ch. 235 became effective on April 23, 1990, pursuant to Utah Const., Art. VI, Sec. 25.

(d) promote student performance in the basic curriculum areas of mathematics and reading and encourage achievement in other curriculum areas identified by each local school board;

(e) focus public and private funding on critical educational areas that directly support student achievement and economic development;

(f) support the development of educational technology in Utah and encourage the expansion of high technology industry in the state; and

(g) are available to each school district so that all students enrolled in the state's public elementary and secondary schools may have access to educational technology programs.

(2) School districts and colleges of education are authorized and encouraged to develop and establish educational technology programs in conjunction with the guidelines provided in this part.

53A-1-702. Appropriation — Allocations — Matches from school districts, the business community, and technology vendors.

(1) There is appropriated for FY 1989-90 $13,500,000 from the Uniform School Fund to the State Board of Education and $1,500,000 from the General Fund to the State Board of Regents to help implement the technology programs authorized in this part.

(2) The appropriation is allocated as follows:

(a) the State Board of Education shall receive $13,365,000 for allocation to the state's 40 school districts, distributed in two parts:

(i) the board shall distribute the first part, 25% of the appropriation, equally among the state's 40 school districts so that each district receives $83,531; and

(ii) the board shall distribute the second part, 75% of the appropriation, based on the ratio of a district's estimated average daily membership for the 1989-90 school year to the state total average daily membership for 1989-90;

(b) the State Board of Regents shall receive $1,485,000 for allocation to the state colleges of education based on each state college's student teacher training enrollment FTE's for 1989-90 as compared to the total student teacher training enrollment FTE's for all state colleges of education for 1989-90; and

(c) 1% of the total appropriation, $150,000, is allocated to the Technology Initiative Project Office established under this part for program administration and coordination costs.

(3) It is the intent of the Legislature that neither the State Board of Education nor the State Board of Regents may establish rules that restrict school districts or colleges of education in their purchases of educational technology under this part or use any of the money appropriated under this section for administrative or overhead costs, other than the allocation provided to the Technology Initiative Project Office under Subsection (2)(c). The monies shall flow through the respective state boards directly to the school districts and colleges, subject to any qualifications established under this part.

(4) It is the intent of the Legislature that the Legislature shall appropriate additional monies for the programs authorized under this part for fiscal years 1990-91, 1991-92, and 1992-93. The additional appropriations are contingent upon matching contributions from federal and business sources and school districts.

(5) School districts and colleges shall match state appropriations for the technology programs on a one to three basis, that is one dollar in local resources for every three state dollars, either through local funding efforts or through in-kind services, which may include

providing an infrastructure, planning services, training services, maintenance, or the use of technical assistance specialists.

(6) (a) The Utah Partnership for Educational and Economic Development shall participate in the program in the following manner:

(i) the partnership shall assist in the solicitation of additional resources for the technology programs authorized under this part from private business and federal sources, with the intent to match the state appropriations from this and other sources on a two to three basis, that is resources having a value of two dollars for every three state dollars;

(ii) the resources raised through the efforts of the partnership shall flow through the State Office of Education and the Office of the Commissioner of Higher Education for allocation to:

(A) the school districts on the basis of a district's average daily membership as compared to the state system's average daily membership; and

(B) state colleges of education on the basis of student teacher training enrollment FTE's;

(iii) the partnership shall establish an Educational Technology Committee comprised of educational technology vendors and others, who desire to participate in the technology program authorized under this part, to provide advisory technical support to the committee and project office.

(b) Monies raised by a school district or college from the private sector for educational technology purposes qualify for the two to three match under Subsection (6)(a)(i) up to the percentage of the allocation a district or college would receive under Subsection (6)(a)(ii).

(7) Vendors who participate in the technology program shall make contributions to the program in terms of vendor discounts, inservice training, and continuing support services under standards established by the Technology Initiative Steering Committee.

53A-1-703. Technology Initiative Steering Committee — Composition — Compensation.

(1) There is established a Technology Initiative Steering Committee, hereafter referred to as the committee, consisting of 13 members selected or appointed as follows:

(a) three business members of the Utah Partnership for Educational and Economic Development selected by the partnership;

(b) one member appointed by the governor, representing the executive branch;

(c) the state chief procurement officer or his designee;

(d) the state superintendent of public instruction or his designee;

(e) a school district superintendent, appointed by the Utah School Superintendents Association;

(f) a local school board member, appointed by the Utah School Boards Association, except that the board member and district superintendent may not be from the same school district;

(g) two public school classroom teachers who have experience and expertise in the use of educational technology, one selected by the other members of the committee and one selected by the state's largest teacher association;

(h) the commissioner of higher education or his designee; and

(i) two members who have experience and expertise in the use of educational technology, one appointed by the speaker of the House of Representatives and one by the president of the Senate.

(2) The committee shall appoint one of the three business members from the partnership to serve as chairman.

(3) Members of the committee shall serve without compensation.

(4) A majority of the committee is a quorum for the purpose of conducting business. Members are appointed or selected for four-year terms.

(5) Members of the committee may not benefit financially, either directly or indirectly, or receive payments for goods or services, or be affiliated with any vendor that may benefit financially from this act.

53A-1-704. Duties and responsibilities.

(1) The committee has the following duties and responsibilities:

(a) to establish a Technology Initiative Project Office, which shall cease to exist on June 30, 1993, unless reauthorized by the Legislature;

(b) to appoint a director for the project office who is not affiliated with any technology vendors;

(c) to review and approve school district and college of education plans and reports related to the technology programs authorized and funded under this part, incorporating broad, objective, functional requirements and guidelines within the approval process;

(d) to review and provide criteria on an ongoing basis for technology products to be used in the programs, which criteria shall give consideration to at least any one or all of the following:

(i) technology that emphasizes instruction;

(ii) technology discounts, which may include installation and maintenance of a technology product;

(iii) a sound inservice component for educators;

(iv) upgrading of options in the original technology, at the same discount rate as given in the original purchase or lower for at least five years after the purchase of the original technology;

(v) technology of proven worth;

(vi) available technology evaluations;

(vii) submission of technology for evaluation by a committee of instructional software users;

(viii) cost effectiveness of the technology being offered;

(ix) identification of discontinued technology;

(x) compatibility of the technology with other technology products, using industry-wide standards; and

(xi) identification of the closest multiple sites and contact persons where the technology is being used and can be observed;

(e) to coordinate raising of funds from federal and private sources to supplement the appropriation authorized under this part for technology programs in the public schools and colleges of education;

(f) to verify that an appropriate evaluation of each plan is included in the plan itself; and

(g) to receive advisory input from the Educational Technology Committee established by the Utah Partnership for Educational and Economic Development.

(2) The project office has the following duties:

(a) to assist the committee in fulfilling its duties set out in Subsections (1)(c), (d), (e), and (f) as directed by the committee; and

(b) to establish a technical review committee in the project office, consisting of volunteers who have educational technology expertise and are not affiliated with any vendors participating in the technology programs.

53A-1-705. Educational technology plans—Components—Review and approval—Reports.

(1) Each school district shall prepare and submit a plan to the committee for review and approval of the district's proposed use of its technology allocation. The approval is of the plan and not of specific products or technology.

(2) The plan shall include the following components:

(a) the technology purchases to be made and proposed installation, maintenance, and replacement costs;

(b) specific, focused educational goals and measurable academic objectives to be accomplished in the district with the program, giving consideration to the respective size and needs of both student and teacher populations;

(c) valid instructional strategies, including inservice training for teachers;

(d) procedures to optimize the cooperation of all levels of education in the program, particularly in the planning process, including principals and teachers;

(e) methods to evaluate the program; and

(f) details of how the new technology will integrate with existing technology in the district.

(3) Each college of education shall prepare and submit a plan to the committee for review and approval of the proposed use of its appropriation. The plan shall focus on training teachers and prospective teachers to use the technology which school districts may acquire under this part.

(4) A school district or college of education may not spend any of the monies appropriated under this part until the plans for its technology program have been reviewed and approved by the committee.

(5)   (a) Each school district and college of education shall prepare and submit a report to the committee on the actual use of its allocation under this part.

(b) The reports shall include information on how the technology is being used to reach the performance goals established under Subsections (2)(b) and (4) and the progress on attaining the goals.

(c) The district or college of education shall submit the report by December 31, 1990, and send a copy of the report to the governor and the Legislature.

(d) The districts and colleges shall submit additional annual reports for each year the Legislature provides appropriations for the technology programs.

(e) The committee shall make regular reports to the Education Interim Committee of the Legislature on the status of the programs authorized under this part.

53A-1-706. Purchases of educational technology.

(1) A school district or college of education shall comply with Chapter 56, Title 63, the Utah Procurement Code, in purchasing technology under this part.

(2) A school district or college of education may purchase technology through cooperative purchasing contracts administered by the state Division of Purchasing or through its own established purchasing program.

This act was introduced by Representative Richard Bradford on February 15, 1990, as Utah House of Representatives Bill 468, Educational Technology in Public and Higher Education. The effective date of the act was April 23, 1990, pursuant to the Utah Constitution, Article VI, Section 25. The act is published in the Utah Code as Part 7, Section 53A, 1990 Supplement, and is titled Educational Technology Programs.

NOTES

1. *Freedom and Equality of Access to Information: A Report to the American Library Association by the Commission on Freedom and Equality of Access to Information* (Chicago, Ill.: ALA, 1986), frontispiece.

2. *Computers in the Workplace: Selected Issues* (Washington, D.C.: National Commission for Employment Policy, 1986), 19.

3. Don C. Smellie et al., "Teaching and Technology: A Critical Link," Association for Educational Communications and Technology-sponsored teleconference to 103 downlink sites in the United States and Canada, March 14, 1990. Dr. T. H. Bell was the major panel member for this international teleconference.

4. Jack E. Bowsher, *Education America: Lessons Learned in the Nation's Corporations* (New York: Wiley, 1989), 76-86.

5. Patricia A. Galagan, "IBM Gets Its Arms around Education," *Training and Development Journal* (January 1989): 35.

6. Robert Heinich, "The Proper Study of Instructional Technology," *Educational Communications and Technology Journal* (Summer 1984): 67-88.

7. William Ridley, "Interview," *Tech Trends* (February/March 1985): 23.

8. John Kenneth Galbraith, *The New Industrial State* (New York: Houghton Mifflin, 1967), 12.

9. Robert Heinich, Michael Molenda, and James D. Russell, *Instructional Media and the New Technologies of Instruction*, 3d ed. (New York: Macmillan, 1989), 444.

10. Charles W. Case and William A. Matthes, eds., *Colleges of Education: Perspectives on Their Future* (Berkeley, Calif.: McCutchan, 1985) and Shapour Rassekh and George Vaideanu, *The Contents of Education: A Worldwide View of Their Development from the Present to the Year 2000* (Paris: United Nations Educational, Scientific and Cultural Organization, 1987).

11. *To Improve Learning: A Report to the President and the Congress of the United States by the Commission on Instructional Technology (House Committee on Education and Labor)* (Washington, D.C.: Government Printing Office, 1970), 5.

12. James A. Mecklenburger, "Educational Technology Is Not Enough," *Phi Delta Kappan* (October 1990): 106.

13. Charles M. Reigeluth, "The Search for Meaningful Reform: A Third-Wave Educational System," *Journal of Instructional Development* 10, no. 4 (1987): 3-26.

14. Alvin Toffler, *The Third Wave* (New York: William Morrow, 1980).

15.   John I. Goodlad, *A Place Called School: Prospects for the Future* (New York: McGraw-Hill, 1984).

16.   *Educational Technology: NEA Special Committee Report* (Washington, D.C.: NEA, 1989). The report is available from NEA, 1201 Sixteenth Street, NW, Washington, DC 20036.

17.   *Linking for Learning: A New Course for Education* is a 26-minute videotape released October 1, 1990, by S L Productions, Box 1243, Manhasset, NY 11030, produced for the U.S. Congress Office of Technology Assessment. The tape is available in VHS or Beta for $30. An earlier videotape also produced for the U.S. Congress OTA, *Power On! New Tools for Teaching and Learning* with the *Promise of Educational Technology* is also available at the same cost from S L Productions. Both supplement printed studies about educational technology that were published by the U.S. Congress Office of Technology Assessment as U.S. government documents.

Computers in Schools and Universities
in the United States

Donald P. Ely
Professor
Instructional Design, Development and Evaluation;
Associate Director
ERIC Clearinghouse on Information Resources
Syracuse University
Syracuse, New York

When it comes to education, no one person or body speaks for the United States. When it comes to computers in education in the United States, diversity defies description with more than 109,000 public and private primary and secondary schools and more than 3,500 tertiary institutions. The common thread is that virtually every student, teacher, and administrator has computer access, but beyond that one similarity, all other aspects are different.

This article will describe four aspects of computer technology in education in the United States: (1) the quantitative story: how many computers are available to students and teachers; (2) the qualitative story: where these computers are located and how they are used; (3) the impact of computer use; and (4) hypotheses about nonuse, limited use, and inappropriate use.

THE QUANTITATIVE STORY

Ninety-six percent of the elementary and secondary schools in the United States have microcomputers (Quality Education Data, 1990). The numbers that are more interesting are the microcomputer densities, that is, the ratio of students to computers. Eight percent of the schools have 1 to 9 students per computer, 23 percent have 10 to 19 students per computer, 20 percent have 20 to 29 students per computer, 24 percent have 30 to 59 students per computer, and 26 percent have 60 or more students per computer. Of that 26 percent, 17 percent have 90 or more students per computer. Apple computers are found in 91 percent of the schools, IBM (or compatibles) in 36 percent of the schools, Radio Shack in 33 percent, and Commodore in 26 percent. Macintosh computers are found in only 8 percent of the schools.

Who controls the computers? Most frequently, there is a computer supervisor (13,569), next, special education personnel (9,386), then curriculum and instruction staff (probably school media specialists are the dominant group) (6,594), and finally reading teachers (4,690) and business education staff (3,368).

Comparable data are not available for higher education, although it is not overly optimistic to estimate that almost every institution of higher education in the United States has computers that are available to students, faculty, and administrators. But there is a mystery about the nature and amount of software available that is oriented to higher education alone. A recent article (Turner 1990) indicates that "higher education barely makes a dent in the $3.4 billion software-publishing industry." Business accounts for about 80 percent of that amount, 10 percent is estimated for "recreational" software (games, etc.), and 10 percent for education, most of it elementary and secondary. The article further reports that "professors around the country are writing their own software" and "most of them are happy to share their work with their colleagues." As for access and distribution of the software, 10 agencies have been established for the purpose of software dissemination in higher education circles. Some of the organizations have received support from commercial computer manufacturers, and others have support of federal agencies, foundations, and the universities themselves.

SOFTWARE USE IN ELEMENTARY AND SECONDARY SCHOOLS

In a recent study of computer-using teachers (n = 608) who have integrated computers into classroom practice, K. Sheingold and M. Hadley (1990) discovered that software was used in the following manner:

Text processing tools	95%
Instructional software	89%
Analytic and information tools	87%
Programming and operating systems	84%
Games and simulations	81%
Graphics and operating tools	81%
Communications	49%
Multimedia	25%

Within the area of instructional software, the following uses prevailed:

Problem-solving program	75%
Tutorial programs	73%
Drill and practice programs	72%
Software accompanying a textbook	37%
Conceptual tools	30%

These figures are confirmed by T. Plomp and W. J. Pelgrum (1990), who studied school computer use in eight countries for the International Evaluation Association. They discovered that the type of software programs most commonly available in U.S. schools were (1) word processing (93 percent), (2) drill and practice (92 percent), (3) educational games (91 percent), and (4) tutorial programs (81 percent) (Plomp and Pelgrum 1990, appendix, 6).

The dominant use, by far, in the Sheingold and Hadley study (1990, 9) was word processing, which was used by 9 out of 10 teachers who participated. "They are used at all grade levels. Not only do teachers use these tools, but, when asked to give examples of their 'most productive and interesting use of the computer in the curriculum they teach,' those who responded (75 percent of the sample) gave more examples of writing and language projects than of any other uses."

OTHER QUANTITATIVE INDICATORS

There are 13 journals completely devoted to computers in education that are widely read in the United States. Other professional journals contain additional articles devoted to computer-based instruction. There also are journals devoted to computers and specialized fields such as the humanities, science, engineering, information science, and others.

In 1989, ERIC, the national education information system, entered 507 items into the database, from which 323 were selected for the publication *Computer-Based Education: The Best of ERIC 1989* (McLaughlin, 1989). These are documents only, not journal articles.

In addition to the Association for the Development of Computer-Based Instructional Systems (ADCIS), there are a growing number of professional associations devoted largely to computers in education: the National Education Computing Conference (NECC), the Society for Advanced Learning Technology (SALT), and the Association for Educational Communications and Technology (AECT). Other professional meetings include many sessions devoted to the use of computers in special subjects and fields.

There is no doubt that computers are ubiquitous in schools and institutions of higher education in the United States. Why is it so?

RATIONALE FOR COMPUTER USE IN SCHOOLS

In a recent book by D. Hawkridge, J. Jaworski, and H. McMahon (1990, 16-17), four basic rationales for computers in schools are proposed:

The social rationale. Policy makers want to be sure that all children should be "aware and unafraid of how computers work." Because "computers are pervading industrial societies and are likely to be important in all countries," learners should be prepared to understand computers and be aware of their role in society.

The vocational rationale. Learning to operate computers is an important competency. "Teaching children programming gives them some confidence in their ability to control computers, and may be a foundation for a career in computer science." There will be employment opportunities for individuals who have the proper computer skills.

The pedagogic rationale. Students can learn from computers: "computers can teach." There are advantages over other traditional methods to using computers to learn.

The catalytic rationale. "Schools can be changed for the better by the introduction of computers." Computers facilitate change. They are symbols of progress. They encourage learning. "Computers are seen as catalysts, enabling desired change in education to occur."

In the United States, the social and vocational rationales seem to dominate. The relatively rapid and extensive adoption of computers in almost every school in the country reinforces the notion that computers are symbols of modern schools and that awareness of computers, usually through familiarization (computer literacy) classes, will confirm the fact that the schools are up-to-date. In some schools, learners acquire competencies of computer operation with the idea that there are increasing numbers of jobs in the information industry. These individuals who are trained to operate computers may do some programming in BASIC, but they generally do not acquire the conceptual competencies required for creative problem solving.

The pedagogic rationale does not appear to be as strong as the social and vocational rationales. The study of Plomp and Pelgrum (1990, appendix, 8) shows from the sample population that 53 percent of the mathematics teachers, 43 percent of the science teachers, and 44 percent of the English teachers in U.S. secondary schools use computers in teaching. The extent of use is not indicated. Sheingold and Hadley (1990, 2) conclude that "overall in United States schools computers are not an integral part of subject matter instruction."

The catalytic rationale is more difficult to understand. Essentially it says that computers are vehicles for change. There is some evidence that teachers change in their motivation and commitment to their students' learning (Sheingold and Hadley 1990, 23). J. D'Amico (1990, 106) reported that teachers involved in a year-long study of computer use in small community elementary schools made "their instructional planning tasks easier and more effective and many were anxious to push their own and their students' use beyond drill and practice." Most teachers who become involved in computer-based instruction are never the same again. But in the United States, that number is relatively small when compared with the entire population of elementary and secondary teachers and university professors.

IMPACT OF COMPUTERS IN EDUCATION

On a national scale, one would have to conclude that computer-based instruction in U.S. schools and universities has had minimal impact. By any measure of learning achievement, of significant changes in styles of teaching and learning, or of curriculum reform, the conclusion is "little or no effect." However, where deliberate efforts have been made by individual teachers or by entire institutions (schools or universities), one would have to say that in those circumstances, the teachers and learners will never be the same again. They have gained new skills, new perceptions of how to learn, increased motivation, and renewed enthusiasm for teaching and learning. The sheer numbers of computers in schools and universities can be misleading, as can the results of research on student learning that show, in most cases, no significant difference between learning through computer-based instruction and traditional teaching. Just because virtually every school and university has computers and many of them are used in some educational context does not mean that they are being used optimally or for the appropriate learning objectives. Justification for computer use is often sought in research findings that "prove" the value of computers in acquisition of knowledge as tested by traditional means. Perhaps there are other measures of success that have not been tested or are beyond testing, such as attitudes toward learning, willingness to pursue problems until they are solved, and changing the role of the teacher from a presenter of information to a facilitator of learning. Perhaps the right questions have not been raised.

If insights into impact are to be found, the literature reporting the behaviors and outcomes of computer-using teachers is more useful than some of the quantitative reports. For example, Sheingold and Hadley (1990, vii, viii) discovered:

1. Teachers "devote considerable time and effort to teaching with computers in their classrooms, and are supported in their efforts."

2. "The key incentive for them in teaching with computers is their students' using these tools effectively for their own learning."

3. "These teachers work in schools that have extensive technology as well as experience in using technology for instruction."

4. "These teachers use the computer as a multipurpose tool."

5. "Using the computer has changed their teaching."

6. "It takes time for these teachers to master computer-based practices and approaches—fully five to six years of teaching with computers."

7. "Although barriers to the integration of computers have lessened for most of these teachers over the years, significant barriers still remain."

D'Amico (1990, 106) echoes some of the same findings after considering his first year of running a computer-based instructional program in two elementary schools located in small communities:

The value of a CMI system is student achievement gains over time, consistent improvement year-after-year.

As for teacher use of CMI ... I will evaluat[e] whether they move from a mechanical instructional application to one more sophisticated and experimental. And I will analyze the degree to which they integrate CMI content with the content of their own lessons and curriculum.

I will ... look at each student's progress relative to previous performance.... I will examine teacher training with a different emphasis, too, evaluating to what degree it helps teachers to move beyond awareness and comfort and challenges them to experiment.

HYPOTHESES ABOUT NON-USE, LIMITED USE, AND INAPPROPRIATE USE

Barriers seem to fall in several categories: (1) software quality, (2) time for teacher learning and planning, (3) hardware availability, and (4) adequate administrative support. Sheingold and Hadley (1990, 21) gave 608 computer-using teachers a list of 35 barriers to the use of computers in teaching. The 5 highest barriers follow:

1. Teachers lack enough time to develop lessons that use computers. (Mean 4.22)

2. Problems scheduling enough computer time for different teachers' classes. (Mean 3.69)

3. Too few computers for number of children. (Mean 3.56)

4. Not enough place in the school schedule for more computer-based instruction. (Mean 3.53)

5. Inadequate financial support for computers from the school and/or district. (Mean 3.51)

Note: 6-point scale: 1 = not a major barrier
6 = a major barrier

The time factor was a major finding in D'Amico's study (1990). Throughout his list of lessons learned, he constantly refers to teachers' lack of time to prepare and to integrate computer-based instruction and time to study students' learning over a longer span.

Scheduling problems usually refer to the facility where the computers are located, usually a laboratory in a separate room. In U.S. schools, that room is often the school library or a room reserved only for computer use. In either case, the facility must be reserved for students' use during the school day and often at the end of the day. Gavriel Salomon, in his article "The Computer Lab: A Bad Idea Now Sanctified" (1990, 51), spells out the deficits of the separate-room strategy. He discusses four erroneous assumptions about the computer laboratory that serve as barriers to optimum use:

1. "The computer is an entity in and of itself, and thus deserves a special laboratory, a special curriculum, and a special teacher to teach it."

2. "Computer use is to be learned as a topic unto itself."

3. "The computer can just be added to otherwise unchanging instructional practices."

4. "Effective computer use depends solely on the quality of the software and course-ware used."

This facility and the assumptions that go with its use certainly form major barriers to the optimum use of computers in schools and universities.

Plomp and Pelgrum (1990, appendix, 9) asked computer coordinators to indicate software problems only. The two top responses in the United States were "not enough software for instruction" (48 percent) and "software not adaptable enough" (22 percent). Of less importance in the United States but of more importance in the seven other countries studied were "lack of information about software" and "poor quality of manuals."

These barriers, however, apply mostly to those who are already using computers in education. What about the vast majority who do not use computers in the classroom? There appears to be another set of conditions that facilitate the implementation of innovations in general and computers specifically. D. Ely (in press) describes these conditions as follows:

1. *Dissatisfaction with the status quo.* One of the first steps to initiate change in an education environment is a dissatisfaction with things as they are. Dissatisfaction often begins in classrooms.

2. *Knowledge and skills.* The people who will ultimately implement any innovation must possess sufficient knowledge and skills to do the job.

3. *Availability of resources.* Without the hardware and software, it is almost impossible to implement changes that require such support materials.

4. *Availability of time.* Time must be made available for implementation to occur — "good" time, "company" time, paid time.

5. *Commitment by those who are involved.* Commitment communicates support, and any individual who is trying a new material or procedure wants to know that there is support from a higher level.

6. *Evidence of leadership*. Even though individuals act alone, especially in classroom endeavors, they need the inspiration and continuing support of those they respect.

7. *Existence of rewards or incentives for participants*. For some it may mean satisfaction for a job well done; for others, it may mean more help, more (or better) resources, and, in some cases, increased salaries and professional opportunities.

8. *Expectation and encouragement of participation*. This means shared decision making, communication among all parties involved, and representation where individual participation is difficult. Each person should feel that he or she has had an opportunity to comment on innovations that will directly affect his or her work.

According to Ely, these conditions provide guidelines for implementing computer-based instruction where it has been unused or underused. The factors are applicable in almost any culture. Once the implementation has begun, other barriers emerge and must be confronted.

CONCLUSION

The use of the computer in educational settings is solidly established in the United States. Although the extent and nature of that use is not fully known, studies of computer-using teachers indicate that computers are used most frequently for word processing and least frequently for integrated subject-matter instruction. Most students in most U.S. elementary and secondary schools have some access to computers, but it is usually on a very limited basis. The most frequently taught course using computers is computer literacy—a course about computers. Computers are probably adopted by many schools as symbols of modernization and change (social and catalytic rationales). There is a genuine desire to adopt computer use in many schools, but the conditions for implementation are not always present; there is no national plan or strategy for implementing computer use or for fully utilizing computers' instructional capabilities in the schools and universities of the United States. Presently, computer enthusiasts (such as those attending the ADCIS conference) are the primary resources for those who seek to promulgate computer use in U.S. education.

REFERENCES

D'Amico, J. J. 1990. "Three Lessons I Learned from a Year of Computer-Based Instruction." *Journal of Computer-Based Instruction* 17, no. 3 (Summer): 103-9.

Ely, D. P. In press. "Conditions That Facilitate the Implementation of Educational Technology Innovations." *Journal for Research on Computers in Education*.

Hawkridge, D., J. Jaworski, and H. McMahon. 1990. *Computers in Third World Schools*. London: Macmillan Press.

McLaughlin, Pamela. 1989. *Computer-Based Education: The Best of ERIC 1989*. Syracuse, N.Y.: ERIC Clearinghouse on Information Resources.

Plomp, T., and W. J. Pelgrum. 1990. "Introduction of Computers in Education: State of the Art in Eight Countries." Paper presented at EURIT 90, Herning, Denmark, April, 1990.

Quality Education Data. 1990. *Catalog of Educational Mailing Lists and Marketing Services*. Denver, Colo.: QED, 24-25.

Salomon, G. 1990. "The Computer Lab: A Bad Idea Now Sanctified." *Educational Technology* (October): 50-52.

Sheingold, K., and M. Hadley. 1990. *Accomplished Teachers: Integrating Computers into Classroom Practice*. New York: Center for Technology in Education, Bank Street College of Education.

Turner, J. A. 1990. "Colleges, Scholarly Societies, and Foundations Create Software-Dissemination Projects to Share Expertise." *Chronicle of Higher Education* (October 17): A17-20.

A Review of the Research Issues in the Use of Computer-Related Technologies for Instruction

An Agenda for Research

Carol J. Williams
Eastern Connecticut State University and
The University of Connecticut

Scott W. Brown
The University of Connecticut

Teachers, administrators, and the media greet each new educational technology with a wave of enthusiasm and optimism about the potential of the innovation to transform the teaching/learning enterprise. Educational researchers have eagerly designed experiments which compare instruction delivered by the new technology with traditional classroom instruction. As far back as the 1940s and 1950s, instructional films were being compared with conventionally delivered instruction. Technology-based educational research has been dominated by the comparative research paradigm in which a media-based instructional design is pitted against a nonmedia-based design. Reeves (1986) points out that despite 25 years of criticism and marginally useful results, research studies using experimental and quasi-experimental designs to compare one instructional technology with traditional instruction continue to be conducted and published. Computer-based instruction (CBI) and computer-assisted interactive video (CAIV) are among the current technologies being studied by means of this comparative paradigm.

Since the early 1970s a number of research syntheses on the effectiveness of computer-based instruction have been published. These studies have examined instruction at all levels, from elementary through college and adult. A variety of computer uses or modes have been studied. Niemiec and Walberg (1987) provided a taxonomy of computer usage as it is commonly found in the literature. Computer-assisted instruction (CAI) includes drill and practice, where the computer is used to reinforce concepts introduced in the classroom; tutorial, where the computer is used to introduce concepts as well as reinforce them; and dialogue, which not only presents lessons and practice exercises but also allows the learner to ask questions in natural language. In dialogue, the most sophisticated instructional usage, the sequence of instruction is largely controlled by the learner's interaction with the computer. In computer-managed instruction (CMI) the computer serves as a manager of instruction rather than as a teacher or tutor. In CMI, where the computer

A version of this article was originally published in the *International Journal of Instructional Media* 17, no. 2, and is reprinted with permission.

tracks and guides students to mastery level, the curriculum is task analyzed, and the student is tested for mastery at appropriate points. Once students have mastered a unit they proceed in a predefined sequence. The term "computer-enriched instruction" (CEI) refers to the use of computers to enrich or enhance instruction as in the simulation of laboratory conditions or the simulation of an airplane cockpit.

Over the years, computer-assisted learning effectiveness has been defined in several ways. The most common measure has been enhanced achievement, such as improved test scores, but other measures of effectiveness have been employed as well, including heightened affective responses, or better attitudes, reduced learning time, higher course completion rates, length of time learning is retained, and, finally, cost (Niemiec and Walberg 1987).

WHAT HAVE WE LEARNED FROM THE RESEARCH COMPARING COMPUTER-ASSISTED INSTRUCTION WITH CONVENTIONAL INSTRUCTION?

The best known of the meta-analytic research studies on CAI are by the Kuliks and their colleagues at the University of Michigan. Using Glass' (1976) approach to meta-analysis, these researchers have attempted to assess what the literature reveals about CAI, CMI, and CEI as it has been implemented at all levels of instruction including elementary, secondary, college, and adult (Bangert-Drowns, Kulik, and Kulik 1985; Kulik and Kulik 1986; Kulik, Kulik, and Bangert-Drowns 1985; and Kulik, Kulik, and Shwalb 1986). A total of 199 comparative analyses were included in these studies: 32 in elementary schools, 42 in high schools, 100 in universities and colleges, and 24 in adult education programs. In addition to calculating and reporting effect sizes for comparative studies, the researchers looked for significant relationships between independent variables and dependent measures across studies. Each study included in a meta-analysis was coded on a number of quantitative dimensions (e.g., duration of CAI) and categorical variables (e.g., random versus nonrandom assignment of subjects and control for instructor effects). For example, Kulik and Kulik (1985), in their study of the effects of CAI in college applications, coded 17 independent variables of each study. These variables represent differences in treatment application controls for validity and differences in publication type. The following variables were coded: type of application—tutorial, drill, and practice, etc.; duration of study; author of program—local or other; type of computer interaction—offline, terminal, or micro; subject assignment—random or nonrandom; control for instructor effect; control for history; control for test-author bias; control for bias in test scoring—objective or nonobjective; control for evaluator involvement; field-tested computer materials—yes or no; emphasis on science—hard or soft; emphasis on knowledge—pure or applied; emphasis on systems—life or nonlife; subject ability level—low, average, or high; year of report; and source of study—dissertation, professional journal, or technical report. Parametric tests were subsequently applied to identify relationships between outcomes of the study and these coded features.

In a 1987 synthesis of their meta-analytic studies of CAI at various educational levels, Kulik and Kulik (1987) reported the following overall results:

- Students learned more in classes where they had some form of computer assistance. The average effect over 199 studies was to raise exam scores by 0.31 standard deviations, that is, from the 50th to the 61st percentile.

- The 28 studies which explored possible reductions in instructional time revealed an average reduction in instructional time of 32 percent.

- Students liked instruction more when they had instructional help from a computer. The 17 studies which examined this aspect yielded an average effect size of 0.33 and effected a positive change in attitude-toward-instruction of .28 standard deviations.

- Attitude toward subject matter, examined in 29 studies, did not seem to change significantly.

The coding of study features allowed Kulik and Kulik (1987) to analyze relationships of these features to study outcomes. A few study features revealed significant patterns:

- Results were stronger in published studies (p < .01). In published studies the average effect size increased by .46 standard deviations, while in unpublished studies the average effect size increased by only .23 standard deviations.

- Effects were larger when different teachers taught the experimental and control sections (p < .05). Same teacher designs yielded an average ES of 0.24 standard deviations, while different teacher designs yielded an average ES of 0.40 standard deviations.

- Effects were larger in more recent studies and smaller in older research (p < .05). Studies before 1975 resulted in average increased exam scores of 0.24 standard deviations, while studies from 1975 on showed an average increase in exam scores of 0.36 standard deviations.

- Effects were larger in studies of short duration and weaker in longer ones (.10 < p < .20). The average ES for studies of short duration was 0.36, for studies of longer duration, 0.27.

Over the past 12 years a number of writers have reviewed the research syntheses exploring the effectiveness of computer-based instruction. Niemiec and Walberg (1987, 32) examined all previous literature reviews of CAI where either achievement, affective response, or measures of both were assessed. Sixteen reviews met their criteria for inclusion. Thirteen of the studies were quantitative (eleven were meta-analytic and provided overall numerical estimates of effects) and three were traditional, nonquantitative box-score type reviews. Eight reviews dealt with studies at the elementary and secondary levels, five with college, and three with selected populations. While the number of primary research citations was over 500, because of overlap, the actual number of studies included was approximately 250.

Niemiec and Walberg (1987) provide a summary table of the various effect sizes and percentages of positive studies found by the thirteen quantitative reviews. These effect sizes measure the average superiority (or, if negative, the inferiority) of CAI as compared to traditional instruction in standard deviation units. For the thirteen reviews, the mean and median effect sizes were both 0.42 (standard deviation = .08). The average effect of CAI was to raise the average student in the CAI group to the 66th percentile of the control group. The mean percentage of studies in the Niemiec and Walberg review, which favored CAI, was 81.9 (median = 84; standard deviation = 13.0).

While both box score analyses and meta-analyses provide some evidence that well-designed computer-assisted instruction can be more effective than traditional instruction, the practical significance of CAI as reported by these studies seems hardly enough to justify the costs of purchasing hardware and the tedious and costly development of software. The fact that effect sizes are smaller in longer studies suggests that short-term research may be affected by novelty and Hawthorne effects. While most of the meta-analyses report moderately positive, highly generalized results, for those who expected computer-based instructional technology to effect a revolution in learning, research comparing computer-based instruction with traditional instruction to date has been disappointing.

Furthermore, one must be careful in interpreting the results of meta-analyses with regard to impact on learning because almost all of the research syntheses include computer applications which are in addition to regular classroom instruction compared with regular classroom instruction alone. For example, the meta-analysis by Kulik and Kulik (1985) of 101 research studies on college-level, computer-based education (the largest of the meta-analyses) showed an average effect size of 0.26 (standard error 0.051). In other words, in the typical study, performance of students in computer-assisted groups was 0.26 standard deviations above performance of the control group. A closer examination of the studies included in the meta-analysis raises serious questions about their significance. If one looks separately at the studies categorized as "tutorial," in which the computer is used as a partial substitute for conventional instruction, one finds that out of 50 studies, only 16 had an effect size greater than .40 (the standard which some researchers believe to represent practical significance) and 16 tutorial studies had negative effect sizes. How successful is an experimental treatment when half the studies yield negative results? Examination of the meta-analyses at other grade levels reveals a similar pattern of uneven results for learning outcomes of computer-based instruction as a substitute for conventional instruction.

Kulik and Kulik (1987, 224) are careful and judicious in reporting their results: "Students generally learned more in classes when they received help from computers." Still, the impression is created that computer-assisted instruction is more effective than traditional classroom instruction. Edwards et al. (1974) demonstrated that effectiveness of CAI depended on how it was used in relation to instruction. In studies where CAI was used to supplement regular instruction, gains in achievement were "fairly consistent" (Kulik and Kulik 1987, 122). When CAI was substituted for traditional instruction, achievement results were mixed.

In an article reviewing developments in meta-analytic methods, Robert Bangert-Drowns (1986) noted that the meta-analysis procedure can be subject to criticism of an apples-and-oranges-type approach to the level of the independent variable. By collapsing subgroups of studies into superclasses, a meta-analytic approach may obscure critical differences among subgroups of studies. This paper argues that compression of subgroups that differ in terms of the extent to which the computer is used as a substitute for traditional instruction into superclasses of computer-assisted versus conventionally taught groups has led to confusion in the interpretation of the effectiveness of the computer as a substitute for traditional instruction.

One wonders whether any instructional treatment that is in addition to regular instruction would not yield more learning. Few people would contest the view that computers serve a meaningful role in the contemporary classroom as supplements to traditional teaching methods. Computers have been used for a number of years now to reinforce and expand classroom instruction, but despite the amount of research effort devoted to the comparative research paradigm, computers have not yet been shown to teach significantly better than the normative classroom teacher or even better than written programmed instruction. Yet as Hagler and Knowlton (1987) point out, there remains a prevailing research "set" that CBI, if well done, should be able to out perform the classroom teacher. And this expectation is now being extended to computer-assisted interactive video (CAIV), the most exciting educational technology on the contemporary scene.

When one examines the research literature on the computer as a teaching tool, one finds that most early studies used mainframe computers not micros; and the literature continues to draw on these older studies. All but two of the more than 200 studies in the Kulik, Kulik, and Bangert-Drowns (1985) and the Niemiec and Walberg (1987) meta-analyses were published before 1983. Becker (1988) examined the research literature on the effectiveness of microcomputers using best-evidence synthesis (Slavin, 1986), which like meta-analysis generates an effect size. Becker examined published and unpublished studies produced since 1984 that used microcomputers, had achievement as one of the outcome measures, and compared computer learning to traditional learning. After discarding studies that had experimental design flaws and those that lasted fewer than eight weeks, Becker was left with 17 studies. Becker found one study conducted in grades 1-6 with an average effect size of + 1.00 and a study on mathematics instruction in grades 3 and 5 that yielded an ES of + .48 in the third grade and an ES of + .31 in the fifth. The rest of the studies had much smaller effect sizes, some even negative. In addition, Becker reports problems with most of the studies either in terms of the study or the reporting of the study. Important details about what was done were often omitted and important statistics often left out. According to Becker, we are far from being able to prescribe under what circumstances computers should be employed in the classroom.

PROBLEMS WITH THE COMPARATIVE PARADIGM FOR ASSESSING TECHNOLOGY-BASED EDUCATIONAL EFFECTIVENESS

Thomas Reeves (1986) makes a strong case against the comparative research paradigm for assessing the effectiveness of computer-related technologies for instruction, citing conceptual, methodological, and analytical problems. Often there is a failure to adequately define the instructional treatment. All CAI or CAIV packages are not alike. A computer simulation of a biology experiment is quite unlike a drill and practice session on multiplication. Yet as Salomon (1981) points out, there is a tendency to treat each medium as a more or less invariant entity with fixed clusters of attributes. Psychological and educational research on media, Salomon contends, requires more subtle distinctions. It is not the medium but rather the attributes that make a difference in learning. Classes of media attributes common to various types of media instruction include contents; symbol systems that structure and code the content; technologies that gather, encode, sort, and convey content; and situations in which the medium is used.

Most researchers have failed to define adequately the experimental treatment, and they have generally tended to ignore the differences and commonalities between the experimental treatment and traditional instruction. Educational researchers have viewed their treatments as distinct wholes that can be controlled in a scientific way. Most instructional treatments, as Reeves (1986) points out, lack such cohesion, and "factorial research designs cannot reflect the degrees of convergence or divergence among instructional treatments" (Reeves 1986, 103). Factors of a particular medium that can contribute to learning may not always be present when the medium is used. For example, Salomon (1981) cites slow motion as an available film technique that is not always used in media instruction. To the extent that slow motion can be used to deliver information to learners who need it, slow motion can be expected to facilitate learning; however, not all films utilize slow motion, not all slow motion carries critical information, and not all learners need slowed-down visualization. There are subtle interactions between components of media, individual characteristics, and learning outcomes that preclude treating an instructional medium, whether computer, interactive video, or lecture, as a distinct and cohesive whole.

Another problem that continues to plague comparative research is that researchers often fail to measure the degree to which a treatment is implemented as the researcher intends. Control groups are often given homework problems designed to fill the time used by the experimental group on CAI or CAIV supplements. If the control group fails to complete the exercises, we would not expect them to learn as much as the experimental group. Also, CAI and CAIV are subject to numerous technical flaws that may interfere with learning. Long pauses in accessing programs and extraneous noise are not uncommon. Reeves (1986, 103) calls for more sensitive research methods that "seek out and account for unavoidable variance in the implementation of instruction."

The comparative research paradigm, while ostensibly of interest to the practitioner curious about comparisons between technology-based instruction and conventional instruction, yields little information to help guide the classroom teacher. Unless one's goal were to replace all classroom teachers with a superior and cheaper technology, determining statistically reliable results in rejecting or failing to reject a null hypothesis provides marginal information to guide the development of improved instructional enterprise. Often one method works only slightly better than another, and hardly ever does the researcher speculate on why the experimental method should work better in terms of what we know about cognition or memory. In addition, meta-analyses have compounded this confusion by collapsing studies on totally different kinds of learning outcomes. Studies of math and computer science programs are lumped together with such things as pilot training and computer-assisted programs to teach education majors to identify students needing special education. While such disparate programs may lead to improved student performance, the individual instructional design elements that lead to improved performance are probably quite different.

The most serious problem with the comparative research model for studying the effectiveness of CAI and CAIV is what is called the invalid implicit assumption. The implicit assumption that instructional media represent meaningful experimental variables independent of instructional content or strategy may, in fact, be invalid. Hagler and Knowlton (1987) call for a differentiation between medium and message. The message is the body of symbols, usually words and pictures, organized to carry meaning. The medium is the physical means of coding and transmitting the body of organized symbols, such as the book, lecture, or computer. As you will recall, Kulik and Kulik (1987) found greater effect sizes favoring CAI when different teachers taught the CAI and conventional groups; when the same teacher taught both sections, differences between the two groups were smaller. The authors suggest that when teachers developing CAI outline objectives, construct lesson plans, and prepare evaluation materials, they may also do a better job in their conventional teaching responsibilities. Hagler and Knowlton (1987) suggest another explanation: when the same teacher teaches the same material in the same organized way via both media, the same learning is achieved in both groups.

Most comparative research on computer-related technologies for instruction will compare a lecture format with an interactive CAI or CAIV package that gives prompt feedback to students and may even branch to feedback according to the learner's attempted response to questions. The lecture format with which the computer-related technology is being compared often does not allow for the lecturer to question or give feedback to the students. An essential component of the instructional design is left out in the lecture group. If the lecture group provided for interaction with the students, one wonders whether the teacher-taught group might not surpass the computer-assisted group on measures of achievement.

When researchers compare CAI to traditional instruction such as a lecture, they are primarily comparing messages rather than media. They may be comparing more instruction with less instruction, as when a comparative research design allows computer instruction to supplement traditional instruction; or they may be comparing more efficient or effective instruction with instruction that is inferior, as when a well-designed CAI package is compared with a traditional classroom approach taught by a less-than-effective teacher; however, the medium is largely neutral. In most cases, either of the media being compared could carry either of the messages being delivered. As Hagler and Knowlton (1987, 84) remind us:

> A quarter of a century ago, in reference primarily to the early studies of instructional motion picture film, Knowlton (1960; 1964) wrote of these problems in detail and showed that they were inherent in all comparative media research wherein the dependent variables were some measure of learning. Stolurow (1962) made the specific case for the teaching machine medium. Feldhusen (1963) suggested that research has taken this media comparison approach because school people want to know how well the new method works in comparison with what they are doing. Renewed attempts have recently been made by Avner, Moore, and Smith (1980), and most notably by Clark (1985), to remind the field of this error.

Media are not inherently inferior or superior; they are "only more or less well suited to the learner and/or the message" (Hagler and Knowlton 1987, 85). Clark (1985a) concluded that when media are compared with one another holding all variables other than media constant, including content and curriculum method, there is no reason to expect learning advantages for one medium over another.

Must we conclude that technology-based educational alternatives should be abandoned in favor of simpler, less costly conventional instruction? Should we give up on efforts to support conclusively the value of instructional technologies as Cronbach (1975), Clark (1983) and others have suggested? Thomas Reeves (1986), while asserting that computer-related instructional technologies, particularly intelligent interactive videodiscs, can be effective and efficient alternatives to existing conventional approaches, argues for the abandonment of comparative experimental and quasi-experimental designs as a way to test the merits of computer-assisted instructional video. To support his point, Reeves (1986) cites a number of studies that have used the comparative research paradigm to evaluate interactive video as a teaching tool. Bailio and Kellock (1981) compared the effects of a biology videodisc with similar instruction delivered by conventional classroom lecture. Schroeder (1982) compared videodiscs with role-playing and programmed texts in teaching leadership and counseling skills. A number of military training applications using videodiscs have been evaluated. Holmgren, Dyer, Hilligoss, and Heller (1980) compared the effectiveness of videodisc and Super 8 filmstrips for instruction in army courses. Ketner (1982) compared the effectiveness of videodisc training versus hands-on in learning to work with sensitive military equipment. Giunti and Kimberlin (1982) compared intelligent videodiscs with CBI for military weapons training, and Reeves and King (1986) compared videodisc simulations with actual tactical field exercises. Reeves (1986, 102) remarks that while some of the studies cited reported reduced time spent in instruction or enhanced student attitude toward programs, "they were unanimous in their failure to detect statistically significant differences in instructional effectiveness." Again, as with computer-assisted instruction, the invalid implicit assumption that delivery system alone can make a difference in learning must be considered.

THE NEW AGENDA FOR RESEARCH

This paper will argue that while standard comparisons of CAI or CAIV with conventional instruction and perhaps even meta-analyses of such research are no longer particularly meaningful, there are a number of potentially fruitful lines of research that will add to our knowledge about teaching and learning as well as to our understanding about how best to use computer-related technologies in the classroom. We must turn our attention now to utilizing what we know from cognitive science and instructional psychology to design more effective instructional strategies. Computer-related technologies for instruction must be integrated with the larger body of instructional technology as Robert Gagne (1987) has defined it. In Gagne's model, instructional technology seeks to provide the conditions that are optimally effective for human learning. Gagne's model grows out of a number of comprehensive generalizations about instruction that have evolved from the work of practitioners and researchers. These generalizations form a framework in which the systematic study of instruction, including instruction delivered by technologies, can proceed. Gagne summarizes the continuing beliefs that characterize the field of instructional technology:

1. Inventions in communications media that may have been designed for other purposes often provide new opportunities for delivering instruction. Instructional technology seeks to investigate, refine, evaluate, and promote such applications.

2. Because the purpose of instruction is learning, the primary focus of instructional techniques must be the human learner, and thus sound instructional techniques must take into account learner characteristics including "innate capacities, experiential maturity, and current knowledge states" (Gagne 1987, 5). These factors form the parameters of instructional design.

3. Procedures to promote learning may be either closely tied to hardware features (such as motion displays) or independent of hardware (such as feedback and provision for review).

4. Research in the field of instructional technology has the purpose of explicating: (a) the most effective ways of using media to promote human learning, (b) the conditions of optimal learning, including properties of media that can help establish such conditions, and (c) novel techniques of instructional design and delivery that can be shown to improve effectiveness.

5. Media selected for instructional uses should be those that best provide the conditions of learning for a given population.

6. Evaluation studies, that have often failed, as we have seen in this paper, to show an advantage for media-based versus nonmedia-based instruction, may have been inadequately formulated. Studies that investigate innovative ways to utilize special features of media such as audio and visual coordination, pacing of learner responses, various feedback strategies, elaboration of factual knowledge, and so on hold great promise for maximizing learning.

7. The goal of research and development in instructional technology continues to be the ability to specify characteristics of a system of instructional delivery that would provide a set of conditions for optimally effective learning that would exceed the capabilities of nonmedia-based instruction.

The agenda for future research on computer-related technologies for instruction must include two types of separate yet related research efforts. One type of research is needed to speed up the classroom application of effective computer-related educational methodologies in the classroom. The other must concentrate on basic research tied to cognitive models of learning and teaching. At a 1982 research conference on "Computers in Education: Realizing the Potential," a panel on science and mathematics education outlined a number of promising applications of computer technologies in the classroom (Reif 1985). The panel called for prototype research to further the application of computers in the classroom by demonstrating the effectiveness of relatively small-scale projects. The advantages of such prototype development include flexibility to make modifications and the ability to try many different approaches. Mistakes made on such a small scale are relatively harmless, easily diagnosed and remedied. Successful working prototypes, when well publicized, may persuade people to adopt these new approaches faster than would published articles. Prototype research should focus on computer-related technologies that are particularly effective in bringing about desired learning outcomes.

Prototype projects must be of high quality. They should be carried out under well-controlled conditions and treated like experiments guided by theoretical ideas about teaching and learning. If not of high quality, prototypes may do more harm than good by discrediting promising ideas that have been poorly implemented. Evaluation of prototype projects should give thoughtful consideration to why things worked or did not work, and thus they may contribute to theoretical insights or to the refinement of theory in the future. Classroom prototypes should pay particular attention to not only technological or cognitive aspects but also to psychological and social factors inevitable in the classroom, including motivational factors that affect student learning. A review of current journals in the field of educational applications of computer-related technologies reveals that careful prototype research is being conducted and reported.

BASIC RESEARCH ISSUES FOR INSTRUCTIONAL TECHNOLOGY

Early studies of computer-related technologies for instruction were often based upon the behavioral paradigm of stimulus-response learning. Instructional designs tended to emphasize the role of association in learning and often were based on written programmed instructional packages. Instruction emphasized the learning principles of contiguity, reinforcement, and practice. Thus one finds in CAI programs a preponderance of drill-and-practice programs, frequent testing, and an emphasis on mastery learning. Because the subject matter lends itself to being delivered in a bottom-up, incremental fashion, one finds many more CAI programs in math and computer science than in other areas.

An extremely important variable often overlooked in earlier CAI studies and even in the meta-analyses was the type of learning task being required. Gagne (1985) has distinguished among five different categories of learned capabilities and the differential requirements needed to support encoding these capabilities. The instructional arrangements needed to promote effective learning of motor skills obviously differs from those that would support the encoding of attitudes. Similarly, the design of instruction to support encoding of verbal information differs from that needed for procedural knowledge (intellectual skills). To date, meta-analyses have lumped together studies exploring very different learning tasks. Studies measuring changes in student attitudes have been grouped together with studies of the effects of drill and practice in mathematics and such procedural learning tasks as simulated practice in piloting an airplane. Because the cognitive requirements of these different types of learning are so different, researchers must be sure to categorize the type of learning being examined. Gagne and Glaser (1987, 64) have provided an abbreviated summary of some of the principal differential instructional requirements for fostering the five categories of learned capabilities he has described.

Although certain principles from early learning theory, such as the importance of reinforcement, still underpin school learning, we are beginning to grasp complex aspects of human learning that cannot be explained by a strict behavioral view of learning. Instructional design needs to be evaluated in terms of more complex theoretical models. Cognitive science and Bandura's (1977) social learning theory provide two such avenues for research.

Several areas of basic cognitive research provide fertile ground for the development of hypotheses about instructional technology. Three overarching issues are (1) the implications of the information-processing model of cognition, especially the characteristics of short-term memory, working memory, and long-term memory for instructional technology; (2) the implications of cognitive strategies for instructional technology, including strategies for learning, for remembering, and for problem solving; and (3) implications of knowledge organization for maximizing learning.

IMPLICATIONS OF THE INFORMATION-PROCESSING MODEL

Current cognitive theory views learning as a set of processes that function to process information. Several phases of processing are hypothesized to intervene between the input of stimulation to the senses and the output of human behavior. Input that enters the human information processing system must, if it is to be retained, be processed through and stored in memory. An important distinction of the information-processing model is the conception of short-term memory (STM). In addition to its storage of limited amounts of new information for a brief time, the STM also is conceived of as having a function called "working memory," where newly received information is integrated with information already established in long-term memory (LTM). In working memory, new information is compared with existing information in LTM, integrated with organized information in LTM (called schemata), and rehearsed. Rehearsal can be simple repetition of new information or it can be elaborative, that is, invested with additional semantic meaning, perhaps from existing knowledge. The limitations of STM in terms of both time and number of items of information that can be processed at one time provide important parameters for instructional technology.

Gagne and Glaser (1987) refer to four important conceptualizations regarding long-term memory. They are (1) how images are represented, (2) the distinction between declarative and procedural knowledge, that is, between "knowing that" and "knowing how," (3) the organized structures called schemata, and (4) the idea that structures in LTM constitute human capabilities. Each of these concepts about LTM need to be taken into consideration when designing computer-related technologies for instruction. For example, CAIV, with its great capacity for visual images, should be able to expand and refine our knowledge about the value of visual images in the recall of material and the differential effect of such images on different groups of learners. Some evidence suggests that the coupling of visual images with semantic information may be of particular benefit for individuals low in verbal ability (Cronbach and Snow 1977; Salomon 1981).

Traditionally, education has tended to emphasize declarative knowledge ("knowing that") much more than procedural knowledge ("knowing how"). Part of this skewed emphasis on verbal learning has had to do with the difficulty of setting up learning environments to teach and assess procedural learning. Computer-related technologies can be used to create much more active learning environments that may better prepare students for performance in the world of work. Computers have the capacity to provide students with access to real data (such as data about populations and demographic trends or economic forecasting data) and the ability to make projections and computations from such data. This allows students to work with pertinent data in realistic contexts while still in school. Computer "laboratories" can be set up to simulate real situations with the following advantages: they are less expensive than the real laboratory, they allow for quick results and for the systematic variation of relevant parameters (e.g., genetics experiments can be simulated without waiting weeks for biological organisms to replicate and mature), they allow active exploration of dynamic processes without danger to students, they allow students to focus on the key experimental issues without the distractions of time-consuming pragmatic details of real experiments, they allow for the exploration of phenomena outside the range of normal experience (e.g., simulations of outer space and of physical forces at speeds approaching the speed of light), and simulated labs allow learners to explore hypothetical situations not encountered in the real world (Reif 1985).

IMPLICATIONS OF COGNITIVE STRATEGIES FOR INSTRUCTIONAL TECHNOLOGY

Cognitive strategies can be used to facilitate learning and remembering. Learners can be encouraged to attend to particular portions of text by interspersed questions (Rothkopf 1971) and by including learning objectives (Kaplan and Rothkopf 1974). Readers can be taught to summarize, question their comprehension, and anticipate what is to come in text (Palincsar and Brown 1984). Strategies for encoding, such as instructions to make a diagram or to use elaborations, can be requested of the learner. Other aids to encoding, such as variations in typography of prose, highlighting, and so on, can be employed by designers of instructional technology to better organize learning materials (Glynn and DiVesta 1977).

Problem-solving strategies can be explicitly encouraged by instructional technology. For example, children have been successfully taught to employ strategies for performing arithmetic operations (Resnick 1981) and for constructing geometric proofs (Greeno 1978). Careful design of instructional technology, by building in specific cognitive strategies for remembering and problem solving, may be more successful than conventional instruction in actually getting learners to engage in cognitive strategies. Learning environments can be created with CAI and CAIV to prompt a student's learning by discovery and then can be made increasingly more complex as the student's knowledge base grows more sophisticated. Students can be coached to form hypotheses, perform experiments in the computer environment, and use the results to modify the original hypotheses. Such designs need to be tested to assess their relative effectiveness.

Early applications of computers as tutors, including most of those included in the meta-analyses referred to in this paper, were fairly primitive, usually little more than technologically presented rote drill and practice. In recent years artificial intelligence has endowed technological tutors with more human-like intelligence. Computers can now be programmed with genuine expertise about a given subject and can use student responses to diagnose a student's understanding at a given stage and then provide appropriate tutorial support. Several intelligent computer tutors (see chapter 9 of Barr and Feigenbaum 1982 for summaries of these and other applications) have been designed to teach arithmetic (e.g., the game of WEST), electronics skills (SOPHIE), and skills in medical diagnosis (GUIDON). Prototypes using AI-based tutorial systems, as well as less powerful, more easily constructed tutorials compatible with existing microcomputers, are worthy of more study.

Metacognitive strategies, too, hold great promise for improving the efficiency of learning. A number of training programs have been developed to teach explicit, self-regulatory skills. Examples are provided by Whimbey and Lochhead (1980), Feuerstein et al. (1980), De Bono (1985), Rubinstein (1975), Wickelgren (1974), and Hayes (1981). The potential of computer-related technologies for extensive feedback, individualization, and interactivity make them ideal tools for further study of metacognitive strategies.

IMPLICATIONS OF KNOWLEDGE ORGANIZATION FOR MAXIMIZING LEARNING

Recent work in cognitive science has demonstrated that the way in which knowledge is structured can greatly influence the ease or difficulty of using that knowledge. It is important to understand how the organization and symbolical representation of knowledge affects people's ability to remember, retrieve information relevant to a particular situation or problem, regenerate knowledge that has been forgotten, and modify existing knowledge. The impact of knowledge structure on procedural learning has recently received considerable attention. Differences in expert versus novice performance have revealed an interplay between knowledge structure and processing abilities mediated by the quality of representation of the problem (see Simon 1973; Simon and Gilmartin 1973; Reitman 1976; and Chi, Feltovich, and Glaser 1981). Problem representation seems to be constructed by the expert on the basis of domain-related knowledge and its organization. Once a problem solver has represented a problem, then the proper problem-solving procedures (which can be thought of as a kind of schema) must be retrieved from long-term memory. Problem-solving deficiencies of novices have now been attributed more to the nature of the novices' knowledge base and less to the limitations of their general problem-solving strategies.

Computers, if they are programmed adequately to analyze cognitive processes underlying a particular subject matter, can be used to diagnose a learner's current knowledge and intellectual skills and their misconceptions. The computer program BUGGY has been used successfully to detect underlying misconceptions responsible for seemingly erratic errors in adding or subtracting multiple-digit numbers (Brown and Burton 1978). Such diagnostic applications may be especially important because they can contribute to theory about cognitive processes.

One way of organizing knowledge for effective use is reliance on a mental model—a relatively simple conceptual device used to explain or predict behavior or phenomena. Such explanations and predictions may be primitive and scientifically naive yet very useful for inferencing and thus for problem solving and for dealing with complex phenomena and devices such as computers, calculators, digital watches, engines, and so on. Instructional technology needs to build upon what we know about mental models. First of all, we need to identify the types of models learners bring to the instructional situation. These naive models have been shown, in the case of physical phenomena, to impair problem solving and learning and to be remarkably resistant to modification (McCloskey 1983; McCloskey,

Caramazza, and Green 1980). We must first discover the kinds of models learners bring to the instructional environment before we can effect changes in their conceptual models that would improve their performance. Current research needs to focus on theoretical analysis of why these misconceptions are so resistant to change, how conceptual structures can be effectively modified, and how to predict common conceptual difficulties that students have. It is even possible to create a simulated environment that models the naive conceptions of novice students. A learning process that first allows students to discover, on their own, the limitations of their current conceptions to explain phenomena in the real world may turn out to be more effective in fostering retention and/or transfer than traditional instruction. Causal models predicting which instructional strategies will be most effective in breaking through these misconceptions can be tested using CAIV to deliver the instruction and evaluate the learning.

Second, we need to track the development of models during the transition from novice to expert performer. If the elaboration of models over the course of learning follows a standard pattern, by understanding the sequence of models, appropriate next steps for instruction can be developed. Finally, we need to teach explicitly models that can facilitate the learner's performance. Kieras and Bovair (1983) have demonstrated success with this strategy in teaching students about the operation of an electrical control device. Students who were taught using an explicit model learned the procedures faster and showed better retention, and they were better able to make faster and more direct inferences about the system's operating procedures.

COMPUTER-RELATED TECHNOLOGIES AS TOOLS FOR RESEARCH

The properties of modern media and computer equipment coupled with knowledge about human cognition provide many opportunities for the development of media-based systems for optimal instruction. Just as importantly, research in support of the advance of instructional technology will contribute to model building in cognitive science. The use of CAIV instructional packages, in particular, allows the researcher to control, better than ever before, the myriad variables bearing upon teaching and learning. The confounding effects of teacher, content, delivery system, and so on can be eliminated. Holding content and delivery system constant, only the variable of interest is made to vary systematically.

Such research is only now being systematically undertaken. A 1987 meta-analysis by Gillingham and Guthrie reviewed all computer-assisted instruction research published since 1980 (dissertations and unpublished papers were excluded). Only 13 studies reported data that could be used to assess a positive or negative effect of CBI on learning (12 of the 13 had a positive effect), and of these 13 studies, only 6 compared two versions of CAI (mean effect size = 1.05; range = 3.28). The remainder of the 13 studies compared computer versus traditional, computer and traditional versus computer, or computer versus no control. Of the 6 studies that compared two forms of CAI instruction, 4 were carried out by Tennyson and his associates in Minnesota. The mean effect size (ES = 1.05) of research comparing two versions of a CAI package reveals by its strength that elements of the instructional package can indeed be varied to provide more optimal learning conditions.

MODELS OF INSTRUCTION AND LEARNING

Ultimately, basic cognitive research using computer-related technologies must be tied to theoretical models if it is to be truly meaningful. The comparative research paradigm, used for many years to evaluate the effectiveness of computer-related versus traditional instruction, was rarely set within a theoretical framework, and thus it yielded little information about why a particular approach was or was not effective with a population of learners. Ironically, computer-related technologies, with their superior controls over a number of instructional variables, offer an ideal research tool for such model testing. When tied to cognitive models of human learning, such studies offer the promise of advancing what we know about how people think, learn, remember, and transfer learning to new situations.

Several new approaches to understanding instructional interactions have been suggested. Reeves (1986) recommended several alternative research and evaluation approaches for computer-assisted interactive video. Citing its practicality in the real world of the classroom, where tight controls are either impossible or too costly, Reeves recommends the approach called by Cooley and Lohnes (1976) "the method of controlled correlation." This methodology requires two major steps. First, differences among learners must be assessed in four domains: (1) characteristics of learners, (2) contextual variables, (3) dimensions of instructional treatment, and (4) criteria or outcomes. Second, the measured differences must be analyzed to answer two questions: (1) how much of the variance in the outcomes can be attributed to each of the predictor domains (student ability, context, and treatment) and (2) how much of the variance is attributable to interactions among the predictors? According to Cooley and Lohnes (1976) better statistical procedures, including commonality analysis and path analysis, are able to estimate the percentage of achievement variance attributable to each of the predictor domains. (For more information on commonality analysis, see Kerlinger and Pedhazur 1973 and Kenny 1979.) These more sensitive procedures allow the assessment of unique effects as well as interactions, and, because of the use of the squared correlation coefficient, can reveal the degree of strength of relationships (Kenny 1979). Controlled correlation, to be meaningful, requires the development of causal models for the influence of the components of the instructional treatment on outcomes (Leinhardt 1980). Cooley and Lohnes (1976) suggest a "model of classroom processes" that includes the dimensions of opportunity, motivators, structure, and quality of instructional events. Reeves (1986) points out that if controlled correlation is to be used to evaluate interactive video, then models of the causal influence of the instructional dimensions of CAIV on outcomes must be developed. While many authors have attempted to list the instructional capabilities of CAIV, none have yet developed a causal model indicating how the dimensions of CAIV interrelate with the other elements in the learning equation.

Instructional Events Model

One approach to model building via controlled correlation suggested by Reeves (1986) would be to utilize Gagne's (1985) model of the critical events of instruction. Gagne, Wager, and Rojas (1981) indicated nine events that are necessary for CBI to be effective. They are (1) gaining attention, (2) informing the learner of the objectives, (3) stimulating recall of prior knowledge, (4) presenting stimuli with distinctive features, (5) guiding learning, (6) eliciting performance, (7) providing meaningful feedback, (8) assessing performance, and (9) enhancing retention and transfer of learning. Reeves suggests that a model of the causal relationships of these events could be integrated with the Cooley and Lohnes (1976) evaluation research model by programming the computer to record frequencies and duration of instructional events required by learners with different abilities and characteristics. Reeves (1986, 104) describes the promise this way:

If sufficient instructional options and branches were designed into the interactive video instruction, variation in learner paths through the instruction would provide considerable data for analysis with multiple regression procedures. On the other hand, designer-specified variations in instructional events might be programmed into the instruction to investigate the effects of particular instructional variables, such as stimulating recall of prior learning.

Cognitive Models

Another avenue of model building for computer-related instructional technologies suggested by Reeves (1986) is provided by information processing variables described by cognitive psychologists. Corresponding to the external instructional events described by Gagne (1985) are internal cognitive processes that have been described by Estes (1978) and Klatzky (1980) as well as by Tobias (1982), who discussed cognitive or "macroprocesses" (e.g., review, summarizing, feedback). As an example, the external instructional event of gaining attention requires internal learner alertness to be effective. Reeves (1986, 104) points to an important potential for computer-related technologies in this regard:

> If a non-interactive instructional event can be hypothesized to encourage or permit a particular macroprocess, can an interactive video program be designed which will require that process? For example, if the inclusion of questions at the end of a chapter of text encourages the macroprocess of review, can intelligent videodisc instruction be programmed so that review is required when diagnosis of student learning indicates it is needed?

CONCLUSIONS

What have we learned from two decades of research on technology-related instruction? Basically, we have established that computers and computer-related technologies can be used to teach effectively, sometimes more effectively than a classroom teacher, sometimes not. We have seen that research on the effectiveness of computer-related technologies for instruction has been consumed by the desire to compare the technological delivery system with conventional instructional design. Unfortunately, as Becker (1988) points out, the majority of those who have conducted research on various aspects of computer teaching have been more comfortable with computers than with research methodology, and thus even published studies often contain serious design flaws. Meta-analyses have collapsed together experiments utilizing very diverse applications, which results in different kinds of learning outcomes. The most serious flaw in the design comparing media-based versus nonmedia-based instruction is the invalid implicit assumption that instructional media represent meaningful experimental variables independent of instructional content or strategy. If all variables other than medium of delivery are held constant, we should expect little or no difference in learning. For example, if inserting interactivity into a linear videotape presentation with inserted questions and branching for feedback enhances learning and retention, in all probability, so would inserting interactivity into a lecture by asking the same questions and responding to students' answers.

While research has demonstrated that computers are beneficial adjuncts to instruction at various educational levels, we are just beginning to explore how computer-related technologies for instruction can best be utilized and for what kind of learning tasks.

Unfortunately, the dominant comparative research paradigm has tended to preclude more important research questions such as how computer-related technologies can provide the optimum conditions for learning and which components of instruction foster more effective learning for which types of learners.

Research about the effectiveness of computer-related technologies for instruction needs now to be tied to models or theories of learning. Using the framework provided by cognitive science, we should begin to investigate the impact of special features of media such as audio and visual coordination, pacing of learner responses, various feedback strategies, optimum elaboration of factual knowledge, and so on.

In addition to examining how computer-related technologies can be used to provide optimal conditions for learning, the agenda for research should also take advantage of the potential of computers as research tools for helping to unravel the complexities of human learning. The computer-related technologies of CAI and CAIV offer the most precise research tools available to date. Using CAI and CAIV it is possible to hold constant all variables such as content, instructional design, and delivery system. The impact of the variable of interest can then be assessed. CAIV offers an exciting potential to explore in depth the important variables of pacing, feedback, interactivity, role and placement of advance organizers, audiovisual coordination, and so on. When placed in a cognitive framework, such studies will allow us to test research questions bearing on some of the most critical issues in learning psychology, such as What is the impact of the structure of knowledge on acquisition and retrieval of learning? Which is a better model for encoding learning, elaboration or levels of processing? Are procedural and declarative knowledge stored together in LTM? What is the role of interactivity in learning? What is the role of prior knowledge? Is information stored in LTM in one abstract code or in both an abstract and a visual code? Which concepts better describe the structure of knowledge, schemas or propositions and productions?

In short, we have only begun to exploit the potential of computer-related technologies for teaching and for the study of teaching/learning phenomena. Rather than being discouraged by the lackluster results of poorly designed studies comparing human and computer-based teaching, we should take heart from the few studies that have manipulated microelements of the instructional design, such as pacing, to reveal significant increases in learning. Computer technology, with its potential for interactivity and individualization, may yet allow us to create powerful instructional designs capable of optimizing learning. Furthermore, carefully formulated research designs using computer technologies have great potential to add to our knowledge about how people learn.

REFERENCES

Avner, A., C. Moore, and S. Smith. 1980. "Active External Control: A Basis for Superiority of CBI." *Journal of Computer-Based Instruction* 6, no. 4: 115-18.

Bailio, B., and A. Kellock. 1981. "Improving Learner Productivity through the Use of Intelligent Videodisc." WICAT Inc., Background information paper prepared for School Division, Association of American Publishers Annual Meeting, Washington, D.C.

Bandura, A. 1977. *Social Learning Theory*. Englewood Cliffs, N.J.: Prentice-Hall.

Bangert-Drowns, R. L. 1986. "Review of Developments in Meta-Analytic Method. *Psychological Bulletin* 99: 388-99.

Bangert-Drowns, R. L., J. A. Kulik, and C.-L. C. Kulik. 1985. "Effectiveness of Computer-Based Education in Secondary Schools." *Journal of Computer-Based Instruction* 12: 59-68.

Barr, A., and E. A. Feigenbaum. 1982. *Handbook of Artificial Intelligence*. Vol. 2. Los Altos, Calif.: William Kaufman.

Becker, H. J. 1988. *The Impact of Computer Use on Children's Learning: What the Research Has Shown and What It Has Not*. Baltimore, Md.: Center for Research on Elementary and Middle Schools, The Johns Hopkins University.

Brown, J. S., and R. R. Burton. 1978. "Diagnostic Modes of Procedural Bugs in Basic Mathematical Skills." *Cognitive Science* 2: 155-92.

Chi, M. T. H., P. J. Feltovich, and R. Glaser. 1981. "Categorization and Representation of Physics Problems by Experts and Novices." *Cognitive Science* 5: 121-52.

Clark, R. E. 1983. "Reconsidering Research on Learning from Media." *Review of Educational Research* 53: 445-59.

Clark, R. E. 1985a. "Confounding in Educational Computing Research." *Journal of Educational Computing Research* 1: 137-48.

Clark, R. E. 1985b. "The Importance of Treatment Explication: A Reply to J. Kulik, C.-L. Kulik and R. Bangert-Drowns." *Journal of Educational Computing Research* 1: 389-93.

Cooley, W. W., and P. R. Lohnes. 1976. *Evaluation Research in Education: Theory, Principles, and Practice*. New York: Irvington.

Cronbach, L. J. 1975. "Beyond the Two Disciplines of Scientific Psychology. *American Psychologist* 30: 1-13.

Cronbach, L. J., and R. E. Snow. 1977. *Aptitudes and Instructional Methods: A Handbook for Research on Interactions*. New York: Irvington.

De Bono, E. 1985. "The CORT Thinking Program." In *Thinking and Learning Skills: Relating Instruction to Basic Research*, vol. 1, eds. J. W. Segal, S. F. Chipman, and R. Glaser. Hillsdale, N.J.: Lawrence Erlbaum.

Edwards, J., S. Norton, S. Taylor, R. van Dusseldorp, and M. Weiss. 1974. "Is CAI Effective?" *Association for Educational Data Systems Journal* 7: 122-26.

Estes, W. K. 1978. "The Information Processing Approach to Cognition: A Confluence of Metaphors and Methods." In *Handbook of Learning and Cognitive Processes*, vol. 5, *Human Information Processing*, ed. W. K. Estes. Hillsdale, N.J.: Lawrence Erlbaum.

Feldhusen, J. 1963. "Taps for Teaching Machines." *Phi Delta Kappan* 44: 265-67.

Feuerstein, R., Y. Rand, M. B. Hoffman, and R. Miller. 1980. *Instrumental Enrichment: An Intervention Program for Cognitive Modifiability*. Baltimore, Md.: University Park Press.

Gagne, R. M. 1985. *The Conditions of Learning*. 4th ed. New York: Holt, Rinehart & Winston.

Gagne, R. M. 1987. "Introduction." In *Instructional Technology Foundations*, ed. R. M. Gagne. Hillsdale, N.J.: Lawrence Erlbaum, 1-9.

Gagne, R. M., and R. Glaser. 1987. "Foundations in Learning Research." In *Instructional Technology Foundations*, ed. R. M. Gagne. Hillsdale, N.J.: Lawrence Erlbaum, 49-83.

Gagne, R. M., W. Wager, and A. Rojas. 1981. "Planning and Authoring Computer Assisted Instructional Lessons." *Educational Technology* 21, no. 9: 17-26.

Gillingham, M. G., and J. T. Guthrie. 1987. "Relationships between CBI and Research on Teaching." *Contemporary Educational Psychology* 12: 189-99.

Giunti, F. E., and D. A. Kimberlin. 1982. "Distributed Instructional System." Paper presented at the Association for the Development of Computer-Based Instructional Systems Conference, Vancouver, B.C., Canada.

Glass, G. V. 1976. "Primary, Secondary, and Meta-Analysis of Research." *Educational Researcher* 5: 3-8.

Glynn, S. M., and F. J. DiVesta. 1977. "Outline and Hierarchical Organization as Aids for Study and Retrieval." *Journal of Educational Psychology* 69: 89-95.

Greeno, J. G. 1978. "A Study of Problem Solving." In *Advances in Instructional Psychology*, vol. 1, ed. R. Glaser. Hillsdale, N.J.: Lawrence Erlbaum.

Hagler, P., and J. Knowlton. 1987. "Invalid Implicit Assumption in CBI Comparison Research." *Journal of Computer-Based Instruction* 14: 84-88.

Hayes, J. R. 1981. *The Complete Problem Solver*. Philadelphia: Franklin Institute Press.

Holmgren, J. E., F. N. Dyer, R. E. Hilligoss, and F. H. Heller. 1980. "The Effectiveness of Army Training Extensions Course Lessons on Videodisc." *Journal of Educational Technology Systems* 8: 263-74.

Kaplan, R., and E. Z. Rothkopf. 1974. "Instructional Objectives as Directions to Learners: Effect of Passage Length and Amount of Objective-Relevant Content." *Journal of Educational Psychology* 66: 448-56.

Kenny, D. A. 1979. *Correlation and Causality*. New York: Wiley.

Kerlinger, F. N., and E. J. Pedhazur. 1973. *Multiple Regression in Behavioral Research*. New York: Holt, Rinehart & Winston.

Ketner, W. D. 1982. "Videodisc Interactive Two Dimensional Equipment Training." In *Proceedings of Fourth Annual Conference on Video Learning Systems*. Warrenton, Va.: Society for Applied Learning Technology, 18-21.

Kieras, D. E., and S. Bovair. 1983. *The Role of a Mental Model in Learning to Operate a Device*. Technical Report No. 13. University of Arizona.

Klatzky, R. L. 1980. *Human Memory: Structures and Processes* 2d ed. San Francisco: Freeman.

Knowlton, J. 1960. "The Need for a Conceptual Rationale for the Audio-Visual Field." In *New Directions in Audio-Visual Communication: Bulletin of the School of Education*, ed. H. Bern. Bloomington: Indiana University, 41-61.

Knowlton, J. 1964. "A Socio- and Psycho-Linguistic Theory of Pictorial Communication." NDEA Title VII-B, Contract No. OE-3-16-019. Mimeograph. Washington, D.C.: U.S. Office of Education.

Kulik, C.-L. C., and J. A. Kulik. 1985. *Effectiveness of Computer-Based Education in Colleges*. Report No. IR 011 876. Paper presented at the annual meeting of the American Educational Research Association, Chicago. (ERIC Document Reproduction Service No. ED 263 890).

Kulik, C.-L. C., and J. A. Kulik. 1986. "Effectiveness of Computer-Based Education in Colleges." *AEDS Journal* 19: 81-108.

Kulik, C.-L. C., J. A. Kulik, and B. J. Shwalb. 1986. "Effectiveness of Computer-Based Adult Education." *Journal of Educational Computing Research* 2: 235-52.

Kulik, J. A., and C.-L. C. Kulik. 1987. "Review of Recent Research Literature on Computer-Based Instruction." *Contemporary Educational Psychology* 12: 222-30.

Kulik, J. A., C.-L. C. Kulik, and R. L. Bangert-Drowns. 1985. "Effectiveness of Computer-Based Education in Elementary Schools." *Computers in Human Behavior* 1: 59-74.

Leinhardt, G. 1980. "Modeling and Measuring Educational Treatment in Evaluation." *Review of Educational Research* 50: 393-420.

McCloskey, M. 1983. "Naive Theories of Motion." In *Mental Models*, eds. D. Gentner and A. L. Stevens. Hillsdale, N.J.: Lawrence Erlbaum.

McCloskey, M., A. Caramazza, and B. Green. 1980. "Curvilinear Motion in the Absence of External Forces: Naive Beliefs about the Motion of Objects." *Science* 210: 1,139-41.

Niemiec, R., and H. J. Walberg. 1987. "Comparative Effects of Computer-Assisted Instruction: A Synthesis of Reviews." *Journal of Educational Computing Research* 3: 19-37.

Palincsar, A. S., and A. L. Brown. 1984. "Reciprocal Teaching of Comprehension-Monitoring Activities." *Cognition and Instruction* 1, no. 2: 117-75.

Park, O., and R. D. Tennyson. 1980. "Adaptive Design Strategies for Selecting Number and Presentation Order of Examples in Coordinate Concept Acquisition." *Journal of Educational Psychology* 72: 362-70.

Reeves, T. C. 1986. "Research and Evaluation Models for the Study of Interactive Video." *Journal of Computer-Based Instruction* 13: 102-6.

Reeves, T. C., and J. M. King. 1986. *Evaluation of a Group-Based Interactive Videodisc System for Military Training*. Paper presented at the annual convention of the Association of Educational Communications and Technology, Las Vegas, Nev.

Reif, F. 1985. "Exploiting Present Opportunities of Computers in Science and Mathematics Education." *Journal of Computers in Mathematics and Science Teaching* (Fall): 15-26.

Reitman, J. S. 1976. "Skilled Perception in Go: Deducing Memory Structures from Inter-Response Times." *Cognitive Psychology* 8: 336-56.

Resnick, L. B. 1981. "Instructional Psychology." *Annual Review of Psychology* 32: 659-704.

Rothkopf, E. Z. 1971. "Experiments on Mathemagenic Behavior and the Technology of Written Instruction." In *Verbal Learning Research and the Technology of Written Instruction*, eds. E. Z. Rothkopf and P. E. Johnson. New York: Teachers College Press.

Rubinstein, M. 1975. *Patterns of Problem Solving*. Englewood Cliffs, N.J.: Prentice-Hall.

Salomon, G. 1981. *Interaction of Media, Cognition, and Learning*. San Francisco: Jossey-Bass.

Schroeder, J. E. 1982. "U.S. Army VISTA Evaluation Results." *Proceedings of Fourth Annual Conference on Video Learning Systems*. Warrenton, Va.: Society for Applied Learning Technology.

Simon, H. 1973. "The Structure of Ill-Structured Problems." *Artificial Intelligence* 4: 181-201.

Simon, H., and K. Gilmartin. 1973. "A Simulation of Memory for Chess Positions." *Cognitive Psychology* 5: 29-46.

Slavin, R. 1986. "Best-Evidence Synthesis: An Alternative to Meta-Analytic and Traditional Reviews." *Educational Research* 15: 5-11.

Stolurow, L. 1962. "Implications of Current Research and Future Trends." *Journal of Educational Research* 55: 519-27.

Tennyson, R. D. 1981. "Use of Adaptive Information for Advisement in Learning Concepts and Rules Using Computer-Assisted Instruction." *American Educational Research Journal* 18: 425-38.

Tennyson, R. D., D. L. Christensen, and S. I. Park. 1984. "The Minnesota Adaptive Instruction System: An Intelligent CBI System." *Journal of Computer-Based Instruction* 11: 2-13.

Tennyson, R. D., and S. I. Park. 1984. "Process Learning Time as an Adaptive Design Variable in Concept Learning Using Computer-Based Instruction." *Journal of Educational Psychology* 76: 452-65.

Tennyson, R. D., O. Park, and D. L. Christensen. 1985. "Adaptive Control of Learning Time and Content Sequence in Concept Learning Using Computer-Based Instruction." *Journal of Educational Psychology* 77: 481-91.

Tobias, S. 1982. "When Do Instructional Methods Make a Difference?" *Educational Researcher* 11, no. 4: 4-9.

Whimbey, A., and J. Lochhead. 1980. *Problem Solving and Comprehension: A Short Course in Analytical Reasoning*. Philadelphia: Franklin Institute Press.

Wickelgren, W. A. 1974. *How to Solve Problems*. San Francisco: Freeman.

Virtualities

Brockenbrough S. Allen
Professor of Educational Technology
San Diego State University

> To simulate night flying, small electric stars are fixed in a wire cupola overhead. For daylight flying, terrain photographs are projected on a silk screen below. The operator of the trainer may control all of the natural variables of flight: clouds, haze, bumpy air currents and wind drift. After the plane has been piloted to a hypothetical objective, the bombardier may drop his bombs, with pinpoints of light on the screen below marking spot[s] where they have landed.
>
> "Synthetic Sky"
> *Life Magazine* 1944

As we enter the 1990s, computers have become so ubiquitous, so powerful, and so cheap that observers hesitate to identify long-term trends for the same reason that one hesitates to predict the trajectory of a Fourth of July rocket: there will be an explosion, in this case an explosion of possibilities—new demands, new markets, and new niches for hardware and software. But the processing and display capabilities of educational computers have followed a general evolutionary path for 40 years, from number processing to word processing to image processing to (in the nineties) spatial processing. It's clear that the widespread use of real-time, three-dimensional graphics—one of the most important simulative capabilities of computers—has been constrained by the limited memory and processing power of the 1980s. The next decade will bring radical changes in the way we think about the interactive and communicative capabilities of machines and the way they challenge our educational use of visualization and envisionment.

A HERITAGE OF SPATIAL THINKING

> The means of achieving desired shapes [300,000 years ago] were much more effective than those evident at 1.2 million [years ago]. The hominids employed artifact designs that require perspective, the control of spatial quantity, and an understanding of composition, in the sense of constituent elements.
>
> Thomas Wynn
> *The Evolution of Spatial Intelligence*

Human ability to think about the movement, location, and relationship of objects extends far into our primate past and, in the case of our individual selves, to our earliest childhood. But the ability to interpret mediated presentations such as photographs, motion pictures, and computer screens is a learned skill. Visual literacy requires mastery of complex rules for inferring three-dimensional relationships from two-dimensional cues such as shading, apparent size, perspective, and occlusion of objects. There are cultural conventions, too. Television viewers in different cultures begin scanning a shot or scene in the corner where they would start to read text: upper left for readers of English and romance languages, lower-right for those of Hebrew and Farsi. As occupants of "carpentered" environments, we are easily misled by optical illusions that play on our assumption that floors and ceilings are parallel and openings in walls are usually rectangular. Non-Westerners are not always so easily fooled.

Visuospatial abilities are highly teachable. Indeed, proper development of human vision requires tens of thousands of hours in which an individual's visual system is directly coupled with a visual environment that responds consistently to voluntary changes in position and location. Without this linkage, mammals don't learn to see properly. Kittens moved about in a visual environment never learn to see well unless they themselves control the movement. When humans put on lenses that turn the world upside down, they adapt within weeks. But not if they are prevented from actively controlling their own locomotion. Restored to physiological sight, the congenitally blind see only blobs and blurs at first; interpretation and understanding come much later.

The available evidence suggests that in order to recognize and understand the flat world of the television monitor and the motionless world of the photograph, viewers must have first learned to navigate in three-dimensional space. In order to "see," we must construct mental models of the real world. And this requires millions of tiny experiments in which we predict the relationship between our movement through space and resulting changes in the visual field.

The eye may resemble a camera in some ways, but most cognitive psychologists are extremely skeptical about the commonplace notion that we store images as mental photos, raster scans, or bit maps the way machines do. Rather, we are searchers for patterns, meanings, and anomalies, guided in highly selective eye movements by internalized standards of significance. To be a trained observer is to know in advance what to look for. We abstract details that seem important at the time of visual inspection and forget the rest almost completely.

SPACE AS A PLACE FOR KNOWING

> Describing the evolutions in the dance of these gods, their juxtapositions and their advances, to tell which came into line and which in opposition, describing all this without visual models would be labor spent in vain.
>
> Plato, *Timaeus*

Visualization—so critical to the reconstruction of experience, to our faculties of imagination, and to our ability to solve everyday problems—is quite different from the notion of pictures in the head. Visualized concrete images are less crisp and more malleable than real-world counterparts, represented in a kind of "problem space" where they can be rotated, folded, segmented, rearranged, and so on.

Descriptions of scientific and engineering phenomena are often based on instrument readings and other indirect evidence and cannot be described without using spatial metaphors. The history of discovery is replete with examples of specially imagined spaces, many of them charged with the creative vitality of this dream revelation of Friedrich Kekulé, who proposed the structure of the benzene ring: "The atoms were gamboling before my eyes ... all twining and twisting in snake-like motion. But look! What was that? One of the snakes had seized hold of its own tail and the form whirled mockingly before my eyes. As if by a flash of lightening I awoke" (quoted in R. H. McKim 1980, 11).

Biderman (1987) argues that there is a finite set of visual primitives that constitutes the basis for our perception of words and sentences. It appears that our schemata for classifying objects depend heavily on segmentation (at perceived vertices) into components that objects depend heavily on segmentation (at perceived vertices) into components that Biderman calls *geometric icons*, or *geons*. Surface characteristics such as hue, intensity, and texture typically play a secondary role. Humans, like other organisms, have a finite capacity for processing visual information; three-dimensional imagery is particularly demanding. Extracting component features and encoding them may reduce this demand.

Linguists and sociobiologists have argued that the ability to conceptualize three-dimensional space formed a foundation for language ("Where is the prey?"). Our speech is studded with spatial metaphors: prices go up, problems get bigger, careers rise, we open our hearts (or close our minds); thus many ideas are understood—often at a deeply subconscious level—as things moving through a sort of mental ether. Such figures of speech are, according to philosopher Mark Johnson (1987, xix), more than just mundane forms of poetic license; they are indicators that human thought and language are profoundly empowered and constrained by the way we understand our own bodies: "We human beings have bodies. We *are* 'rational *animals*,' but we are also '*rational* animals,' which means that our rationality is embodied.... Our reality is shaped by the patterns of our bodily movement, the contours of our spatial and temporal orientation, and the forms of our interaction with objects. It is never merely a matter of abstract conceptualization and propositional judgments."

INTERACTION OR NAVIGATION?

> How much a dunce that has been sent to roam
> Excels a dunce that has been kept at home.
> William Cowper
> *The Progress of Error*

How should computers represent spatial relationships? Even more important, how should computers use spatial metaphors to represent nonspatial relationships? These will emerge as two of the most fundamental issues in educational computing of the 1990s. By the end of the century, we can expect a vastly expanded repertoire of affordable hardware and software options for spatial representation of data and ideas.

The Macintosh-style graphical interface of the 1980s combined features such as windows, icons, and mouse-driven movement to offer a serious alternative to text-based interpreted commands, adding, in a sense, an extra dimension to the notion of a command *line*. But there is more to a Mac-style graphical interface than an X-Y coordinate system and a pointer. Additional dimensions are represented by spatial metaphors. Multiple windows, open to different applications, are represented as "layers." Files are organized by putting them "into" folder-like icons.

Graphical interfaces raise questions about our notions of interactive systems. The first major advance in computer interfaces involved a shift from batch processing to conversational computing. In earlier days, computer users submitted programs and data files on a stack of punch cards. As an undergraduate at Berkeley, I sometimes had to wait several days to get a reaction from the campus mainframe. I was amazed several years later to be able to sit at a glass teletype, key in BASIC commands, and get immediate responses. It was all very language-like. Type something and the computer types something back. It is this notion of computing, perhaps, that led Alan Turing (1950) to propose his famous test of machine intelligence: if you could hold a conversation with a machine and couldn't distinguish the responses from those which a human might make, then the machine was "intelligent."

We think of conversation (and interaction) when there are at least two systems (even if one is a computer) and when each system influences the behavior of the other(s). Most people would also agree that controlling a machine through knobs and levers is also a form of interaction. But in driving to work, does one interact with the roads? In reading a book, does one interact with the pages? Why do we continue to refer to certain types of videodisc machines as Level I Interactive Video when they are merely a means for finding frames and "paging" through them at various speeds.

It might help if we distinguished clearly between the verbs *interact* and *navigate*. *Interact* means "to act upon one another," and *navigate* means "to steer a course through a medium" (*Webster's Ninth New Collegiate Dictionary*). The distinction will become more important as we attempt to build systems that give us greater freedom to organize and explore information. Trying to understand complex systems (whether they be systems of thought or systems of physical objects) without being able to navigate through them may be impossible. Or perhaps just foolish.

In any case, as we continue our trek into the information jungle, we're going to need devices to help us find our way. The utility of navigation as a computer metaphor rests on our experience as a species, as a culture, as individuals in moving through real three-dimensional space. But navigation tools are of much greater value when computers are powerful enough to provide many choices of "places" to go and interfaces that represent spatial relationships so that they can be grasped intuitively, even viscerally.

Early personal computers, of course, did not have the memory and processing power required for high-resolution graphical interfaces. Nor were they capable of representing complex three-dimensional objects moving through space; this function was assigned to videodisc systems with their huge storage capacity. Simply stated, the principle drawback of conventional videodiscs as a means of representing reality is that they don't allow real-time manipulation of objects or unconstrained navigation through the space that contains the objects.

We've seen some memorable but inherently limited attempts to use interactive video as a navigable medium; most notable are the surrogate travel discs. The classic example is MIT's Movie Map (Lipman 1980), a system that permits viewers to select videotaped routes through a constrained spatial framework consisting of streets and intersections. Movie Map affords optional perspectives such as front and side views of street travel, aerial photos, and still-image tours of buildings. Viewers can navigate through time, too, using the Winter/Spring and Now/Then buttons.

Another approach to the problem of video navigation involves a technique called *interleaving*, introduced by Phillips (the Dutch electronics giant) in 1985. Video, shot simultaneously from several viewpoints is laid down on the disc as a series of very short alternating segments: $A_1 B_1 C_1 A_2 B_2 C_2 \ldots A_n B_n C_n$. The viewer can instantly select any one of the viewpoints (three in this case) as the action continues. A standard disc side can store 10 minutes of action viewable from 3 perspectives (or 1 minute of action viewable from 30 perspectives).

Intel Corporation's DVI (Digital Video Interactive) technology offers some new solutions to the "navigation" problem. An anamorphic lense is used to record a 360-degree panoramic image that is then stored on a DVI disc. Because DVI encodes "natural" video in digital form, images can be manipulated under computer (and viewer) control in real time. The viewer can pan through the reconstructed image at will in either direction and zoom in on details.

Another DVI technique involves adding new spatial metaphors to ordinary video. Motion picture "tiles" or "windows" are embedded in a computer-managed spatial framework through optical animation. Televised "infotainment" programs such as "Night-line" and "Crossfire" make modest use of this technique when they angle tiled images of newsmakers in different studios so that they appear to be facing each other. With DVI, a viewer could use a mouse or joystick to roam through computer-managed space, inspecting tiled images from various distances and angles, much as one would wander through a museum or art gallery.

FRAMELESS NAVIGATION

> In a car you're always in a compartment, and because you're used to it you don't realize that through that car window everything you see is just more TV. You're a passive observer and it is all moving by you boringly in a frame. On a cycle the frame is gone. You're completely in contact with it all. You're *in* the scene, not just watching it anymore, and the sense of presence is overwhelming.
>
> Robert Pirsig
> *Zen and the Art of*
> *Motorcycle Maintenance*

Given very powerful computers (and fairly large amounts of money), it is now possible to extend the navigational metaphor to three-dimensional computer models of complex objects and arrays. Some simulations of atmospheric phenomena, earthquate faults, atom splitting, and air tunnel tests are so complicated that they must be conducted in super-computers. How do scientists inspect the results? Often the information is so unfathomable that more can be understood through visual inspection and spatial manipulation of computer-generated three-dimensional models than from even the most sophisticated statistical analysis. Apparently, nothing can yet beat the ability of a well-trained human viewer for detecting certain types of unanticipated patterns and anomalies.

The line resolution of high-end monitors is now approaching the angular resolution of the human eye. It appears that computer-generated displays of simple objects will soon be indistinguishable from real objects, provided that cues from stereoscopic vision and motion parallax are eliminated. On the horizon are powerful techniques for creating highly realistic, real-time three-dimensional simulations of the "ordered chaos" represented by scenes of mountain terrains and forests. Much more challenging is the problem of simulating the movement of fluids or the complex volitional movements of sentient life forms.

This problem aside, those who are engineering the computer simulations of the future must confront the limitations of the framed view (the monitor or computer screen). The frame is both an anchor for the timid armchair navigator and the bane of the truly intrepid. It is the *idée fixe* for almost every filmmaker, videographer, and software designer and has been the dominant scheme for a thousand years of Western painting and architecture.

But the frame began to fade several years ago at NASA's Ames Research Center when Scott Fisher and his associates developed a lightweight helmet housing two wide-angle stereoscopic LCD displays and a device for tracking the position of the user's head (see Fisher 1990). As one "looks around," the computer-generated imagery changes accordingly, maintaining the viewer's three-dimensional perspective. A *data glove* senses gestures and represents them as a computer-generated virtual "hand" for directing events and manipulating computer-generated objects. (Advanced versions use a *data suit* for sensing body positions.) The system also includes speech recognition and synthesis capabilities.

Futuristic? Not really. VPL Research is now marketing a commercial version of the NASA system for about $250,000. Many observers expect prices to decline rapidly as custom chips are developed and as costs for specialized hardware and software are amortized. Autodesk, Inc., of Sausalito, California, plans to market a system next year for about $30,000. One engineer predicts that $2,500 no-frills hobbyist systems will be available within two years.

VIRTUAL REALTIES

> We do not see things as they are;
> we see things as *we* are.
> the Talmud

Interactive technology and communications are merely aspects of a revolution that will soon project computer users into *virtual realities*. The phrase (which sounds at first like an oxymoron) refers to environments in which visual, aural, or other stimuli generate in the mind of the user a sense of navigable, frameless, three-dimensional space. Ted Nelson, who coined the terms *hypertext* and *hypermedia*, prefers the word *virtualities*.

West Coasters have adapted the jargon of science fiction writer William Gibson (*Neuromancer* and *Mona Lisa Overdrive*) and talk about *cyberspace* and, yes, *cybernauts*. Presumably these words derive from *cybernetic*, introduced by Norbert Wiener to refer to the study of communication and control systems. But regarding earlier discussion about navigational metaphors, it should be noted that the root-word, *cyber*, descended from the Greek *kybernetes*, pilot or steersman.

Cybernauts "map" their actions into *cyber domains* through the use of puppets. Do not be misled by the choice of words. In this context, a puppet is more than a Pinocchio-like doll. Autodesk's Randal Walser calls it "a sort of vehicle for your mind." Any object controlled by a remote intellect is a puppet. As Walser (1989, 00) explains,

> Looking through a puppet's "eyes," your sense of self merges with it.... You can place your mind within this or that puppet, moving your center of awareness instantly from place to place within a space (or back out to your physical body in the real world).... We distinguish a special disembodied puppet called a spirit which is basically just a viewpoint and control center in cyberspace. Think of a spirit as a manifestation of a cybernaut's personality or character, projected into cyberspace, where it can inhabit any object, or simply roam free.

Gibson, the science fiction writer, originally conceived of cyberspace as a huge computer-based "consensual reality" with millions of users, ranging from lonely hackers to huge corporations. Early experiments suggest that consensual use of cyberspace is not only possible but also fun—leading, for example, to sophisticated games of tag and hide-and-seek.

How would one know whether an object was occupied by a spirit representing a human co-worker or inhabited by some machine intelligence? It might be very difficult. The notion of virtual realities challenges Turing's test of artificial intelligence. Why should the key to earning our respect, the proof by example, be restricted to conversing? Why not intelligent miming or gesturing, dancing or gamboling, or serving as silent guide to new perspectives?

At Autodesk, there's also talk of *Cyberia*—a set of cyberspace domains controlled from a room equipped with various props and devices including data suits, joysticks, keyboards, bicycles, rowing machines, steering wheels, musical instruments, and so on. As patrons of their personal domains, cybernauts would use these devices to map their actions into virtualities, much as people go to museums, theaters, and health clubs but with the power to reshape the electronic environment as they wish. Medical students would roam through electronic cadavers, reconfiguring their self-representation at will (as a scalpel, for example, or a microbe) and changing their scale of action from normal to microscopic. Architects and designers would escort clients through cyberspace mockups of buildings and products, rearranging or reshaping components through gestures. Autodesk's Eric Gullichsen raises the specter of cyberspace realities (in a couple of decades) that are so realistic that "a client could have a house built for him in the machine, invite his friends over and enjoy it in the machine." If housing continues to get more expensive, consider moving to Cyburbia.

REFERENCES

Biderman, I. 1987. "Recognition-by-Components: A Theory of Human Image Understanding." *Psychological Review* 94, no. 2: 115-47.

Fisher, S. 1990. "Virtual Environments: Personal Simulations and Telepresence." *Multimedia Review* 1, no. 2: 24-29.

Foley, J. D. 1987. "Interfaces for Advanced Computing." *Scientific American* (October): 126-35.

Gibson, W. 1984. *Neuromancer*. New York: Ace Science Fiction.

Gibson, W. 1988. *Mona Lisa Overdrive*. New York: Bantam Books.

Johnson, M. 1987. *The Body in the Mind: The Bodily Basis of Meaning, Imagination, and Reason*. Chicago: University of Chicago Press.

Lipman, A. 1980. "Movie Maps: An Application of the Optical Videodisc to Computer Graphics." *Computer Graphics* 14, no. 3.

McKim, R. H. 1980. *Thinking Visually: A Strategy Manual for Problem-Solving*. Belmont, Calif.: Wadsworth Publishaing.

Turing, A. 1950. "Computing Machinery and Intelligence." *Mind* 59 (October): 230-65.

Walser, R. 1989. *The Emerging Technology of Cyberspace*. Unpublished manuscript. Sausalito, Calif.: Autodesk, Inc.

Wynn, T. 1989. *The Evolution of Spatial Intelligence*. Chicago: University of Chicago Press.

Video Technology Revisited
in Teacher Training

Rolayne Wilson
Utah State University
Department of Health, Physical Education,
and Recreation
Logan, Utah

The use of video technology in teacher training began in the early 1960s at Stanford University. Those were the days of bulky cameras, microphones with long cords, and playback units. It was no easy task to transport this equipment to classrooms, gymnasiums, or out-of-doors to preserve the microteaching experiences of preservice teachers. Video cameras have now become lightweight, fairly inexpensive, easily accessible to all teaching environments, and wireless microphones have improved the quality and volume of the voice on tape. Instructional technologies continue to change incredibly quickly, with new innovations constantly being introduced in the educational arena. The purpose of this essay is to revisit an existing technology that continues to be a valuable and reliable utility in the training of preservice teachers, specifically in the area of physical education.

Orme, McDonald, and Allen (1966) compared the use of videotape and written models in teacher training. They found that students performed the desired teaching behaviors better after viewing the videotaped performance of a master teacher. The study also revealed that better teaching behaviors occurred in a later microteaching lesson when the instructor provided feedback while the preservice teachers viewed their first microteaching tape than did the group of preservice teachers who viewed their first microteaching tape alone.

Fuller and Manning (1973) conducted an exhaustive literature review related to the use of videotapes. One section of the review focused on microteaching feedback. Fuller and Manning identified two conditions under which the benefits to preservice teachers are maximized: first, when the supervisor has no expectations for immediate improvement in teaching by the preservice teacher, and, second, when feedback from the supervisor is unambiguous and is related to performance goals identified before the preservice teacher views the videotape.

Allen (1967) reported that after an eight-week microteaching program consisting of approximately 10 hours per week, secondary school interns performed more competently than did a comparable group of student teachers who spent 20 to 25 hours a week receiving traditional instruction with related experience as teacher aides. Koran, Snow, and McDonald (1971) found that videotape feedback was more effective than written feedback in training preservice teachers.

Martin (1987, 82) concluded his study with the following comment: "The use of stimulated recall in reviewing videotapes of student teachers can provide meaningful feedback to student teachers on their actual performance, can provide university supervisors a technique for assisting student teacher growth, and can provide a means for accumulating valuable video tapes to be used in the preservice training of future teachers."

Legge and Aspen (1972) concluded from their study that microteaching, used in conjunction with a video camera then followed with an intervention session, provides significant improvements in teaching skills for preservice teachers. Peck and Tucker (1973, 951) describe microteaching as "a conceptual system for identifying specified teaching skills with the use of videotape feedback to facilitate growth in teaching skills."

The literature reviewed found video technology to be a viable tool in increasing the effectiveness of the teaching skills of preservice teachers. Video technology in teacher training provides several benefits:

- It shows the lesson as it really is.

- It promotes an objective analysis of the lesson.

- It allows important segments of the lesson to be reviewed over and over.

- It provides visual as well as verbal evidence of how the lesson was executed.

- It allows for self-evaluation.

- It allows the results of the lesson to become immediately available.

- It heightens student interest and motivation.

- It develops self-confidence for student teaching.

Video technology can help develop sports skills in physical education preservice majors. For example, a student might be videotaped while performing groundstrokes in tennis. The student's performance would be subjected to a biomechanical analysis by the instructor while the student viewed the videotape. The student would then receive feedback on correct and incorrect tennis groundstroke execution. Skill development, however, is only a part of the training of physical education majors.

Another area of training is the development of effective teaching skills. Learning to teach, like learning sports skills, requires repetition. Anderson (1980) provides an in-depth discussion of the analysis of teaching in physical education. Several observation instruments are presented and discussed. The observation instruments provide feedback for preservice teachers on how effective their teaching skills are in a microteaching situation. Coding a student's teaching performance in a live setting requires extensive training. Anderson suggests that coding from a videotape provides better reliability and validity. Metzler (1980), Siedentop, Tousignant, and Parker (1982), Placek and Silverman (1983), Rink (1985), and Taggart (1988) agree that preservice physical education majors need to have several field experience opportunities to practice their teaching skills. The preservice teacher's lessons were videotaped and subsequently coded using an observation instrument. Taggart (1988, 75) said:

> Teacher training based on a behavior analysis approach demands that student teachers understand the research base and relevance of the teaching skills they will be expected to demonstrate. It also requires adequate opportunities to develop competency in the implementation of these skills in a variety of settings with a variety of clients.

The physical education teacher education program at Ohio State University utilizes videotape as its primary means of evaluating the progress of the acquisition of teaching skills among preservice teachers (Taggart 1988). This program encourages the development and implementation of preservice programs that are clearly identifiable in both product and process measures. Videotaped lessons allow the student and the instructor to evaluate the product and process measures of the teaching experience.

Knowledge of research results with videotaped preservice experiences and the positive impact these experiences have on the acquisition of teaching skills were the catalysts for the Health, Physical Education, and Recreation Department at Utah State University in Logan, Utah, to implement a similar program. The physical education teaching methods courses require the students to teach several microlessons. The class titled "Introduction to Teaching Physical Education" provides the preservice teacher an opportunity to learn and practice teaching skills. The students teach two 10 to 15-minute lessons while being videotaped. After each lesson, the student meets with the instructor for an intervention session. During the session, the student recalls what went well with his or her lesson, indicates what areas need improvement for the next lesson, and reflects on how he or she felt about the lesson. The intervention then focuses on the following areas of teaching effectiveness as the student and instructor view the videotaped lesson:

- Wait time versus activity time
- Verbal crutches
- Modeling of the skill and/or drill
- Management skills (grouping of students, equipment distribution, class formations, drill formations, effective use of space and equipment)
- Proper progression of skill
- Accomplishment of lesson plan objective
- Creativity in planning the lesson
- Correct lesson sequence (introduction, lesson focus, culminating activity, and review)
- Simple and short teaching cues
- Movement pattern of teacher in the gym or outside
- Safety factors addressed during the lesson

Video technology allows preservice teachers to view their lesson as it was taught. The old adage "a picture is worth a thousand words" certainly applies when using videotape to critique a lesson. Some comments preservice teachers have made about the videotaping and the intervention session follow:

- "I had no idea I said OK so many times while teaching."
- "When I first knew I was going to be videotaped, I was scared to death. After viewing the tape, I have learned so much about what I need to work on to improve my teaching. This was a valuable yet scary experience."
- "I can see where I need to model the skill and drill for the class."
- "I didn't have a clue that those kids were off task while I was walking around the gym."
- "I need to make my explanations shorter. I talk way too much. I'm glad you videotaped the lesson so I could see my strengths and areas I need to improve in."

Videotaping a class, arranging for and conducting an intervention session require a time commitment for both preservice teacher and instructor. The benefits to the students in terms of improving their teaching from the first lesson to the second lesson are worth the effort. The course evaluations for the class have indicated that the students' confidence has increased, they are aware of their strengths and weaknesses, and they are motivated to continue their pursuit of a teaching certificate.

An alternative approach to the intervention session is to have the preservice teacher evaluate the lesson videotape using an observation instrument. The Health, Physical Education, and Recreation Department at Utah State University has developed an observation instrument specifically for the physical education methods courses (see figure 1, page 58) that reduces the time commitment for the instructor. The instructor fills out an evaluation sheet at the conclusion of the lesson after observing the critical points of the lesson. The student then views the tape and completes the evaluation within a specified time frame.

The Utah State University Physical Education Teacher Evaluation form provides an observation instrument that enhances the videotape experience of preservice teachers and teacher educators by providing a behavioral analysis of the teaching experience. An in-depth explanation of the five categories used to evaluate preservice teachers' teaching skills follows:

Explanation of USU Teaching Skills Categories

CONTEXT LEVEL

Management. Time devoted to transition, management, break, or warm-up. It will include such things as team selection, changing equipment, changing stations, teacher explanation of organizational arrangement, taking attendance, lecturing about appropriate behavior, getting a drink of water, telling jokes, and activities designed to prepare students for further activity but not to alter their physical state on a long-term basis—light exercises to begin class, stretching exercises prior to class, and cooling down activity.

Instructional. Time devoted to technique, strategy, rules, social behavior, or background. It will include such things as watching a motor-skill lecture or demonstration, explanation of strategy, explanation of an individual move, discussion on how to move the ball down field, explanation of the rules of the game, viewing a film on rules or a skill, explanation of sportsmanship, reporting one's own violations in a game, information on history, tradition, heroes, records, or relationship to fitness.

Active learning. Time devoted to skill practice, scrimmage, game, or fitness. It will include such things as a circle drill in passing a volleyball, practicing a dance step, one-on-one dribbling, half-court five on five, practice of free throws, application of skills in a game, running the half-mile, activities whose purpose is to alter the physical state of the individual in terms of strength, cardiovascular endurance, or flexibility—aerobic dance, distance running, and weight lifting (should be of sufficient intensity, frequency, and duration).

(Explanation continues on page 59.)

USU Physical Education Teacher Evaluation

Teacher_____ School_____ Grade_____ Date_____

Activity_____ # of students_____ Starting_____ Ending_____

Context Level
Management (M)   Transition, management, break, warm-up
Instructional (I)   Technique, strategy, rules, social behavior, background
Active Learning (A) Skill practice, scrimmage, fitness

```
 :  :    :  :    :  :    :  :    :  :    :  :    :  :    :  :    :  :

 :  :    :  :    :  :    :  :    :  :    :  :    :  :    :  :    :  :

 :  :    :  :    :  :    :  :    :  :    :  :    :  :    :  :    :  :
```

M=_____ min____ %   I=_____ min____ %   A=_____ min____ %

EXPLANATION/DEMONSTRATION   TEACHER TRAITS

	1	2	3		Y	N
Everyone attentive				"With-it-ness"		
Major pts. stressed				Smoothness		
Skill level appropriate				Overlapping		
Slow-normal speed				Reviewing		
Level of understanding				Objectives		
Amount verbalization				Hustles/prompts		
Questions allowed				Momentum		
Clearly defined tasks				Group alerting		
Timing				Appropriate equipment		
Safety				Appropriate dress		
Clarity/simplicity				Promptness		

INTERACTION

Verbal Teacher Feedback to Student

Positive	
Constructive	
Negative	
First names	
Questions	

PC/N Ratio_____
Total_____

Nonverbal Teacher Feedback to Student

Positive body gestures	
Negative body gestures	
Body contact	

P/N Ratio_____
Total_____

Verbal Student Feedback to Teacher

Questions	
Positive	
Negative	

Total_____

PLACEK

1. Number of Students_____ Number Engaged_____ % Engaged_____ Change_____

2. Number of Students_____ Number Engaged_____ % Engaged_____ Change_____

3. Number of Students_____ Number Engaged_____ % Engaged_____ Change_____

Figure 1. USU Physical Education Teacher Evaluation.

EXPLANATION/DEMONSTRATION

Everyone attentive. The students are within visual and auditory distance of the teacher and everyone is present, attentive, and focused on the teacher.

Major points stressed. The teacher verbalizes and demonstrates correct and/or incorrect features as defined in the lesson plan.

Skill level appropriate. The verbal explanation and movement demonstration are appropriate for student skill and knowledge level.

Slow-normal speed. The skill demonstration is initially performed in slow motion and is followed by a demonstration at normal speed.

Level of understanding. Based on student reaction, are the students understanding what the teacher is saying? If students have quizzical looks on their faces or ask a lot of questions, the level may be too difficult.

Questions allowed. To what degree are students given an opportunity to ask questions?

Clearly defined tasks. Tasks are so defined that students can move into formation and begin their tasks without asking questions and without having to be physically manipulated into the correct formations.

Timing. Refers to the time between task definition and when students actually begin the task. Appropriate timing would be to introduce one task and then let students practice the task. Inappropriate timing would be to explain three tasks at one time and then let the students practice the tasks. By the time the students reach the third task, they may have forgotten the task, so the teacher must take the time to repeat the instructions.

Safety. The degree to which the teacher removes or takes precautions to limit hazards in the playing area and alerts students to the inherent risks of the drill or activity.

Clarity/simplicity. The teacher presents clear directions and instructions in logical, step-by-step sequences at an appropriate level of vocabulary.

TEACHER TRAITS

"With-it-ness." The ability to know what students are doing at all times. In short, having eyes in the back of one's head.

Smoothness. The ability to keep the lesson free from stops or breaks in the flow of activities.

Overlapping. The ability to deal effectively with two issues at the same time.

Reviewing. Does the teacher, at the beginning of class, review previously learned material and, at the end of class, review newly learned material?

Objectives. Does the teacher relate the objectives of the day to the students?

Hustles/prompts. Verbal or nonverbal behavior used to energize student behavior and as a reminder of appropriate ways of behaving within the framework of the lesson.

Momentum. The ability to keep the ongoing lesson free from events that slow down its forward movement or hold back student progress in an activity.

Group alerting. The ability to keep all students on task and "on their toes."

Appropriate equipment. Is equipment out and ready for student use? Is the amount of equipment adequate? Is the appropriate equipment being used for the activity?

Appropriate dress. Is the teacher dressed in clothes that are appropriate for the teaching of physical education?

Promptness. Does the class begin on time?

INTERACTION

VERBAL TEACHER FEEDBACK TO STUDENT

Positive. Feedback that includes a positive word or phrase in response to correct, well-executed aspects of the movement skill attempt. May include: "Good!," "Nice!," "You watched the ball that time."

Constructive. Feedback that makes a judgment about past performance or suggests how future performance can be improved without the additional flavoring of a personal put-down. May include: "Snap your wrist when you shoot," "Shift your weight."

Negative. Feedback that includes a negative word or phrase to correct poorly executed aspects of the movement skill attempt with the explicit addition of a personal put-down. May include: "No!," "Don't hit like that!," "That's not right!"

First names. The number of times the teacher used students' first names. Does not include names called during attendance.

Questions. The teacher asks questions about content or procedure that elicit student answers. This does not include rhetorical questions.

NONVERBAL TEACHER FEEDBACK TO STUDENT

Positive body gestures. Teacher smiles, nods energetically with smile, winks, laughs, applauds, laughs to encourage, gives "thumbs up."

Negative body gestures. Teacher grimaces, growls, frowns, drops head, throws head back in derisive laughter, rolls eyes, shakes head, hits, pushes away, bangs table or wall, damages equipment, throws things down.

Body contact. Pats student on shoulder or head, shakes student's hand, embraces joyfully, gives "high five," uses physical manipulation during a skill.

VERBAL STUDENT FEEDBACK TO TEACHER

Question. The student asks questions about content or procedure that require a teacher answer.

Positive. Positive feedback from the student to the teacher. May include: "I like this," "This is fun," "Let me do that again."

Negative. Negative feedback from the student to the teacher. May include: "I hate this!," "This is stupid!," "I don't want to do it again!," "Let's quit!"

PLACEK

Motor-engaged. The teacher quickly glances around the whole class to count the number of students who are engaged in movement performance or directly related behaviors that, in the observer's mind, contribute to a positive learning environment. For example, twelve students are waiting in line, five are shooting baskets, two are listening to the teacher answer a question, and three are hitting each other. In this example, nineteen students are motor-engaged and three students are off-task.

Appropriately motor engaged. The teacher quickly glances around the whole class to count the students who are actually moving and practicing the teacher-designated movement tasks. From the example above, only the five students shooting baskets would be included here. The other seventeen students are inactive or involved in other kinds of activity that is not classified as appropriately motor-engaged.

The instructor's evaluation and the preservice student's evaluation would be compared to see where evaluation agreements and disagreements occurred. If the instructor felt there was a discrepancy in perception of the lesson, a follow-up intervention session could be scheduled, if necessary. Using video technology allows the student to do a thorough evaluation of the lesson, because the tape can be stopped, allowing the student to ponder what was just viewed. If the action of the class or the teaching cues occurred too quickly, the tape can be replayed to verify the incident before evaluating the episode.

In the Health, Physical Education, and Recreation Department at Utah State University, video technology has been valuable in helping physical education preservice teachers acquire effective teaching skills. As new technologies develop — and certainly there is a place for their use in educational settings — it would be a mistake to abandon videotape, a proven technology for instruction. The old need not be replaced by the new, especially when the potential of videotape technology for teacher training may not have been adequately explored or developed.

REFERENCES

Allen, D. W. 1967. *Micro-teaching: A Description*. Stanford, Calif.: Stanford University, 1-11.

Anderson, W. G. 1980. *Analysis of Teaching Physical Education*. St. Louis, Mo.: C. V. Mosby.

Fuller, F. F., and B. A. Manning. 1973. "Self-Confrontation Reviewed: A Conceptualization for Video Playback in Teacher Education." *Review of Educational Research* 43, no. 4: 469-528.

Koran, M., R. E. Snow, and F. J. McDonald. 1971. "Teacher Aptitude and Observational Learning of a Teaching Skill." *Journal of Educational Psychology* 62: 219-28.

Legge, W. B., and L. Aspen. 1972. "The Effect of Videotaped Microteaching Lessons on the Evaluative Behavior of Pre-Student Teachers." *Journal of Teacher Education* 23, no. 3: 363-66.

Martin, D. V. 1987. "Use of Stimulated Recall in Videotape Analysis of Student Teacher Performance." *Action in Teacher Education* 9, no. 3: 71-83.

Metzler, M. W. 1980. "The Measurement of Academic Learning Time in Physical Education." *Dissertation Abstracts International* 40: 5,365A. University Microfilms No. 80-90, 314.

Orme, M. E. J., F. J. McDonald, and D. W. Allen. 1966. "The Effects of Modeling and Feedback Variables on the Acquisition of a Complex Teaching Strategy." Unpublished paper. ERIC Document Reproduction Service No. ED 014 441.

Peck, R. F., and J. A. Tucker. 1973. "Research on Teacher Education." In *Second Handbook of Research on Teaching*, ed. R. M. Travers. Chicago: Rand McNally.

Placek, J. H., and S. Silverman. 1983. "Early Field Teaching Requirements in Undergraduate Physical Education Program." *Journal of Teaching in Physical Education* 2, no. 3: 48-54.

Rink, J. 1985. *Teaching Physical Education for Learning*. St. Louis, Mo.: Times Mirror/ Mosby.

Siedentop, D., M. Tousignant, and M. Parker. 1982. *Academic Learning Time: Physical Education*. Columbus: Ohio State University.

Taggart, A. C. 1988. "The Systematic Development of Teaching Skills: A Sequence of Planned Pedagogical Experiences." *Journal of Teaching in Physical Education* 8, no. 1: 73-86.

The Year in Review

John Sayers
and
Rockley Miller
Editors
The Videodisc Monitor

What will undoubtedly prove to be the decade of multimedia got off to a strong start in 1990 with the computer companies moving digital video, windows, and CD formats to the public spotlight under the growing banner of multimedia.

But the now-old standby analog videodisc showed that it was not quite ready to exit stage left. Indeed, while all the excitement seemed to be digital, all the real product seemed to be videodisc.

With technology always pushing the latest and greatest into a market for tried and true, we may be in for a period where digital multimedia gets all the attention while analog videodisc gets all the work done.

A BAKER'S DOZEN OF TOP STORIES OF 1990

- In February, IBM unveils its M-Motion Video Adapter/A, the long-awaited successor to InfoWindow, continuing along a path of unbundling its multimedia offerings and moving video into new windows of opportunity.
- In March, Hearst/ABC-Viacom Entertainment Services (HAVES) launches Healthlink Television, promising to bring patient education videodiscs into 20,000 doctors' waiting rooms. This is followed in May by Whittle Communications' plan to do exactly the same thing with Special Reports.
- In April, Panasonic introduces the first commercially available rewritable analog videodisc recorder based on magneto-optic technology.
- In April, the National Institute of Standards and Technology makes plans to establish standards for multimedia courseware portability, building upon the work of the Interactive Video Industry Association Compatibility Committee in the form of its *Recommended Practices for Interactive Video Portability Release 1.0*, formally published the following month. Subsequent Release 1.1 is adopted as a Department of Defense standard for multimedia systems and programs.
- In June, Commodore announces Commodore Dynamic Total Vision (CDTV) in a bid for the CD-based interactive consumer market. Nolan Bushnell is named general manager for the effort.
- Also in June, Pioneer breaks the $500 price barrier with its CLD-980 combination CD/videodisc player spurring strong growth in the consumer market.

Reprinted from *Multimedia & Videodisc Monitor*, January 1991.

- In August, Empruve unveils Cornucopia, a breakthrough design for a friendly "multimedia appliance" based on the book metaphor and that uses a separate digital video screen to augment a page-like text display.
- Also in August, the Florida education commissioner announces an intention to place Pioneer LD-V2200 videodisc players with bar code readers in every school in the state.
- In September, Kodak announces Photo CD, another format that promises to let the average home photographer put up to 100 photos on a compact disc for subsequent display on a television set.
- Also in September, Sony wins a record contract from the Defense Electronics Supply Center (DESC) for as many as 91,000 dual drive CD-ROM units.
- In November, the Texas State School Board formally adopts the Windows on Science videodisc-based curriculum from Optical Data Corporation for use in Texas schools—thus allowing traditional textbook funds to be spent on educational technology for the first time. Adoption may lead to sales of 10,000 to 15,000 players to Texas schools within the first year.
- Also in November, digital video moves to the chip level as Chips and Technologies announces PC Video for real-time video windowing and Intel announces the availability of DVI i750 chip sets.
- In December, Microsoft rallies the computer industry around its proposed multimedia extensions to the successful Windows graphic user environment and seemingly gets most key players peddling in the same direction.

1990: MONTH-BY-MONTH NEWS SUMMARIES

January

- The American karaoke market heats up as Daiishi Kosho forms a new U.S. subsidiary (DK Karaoke) to market the karaoke sing-along systems and software to clubs, restaurants, universities, and other public locations.
  Also, Ted Karasara, president of rival karaoke firm Pioneer Laser Entertainment, indicates that there are 600 of its disc-based karaoke systems in place in the United States. Pioneer plans to bring the installed commercial base to 1,500 to 2,000 units by the end of 1990.
- IVEX adds its new VDS-2000 disc-based flight simulator to its Visual Display System product line.
- Litigation Sciences introduces a videodisc-based courtroom support system that enables trial lawyers to present electronic exhibits on color TV monitors situated throughout a courtroom.
- London Underground (the subway authority) installs 48 networked interactive video/computer-based training systems (the WITS 2000 from Wicat Systems Ltd.) to train drivers, station supervisory staff, and booking clerks.
- In the consumer market, videodisc players are now (or soon will be) available under the brand names of Magnavox, NEC, Panasonic, Philips, Pioneer, Sharp, Sony, and Yamaha. Of those firms, Pioneer USA claims the largest market share.
  Pioneer USA president Setsujiro Onami says 150,000 consumer videodisc players were sold in the United States in 1989—100,000 of which were Pioneer. He set 1990 Pioneer consumer player sales at 150,000 to 200,000 for 1990.

- Pioneer announces agreements with AIMS Media and American School Publishers to bring some 200 educational videodisc titles into the market. All the software employs Pioneer's bar code technology, which uses a scanner pen and bar codes in printed instruction manuals to access information on the videodisc.
- Sony, Dai Nippon Printing, and 14 other firms form a consortium in Japan to "develop multimedia computer systems."

February

- Commodore introduces the Amiga Vision authoring system, an icon-based, flowchart metaphor authoring system that offers a full relational database and Dbase compatibility. The system takes advantage of all the features of the Amiga computing platform, such as multitasking.
- With its new M-Motion Video Adapter/A adaptor card and related software program for the IBM PS/2 Micro Channel systems, IBM takes the wraps off the long-awaited successor to its InfoWindow system and continues along its path of unbundling or "granularizing" multimedia systems and software to meet a variety of market requirements.
- The Interactive Video Industry Association Compatibility Committee completes initial work on a Proposal for Interactive Compatibility (PIC 1.0), a set of recommended practices that are meant to facilitate courseware portability across different interactive hardware platforms.
- The Northeast Regional Board of Dental Examiners (NERB) plans a videodisc-based encyclopedia of dentistry which, when complete, will provide licensure candidates with a thorough review of the procedures, requirements, and content area of the NERB examination.
- Panasonic and Disctronics produce a 12" OMDR recordable videodisc master for Dow Chemical USA in what Panasonic calls the first known transfer of write-once videodisc to LaserVision.
- The terms *CDV* and *CD Video* pass from the limelight as their only proponent, Philips, announces that "the videodisc system will, in the future, be called the Laserdisc system."
- Pioneer, through its Dutch holding company, plans a British subsidiary to build a $28 million plant for the manufacture of audio and video equipment. The plant, to go online in Wakefield, England, in May 1991, will press videodiscs and assemble videodisc and compact disc players.
- More than 1,500 attend concurrent conferences hosted by the Society for Applied Learning Technology in Orlando, Florida.
- Sony introduces the LDP-1450 videodisc player ($995), which features a worst-case access speed of two seconds and offers the same 30-character display as the Sony LDP-1200; and the LDP-3600D player ($2,495) plays either the PAL or NTSC video formats.
- The Tech 2000 permanent gallery of interactive applications formally opens to the general public.
- Trivision introduces its Messenger System, a new videodisc-based system that allows advertisers to pump messages into drivers while drivers pump gas into their cars. The system will roll out to 132 Texaco Food Marts in Florida.
- The U.S. Air Force Operational Contracting Division at Vandenberg Air Force Base awards Dense-Pac Microsystems a contract totalling $400,000 to provide the Air Force with a Ballistic Missile Instructional System II.

• The United Auto Workers-General Motors Health and Safety Training Center, set up in 1986, adds an additional 150 Visage interactive video systems at GM plants throughout the United States and Canada. This brings the total number of Visage systems installed by UAW-GM to more than 1,500 units.

March

• The American College of Radiology announces plans to publish its library of teaching films (the ACR Learning File) on videodisc. Most of the 8" videodiscs will be comprised of still frames of black-and-white pictures and X-rays.

• Hearst/ABC-Viacom Entertainment Services (HAVES) launches Healthlink Television, an advertiser-supported patient education service to be shown in physician waiting rooms. Initially, hour-long programs of health care information (including nine minutes of commercials) will be distributed monthly via videodisc. The firm expects that its service will penetrate 20,000 waiting rooms by the end of its first year.

• At the Microsoft CD-ROM conference, Intel introduces ActionMedia 750, a family of DVI authoring and delivery platforms and boards. Also, Intel and Olivetti Systems and Networks will develop a multistandard digitizer board compatible with SECAM, PAL, NTSC, and YC video standards.

• Microsoft's Fifth International CD-ROM Conference and Exposition draws 2,600 to San Francisco.

• The Optical Publishing Association announces 16 awards for excellence in optical technology at the Microsoft CD-ROM conference.

• Philips Interactive Media Systems announce a CD-I Starter System, a low-cost (under $10,000) editing system using the CD-I player as its host, as well as several CD-I authoring systems for Apple Macintosh, PC, and Sun SPARC platforms.

• At the Microsoft CD-ROM conference, Pioneer demonstrates LD-ROM, an extension to the LaserVision Videodisc format that allows digital data in the ISO-9660 CD-ROM format to be encoded along with the normal stereo audio and video information on a standard videodisc.

• Bermac completes what it contends is the first working CD-ROM XA application for a major client, TetraPak. The application marries CD-ROM XA with videodisc on a Sony View system, using the CD to provide multiple language support for the videodisc.

• Video Associates Labs offers a new MicroKey Digital Audio Card for the AT computer architecture that features multiple input digitizing, sampling rates of 8, 16, or 32 KHz, input level control, and microphone input and headphone output jacks. The $395 card comes with software drivers that automatically manage all the digital audio functions in background mode and provide a variety of support commands.

April

• C-Cube Microsystems introduces the CL550 single-chip image compression processor that implements the proposed JPEG (Joint Photographic Experts Group) standard for image compression. The firm said its processor compresses still images or motion video by a factor of 20 without visible degradation in quality.

• Capitol Disc Interactive, a 50/50 joint venture between Philips Interactive Media Systems and Capitol Video, develops the first U.S. commercial applications of compact disc-interactive: an opening segment for U.S. Defense Communications' Annual Forecast to Industry and a museum application for the Amparo Foundation of Mexico, which will use 26 CD-I visitor information kiosks in its museum.

• Marketing by Laser, a software development and marketing organization specializing in the travel industry, plans to place 1,000 interactive systems in travel agencies nationwide in the near future. The systems will deliver videodisc-based hotel, travel, and destination information sponsored by participating advertisers.

• The National Institute of Standards and Technology seeks to establish standards for multimedia courseware portability.

• At the National Association of Broadcasters show, Panasonic introduces the first commercially available rewritable analog optical disc recorder. The LQ-4000 uses magneto-optical recording technology and offers a minimum 10-year life and one million erase-and-write cycles.

• The Royal Mail (U.K.) plans to train 20,000 workers via an interactive video package designed to introduce the RM's new performance and development review system. The program, produced by Epic Interactive Media, will be delivered on the RM's existing network of 200 interactive video work stations.

• Xerox expands its commitment to internal interactive training with the purchase of 73 new videodisc systems that will "seed" new training areas nationwide.

May

• Commodore launches its "new standard for multimedia platforms," the Amiga 3000, a multitasking PC that features a new AmigaDOS 2.0 operating system, a 16 or 25 MHz, 68030 processor, 68881 or 68882 math coprocessor, 32-bit architecture, two MB of memory standard, 40 MB hard drive, 3.5" floppy disk drive, and SCSI interface for added communication capability.

• More than 375 delegates attend the eighth annual Electronic Marketing Conference in Orlando sponsored by Deloitte and Touche.

• Presser Digital Audio Disc Corporation delivers its first laser videodisc titles to Image Entertainment. The plant will press 100,000 discs monthly.

• Disc Information Systems Corporation reports that it now has more than 1,000 of its disc-based video Select-a-View kiosks installed in video stores throughout the United States and Canada.

• The Interactive Video Industry Association Compatibility Committee officially launches its Recommended Practices for Interactive Video Portability (release 1.0).

• The Nebraska Videodisc Design/Production Group holds its tenth annual Nebraska Videodisc Symposium in Lincoln, Nebraska.

• The Principal Financial Group uses CD-I to inform pedestrians in Des Moines, Iowa, and some 6,000 PFG employees about the firm's structure, products, and markets. Also, CD-I technology is used for information displays at Japan's six-month Flower and Green Exposition.

• Quixote reacquires total ownership of videodisc and CD pressing firm Disctronics Manufacturing from Disctronics of Australia.

• The Smithsonian Institution opens Information Age: People, Information and Technology, one of the largest multimedia exhibitions ever mounted by the museum. The exhibit employs 50 Pioneer LD-V8000 players in 19 video displays and 40 work stations.

• The U.S. Defense Mapping Agency begins a two-year research and development project to create The Digital Chart of the World on CD-ROM.

• VideoLogic releases an InfoWindow emulator software package for use with its DVA-4000/MCA and DVA-4000/ISA digital video adaptors. The package allows owners of InfoWindow courseware to run applications on both ISA and MCA platforms using VGA monitors.

• Whittle Communications, a leading publisher of medical magazines intended specifically for physician waiting rooms, plans to install 20,000 videodisc systems in medical reception areas by January 1991. The project, dubbed Special Reports TV, is a spin-off of Whittle's Special Reports magazine already in 19,000 doctor's offices.

June

• More than 200 delegates attend the International Laserdisc Conference 1990 in Calgary, Alberta (Canada), cosponsored by the Alberta Laserdisc Committee and Access Network.
• Apple releases HyperCard 2.0, the first major new revision of its HyperCard software since the product was introduced in 1987.
• Commodore announces Commodore Dynamic Total Vision (CDTV), an $895 interactive multimedia player targeted for the home consumer.
• More than 500 delegates travel to London for the first Multimedia Conference on Interactive CD, sponsored by Philips and its partners.
• Pioneer introduces the CLD-980, the industry's lowest priced combination CD/videodisc player with a suggested retail price of $500.
• **Stan Cornyn of Warner New Media shows a prototype modified consumer laser** videodisc player — code-named "Magilla" — which he said incorporated the "greatest hits of audience testing," for what people want in an interactive home system. The unit shown was a functioning combi-player that combines the attributes of a Pioneer LD-V8000 videodisc player with CD-ROM XA or CD-I audio, and a four-field interleave decoder.

July

• The Discovery Channel releases the first six educational videodiscs in a projected library of 100 programs to be produced by 1995.
• The European Laserdisc Association is formed by Bertelsmann/Telemedia, Panasonic, Philips, Pioneer, PolyGram, and Warner Home Video to promote consumer videodisc market penetration in Europe.
• IBM forms a new Multimedia and Education Division to be headed by IBM vice president Lucy Fjeldstad. The division is divided into IBM Educational Systems, Academic Information Systems, and Multimedia.
• Graphic display manufacture Radius introduces Radius TV, a $2,795 integrated computer/television subsystem that represents a complete merging of television functionality into the Macintosh II environment.
• Sony merges its Direct Markets Company, JumboTron, Intelligent Video, Duplication, Security, and Video Conferencing divisions with the Broadcast Products, Professional Video, Professional Audio, and Data Recording divisions to form a new Sales and Marketing Company.

August

• Empruve unveils Cornucopia, a prototype multimedia "electronic book" that employs DVI, CD-ROM, and other emerging technologies.
• Florida education commissioner Betty Castor announces that Florida will purchase Pioneer LD-V2200 videodisc players with bar code readers for each of the state's approximately 2,500 public schools (K-12).

• Intel and PictureTel agree to combine their digital video compression algorithms and processor architecture technologies to create products that will deliver multimedia and video conferencing to the desktop.

• The state of New York awards a five-year, $2 million contract to Lexitech to provide public self-service information kiosks for an innovative electronic job information service called "Jobs Plus." One hundred kiosks will be placed in Community Service Centers throughout the state.

• San Juan Capistrano Unified School District buys 180 multimedia systems (Apple Macintosh and Pioneer LD-V2000 videodisc player) to teach science to upper elementary grades four through six.

• A record 2,500 participants attend concurrent conferences in Washington, D.C., sponsored by the Society for Applied Learning Technology.

• Turner Educational Services and Floyd Design enter into an agreement to market to schools interactive videodisc programs based on CNN news programming.

• Video Associates Labs introduces its MicroKey/A board, which combines VGA graphics, digital audio recording, and the ability to output the graphics and recorded sound to videotape for customized client presentations.

September

• Eastman Kodak announces "Photo CD," an electronic photography system that will transfer 35mm film images to CD-ROM for subsequent television display. The system — which is not expected to become commercially available until 1992 — will be capable of storing up to 100 high-resolution images per disc.

• The Interactive Video Industry Association (IVIA) votes to change its name to the Interactive Multimedia Association (IMA).

• In New York, 150 participants gathered for the International Multimedia Conference sponsored by Multimedia Computing Corporation.

• NewTek announces the Video Toaster, a video processing card for the Commodore Amiga that combines numerous professional post-production capabilities including digital video effects, character generation, color processing, production switching, output previewing, and three-dimensional rendering.

• The Optical Publishing Association officially submits a proposed standard for the transfer of multimedia data to compact disc (including CD-ROM) to the National Information Standards Organization (NISO), which is considering adding the proposal to its working group.

• Pioneer buys about 10 percent of independent film producer Carolco Pictures for $60 million, in exchange for worldwide videodisc rights to Carolco's movies.

• Sears installs 87 Florsheim Express Shop interactive terminals, and 200 units were targeted for installation by year's end.

• Sony wins a record $12.1 million contract from the Defense Electronics Supply Center (DESC) for an estimated 21,000 CDU-625 dual drive CD-ROM units with options allowing the purchase of up to a total of 91,000 units for a total of $34.4 million over a four-year period.

• Sony introduces the MDP-1000, the first industrial player to accommodate both 12" and 8" videodiscs, as well as CD audio discs.

• The Texas State Textbook Committee unanimously recommends the adoption of Optical Data Corporation's Windows on Science videodisc-based curriculum for use in Texas school districts. The disc-based curriculum was formally adopted in November and is the first videodisc program to be adopted by any state.

October

• Interactive Video and Educational Systems begins conversion of its extensive library of electronics training programs to interactive video.

• The Interactive Multimedia Association publishes *Recommended Practices for Interactive Video Portability (Release 1.1)* and issues three Industry Advancement Awards at a special reception at the Multimedia Expo in San Francisco.

• Matrox enters the videodisc player hardware market with its LVP-1080 player, which features instant track jump and one-second random access. The unit will be incorporated as a running upgrade to systems delivered to the U.S. Army under the EIDS contract and replaces the earlier series of units manufactured by Hitachi.

• Nearly 5,000 visit **The Interactive Media Event (TIME)** in London, sponsored by the National Interactive Video Centre.

• During the TIME conference in London, Philips Interactive Media Systems previews the VP380 multistandard omni-player that will accommodate all laser videodiscs, as well as 5" CD and CD-V formats and 3" CD singles in both PAL and NTSC formats. The player includes an RS-232 computer port and RGB output.

• Also, Philips IMS unveils its CDI 601 and CDI 602 integrated single-box professional CD-I players. Both units provide digital video and audio processing with multistandard TV in RGB, Y/C, or CVBS for PAL and NTSC formats.

• Progressive Insurance develops an interactive video CDL (commercial drivers license) training and testing course. The course comes in two versions—one for bus drivers (approximately four hours of instruction) and one for truck drivers (four to eight hours depending on endorsements required).

• Sony shows a prototype portable CD-I unit that incorporates a full color 4" display, CD-I processor, and new three-button user control interface.

• Also, Sony demonstrates a CD mastering system capable of supporting CD audio, CD-ROM, CD-ROM XA, and CD-I formats. The system is based on the Sony 20-mips News RISC 3860 work station and a recordable CD unit.

• VideoLogic ships an Apple Macintosh version of its DVA-4000 digital video card and its MIC System II software.

• In addition, VideoLogic previews two new extensions of the DVA-4000 technology: "Cyrus," a PC-based symmetrical audio/video compression/decompression board that links to the company's DVA-4000 boards (with Mac version "Phoebe"), and "Chimera," an external format conversion box that will take an incoming VGA or Macintosh RGB signal and output it in NTSC or PAL video formats for recording onto High-8, Super VHS, or VHS tape or for display distribution to standard TV monitors.

November

• Chips and Technologies enters the multimedia market with PC Video, a new integrated circuit that dramatically reduces the cost of real-time video windowing by integrating the windowing control logic on a single $40 VLSI chip. The first implementation of the technology comes from New Media Graphics, which licensed its Video Windows technology to CT for the development of PC Video.

• The Digital Audio Visual Interactive Media Society (DAVIS) is established by 55 firms in Japan.

• IBM announces a new XGA (Extended Graphics Array) graphics standard and several enhancements to its multimedia line.

- Intel announces the availability of its i750 video processor chips for $85/unit in 10,000 unit quantities.
- MacroMind proposes its MacroMedia standard programming data format for multimedia developers.
- Maxwell Communication and Philips establish Maxwell Multi Media, a multimedia publishing company that will produce and sell language courses using CD-I technology.
- Philips and Du Pont Optical is dissolved. Philips agrees to purchase Du Pont's interest in the consumer side of the business.

December

- ARES, in conjunction with Realtron multiple listing service, begins installation of disc-based real estate systems in several Florida districts. Forty out of a potential 1,500 systems are installed in the Fort Lauderdale area.
- Commodore Business Machines and Philip/American Interactive Media delay widespread distribution of their respective consumer-oriented formats, CDTV and CD-I, till 1991.
- The State of Florida, Intelex, and Network Technology Corporation install Florida TouchGuide roadside tourist information systems throughout Florida. The kiosks are the first commercial public access touch-screen-based kiosk information systems to use Intel's DVI technology.
- The German Bundespost (Post Office) orders 1,000 interactive systems for the delivery of post office operations training. As part of the contract, VideoLogic will supply its DVA-4000 digital video adaptor boards. VideoLogic's part of the contract alone is valued at $1.9 million.
- Microsoft releases preliminary specifications for PC-based multimedia computing standards and multimedia extensions for Windows and OS/2 at the Microsoft Multimedia Developers Conference. More than 600 developers attended.
- Optical Data Corporation stirs controversy with its decision to subsidize videodisc player sales to Texas schools that purchase Optical Data's *Windows on Science* program. The cost to schools is $199/unit. However, the subsidized players have no RS-232 port—making Level Three programming an impossibility.
- Unisys Corporation develops the ST-1000 series of turnkey interactive self-service terminals.

AECT

The Year in Review

Lucy E. Ainsley
Coordinator of Media & Technology
Birmingham (Michigan) Public Schools

OPERATIONS

During 1990, AECT continued to grow. Attendance at the national convention and other association conferences rose, as did subscriptions to the association's two journals, *TechTrends* and *Educational Technology & Development*. There are now more than 4,800 AECT members worldwide.

Following a successful convention, AECT sponsored a national teleconference in March. "Teaching and Technology: The Critical Link" featured former U.S. Secretary of Education Terrill Bell, AECT Past President Don Smellie, and AECT members Doris Pretlow and Stanley Huffman. The program was endorsed by the National Education Association. Viewed by more than 10,000 educators throughout the United States and Canada, the teleconference highlighted innovative uses of technology in classroom settings.

LEADERSHIP

The 1990 AECT Professional Development Seminar, "New Directions in Developing Interactive Instruction," was held July 21 to 25 at the University of Georgia, Athens. AECT members joined representatives from private industry, government, and the military at the conference, which focused on interactive video. Speakers from around the country shared their expertise and experience in developing interactive learning materials for education and training.

The seminar featured the second national teleconference of the year for AECT. The teleconference, originating from the University of Georgia, featured a two-way link with participants at Wayne State University. This teleconference, directed at both education and the corporate sector, was viewed at more than 80 locations throughout the United States and Canada.

AECT's Summer Leadership Conference, held in Kansas City August 2 to 5, brought more than 150 AECT members and AECT affiliates together for three days of intensive meetings and social interaction. The conference, while focusing on leadership development training, also served as the midyear meeting for the AECT board of directors, the ECT foundation board of trustees, and various AECT divisions and committees. Conference participants also enjoyed the spirited competition of the first annual "Grasshopper Open" golf tournament.

Throughout the year, the association was represented by officers and staff at conventions and conferences around the country. From Georgia to Oregon and Minnesota to Texas, AECT was visible at meetings of other national associations, including the American Library Association, the National School Boards Association, and the Health Science Communications Association, as well as various AECT national affiliate, state affiliate, and regional conferences.

NEW EXPOSITION

AECT has begun developing a new exposition that will debut in February of 1994 in conjunction with its national convention. The exposition will showcase educational technology, hardware and software being used by educators in schools today, and products being developed for future educational applications. The new exposition represents an opportunity for the association to direct the perspective of the education community toward the role instructional technology plays in the process of school improvement and reform. It also represents an expanded opportunity for professional development activities by AECT members and other educators. Several national associations have expressed interest in holding their annual meetings concurrently with AECT so their members can attend the new exposition.

GOVERNANCE

Internally, AECT continued to prosper. Increased activities by divisions and committees have resulted in additional presentations end activities during the national convention, new features in *TechTrends*, and work beginning on new nonperiodic publications. AECT has increased it's potential for more nonperiodic publications by securing the rights to the Copyright Information Services, previously headed by Jerome K. Miller. Additionally, the number of AECT chapters expanded to seven, with chapters now located in Southern Wyoming, Central Pennsylvania, Southwest Virginia, West Central Wisconsin, the Twin Cities, the Utah Valley, and at Utah State University. In addition, two new AECT committees have been set up. Susan Stafford is chairing the committee on Special Needs for Handicapped Persons (at convention), and she is also helping set up a much-needed committee to revise the ALA/AECT publication *Information Power*, the national school guidelines. This committee is currently chaired by Sandy Patton.

As the nation confronts the challenge of school improvement through educational reform in the 1990s, AECT will maintain a position of leadership, demonstrating that instructional technology and educational media are powerful tools for improving the curricula in our nation's schools.

Part Two

Reports from the States

Introduction

The editors wrote to all states asking them to submit state-of-the-art reports concerning initiatives for educational technology. Most states replied with documents, plans, and legislation that is currently underway. This section includes excerpts of materials received from selected states. These documents demonstrate that serious plans are being considered nationwide to incorporate technology into classrooms by implementing a coordinated plan, often backed by state funding, to ensure that progress is made toward stated goals.

Plans are included here in enough detail to allow readers to see what others are doing in the hope that good ideas from one state may have an impact on the plans of another.

California
Educational Technology
Program Highlights
1984 to 1990

Assembly Bill 803 (Chapter 1133, Statutes of 1983), the Educational Technology Local Assistance Program, and Assembly Bill 1470 (Chapter 1334, Statutes of 1989) as amended by Senate Bill 1201 (the Farr, Morgan, Quackenbush Educational Technology Act) have provided approximately $115 million for educational technology programs and activities since 1984. Funding priorities were set by the state board of education, based on recommendations from the California Department of Education and the Educational Technology Committee, which was established in Assembly Bill 803 and continued in Assembly Bill 1470. Assembly Bill 1470 also established the California Planning Commission for Educational Technology, which is responsible for developing a state master plan for educational technology prior to January 1, 1992. The major programs and activities funded from 1984 to 1990 follow:

ADOPTION/ADAPTATION/ EXPANSION GRANTS

Approximately $66 million has been used to fund more than 6,000 site-based grants to encourage schools to begin or expand their efforts to improve instruction through the use of educational technology and to facilitate the completion of district-level technology plans.

LEVEL I MODEL TECHNOLOGY SCHOOLS

Six Level I Model Technology Schools receive $500,000 per year over a five-year period (the schools are currently in their fourth year) to create models of using technology for improving all aspects of the school environment. Important to the overall process is the development of business and research partners at each site. These projects are expected to produce information on the use of technology as a tool in improving curriculum, instruction, and administration for educational decision makers at both the state and local levels. After five years of funding to produce research-based instructional data, the sites are intended to become centers for dissemination, demonstration, and training.

LEVEL II MODEL TECHNOLOGY SCHOOLS

Initially, 10 projects received an average of $80,000 per year for two years to use technology in specific subject areas and at specific grade levels. Each project focused on aligning instruction with the state's curriculum framework. Each was expected to produce educational products (for example, curricula, lesson plans, and training) for other California schools that may wish to adopt or adapt the products. Currently, 6 of these projects have received additional funding for dissemination purposes.

INSTRUCTIONAL TELEVISION
REGIONAL AGENCIES

Seven instructional television regional agencies receive grants, with amounts based on the number of students enrolled in each region, to broadcast curriculum-relevant instructional television series. The agencies: (1) distribute program guides listing broadcast times and descriptions of programs, (2) maintain duplicating services, allowing schools to purchase videocassettes, and (3) conduct extensive staff development programs. The agencies offer video programming and support services that enhance curriculum in virtually all subject areas.

INSTRUCTIONAL MATERIALS
DEVELOPMENT

Recognizing the need for technology-based materials that are consistent with the state's curriculum framework, program funds are used to establish partnerships between developers and the California Department of Education. These grants are intended to bring to the marketplace technology-based instructional programs that would not otherwise be developed, at least in the short term. All local educational agencies and all nonprofit or for-profit companies are eligible to compete for these development grants. The products will serve as models for all publishers of instructional materials. Three award-winning products are already available:

1. GTV, the American Experience: A Geographic Perspective, was produced by the National Geographic Society in collaboration with Apple Computer, Inc., and Lucasfilm Learning Systems. The program combines computer graphics, laser disk technology, and text.

2. World Geography, produced by MECC, develops students' study skills, such as acquiring, organizing, and interpreting information. Students use this tool to acquire and produce in-depth information pertaining to all countries.

3. Explorations in Middle School Science: The Physical Science Program, produced by Josten's Learning Corporation, consists of 36 computer-simulated laboratory activities for grades 6-9 keyed directly to what students are learning in the classroom.

The newest program, still in development, is Science 2000, a complete technology-based resource management system for teaching science in grade 7. The resource management system will be **aligned** with the California Science Framework and will demonstrate how a variety of materials and programs (for example, computer software, films, video and audio tapes and disks, hands-on materials, text, and telecommunications) can be configured to provide students with the opportunity to experience an optimum science curriculum. Decision Development Corporation, in partnership **with** the National Geographic Society; Dinamation Corporation; IBM; Apple Computer, Inc.; the University of California at Irvine; Pacific Bell; and several school districts in California, expects to complete the program by June 1991.

All contractors provide substantial matching funds, California schools receive discounts, and the state receives royalties and other services for schools based on the companies' out-of-state sales.

CALIFORNIA TECHNOLOGY PROJECT

The California Technology Project was initiated in the spring of 1989 as a partnership between the California Department of Education, the California State University system, county offices of education, and school districts. The California Technology Project is a coordinating mechanism for a wide variety of decentralized, educational-technology-oriented services throughout the state, including:

1. Locally planned staff development programs and extensive school-based planning services and program implementation assistance, provided under the auspices of 13 regional consortia/councils.

2. Cooperative pilot projects with the state's subject-area curriculum projects.

3. Electronic communications networking via CSUNet/TRIE (Technology Resources in Education) with three primary components/programs: information resources (for instance, data on exemplary materials), electronic conferencing, and electronic mail services.

4. Information collection/assessment/evaluation support, including state-of-the-art school surveys, reports, and evaluation guides.

INSTRUCTIONAL TELEVISION LICENSES/ PROGRAM ACQUISITIONS

The program has used more than $1.5 million to acquire multiyear licenses for approximately 50 ITV series and two computer software packages. If individual schools had been required to purchase these series directly from the distributing companies, the cost would have been many times greater. These license agreements encourage extensive legal use of video programming of high quality. The selection process for materials is carefully coordinated with existing curriculum priorities, with identified gaps in available programs, and with the needs identified by teachers, media directors, and ITV personnel.

CALIFORNIA VIDEO AND SOFTWARE CLEARINGHOUSES

The clearinghouses, with the assistance of county media centers and regional software preview centers, evaluate K-12 video, software, laser disk, and CD-ROM materials to determine their consistency with the state's curriculum framework and exemplary instructional practices. The resulting data are provided to schools across the state via CSUNet, the primary dissemination vehicle.

VCR DISTRIBUTION PROJECT

During the summer and fall of 1985, the state purchased and distributed more than 7,000 VCRs, one to every school in California. The county offices of education provided training to the schools when they came to claim their VCRs.

TECHNICAL ASSISTANCE GRANTS TO TECC
(Teacher Education and Computer Centers)

The Teacher Education and Computer Centers, which no longer exist, received funds based on student attendance in their regions to provide information and planning assistance to districts and schools applying for and receiving educational technology program grants. The centers also provided demonstrations to school and district personnel on the use of technology in the curriculum.

TECHNOLOGY IN THE CURRICULUM
(TIC) GUIDES

The state, with the assistance of the Teacher Education and Computer Centers (TECC), developed resource guides in six curriculum areas that include a curriculum outline, annotated descriptions of software and video materials, model lesson plans, and information on how to obtain the resources. Each school received a set of the guides.

SUMMER TECHNOLOGY TRAINING INSTITUTES

From 1985 through 1987, institutions of higher education received grants to provide four weeks of intensive instruction to cadres of teachers and other education professionals during the summer and to provide follow-up support during the school year.

TEACHER TRAINING VIDEO PROJECT

In 1987, the Sacramento Educational Cable Consortium received funding to train and support 35 high school teachers in the Sacramento area. With training in video production design and filming techniques, these teachers produced more than 100 programs which were distributed via cable television.

THE INSTITUTE OF COMPUTER TECHNOLOGY

The Institute of Computer Technology is a unique California program devoted to teaching about computers. Located in Santa Clara County, the institute was formed by the Fremont Union High School District, the Los Gatos-Saratoga High School District, the Sunnyvale Elementary School District and more than 50 technology companies to provide technological training, to facilitate the use of technology in education, to foster cooperation between industry and education, and to experiment with innovative techniques and computer applications.

OTHER PROJECTS AND ACTIVITIES

The CSU chancellor's office received a grant for the Mechanical Universe project to train high school physics teachers, ETN (Los Angeles County Office of Education) provided staff development via telecommunications, and a variety of dissemination and communication activities were supported with program funds.

Although not funded by the Educational Technology Act,* the IBM California Education Partnership projects are generating a great deal of excitement in California. IBM has committed $20 million in equipment, software, and technical support to the two-year partnership. The California Department of Education, the state's local educational agencies, and the California State University system are contributing executive and technical support. The major components of the partnership include:

1. Joint development projects for creating multimedia instructional materials and teacher guidance materials aligned with California's curriculum framework.

2. Staff development laboratories in selected schools, districts, and county offices of education to serve as curriculum libraries where teachers can review technology-based instructional materials. Some of the laboratories will have development capabilities.

3. A pilot telecommunications network that links the California Department of Education, more than 80 school district superintendents, and 20 California State University campuses.

4. An IBM employee volunteer program that encourages IBM's 21,000 active employees and 5,000 retirees in California to become involved in supporting education.

For additional information, call or write the Office of Educational Technology, California Department of Education, 721 Capitol Mall, Sacramento, CA 95814. (916) 445-5065.

---

*Anticipated 1991-92 funding for the Educational Technology Act is approximately $14 million.

Connecticut
Instructional Technology in Connecticut
A Status Report

AUTHORIZING LEGISLATION

Several pieces of existing and pending legislation relate to the state department of education's responsibilities for instructional technology. In summary, legislation exists as follows.

Section 10-4. This section gives the state board of education responsibility for the general supervision and control of the educational interests of the state. Among these responsibilities are the services relating to the provision and use of instructional technology by school districts (including instructional television) and development of guides with recommendations for instructional technology resources. Since 1981 the Connecticut Board of Education has assumed full responsibility for instructional television services for Connecticut schools. A description of these services may be found below under the heading "Instructional Television." This section also directs the board to prepare every five years a five-year comprehensive plan for elementary, secondary, vocational, career, and adult education. Included in the current plan, "Challenge for Excellence," are statewide goals for students in the area of learning resources and technology.

Section 10-4e. This section establishes the Joint Committee on Education Technology and defines its membership: representatives of the state board of education and the board of governors of higher education, with advice and assistance of the State Library Board and Connecticut Public Broadcasting. This committee had the responsibility for development of a long-range plan and related recommendations for the coordination of educational technology in Connecticut. In 1983, the Joint Committee presented its report and recommendations in *New Directions for Educational Technology: Recommendations of the Joint Committee on Educational Technology.*

Section 10-4h. This section authorizes the state board of education to establish a competitive grant program in each fiscal year for which funds are appropriated. These grants will help local and regional school districts and regional educational service centers develop and expand their use of telecommunications, including instructional television. Thus far there have been three Telecommunications Incentive Grant competitions (in 1986-87, 1987-88, and 1988-89) that resulted in the awarding of 42 projects from a funding total of $251,200. Projects spanned a wide area of application, ranging from classroom activities to the establishment of distance learning capabilities. No state funding has been available for these grants since the 1988-89 fiscal year.

Amendments. Amendments to sections 10-4e and 10-4h are currently proposed in Substitute Bill No. 584: An Act Concerning Educational Technology. Essentially, the changes expand the definition of educational technology and add to the membership of the advisory committee.

Section 16-333g and Section 16-333h. These sections mandate that all cable television franchises in Connecticut offer free basic service to schools and libraries. Such service shall include at least one dedicated instructional television channel.

STATE DEPARTMENT OF EDUCATION
INITIATIVES

Instructional television. The state department of education sponsors annually 400 hours of curriculum-related, instructional television programming during the school year. These 86 series (comprising 1,199 individual programs) provide information in nearly all subject areas and grade levels, from K-12. A comprehensive *Instructional Television Schedule and Resource Guide* is printed each year and distributed to schools in late August. Because they are broadcast over Connecticut Public Television stations, programs are readily available to schools throughout the state. Classroom use of instructional television is flexible because all programs may be recorded and used for at least one year. The department of education supplies teacher guides for many of the series carried. These give teachers an overview of each program and suggest ways to most effectively use the programs and integrate them into classroom activities.

The Knowledge Network (an instructional television fixed service system). In 1989 the state department of education entered into an agreement with Connecticut Public Broadcasting to develop, construct, and operate the Knowledge Network, a two-channel instructional television fixed service (ITFS) system that would provide instructional programming to virtually every school district in Connecticut. ITFS is the identification given by the Federal Communications Commission to television channels set aside for use by schools for the delivery of instruction and instructional materials. It is a relatively low-powered, limited-range system that is private because home television sets cannot receive the signal without the special (but low-cost) receiving equipment available to schools. The state department of education will supply each school district with one antenna and decoder free of charge. At this time there are 27 school districts receiving the ITFS signal. During the 1990-91 school year these districts have had access to instructional television programming, national teleconferences, special programming from PBS and other production agencies, examples of satellite distance learning courses, and in-service programs for teachers. Educators are informed of the Knowledge Network offerings through the *Learning Resources and Technology Newsletter* mailed every other month. Construction of towers to relay the microwave system and installation of antennas is scheduled for completion by the end of 1992. However, this time all bonding and operational funding requests have been eliminated from the governor's budget.

Links to Learning project. This major initiative, a cooperative effort involving the Connecticut State Board of Education and Southern New England Telephone (SNET), became a reality in late May of 1988. This is the first telecommunications partnership between a telephone company and a state department of education of this magnitude in the United States. The project has three major components:

1. Data Link, an application of electronic mail and remote database searching that gives teachers and students access to volumes of research materials and electronic messages via their personal computers

2. SNET Voice Link, which enhances communication between teachers, parents, and administrators by giving them the capability to record or listen to messages by push-button phone 24 hours a day

3. SNET Video Link, which allows teachers and students to share lessons from predesignated locations in different school districts via two-way video and voice transmission over telephone facilities.

SNET continues a financial commitment to the project on a limited basis and also contributes to the telecommunications grant program in the absence of state funding.

Guide to Program Development in Learning Resources and Technology. In keeping with its statutory responsibility to provide guides and recommendations to help local districts provide a quality educational opportunity for each student, the department has published, in 1991, a *Guide to Program Development in Learning Resources and Technology*. The guidelines present planning, implementing, and evaluating learning resources and technology in the teaching and learning process within the context of educational reform and with the growing realization that the literate individual must not only read and write but also know how to locate and use information in a wide range of formats. A fundamental principle for this document is that all learning resources and technologies should be accessible as teaching and learning tools. It encompasses what have traditionally been separate programs: library media, computers, instructional television, and other technology. The guide reflects the concepts and goals found in the *Connecticut Common Core of Learning* and national association guidelines related to learning resources and technology.

MECC (Minnesota Educational Computing Consortium). Since 1980, the state department of education has entered into a state site license agreement with MECC that provides, at substantial savings to school districts, access to a software collection consisting of more than 2,000 programs, manuals, and activity guides covering all subject areas in grades K-12. As participating members, schools are granted unlimited duplication rights to all MECC software and instructional materials. Without the site license, the cost to a school to maintain an equivalent software collection would be in excess of $5,000 annually. The department is assisted by the regional educational service centers, which distribute the software and provide a variety of support services. All schools and districts in the state are eligible to participate in the program. Participation has been increasing each year, with approximately 105 educational institutions involved in the state-run program during the 1990-91 school year.

Learning Resources and Technology Unit. The state department of education maintains a staff of three consultants in a Learning Resources and Technology Unit, a part of the Division of Curriculum and Professional Development. The unit is responsible for the coordination and delivery of the aforementioned services and programs. Additionally, the staff is responsible for technical support to the library media, computer, and technology programs in schools throughout the state. This takes place via school visits, sponsoring statewide conferences and workshops, professional development workshops, work with professional associations and advisory councils, a *Learning Resources and Technology Newsletter*, and a variety of printed materials. The unit is also responsible for library and information services within the department itself.

THE ROLE AND IMPACT OF LEARNING RESOURCES AND TECHNOLOGY ON EDUCATION

We live in an information-intensive society. The technology that brings more information into our homes and businesses is gradually finding its way into the educational process. In an age in which technology already permeates every important facet of American life and promises to become even more pervasive in the future, it is critical that technology is put to the best possible use in the education of Connecticut's children. There is research that indicates that learning resources and technology, when used properly, can have a positive influence on learning:

- A 1989 study of more than 600 teachers in all 50 states reported the following changes resulted from the integration of computers into instruction: heightened expectations of student work and the ability of the teacher to present more complicated material; increased opportunity to provide individualized instruction; and emergence of student-centered classrooms, with teachers acting more as coaches or facilitators than as dispensers of information.

- Elaine K. Didier (1982) found that the benefit of full-time library media specialists resulted in increased student attainment in reading and study skills and that the contribution of the library media specialist to the curriculum development process had a positive relationship to student achievement.

- A 1989 study requested by the Senate Committee on Labor and Human Resources found that distance learning affects the educational process in a number of ways. Students reported having to take greater responsibility for their learning and that their experience helped them to make the transition to higher education. Students also reported that they benefited from exposure to a greater range of ideas, peers, and teachers made possible through an expanded educational community.

- According to a 1985 report from the Southeastern Educational Improvement Laboratory, students at all levels are increasing their technological literacy and already use video as the communications medium of choice.

Throughout Connecticut many schools are employing a wide range of these learning resources and technology (including library media resources, computers, distance learning, and other telecommunications technology) in the teaching and learning process. Unfortunately, there has been no overall state plan or mandates that have guided the integration of these resources into our schools. As a result there is great disparity across our state in the access to and effective use of learning resources and technology. The state department of education has attempted to promote greater equity by means of state guidelines; the statewide delivery of instructional materials through such vehicles as instructional television and the Knowledge Network, which reach or will reach virtually every school district; and statewide contracts such as MECC that provide reduced costs for computer materials for all districts and cooperative arrangements with business.

Not only has the required content for a child's education expanded in recent years, but the approaches and methods of instruction have changed as well. For example, whole language is gaining acceptance as a philosophy of language learning. This kind of initiative relies heavily on literature and nonprint resources to give children authentic language experiences that include reading, writing, listening, and viewing.

Science and math instruction now has a greater emphasis on "hands-on" and "real world" experiences for students. Life skills are becoming as important as facts to be memorized. Information and technology skills help students navigate in a world filled with information. The importance of these information skills for students is reflected by their inclusion as goals two and three of the department's "Challenge for Excellence":

Goal Two: Mastery of the Basic Skills

Connecticut public school students will demonstrate skills necessary to locate and effectively use a variety of sources of information, including print materials, media, computers, and other technology.

Goal Three: Acquisition of Knowledge

Connecticut public school students will acquire the knowledge necessary to use computers and other technologies for learning and problem solving.

LOOKING TO THE FUTURE

There is little doubt that technology will continue to play an increasing role in our everyday lives and in education. In Connecticut renewed planning efforts and a commitment of state resources are necessary if our schools are to (1) make maximum use of learning resources and technology, (2) ensure each student the opportunity to become literate not only in reading and writing but also in using information and technology, and (3) provide equitable access by all teachers and students to the necessary range of learning resources and technology. To achieve these goals, the following steps should be taken:

1. The Joint Committee on Educational Technology should evaluate progress to date on the recommendations made in its 1983 report. It should then develop a long-range, statewide plan for educational technology in Connecticut schools that would serve as the framework for funding and grant programs.

2. Teacher preparation programs must begin to educate prospective teachers in the proper and effective use of learning resources and technology in modern education. Teachers should be comfortable using learning resources and technology themselves, as well as incorporating them into teaching and learning.

3. Existing cost-effective methods for delivering instructional resources on a statewide basis should be maintained or expanded (or in the case of the Knowledge Network, completed). Such projects must become a priority for planning and funding.

4. The state department of education should continue to pursue cooperative arrangements with business and industry to develop model programs and assist in the infusion of technology into the schools.

Florida
1990-91
Instructional Technology
Implementation Plan

INTRODUCTION

The 1990 Florida Legislature appropriated more than $29 million to the department of education to fund a variety of instructional technology activities ranging from software acquisition and technology challenge grants to multimedia product development and instructional technology teacher inservice. These activities are managed by a number of offices in the department including the Division of Public Schools; Division of Human Resource Development; the Division of Vocational, Adult, and Community Education; and the Office of Educational Technology.

Responding to the need to assure that all of the department's instructional technology initiatives were coordinated effectively, Commissioner of Education Betty Castor established a special task force made up of representatives from across the department to develop an implementation plan for the 1990-91 initiatives. The plan was "to address the resources available from the Instructional Strategies Enhancement appropriation, as well as all other department resources that may support the use of technology in schools." To fulfill its charge, the Technology Initiatives Task Force (TITF) developed a vision, goal, and objectives to serve as guides for the various instructional technology initiatives. The TITF also developed implementation plans for each initiative and prepared policy recommendations for specific actions that will enable the department to achieve its objectives. Finally, the Task Force developed budget issue information to facilitate the preparation of the department's budget as it relates to instructional technology.

The Task Force accomplished its mission over the six-week period of July 16 through August 24, 1990. After the group as a whole met for three days in a "lock-in" format, subgroups of the task force worked the following three weeks on developing individual implementation plans for all the initiatives. The full Task Force then assembled again in order to complete its responsibility, meeting in a "lock-in" format for most of the final two weeks of the effort.

The following material presents the thinking of key personnel in the department about the planning and implementation of instructional technology activities to achieve the goal of enhanced learning for all students. It is the hope of this task force that the effects of the initiatives and proposals described in this report will be substantive and long-lasting.

TASK FORCE RECOMMENDATIONS

The Task Force believes that research and development has been underfunded. It is imperative that steps be taken to assure that classroom use of technology *helps students learn*. Only through research will we determine the effectiveness of current and proposed practices. The task force is also concerned that the effects of department initiatives may not be documented well enough to draw the best conclusions. In the future, each initiative is to have an evaluation process built into its plan, the results of which can be used to make policy decisions.

All department initiatives are intended to have long-term impact through thoughtful implementation and continued state support. In order to sustain this support, the task force has made recommendations that address the following areas:

1. Strategic statewide five-year plan for technology use

2. Alternative sources of funding

3. Research, development and evaluation

4. Staff development

5. Technology and restructuring

6. Distance learning

7. Department of education support for technology utilization

Budget requests to support the recommendations include increases in funding for the technology grant program, research-and-development-related initiatives, distance learning, and teacher training efforts. All of these areas can have a positive effect upon learning outcomes. The task force also believes that, if the department is to render the leadership and assistance necessary for a rapidly growing state, the creation of permanent staff positions in the offices most involved in the implementation of technology initiatives is a necessity. Funding at levels close to those recommended, in combination with the restructuring strategies being refined, will enable the department to provide the leadership necessary to affect the dramatic change in school performance that must occur.

The proposed budget is contingent upon identifying an alternative source of funding. Considerable thought has gone into this aspect of our leadership efforts for technology. Several alternatives are presented in recommendation form. It is believed that two or three of these may be viable, thus providing a means of sustaining the momentum that has been created for using technology in the restructuring efforts of schools. We are committed to trying to configure some of these, and perhaps others, to become a resource base for technology in schools.

The convening of this task force and the submission of its report represents the first step in the development of a department plan for the implementation of technology in education. With the continued support of the legislature, state board of education, and the infrastructure recommended by the task force, the momentum that has been generated can be expanded, allowing us to assure that technology will be a significant part of the improvements that will take place in student learning. Following is a list of initiatives designed to implement the use of technology in schools:

Implementation Strategies

1. *Interactive videodisc.* Interactive video has been shown to enhance student learning and productivity through a multisensory and exploratory approach to content. Because of interactive video's unusual capabilities, the department has taken several steps to promote the use of this powerful educational tool. Collaborative efforts with ABC News InterActive have resulted in the availability of an AIDS Education Disc for use in our schools. Other discs on human sexuality and drug education are under development. In addition, we have provided one laser videodisc player to every school in the state as a means of initiating school use of this technology.

2. *Distance learning.* A special effort is underway to promote distance learning (the provision of specialized courses from a remote location) in Florida's schools. An assessment of current capacity for receiving satellite- and/or cable-delivered courses will be conducted, and a plan will be prepared that will outline additional actions to be taken to establish a comprehensive distance learning capability. This will include the production of programming for instruction and inservice, and the eventual creation of an educational television network that will provide learning opportunities to every part of the state.

3. *Model technology schools.* Five schools were selected more than two years ago to serve as sites for exploring various uses of technology in differing educational settings. These schools function in a partnership arrangement with the department, the school district, business partners, parent groups, and higher education institutions in the area. They employ different technology approaches and disseminate the information gained from such efforts. They also provide instructional technology inservice to teachers and other educators.

4. *Codevelopment.* The department has formed partnerships with various technology-oriented companies to jointly develop instructional materials in the form of computer software and interactive videodisc "courseware." These development efforts occur in areas where instructional materials are needed but do not exist. Contractual arrangements call for the department to take primary responsibility for instructional aspects of the product while the partner has primary responsibility for production and marketing. The state will receive royalties from the sale of these products outside of Florida.

5. *Technology Grant Program.* This program provides almost $7 million to school districts to be used in the implementation of innovative instructional technology projects. Funding occurs as a result of proposals submitted by districts to the department. These proposals were examined by a review panel consisting of business and education representatives, and recommendations were made for funding to the commissioner. Districts may receive up to $400,000 per grant.

6. *Software Acquisition Project.* This project results in a state contract containing multiple titles for instructional software from which school districts may purchase. Districts are invited to nominate instructional software titles for consideration. A panel of software experts, most from school districts around the state, reviews the nominations and establishes the final list. Bids are then sought from software companies seeking the best price possible for the chosen software

products. This year videodisc products will be included on the contract for the first time. Almost $3 million will be distributed to districts for use in purchasing from the contract.

7. *Schoolyear 2000.* This project is designed to examine the educational system thoroughly and, working with school districts, identify significant changes in the whole educational process necessary to alter the way we deliver instruction. The outcome of this project is intended to be a substantially restructured system of schooling that will be ready for trial in five to six years. Though the project's primary emphasis will be on instructional strategies, there will be a great reliance on technology.

8. *Teacher inservice.* As technology becomes an integral part of the educational process, teacher preparation becomes essential. This project provides staff development in the following areas: technology in preservice teacher education, computers as classroom tools, integrating technology in curriculum, and technology for school improvement. These training sessions will be offered to teachers and administrators from all school districts and will integrate other department initiatives into the training components. Funds will be provided to districts to allow teams of trainers to attend the staff development sessions.

Indiana
A "Slice" of Tomorrow's School
A Report of a Developmental Program

Nancy A. S. Miller

INTRODUCTION

What is the ideal school of tomorrow? How will it function in the community? What roles will students, parents, teachers, and administrators play in education for the twenty-first century? The Indiana Consortium for Computer and High Technology Education, through the auspices of the Indiana Department of Education, approved $400,000 in 1988 for the planning and implementation of A "Slice" of Tomorrow's School, in which alternative teaching and learning strategies, styles, technologies, and environments would be explored.

A specially formed National Advisory Council for Tomorrow's Schools provided visionary leadership and practical guidance in the planning and development of the "Slice" project. This group met in October 1988 to identify attributes of tomorrow's students, teachers, and educational systems and to help identify characteristics of schools ready to meet the challenge of a restructuring process. Through a selective "Request for Proposal" process, two Indiana school districts were chosen in December 1988 to receive support in the development of their own visions of tomorrow's school: Lafayette School Corporation (Lafayette). and North Adams Community Schools (Decatur).

Two lead teachers from each district were released from classroom duty to manage and coordinate the planning, staff, and program development during the spring semester. Each site team's plan had elements that addressed many of the key attributes identified by the National Advisory Council, including learner-focused programming and management, flexibility, choice, media-rich environments, relevance and connectivity. Through review of literature and visitations to a variety of unique schools, the site teams took the best of available programs, technologies, and strategies and then combined them with identified desirable attributes and outcomes to prepare programs that they felt would be eminently more suitable to their learners' needs than the existing school structure and program.

Each district's first implementation was scheduled for the summer of 1989. This approach allowed the schools to use existing technology resources, to provide greater flexibility in educational facility use, and to allow teachers a traditionally more open and less pressured environment for change. Though many elements of the design and structure of the two schools were held in common, each team customized their program to meet local school and community needs. An overview of each "Slice" project follows.

LEARNINGSPHERE 2008
Lafayette School Corporation

Program Beliefs, Mission, and Objectives

Schools must value and respect their clients and make the learning environment learner centered. Learners must have time to interact and to ponder germinating thoughts and interests. Affection, ownership, and attention to improvement enrich and empower teachers and their learners.

The mission of Lafayette's LearningSphere was to help people to:

- be citizens who can and will communicate, gather, understand, and use information
- engage in creative, responsible decision making
- adapt to challenges of the twenty-first century
- foster positive physical, emotional, and social development in a changing environment

The 1989 summer program provided an interdisciplinary approach to three selected spheres of learning. Each sphere overlapped with the other two spheres, allowing collaborative and cooperative planning, teaching, and learning (see figure 1). Core objectives (for all learners) were covered to facilitate future learning in all content spheres as well as for synthesis of learning within the program. Interest area objectives for learners included demonstrated skills of comparison, understanding, appreciation, evaluation, exploration, and creation within one of the following three areas: (1) Communication: Lafayette's Link to the World, (2) Lafayette's Culture: Its Link to the World, (3) Lafayette's Environment: Its Link to the World.

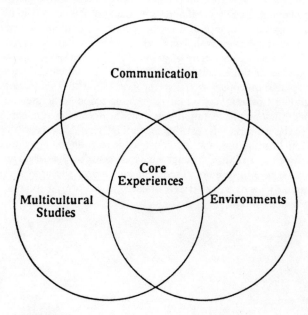

Figure 1.

Learners, Learning Guides, Individual Learning Plans

The LearningSphere program's philosophy and goals were presented to interested parents in April of 1989. The 117 learners were randomly selected from an application pool of 276 students, representing a cross-section of the Lafayette School Corporation student body. Learners represented all neighborhoods and schools in the Lafayette school district as well as students from kindergarten through eighth grade at all ability levels. One child, who is completely blind and had just finished first grade at the Indiana School for the Blind, was also enrolled in the program. The learners were divided into two multiage groups: 5- to 9-year-olds and 9- to 14-year-olds.

Learning guides for the program were selected by the lead teachers and project director based upon ability, interest, and teaching styles. The teachers on the LearningSphere team represent diverse subject-area and grade-level backgrounds, but most were experienced master teachers. It was imperative for successfully meeting project objectives that the teachers could, in fact, work together as a collaborative team within the program. An interdisciplinary approach that utilized special resource teachers as consultants to the sphere teachers demanded cooperation and flexibility among the staff. French language, fitness, music, media and art curricula and activities were closely tied to sphere topics. A full-time guidance counselor became a liaison between the families and the LearningSphere and helped the teachers identify and match learning styles with teaching styles.

The individual learner objectives were jointly established by the student, parent, and staff at a preprogram series of parent conferences. One objective was universal: the learner will exhibit an increase in self-directed learning. Within the program, learners were required to spend eight hours per week on site and complement that on-site work with eight hours of participation per week at home or in outreach explorations of the sphere content. In some cases, the individual learner objectives were based on academic needs and issues; in others, they focused on the social or emotional health of the individual learner.

Program Structure and Implementation

In the LearningSphere vision the school would be flexible in time and learning opportunities and facilities. Learners could select courses of study, choose appropriate times for attendance according to their personal plans, and work independently at any time, day or night. Daycare and meal programs would be available as needed by learners. In the 1989 program, Lafayette offered a modified flexible schedule that was open for participation Monday through Thursday, with evening hours available on Tuesday and Wednesday. The center was closed for the supper hour and reserved for staff development and planning each Friday morning. Students, arriving and leaving at all hours during the day, provided significant challenges to the transportation and student management systems of the district.

A variety of instructional strategies was employed, but great emphasis was placed upon promoting a healthy mind and healthy body and high learner self-esteem. Students met in general assemblies and large group sessions for some core skills training, met in small seminar sessions with learning guides for specific topic exploration, and worked individually or paired with other learners or learning guides for individual study and questions. Lunch and snack programs as well as daycare for the learners before and after learning center use were offered within the facility and program.

At first, more time in the LearningSphere was devoted to core objectives, including several general assemblies and small group training opportunities, than to individual study activities to allow learners to gain an understanding of self-directed learning techniques and to use the technologies made available to them. As the summer progressed, more time was spent on covering the individual learning objectives and development of individual projects. Attention to the content area objectives and small group seminars on the topics contained in the three spheres remained fairly constant throughout the summer program. Two professional staff members were assigned to each sphere. Though intended to be identified as primary and intermediate learning guides, the cultures sphere staff chose to divide responsibilities according to the two cultures to be studied, with each guide taking responsibility for both primary and intermediate learners within that culture topic. Special resource teachers worked with sphere staff to coordinate and facilitate interdisciplinary units and instruction.

Staff Development and Curriculum Planning

Lafayette devoted constant and thoughtful attention to the staff development and curriculum planning needs of the twenty professional staff members involved in the project. The two lead teachers received a paid sabbatical during the second semester to plan the basic structure and core curriculum for the summer program. A two-day retreat to kick off the program was held in March, and periodic planning and development meetings of the whole LearningSphere staff were scheduled throughout April and May. During the summer implementation, each Friday morning was reserved for staff development activities, cooperative planning, and program coordination. Staff development activities included technology training, team building, interdisciplinary instruction, and time to discover and develop curriculum resources for the themes to be offered during the summer program.

Special Programs and Applied Technologies

Special centers and programs added value to the Holistic care/"Well child" programming plan of LearningSphere 2008:

- A Learning Lunch program was designed to provide a relaxed, family-style atmosphere. Centerpieces at each round table, china dishes, and family-style serving were some of the details that made a difference. Learning guides and visiting adults were encouraged to join students (at least one adult at each table). A predetermined topic, such as "A place I would like to visit" or "My most embarrassing moment," was the main item for discussion during lunch. Entertainment was also provided daily and included musicians, clowns, storytellers, celebrity presentations, and guest "fun topic" lecturers to round out the lunch experience.

- The Spa provided supervised activity in strengthening the "well-body" concept and reality. Learners could attend individually during the day, and the Spa learning guide also worked with the sphere teachers to develop fitness activities for group interaction.

- The Daycare Center was provided for the convenience and use of LearningSphere staff's children, as well as learners who needed to come early, stay late, or have a place to go between scheduled learning sessions. It also featured its own high-tech centers, but the daycare enrollees were allowed to visit the LearningSphere media, exploration center, spa, and art centers as well.

- Beginning French instruction was provided to all LearningSphere participants as a core activity. French was selected because of the cultural tie of Lafayette to its namesake and nearby historic French fort. The French teacher prepared audio instruction tapes for student/family loan and a videotape that was aired over the local cable channel to facilitate home learning opportunities within the program.

- Frequent field trips throughout the summer brought additional community and business involvement to the school experience. Excursions included nature hikes, trips to newspaper publishers, television stations, the zoo and The Children's Museum, as well as a family picnic at Fort Ouiatenon including French aviators who were touring all of the cities in the United States with the name "Lafayette."

Supporting the operation and goals of the LearningSphere education program, technology was applied to many aspects of the structure and curriculum. Technology was not the focus but an important tool used to achieve project, learning guide, and individual learner goals and objectives during the summer implementation. In addition, many special field trips, guest lectures, and outreach activities were organized, open both to student and parent participation. Several special activities, centers, and program features utilized the following two advanced technologies to broaden the learners' horizons and strengthen the educational program:

1. Videoconferences—Learners in the cultures sphere participated in a two-way videoconference with students at an international school in Paris. Environment sphere learners participated in one with naturalists in Hawaii, and the communications sphere learners videoconferenced with students from the Los Angeles Open School. GTE North provided facilities, satellite time, and expert assistance to make these high-tech experiences possible.

2. Personalized newspapers—A series of five individualized newsletters for each learner was produced by project staff during the program. Each newsletter featured an article common to all in the LearningSphere, an article common to learners in the individual spheres, and at least one article that was particularly created for that individual learner. Information about learner interests was gathered from the students at enrollment time and was used as the starting point for researching and writing individualized articles.

PROJECT SLICE: A LEARNING COOPERATIVE
North Adams Community Schools

Program Beliefs, Mission, and Objectives

As Hodding Carter observed, "There are only two lasting bequests we can hope to give our children. One of these is roots: the other, wings."

The goals of Project Slice at North Adams follow:

- To promote experiences that foster the development of a child who is able to communicate globally, who is technically literate, and who strives for life-long learning

- To help persons of all ages break conventional educational mindsets and boundaries that impede learning

- To educate the total child—social, emotional, intellectual, and physical—through the direct involvement of the child's home and community environments

Specific objectives for the program included the following:

- Learners will show an increase in self-directed learning by formulating appropriate questions as well as identifying, finding, and using information sources and technologies appropriate to their needs.

- Learners will be able to work effectively in a group by sharing/accepting different viewpoints and by demonstrating their ability to collaborate and compromise.

- Learners will share their explorations by effective organization and display of their work, by communication of their experiences to another audience, and by demonstrating self-assessment of their learning.

A special primary-level option incorporated all of the above goals and a subset of the specific objectives for Project Slice. For these learners the focus was on experiential learning activities using technology and on exploration of physical, tactile, and artistic expression. Through involvement of significant adults in the primary learning strand, an emphasis on group interaction, cooperative learning, and family unity was sought.

Under the umbrella of cooperative learning and through the theme of communication, the Project Slice program components addressed and used the following skills: research, group process, critical/creative thinking, consensus building, interpersonal relations, collaboration, and inquiry. Intermediate learners were offered the option of enrolling in one of the following three "learning families" (see figure 2):

- Social Environments—Explore media and pathways of communication and human interaction (Oral Expression, Kinesthetic Awareness, Visual and Performing Arts, Sign Language, Visual Representation, Signs and Symbols, Interactive Media, Telecommunications). North American Indian, Australian, and Japanese were among the cultures studied.

- Physical Environments—Explore the physical and social dimensions of alternative surroundings (Space Exploration, Inside the Earth, Population Trends, Developing Resources, Aquatic Living, The Earth [Then, Now, Tomorrow], Family Structures, Multicultural Awareness).

- Economic Environments—Explore the internal and external framework of economics (Impact of Decisions; Multicultural Affinity; Monetary Systems; Business, Government, Community, Individual, and Socioeconomic Realities).

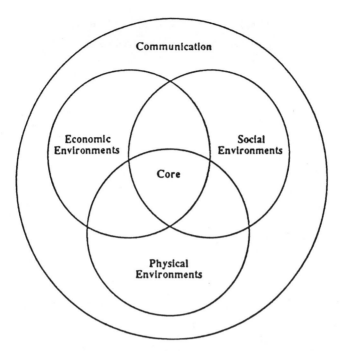

Figure 2. Diagram of the three learning families used for Project Slice in North Adams.

Learning Cooperative Roles

A run-down of the roles of participants in Project Slice follows:

Student
- has responsibility for learning
- has choice in what, when, and how to learn
- participates in self assessment: reviews learning results

Parents
- join in their child's learning, hence embodying the idea of lifelong learning
- actively participate with child in structured learning activities
- assist child in defining, implementing, and assessing the course of study

School
- serves as learning center
- serves as hub around which educational resources are located
- makes available to learners the necessary tools and support staff
- brings the world to the student and the student to the world

Teacher
- facilitates a curiosity and love of learning for students of all ages
- coordinates learning materials and provides avenues to information
- serves as the collaborative hub between the home, the school, and the community

Community
- develops interdependent partnerships with schools
- helps link learning to living
- actively promotes lifelong learning among members

Learners, Learning Guides, Individual Learning Plans

Project Slice was advertised and presented to North Adams families as one of several summer school options. The philosophy behind the enrollment process at North Adams was not to enroll a particular set or cross-section of ages and abilities within their community but to provide the experience for all who wished to participate. The aggregate enrollee group did span a wide range of student interests and abilities. A total of 32 primary learners ages 4 through 6 were enrolled in a four-week Slice program, 89 intermediate learners ages 7 through 14 enrolled in an eight-week program, and an additional 65 intermediate students enrolled in a similar four-week program.

The instructional team for the learning cooperative was made up of certified staff, paraprofessional staff, student interns, consultants, and volunteers. Individuals involved in the program included primary through high school teachers in diverse subject areas. Twenty-one staff members representing a wide range of experience levels were involved in the summer implementation. In each of three Project Slice spheres and in the Mini Slice Primary, a team including a professional teacher, a paraprofessional learning assistant, and a high school student intern was selected. In addition, the two lead teachers, project clerical support staff, and project director provided administration, guidance, and instructional resources for the learning guides.

Staff Development and Curriculum Planning

A comprehensive series of twelve staff development opportunities and work sessions were scheduled in April and May of 1989 for Project Slice staff. All staff members participated in cooperative learning training and spent several evening sessions learning to use new technologies and to write curricula for the summer program. Many of the staff also visited other Indiana schools that were involved the incorporation of technology and vision into educational programs. Preservice staff development and planning culminated a week before the summer program commenced in a two-day staff retreat to brush up on technology skills, review learning materials, and work on team building. Staff development activities and continued sharing among the Project Slice staff occurred throughout the summer implementation.

Program Structure and Implementation

Program Strands (serving 188 students in all)
1. Project Slice: A Learning cooperative (June and July, 8 weeks)—Students in grades 2-8
2. Mini-Slice: Primary (June, 4 weeks)—Students in preschool through grade 1
3. Mini-Slice: Intermediate (July, 4 weeks)—Students in grades 2-8

Project Slice learners and guides were grouped in heterogeneous, mixed-age "family groups" that met for three hours on Tuesday through Thursday mornings. The Mini-Slice Intermediate offered a short (four-week) version of Project Slice without the long-term individual or group project component to facilitate participation by students involved in other summer school or extracurricular programs. Core learning experiences in the use of technology and in cooperative learning were facilitated by the project director, lead teachers, and guest consultants. These core skills were reinforced by "family group" activities within chosen themes as well as through individual exploration and application of the skills within the learning plans.

The intermediate (grades 2-8) learner's weekly schedule consisted of 12 hours of required, structured activities including whole group sessions, "family group" meetings, and seminars. Slice was open an additional 24 hours per week (mornings, afternoons, and evenings) to provide opportunities for open computer labs, exploration and production labs, individual learner consultations, extra "family group" sessions, and staff preparation and development. Each learner was required to schedule an additional four hours per week on site to complete individual projects or learning plans.

Kentucky
The Kentucky Education Technology Plan

Council for Education Technology

INTRODUCTION

The Kentucky Education Reform Act of 1990 created a new vision of education, a vision that requires us to rethink all dimensions of schooling. To plan for this vision, the Reform Act created a nine-member Council for Education Technology to advise the state Board for Elementary and Secondary Education. Recognizing the important role technology can play in enabling the learner to achieve, the reform act directed the council to develop a plan for the equitable and efficient use of instructional and administrative technology in Kentucky schools.

The reform act requires the council to provide the legislature with the broad parameters of a five-year plan by January 1, 1991. Implementation of the first stages will begin as soon as approval is secured. Thereafter, the council is to submit recommendations to the state Board for Elementary and Secondary Education "which shall accept the recommendations or return them to the Council along with suggestions for changes to make the recommendations consistent with Board policies." The council expects to complete the full report on or before June 1, 1991, and to update the five-year plan from time to time as necessary with an annual report to the Legislative Research Commission on or before July 1 each year thereafter.

The Five-Year Plan for Education Technology

The Kentucky Education Reform Act, House Bill 940, Section 22, states that the Council for Education Technology is to develop a "long-range plan for the efficient and equitable use of technology at all levels from primary school through higher education, including vocational and adult education. The plan shall focus on the technology requirements of classroom instruction, literacy laboratories, instructional management, distance learning, and communications as they relate to the Commonwealth's performance outcomes for students."

The Education Reform Act further states that the plan shall "outline the Commonwealth's five (5) year activities related to purchasing, developing and using technology to:

Improve learning and teaching and the ability to meet individual student's needs to increase student achievement;

Improve curriculum delivery to help meet the needs for educational equity across the state;

Improve delivery of professional development;

Improve the efficiency and productivity of administrators; and

Encourage development by the private sector and local school district acquisition of technologies and applications appropriate for education.

The five (5) year plan shall cover all aspects of education technology, including but not limited to, its use in educational instruction and administration, video and computer systems, software and hardware, multiple delivery systems for satellite, microwave, cable, instructional television fixed service, fiber optics, computer connections products, the preparation of school buildings for technological readiness, and the development of staff necessary to implement the plan.

The five-year plan is to include specific recommendations to the state Board for Elementary and Secondary Education for adoption of administrative regulations to establish and implement a uniform and integrated system of standards and guidelines for financial accounting and reporting that is to be used by all school districts. These recommendations are to be submitted to the state Board for Elementary and Secondary Education by January 1, 1991.

Finally, the Education Reform Act requires an "integrated technology-based communication system designed to provide comprehensive, current, accurate, and accessible information relating to management, finance, operations, instruction, and pupil programs which are under the jurisdiction of the Kentucky Department of Education." The system is to be operational by the beginning of the 1991-92 school year.

Context

Technology Currently in Use in Kentucky's Schools

Since Kentucky Educational Television, Inc. (KET) was established in the early 1960s, instructional programming via television has become a familiar feature in Kentucky's classrooms. All school sites now have satellite receivers, and, in many districts, the number of television receivers is approaching one per classroom. Information gathered in the fall of 1990 indicated that more than 21,000, or 70 percent, of Kentucky's teachers used KET for instructional purposes at least once during the fall semester. In its latest technology advance, KET began providing live interactive courses for 720 students in 77 schools in 1990 and is planning additional interactive programming in future years. The Western Kentucky Education Technology Consortium also is experimenting with two-way video for interactive distance learning. The use of video teleconferencing to provide inservice training for teachers, administrators, and school board members is gradually increasing.

Information regarding the use of computers in the schools is much less clear, and the lack of reliable data regarding current use has posed serious problems to the council in the development of preliminary recommendations. To remedy this situation, a detailed survey should be conducted to secure accurate information on the present status of technology use in the public schools. Data from this survey will be used in early 1991 to refine the preliminary recommendations appearing in this document.

EXECUTIVE SUMMARY

The Kentucky Education Reform Act created a nine-person Council for Education Technology to advise the state Board for Elementary and Secondary Education. The reform act directs the council to develop a five-year plan for the equitable and efficient use of instructional and administrative technology in Kentucky schools and to submit the broad parameters to the Legislative Research Commission by January 1, 1991. The plan is to include specific recommendations to the state Board for Elementary and Secondary Education for establishing a statewide financial accounting system by August 1991.

The council gathered information about similar efforts in other states and invited input from technology vendors and users in its consideration of the following areas:

Planning and evaluation. The Council for Education Technology believes that the most effective decisions concerning education occur at the site of learning—the school. The council recommends that release of state funds for the purchase or lease of technology should be contingent upon the development by the school/school district of a complete five-year technology plan based on guidelines provided by the Kentucky Department of Education. Each school will identify a technology committee that will assess the school's instructional and management needs and plan for technology implementation.

Instructional technology. The Kentucky Education Reform Act also created the Council on School Performance Standards in order to establish outcomes expected for all students. Some of these recommended outcomes will require students to use various forms of technology; achievement of other outcomes can be aided by technology. Therefore, every school in the commonwealth will need to provide technology for every student.

The Kentucky Department of Education will provide a variety of services to schools and districts as they endeavor to select, place, and use instructional technology. These services will include regularly updated "Blueprints for Technologically Active Kentucky Schools" as well as a selection guide listing technology and training options from which the schools/school districts may choose. The Kentucky Department of Education will aggregate orders from the selection guide in order to obtain the best price for hardware and software through quantity purchasing.

Training and development. The council recommends that funds be allocated for the support of the initial training effort as well as for the establishment of development sites around the state. These development sites will be used to demonstrate, evaluate, and offer training on hardware and software applications. They will also provide vendors with a testing ground for new applications designed specifically to meet the curriculum needs of the commonwealth.

Education network. The council envisions that by 1996, an education communications network will connect all agents of education in the commonwealth. Requirements for this education network will be provided to the Communications Advisory Council, which will be evaluating the overall communications needs of the state.

In the interim, the Council for Education Technology proposes a phased introduction of the components of the total education network. This approach will allow the council to meet the legislative mandate for state-to-district communications by August 1991 while retaining enough flexibility to adapt to future improvements in the commonwealth's communication system.

In phase I, the council recommends that the existing state communications system that now reaches all 120 counties be extended to school district central offices. Two-way alternative interactive voice and video communication approaches will be piloted at selected sites within the network and expanded as warranted and feasible. During phase II, the state will establish communications from school district offices to schools. Local districts will initiate or expand local-area networks within the school buildings.

Management system. One major purpose of the education network will be the support of an education management system composed of an administrative subsystem (financial and personnel) and a student information subsystem. In view of the limited timeline for the implementation of the financial accounting component of this system, the council recommends that the Kentucky Department of Education and the Department of Information Systems retain the services of a systems consultant who will oversee the development of a technology-based management information system for the state. Needs of all prospective users will be considered through a Management Technology Applications Advisory Committee consisting of representatives of school districts, local schools, and Kentucky Department of Education personnel.

The council expects that most school districts will adopt the state's standard management system, but has recommended other options to meet the needs of school districts that have existing systems or those that contract with an educational service organization to provide computing assistance.

Recommended allocation of funds. The council recommends that the 1991-92 funds be expended to implement the education network, components of the management system, training, evaluation, and the technology development sites. The council also recommends that funds be reserved in anticipation of issues that still require study. All remaining funds should be allocated directly to school districts to be spent in the implementation of local school plans.

The council proposes that funds for instructional technology initially be allocated on the basis of the SEEK formula in the form of "technology credits." This allocation policy will be reviewed on a biannual basis to determine its impact on local schools and school districts.

Louisiana
Louisiana School Telelearning
Project Outreach

Telelearning, Project Outreach, a Louisiana School for Math, Science and the Arts distance education program, is in its fifth year. In 1986, a two-school network was created to test the feasibility of teaching calculus and a survey of the arts to schools using audiographics technology. With 8G Quality Education funds, the state Department of Education, in conjunction with the Board of Elementary and Secondary Education, approved an expansion of the system to reach as many as 114 rural schools in Louisiana. For 1990-91 the actual network size was 84 schools receiving 10 subjects (French I, II, III, Spanish I, II, III, advanced mathematics, calculus, physics, and a survey of the arts). Most of the participating schools are taking two courses through the telelearning network.

The Telelearning program will allow hundreds of graduating seniors the opportunity to attend college where that opportunity was not available before. Some of the students with ACT schools at the top range will receive entrance to LSU as engineering majors because they were given the opportunity to take physics, a course required for entrance to the program. Many of the students will apply to and major in technical areas in math and science because of their exposure to a math or science class through the Telelearning program. Because of the popularity of the program and increase in demand, some 150 high schools, most of them rural, may be served in 1991-92. The Telelearning program is gaining national attention as a model for distance education at the secondary level.

Telelearning clients are primarily rural school students who attend a school with a K-12 population of 0-200. The participating school is deficient in two or more subject areas that may deprive the students of access to programs and scholarship opportunities. Some 700 students in 84 schools are currently being served out of a larger college-bound population (statistics not available). We do know that most (80 percent or more) of the college-bound students at these schools are being served by their choice with the Telelearning system.

A typical telelearning class includes four schools plus the teaching site, with five to seven students per school. The class duplicates a regular classroom in size. Each school has up to five microphones to provide voice contact between the teacher and students. The system not only allows but encourages interaction between the teacher and students. The telelearning program refers to this process as forced interaction. Each participating school provides a proctor to facilitate the class by taking roll and administering materials, assignments, and exams. Audiographics distance education systems can take instruction anywhere. As long as there is a phone line, the classes can be taught. The Louisiana Telelearning program taught a trigonometry class to students in Leumah, Australia, on October 16. The class was technically perfect, with no computer or equipment problems. For two schools so far apart, the class was quite remarkable.

The class is taught with audiographics, a popular distance education technology that includes a personal computer, electronic penpad, audio convener, modem, and high-resolution monitor. The system is a computer-based, interactive audio and graphics system that incorporates graphics and single-frame video images stored in and utilized by a special patented software package that operates the program and its peripherals. In addition, a common telephone line is used to deliver the audio component of the system and digitized computer information. The personal computer controls the system through a modem that separates speech from the computer data. The teacher communicates with the class via an audio convener that processes the sound by sending the teachers' conversation or students' responses via the phone line. The teacher has a bank of computer images stored in a special directory and created with a special graphics package stored in the operating software. The software also includes a video component that allows the user to capture and store any video image provided from a NTSC video signal (for example, video camera, VCR, or videodisc). Besides the keyboard, a second peripheral is the penpad. This component serves as an "electronic chalkboard" for transmitting written information to and from the participating schools. The penpad is also the source device for creating graphics for instruction.

The equipment used in the telelearning system includes:

1. A personal computer*

2. A patented Optel Voice Too Modem (300 baud)

3. An electronic penpad designed for the Optel software

4. Optel Telewriter III operating software

5. An audio convener with up to five microphones per school

6. A high-resolution 27" color monitor

---

*The telelearning system uses a Tandy Model 4016 16 MHZ. IMB STD 80386 with a 3.5, 1.44 disk drive and a 105 MB hard drive. The system uses a dual serial port adapter and 4 additional ports for various peripherals.

Maryland

Joseph L. Shilling

The Maryland Department of Education has recently embarked on an ambitious program to improve the quality of education for all students in the state. As part of this, the state board of education has adopted a set of ten goals for public education to be achieved by the year 2000. These goals include the following:

- 95 percent of Maryland students will start first grade ready to learn.

- Maryland will rank in the top five states in the nation on national and international comparisons of student achievement and other measures of success.

- 100 percent of Maryland students will be functionally literate in reading, writing, mathematics, and citizenship.

- 50 percent of Maryland students will achieve excellence levels in mathematics, science, reading, social studies, and writing/language arts on state-developed assessment measures.

- The number of Maryland students pursuing postsecondary studies in mathematics, science, and technology will increase by 50 percent.

- 95 percent of Maryland students will achieve a high school diploma and will be prepared for postsecondary education, employment, or both.

- 90 percent of Maryland students who drop out of school will secure a high school diploma by age 25.

- 100 percent of Maryland students will be literate.

- Maryland schools will be free of drugs and alcohol and will provide a safe environment conducive for learning.

The state and local school systems must move toward the goal of having one computer for every 10 students enrolled. Those computers need to be configured in a way that permits an integrated learning environment and tracking of student progress. Computer hardware and software are powerful tools that, if used efficiently and effectively, can help reach Maryland's goals for the year 2000. With new developments in both hardware and software, computers are now being used across the curriculum and at all grade levels. The role of the computer has changed from computer-assisted instruction to the computer as a tool for instruction that can benefit every teacher and student.

In the past 10 years there have been many evaluations of the effectiveness of computers. Recent studies at the Waterford Institute (1989), The Maryland Education Project (1989), The Statewide Maryland Education Technology Network Evaluation

(1989), Calvert County, Maryland (1989), and Fredrick County, Maryland (1990) indicate that computer technology is an effective way to meet the developmentally appropriate curricular and instructional needs of students. The most promising applications include:

- Management of classroom activities and recordkeeping
- Understanding abstract mathematics and science concepts
- Developing writing skills with word processors
- Individualized learning through managed interaction/feedback
- Problem-solving skills and "higher order" thinking
- Simulation in science, mathematics, and social studies
- Cooperative learning through networking and telecommunications
- Database management systems to manipulate data for analysis
- General purpose computer skills
- Skills for business and vocational training
- Needs of special education students
- Distance learning for teachers and students in remote areas

A student/computer ratio of 10 to 1 enables each student to use a computer on the average of 40 minutes each school day. Although this is a minimum standard to support a funding strategy, an even smaller ratio is desirable to fully integrate computers into the instructional program at all grade levels and across all curriculum areas.

The current statewide student/computer ratio is 19 to 1, with a range of between 57 to 1 and 10 to 1 at the local school system level. The total number of computers in schools is approximately 35,000. To reach the goal of 10 to 1, an additional 34,400 computers will need to be purchased. Funding for the hardware/software would be shared, with the state providing 50 percent of the cost and the local school systems providing 50 percent. Calculation of the state/local share for each school system would be based on the per-pupil wealth of the system, with the poorer systems receiving a larger percentage of state funds.

In addition to computer technology, the department continues to provide an extensive instructional television service to local school systems. Television is an effective tool that, if used properly, can have a powerful impact on the teaching and learning process. In the past twenty years, the Division of Instructional Technology (INTEC) has leased and produced programming that has been targeted to meet existing curricular needs within the local school systems. Television provides a multisensory learning environment that helps meet the needs of students with different learning styles. Television is able to bring to the classroom experiences that are not possible with traditional methods and tools, such as the lecture, chalkboard, and textbook.

In the early days of ITV, programming was nothing more than a prerecorded lecture. It was designed to take the place of the teacher. Today, ITV takes advantage of a variety of sophisticated technologies and techniques to create programming that is interesting, captivating, motivating, and able to compete with the likes of MTV. ITV provides teachers with resources that supplement and enhance the traditional lecture and texts. ITV allows teachers to demonstrate concepts, such as how cells divide or the structural relationship of the parts of an atom, that cannot be demonstrated with more traditional instructional formats. Students can experience historical events, visit any place in the world, or learn a foreign language as spoken in the country of origin.

The department is in the process of surveying 150 schools throughout the state to study the impact that various technologies are having on the instructional process. Schools from all three levels, elementary, middle, and high, are included as are an equal number of schools with significant technology resources and those with limited resources. The goals of this project are

- to determine how schools are using the various technologies,

- to identify programs, processes, and procedures that facilitate the use of technology that can be transported to the rest of the state,

- to determine why some schools have access to and effectively use technology as part of their instructional program while other schools either lack the resources or use them in ineffective ways,

- to assess ITV utilization,

- to determine effectiveness of current INTEC services, and

- to identify services that INTEC could provide.

This survey will be completed in the third quarter of the 1991 fiscal year.

Michigan
Connections
A Strategy for Michigan's Future
through Telecommunications

PREFACE

Telecommunications is the watchword of the nineties. Every decision maker in business, government, and education is exploring how today's technology can be used to improve efficiency, productivity, accountability, equity, and quality of life. In 1988, Governor James Blanchard asserted the importance of telecommunications to Michigan's future in his state of the state address. Calling for the establishment of a telecommunications task force, the governor first recognized a need to harness technology in schools to educate our state's youth. As planning began, it became apparent that the development of a comprehensive, state-of-the-art telecommunications network would have consequences for those outside school walls as well. Business and industry, state and local government, community and service organizations, libraries, hospitals, colleges and universities all stand to benefit from a coordinated, improved telecommunications "highway system." By accessing a statewide network, our northern, rural, and remote communities will be offered new educational and economic opportunities through instantaneous communication.

To take on this task is a bold mission. Michigan must be established as a technological leader. Its people must be prepared for the jobs of tomorrow and its products ready for global competition. Telecommunications is shaping Michigan's future. The recommendations of the Telecommunications Task Force project a vision of statewide communication. Implementing these recommendations could result in small businesses in Marquette accessing new international markets, the classrooms of Alpena connecting with those of Japan, and employees increasingly conducting business from home. The vision is in place. Now we must act.

Universal, instantaneous electronic communication will revolutionize our lives over the next several years in ways that are, as yet, unforeseeable. To ensure that all of Michigan's residents benefit requires comprehensive planning and prudent investment. This report and recommendations that follow are the first steps in the long-term development of a high-capacity, accessible telecommunications system in Michigan—a system without parallel. It is expected that new initiatives will grow out of those outlined in the report as teachers, businesspersons, community leaders, and government share ideas and strategies.

From the vantage point of the twenty-first century, our efforts will, no doubt, appear somewhat naive, our aim bearing to the left or right of the intended target. Such is the nature of prediction. By daring to travel an unmarked path, however, we can provide a foundation on which our leaders will continue to build and invest.

Michigan's major challenge is to position itself as a technological leader and thereby avoid becoming a technological dinosaur. Together, we must choose evolution over extinction. We must use our telecommunications know-how to build a sophisticated workforce and an equitable education system, ensure governmental accountability, and develop a business climate ripe for innovation and job creation.

The strategy and recommendations presented here represent the concerted effort of a number of people. We would like to thank the members of the Telecommunications Task Force, Electronic Data Systems Corporation, Telecommunications Resource Group participants, and survey, hearing and interview respondents. Their ideas and suggestions have been invaluable and reflect the informational needs of the people of our state. We invite the Telecommunications Resource Group to remain active and help in implementing the recommendations presented here.

Thomas L. Baldini, Co-Chairperson

Janet Blanchard, Co-Chairperson

EXECUTIVE SUMMARY

In 1861, the telegraph's ability to transmit Morse code signals coast to coast rendered the pony express obsolete. In the hundred years following the 1876 patenting of Bell's telephone, some 600 million telephones were placed in the homes of America's families, connecting their communities by a hodgepodge of poles and wire draped across the countryside. Through two world wars, the Great Depression, civil unrest in the sixties, and Vietnam, a young nation found strength in numbers, its telephone network bringing people together again and again for a common cause. Today, America stands poised on the edge of a new and far-reaching frontier. Forming an enormous three-dimensional web comprising hair-thin optical fibers, coaxial cables, copper wire, radio, satellites, cable television, microwave towers and computers, telecommunications resources are crossing land, water, and space to link cities, countries, and continents in a global communication network. Fast-paced and still evolving, telecommunications technology is impacting how America interacts with its world neighbors. Just as the mobility afforded by highways, waterways, and bridges contributed to past prosperity, the mobility of information promises future economic success. The Information Age is more than a futuristic vision. It promises the release of once-sequestered information and greater personal freedom for individuals who demand the right to know and the means to communicate.

Government, with its stores of valuable data, must invest in telecommunication tools to free the global exchange of information and improve the quality of life. A report issued in 1989 by Syracuse University's School of Information Studies entitled *Managing Information Resources: New Directions in State Government*, indicates the progress of state governments in managing information resources through investments in technology. In 1988, 47 states owned a total of 197,300 microcomputers. Nineteen out of 23 states surveyed for telecommunications investments had in place or were planning to establish integrated voice, data, video, and image networks. New investment does not come easily for states that must balance budgets. Unaware of the gains to be made through telecommunications and lacking a strategic direction, government must educate and coordinate if it is to seek technological solutions to communication dilemmas. Telecommunication networking promises unlimited opportunities—electronic mail, home banking, on-screen yellow pages and telephone directory, online libraries, teleconferencing, interactive video instruction, and "smart" vehicles and roadways. More than exciting novelties, such technological applications will alter daily routine and present new education and employment opportunities.

In his 1988 state of the state address, Governor James Blanchard made a commitment to "assure taxpayers that their investments will result in the most integrated, flexible, high-tech telecommunications system in the world." Making good on that promise, the governor's Telecommunications Task Force was formed later that year to identify Michigan's telecommunications resources and services. The task force—comprising representatives from the governor's executive office, the Cabinet Council on Human Investment, the Public Service Commission, and Michigan's departments of commerce, education, labor and management, and budget—was charged with developing a plan to link all areas of the state to sources of high-speed information transmission. Michigan's businesses, schools, and government have already made significant investments in establishing segments of this statewide network. By coordinating the planning and spending of these large consumers and setting statewide standards, a comprehensive backbone system will be established—a system that is accessible and integrated and that incorporates switched broadband technologies. Such a network will ensure the long-term success of Michigan's youth, workers, and entrepreneurs.

The task force contracted Electronic Data Systems Corporation (EDS) to lay the groundwork for the study. Specifically, EDS was to identify existing telecommunications resources and determine how these resources could be improved and expanded to aid Michigan in meeting the challenges of the Information Age. Over the past year, the task force has compiled information from a number of sources, including public hearings held in Marquette, Flint, Novi, Grand Rapids, Roscommon, and Lansing; more than 1,800 surveys distributed and more than 100 private interviews conducted with representatives of schools, businesses, libraries and other organizations; documentation from other states and countries on information management programs; and trade literature. This information is the basis for the recommendations set forth in this report. Components of a comprehensive telecommunications strategy for Michigan, these proposals will offer new educational opportunities, enhance the business climate, build a skilled work force, and ensure efficiency in government.

In the twenty-first century, America's states will be ranked by how well they have defined their informational needs and how aggressively they have worked to meet them. It is the purpose of this report to help Michigan identify its own informational needs; develop an efficient, competitive telecommunication architecture; equalize access to information; and garner new technology-based perspectives on commerce, learning, and governance. The recommendations highlighted in this summary will help Michigan improve, manage and promote its telecommunications resources. They will secure a competitive edge in the new global information society for the leaders and workers of the next century. These recommendations follow.

Task Force Recommendations

- Build and encourage telecommunications partnerships between businesses, communities, governments, and schools.

- Provide quality training programs for educators who use telecommunications technology to deliver instruction.

- Promote telecommunications as a tool to assist in the restructuring of Michigan's classrooms and fostering the implementation of new teaching and learning theories and methodologies.

- Provide incentives and competitive grants to encourage the deployment of telecommunications technology—including interactive video—in Michigan schools.

- Establish a Division of Educational Technology within the Michigan Department of Education to (1) coordinate investments in information technology at all levels (preschool, K-12, and postsecondary), (2) integrate technology-based educational programs into a cooperative delivery system, (3) provide technical assistance to school districts, and (4) encourage, plan, and implement professional training programs for providers and users of distance learning technologies.

- Support the efforts of Michigan's postsecondary institutions in training a marketable workforce, investing in research, and forming consortia of existing networks.

- Encourge the establishment of new entrepreneurial ventures in Michigan that draw upon the untapped potential of telecommunications technology.

- Promote and develop the state as a hub of information services, attracting new business based on accessibility to Michigan's rich store of information resources and services.

- Provide incentives for Michigan's private communications industry to deploy the latest technology—including digital switched broadband technologies like fiber optics and cellular-type radio—in every region of the state.

- Devise a strategy for using telecommunications to market Michigan products and services to the world.

- Transform Michigan state government into a model "telecommunity"—an informational source, a service provider, an organization of "knowledge" workers, and a force for change.

- Encourage the development of a state-of-the-art, hybrid, interactive, switched telecommunications "back-bone" system—comprising multiple broadband technologies—that would serve all institutions and every Michigan citizen.

- Designate two state departments as pilot information innovators. These agencies will determine methods of using technology to improve service delivery, strengthen employee skills, and find ways of using information as a strategic resource. Using these pilot projects as guides, all state departments will be encouraged to follow suit by 1995.

- Recruit and maintain a corps of skilled information workers for state government.

- Initiate a schedule of improvement for state government's telecommunications infrastructure.

- Work with local governments across the state to aid them in managing their information resources and offering improved services to their constituents.

- Solidify the state's role as an information clearinghouse.

- Establish the Cabinet Council on Information Technology to take the lead in planning Michigan's future as a premier center of information-based services.

- Promote the use of technology to eliminate the social and informational isolation of Michigan's handicapped citizens and devise a strategy to bring them into the center of Michigan's workforce.

- Encourage businesses, education institutions, and state agencies to develop tele-commuting policies and other telecommunications programs for those individuals who are not able to be physically present in classrooms or the workplace.

- Support the concept of connecting homes, offices, and schools through a network of switched broadband technologies such as fiber optics, cellular radio, and micro-wave as a national priority, bringing all Michigan residents a new range of informa-tion, education, and employment opportunities.

- Devise a telecommuting policy for state workers, encouraging the private sector to follow suit.

Missouri
Plans for Educational
Technology

This report from Missouri consists of two sections. The first, "A Road Map to School Improvement," was undertaken by the Missouri Technology Task Force and the second, "Video Instructional Development and Educational Opportunity (VIDEO)" by the Special State Instructional Programs Staff, Division of Instruction.

A ROAD MAP TO SCHOOL IMPROVEMENT

Introduction

Parents of today's public school students grew up in a nation that dominated the world with its unprecedented industrial and military might brought about by technological superiority. Yet today, in a marketplace dominated by foreign interests, students in Missouri and the rest of the nation lack the basic competencies to compete in an increasingly complex and technologically dependent global community. Today's learners face challenges that society and, by assignment, the schools must equip them to overcome. The technology that once gave the United States the edge as a global competitor is no longer unique, but it can again give this country the edge in a different arena: the learning environment.

The focus of this report is the learner. Implementation of new technologies and techniques will empower students and thus provide optimal educational opportunities for them. Teaching facts alone is no longer acceptable; we must teach learners how to think and apply knowledge practically.

The teacher, of course, plays a central role in the effective use of technology in the classroom. We must create the expectation that teachers will serve as facilitators of learning, not simply disseminators of information.

We believe Missouri's schools can achieve national prominence by asserting their leadership in the use of technology. Some Missouri school districts are well on their way toward achieving this distinction. Others are only beginning to explore the possibilities technology has to offer.

The report of this task force reflects the collective efforts of individuals committed to excellence in education. This report, the product of their efforts, can serve as a road map for Missouri's schools as they strive to produce motivated students who are well prepared to compete in the technology-rich society of the twenty-first century.

Background

Problems and Issues Facing Educators

Providing equitable access to quality, free public education is a fundamental challenge faced by our society. Advanced curriculum offerings, procurement and retention of qualified teachers, local and state funding, geographic location, and educational facilities are some factors that contribute to this challenge. Although educational concerns and issues have been debated for many years, recent state and national reports, in addition to global factors such as the changes in Eastern Europe and our declining effectiveness in competing in the economic arena highlight the need for state and local authorities to reexamine our education system with an eye toward restructuring for improvement.

Curriculum and instruction should be reevaluated in light of recent events that are changing our world's geopolitical landscape, thus causing educators to consider the teaching and learning environment in a global, rather than a provincial, context. Geographic and even political boundaries are no longer barriers to commerce, education, and the social good. The curricular impact of these changes is as yet unclear; however, support for change is expressed by the *Labor Force 2000: Corporate America Responds* report, which notes "social change [is] as fundamental as the earlier shift from farms to factories. And it requires that tomorrow's workers be equipped with new knowledge, skills, and attitudes." The report *Missouri's Future Is Now: Achieving Competency in Science, Mathematics, and Technology* recommends that "curricula which effectively address competency in science, mathematics, and technology must be established throughout Missouri." These and other recommendations listed by the report suggest that substantial changes are needed in our education system. Indeed, the Missouri state board suggests that "traditional curriculum and instructional practices must be revised to focus on the achievement of desirable outcomes for all students."

In addition to the demands for an enhanced curriculum, teacher shortages have exacerbated the problem of schools being unable to provide needed courses of study. Nationally, teachers constitute 8 percent of our work force. The Missouri State Board of Education's *Missourians Prepared* report notes that in the next decade Missouri's public schools will need to hire an estimated 25,000 new teachers to replace about half of the state's current teaching force.

Beyond these concerns, by nearly every measure, Missouri's public education system is underfunded. The state board report indicates that "despite the significant financial commitment to education by the state and local school districts, it is apparent that current funding for public education in Missouri is simply inadequate." The combination of these forces has created apprehension among educators about the future of our public education system. In response to this concern, many national and state education agencies have initiated campaigns for educational reform. Many of these early reform movements resulted in new standards for achievement and graduation. Other school improvement proposals, such as choice and the year-round school, are being implemented. More dramatic changes may loom in the future as the school restructuring movement gathers support. The Missouri State Board of Education has said that "although we are encouraged by the school-improvement efforts of recent years, it is clear that more fundamental changes will be required for schools to meet the challenges of the 1990's and beyond" (*Missourians Prepared*, 1990).

Technology as a Tool of Tomorrow

Nationally, education has been challenged to respond to the impact of these social, economic, and political changes. National reports suggest that transformations, reconstruction, and revolutions stand to alter the future of education in this country. The Office of Technology Assessment noted that "the infusion of computers and development of advanced interactive technologies coincide with troubled news about American schools, and have been hailed by many as an important catalyst for reform" (*Power On!: New Tools for Teaching and Learning*, 1988). These reports call for changes in our schools that would incorporate technological solutions capable of bringing about more effective and efficient use of existing resources. In Missouri, the Excellence in Education Act is a key indicator of our state's progress in and commitment to public education. However, advancement towards excellence requires our state to examine all domains of teaching and learning, especially the tools that empower the learner and enable the teacher to extend the learning process beyond the confines of hours, walls, and a traditional place called "school."

The emergence of new technologies has the potential to reshape education. Technology has been shown to improve the quality of learning, provide more equitable opportunity and access, and ensure greater cost effectiveness. The Office of Technology Assessment concluded that "the nation's educational system may be on the brink of major change. This results both from a fundamental change in the demand for educational services and from the fact that new technology makes it possible to consider real improvements in the productivity of both teaching and learning." The study also indicates that in combination, "these forces could change what is taught, when it is taught, where it is taught, and the nature of the teaching profession." These changes seem distant, both in terms of time and geography; however, the state board submits that "teachers of the 1990's will be expected to implement new instructional practices including new technologies."

One such new instructional practice utilizes computer technology in combination with interactive laser disk applications. This technology allows students to explore subject areas in pathways that are unique to the individual student. Hypermedia, or highly interactive instructional multimedia, and other hybrid technologies will become more important in delivering curriculum in ways that enrich the learning experience. Another example of an enabling instructional technology growing in use nationwide is communications and satellite technology, which can provide an array of course offerings for critical shortage areas and serve to enrich existing curricula. Educational technologies such as these can create a teaching and learning environment that synergizes the tools of technology and the talents of students and educators to achieve excellence.

Need in Missouri

Availability of potent technological tools in Missouri schools is limited. Toch reported in *Education Week* that in 1983, Missouri ranked forty-second in the percentage of microcomputers available for student use in schools. A comparison of studies by the Missouri Department of Elementary and Secondary Education (1986), Toch (1984), and Rienhold (1986) reveals that the availability of microcomputers in K-12 educational programs in Missouri was one of the lowest in the United States.

The Missouri legislature appropriated $2.5 million for the 1985-86 school year to fund purchases of microcomputers for instructional purposes in the state's public schools. Although these funds provided for the purchase of many computers, this one-time allocation lacked adequate follow-up training and support to prove a significant influence on technology usage in the classroom. The incentive grants program included in the Excellence in Education Act, though not designed specifically for technology, has contributed to the state's funding support for technology in Missouri schools. During the past five years this source has distributed $4.5 million annually for school improvement projects, many including the purchase of technology.

The Video Instructional Development and Educational Opportunity (VIDEO) legislation, enacted in 1989 by Senate Bill 709, was established to encourage all Missouri public educational institutions to supplement educational opportunities through telecommunications technology and satellite broadcast instruction. In the first year the VIDEO program 458 LEAs (local education agencies), 21 higher education institutions, and 5 public broadcasting stations applied for and received approximately $4.7 million in initial access and broadcast grants. This legislation has resulted in the purchase of an additional 400 satellite dishes capable of receiving educational programming from virtually any communications satellite. The VIDEO program will continue to distribute funding for the next four years to provide grants to school districts for the purchase of video-based educational technologies, including satellite equipment, instructional program development, and instructional programs.

Thus, technology is becoming an economic, social, and political issue, and the anticipation for change is increasing in Missouri schools. The challenge to this state's educators and policy makers is to understand the potential of all emerging technologies and provide the leadership necessary to ensure successful learning outcomes.

Need for Planning

All of the state's potential technology funding sources were implemented without a statewide technology vision. To make full progress toward district and state educational goals, schools must understand, plan, and deploy the necessary technological resources. The basis for effective utilization of education technology is careful planning at every level of the educational system. A report entitled *Thinking about Technology in Schools: A 1988 Snapshot* examined 213 technology plans and concluded that although a broad array of technologies were being planned for, most uses were not "well-articulated strategies." The report further concluded that planning efforts at the district level are substandard, noting that "technology planning clearly is a weak area of endeavor in most school districts." While the Missouri state legislature and the State Board of Education can be credited with taking steps to improve the status of technology in the schools, researcher J. D. Layton found that "Missouri is behind other states in many areas, and there are no state, district, or local education agency long range plans to guide the efficacious use of technology." The need for comprehensive planning at all levels is imperative.

Statewide Technology Task Force

It became evident through surveys and direct contact with Missouri school districts that something must be done concerning educational technology in Missouri public schools. In the face of limited funding, attempts to integrate technology into our schools by increasing awareness, providing inservice, and advocating the technology have been disappointing. The logical conclusion was that Missouri needed a plan for educational technology. Missouri educators lacked consensus and needed leadership regarding the best use of technology in the learning environment. Based on these findings, the Missouri Technology Task Force was created.

Purpose of Task Force

The specific purpose of this task force is to develop a strategic plan for technology that will assist state and local authorities in the creative application and appropriate integration of all technologies to achieve the broad educational goals for K-12 Missouri public schools.

Methodology

This report represents the findings of a statewide planning effort that began in April 1989 and concluded in October of 1990. A modified strategic planning format was adopted. A planning team was selected to provide leadership for the overall planning effort. The team developed a mission statement, identified five focus areas, established vision statements, and developed desired outcomes. The planning team included 24 individuals representing decision makers in government, business and industry, and education. Four action teams were established to study the five focus areas developed by the planning team. The action teams were charged with developing strategies to achieve the outcomes identified by the planning team. Action teams consisted of individuals with expertise in the application of technology in various settings. Participants were broadly representative of various geographic and occupational sectors of Missouri.

In addition to the many planning meetings, activities of the task force included conducting an internal and external analysis of other state and district technology plans, as well as selected social, economic, demographic, and political data; identifying strengths, weaknesses, opportunities, and threats; and soliciting input from groups outside of the immediate planning team.

An open forum sponsored by the Task Force provided a unique opportunity for organizations and groups to meet with the Technology Task Force and present their position statements relative to educational technology. The open forum was conducted on April 9th, 1990. Based on comments from task force members and participants and the enthusiasm exhibited by educational support groups, the open forum was successful in furthering the task force's goal of sharing ideas, opinions, and organizational platforms.

Task Force Beliefs

The planning effort was greatly influenced by a collection of basic beliefs. These beliefs had a recurring impact on the planning activity and therefore represent the foundation of this report. These beliefs follow.

- Missouri students can be the best in the nation; achievement at an "average" level is not, and should not be, the expected level of achievement by our students. Prominence is the only acceptable level of achievement for Missouri schools.

- Learning is a lifelong process; schools exist to provide individual learning experiences so that all learners can achieve their potential.

- Schools should provide students access to appropriate educational opportunities and resources; no student should be denied, by virtue of district sparseness, wealth, or location, coursework necessary for employment or postsecondary educational pursuits.

- Schools should be accountable for learning outcomes; Missouri educators should accept the responsibility to define their goals and be held accountable for those goals.

- All citizens have a responsibility in supporting Missouri public schools; parents and communities in general have unique roles in ensuring success for all Missouri students.

- Technology will contribute to accomplishing the educational goals of Missouri; the use of educational technology in teaching and the learning environment is essential to achieving these goals.

- The actions stated in this report, if acted on, will improve the quality of learning, ensure equity of opportunity, enhance accountability, and foster community and parental involvement.

The task force developed the following mission statement: Utilize technology to enable all Missouri students to achieve national prominence in learning essential skills and competencies necessary to be effective citizens, qualified members of the workforce, and lifelong learners.

VIDEO INSTRUCTIONAL DEVELOPMENT AND EDUCATIONAL OPPORTUNITY (VIDEO)

Purpose and Background

The Video Instructional Development and Educational Opportunity Program (VIDEO) enacted by the general assembly in 1988 through SB709 encourages all educational institutions in Missouri to supplement educational opportunities through the use of telecommunications technology, including instructional television programming and satellite broadcast instruction.

Three subprograms within the VIDEO program are

1. grants to public school districts, public institutions of higher education, and public television stations for equipment and instruction;

2. development of instructional programs to be transmitted through the airwaves or by cable television, available free of charge to the public; and

3. development of instructional programs to be made available on a subscription basis.

Five types of grants are available under the program:

1. *Initial Access Grants* in $6,000 units based on student population and number of instructional facilities to be used for:

   - acquisition of television reception and playback equipment such as satellite receivers, ITFS antennas, cable connections, television receivers, and VCRs,

   - subscription fees for instructional television and course fees for media courses broadcast via satellite,

- fees and stipends for staff training,

- equipment maintenance, and

- purchase of videotapes, both commercially prepared and blank (limited to 10 percent of state grant funds received).

2. *Continuation Grants* in $500 units, based on the number of initial access units acquired and expended the previous year(s) to be used for:

- course fees and subscription fees,

- staff training fees,

- telecommunication transmission charges, and

- equipment maintenance.

3. *Broadcast Grants* to be awarded to public television stations for the purpose of increasing the number of subscribing organizations and increasing the time available for on-site educational assistance.

4. *Program Development Grants* to be awarded for development of instructional programming deemed useful according to a statewide needs assessment.

5. *Discretionary Grants* to be awarded for projects that demonstrate innovative uses of video technology.

A 27-member advisory committee meets throughout the year to oversee the program's progression and make recommendations for implementation of program components. The committee is also responsible for issuing a report to the state board of education and the general assembly.

Report

With the completion of the first year of implementation, the success of the VIDEO program can be measured in participation numbers. As of January 1990, 458 local education agencies (LEAs), 21 institutions of higher education (IHE), and 5 public broadcasting stations had applied for and received approximately $4,700,000 in initial access and broadcast grants. The LEA breakdown included 346 districts with populations of less than 1,500, 76 districts with populations between 1,500 and 4,000, 18 districts with populations between 4,000 and 7,500, 8 districts with populations between 7,500 and 12,000, 6 districts with populations between 12,000 and 30,000, and 3 districts with populations of more than 40,000. This translates into live broadcast access for more than 550,000 students in elementary, secondary, and college classrooms. Video instruction in the classroom averaged 10.6 hours per week, targeting science, social studies, and foreign language. In addition, 750 students participated in stand-alone courses that included instruction in foreign language, physics, chemistry, and math. Video technology was also utilized for staff development, board member training, and general community use. The total appropriation for the program was $5,133,240; total expenditures were $4,555,177.

Many LEAs implemented distance learning technology prior to SB709. Cable access was available in 176 districts, satellite dishes were in use in 106 districts, and Instructional Television Fixed Service (ITFS) antennas were installed in 33 districts (see figure 1).

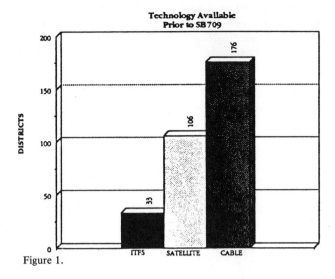

Figure 1.

Initial access grants. Initial access units of $6,000, based on population and number of instructional facilities, are allocated to each LEA and institution of higher education. In year one of the VIDEO program, 50 of the 93 elementary districts in the state (54 percent) applied for and received their total entitlement of $6,000, matching this with $600 of local funds. In years two, three, four, and five, these districts will be eligible to receive continuation funds of $500 per year for each initial access grant to assist with maintenance of the program.

Also in year one, 408 high school districts (90 percent) applied for and received a minimum grant of $6,000, matching 10 percent of their allocation with local funds. Additionally, 126 of that number received $12,000 or more to reflect their larger populations and number of instructional facilities. All of these high school districts will be eligible to apply for additional access units in subsequent years of the program as well as continuation monies available to them. Twenty-one public institutions of higher education (100 percent) applied for and received allocations of $6,000, $12,000, $18,000, $24,000, or $36,000, with one receiving $60,000 (matching with 10 percent of local funds) based on full-time student enrollment and the number of instructional facilities (see figure 2, which represents numbers of grants).

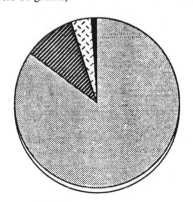

Initial Access Grant Awards

High School Districts	84.8%
Elementary Districts	10.1%
IHEs	4.0%
Public TV	1.0%

Figure 2.

Typically, grant monies from LEAs and IHEs were spent purchasing equipment: satellite receiving equipment, dedicated telephone systems, televisions and VCRs, cable drops, and ITFS antennas (see figure 3). Computers for use with stand-alone courses and interactive videodisc equipment were acquired on a limited basis and are too small in number to be represented on the chart.

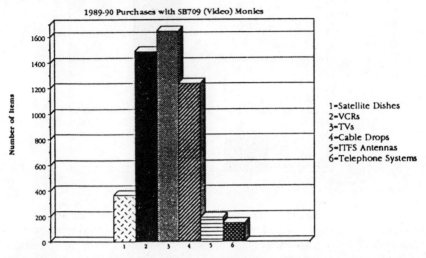

Figure 3.

Broadcast grants. Grants totalling $255,000 were distributed to five public broadcasting stations in year one. Approximately $53,000 was used to hire additional staff to provide inservice to school districts' faculty and staff; $50,000 was spent on equipment purchase and upgrade. The remaining funds were utilized to establish or purchase programming in the following areas: social studies, science, foreign language, language arts, math, technology, and staff development (see figure 4). Additionally, 195 ITFS systems were installed in the St. Louis area as a direct result of SB709 monies.

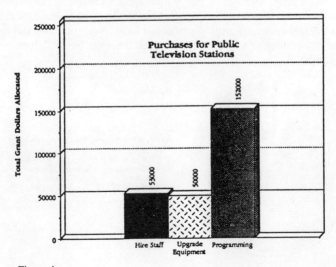

Figure 4.

Continuation grants. Year two of the program marks the implementation of continuation grants of $500 per each initial access unit already received and expended. Districts may apply for both initial access grants and continuation grants, thereby enabling them to acquire services in additional buildings while maintaining those already using video technology. Continuation grants will be awarded throughout all four remaining program years.

Program development grants. Based on a statewide needs assessment, four areas of greatest need were identified: writing skills, basic math skills, teaching strategies for staff development, and Missouri history. Program development grants will award monies to develop or purchase existing programming in these areas. Missouri history is targeted for initial development. Programs developed or purchased under this program will be transmitted free of charge to the public, including public and nonpublic schools.

Discretionary grants. Using a competitive process, projects for innovative uses of video technology will be selected to receive discretionary grant money. The VIDEO advisory committee has recommended that $250,000 be earmarked for this grant category. Public institutions in Missouri are eligible to apply.

Media courses (stand-alone courses). As of April 1990, 11 media courses had been approved by the Missouri Department of Elementary and Secondary Education for use in Missouri high schools. Under the supervision of a teacher/monitor with required qualifications, these classes may be counted toward graduation credit. Courses originate from Oklahoma State University, Kansas State University, and Eastern Washington Service District 101. The content areas offered are

- Math (calculus, trigonometry, analytical geometry)
- Science (physics, chemistry)
- Foreign language (German I, II; Russian I; Spanish I)
- Economics
- English

Instruction was extended to 750 students in 61 districts through stand-alone courses during the first year of the program. Additional districts have indicated they will offer this method of instruction in the coming school year.

Dissemination and technical assistance. During the summer and fall of 1989, 12 informational workshops were held to assist with the initial application process. In March of 1990, 15 workshops were conducted across the state to assist districts in completing final reports, answer questions about participation in the program, and assist application procedures. Technical assistance is also available from department staff on a 12-month basis.

Nebraska
Elementary and Secondary
School Education

INTRODUCTION

Nebraska is characterized by large expanses of land, a few densely populated communities, and a large number of small rural communities. Outside the urban areas, the population of school-age children is scattered over many miles. Because all school districts in the state are funded in large part by property tax revenues and because all districts are not equally wealthy, not all Nebraska students have the rich variety of school programs needed in a complex, modern society. In addition, students in the more sparsely populated regions of the state do not have access to as many educational resources and community services (museums, art galleries, or performing arts programs) as students in urban areas.

Many Nebraska school districts are able to provide only the minimum of courses required by state rules. Therefore, many students have a very limited curriculum from which to choose. This is especially true of advanced courses. For example, only 110 of Nebraska's 365 high schools offer calculus. Only about 60 percent of those schools offer a true advanced placement course equal to the first semester of college calculus. Advanced placement courses are almost nonexistent in high schools with fewer than 250 students.

Some Nebraska school districts have attempted to address economic and equity issues by transporting students or teachers to other districts. In at least one case, an entire junior high school is being transported. Parents have also reported that they are moving or transferring their children to other districts in order to find increased educational opportunities. If Nebraska's school population of more than 300,000 is going to meet the challenges set forth by President Bush and the nation's governors at the Educational Summit, Nebraska policy makers must recognize that our schools need to broaden their course offerings. The following assurances must be made:

1. All learners must have access to high-quality instruction, no matter where they are located in Nebraska.

2. Nebraska teachers must have access to the latest tools and methods in order to improve instruction for Nebraska schoolchildren.

3. All educators in Nebraska elementary and secondary schools must have easy access to information, whether it is located in their local library or in a computer hundreds of miles away.

4. Nebraska communities must be able to provide their work force with quality training and expertise in order to compete in a global economy.

For many Nebraska communities, telecommunications technologies may provide the only access to the high-quality instruction they will need. Telecommunications can supply the interactivity, or two-way communication, that optimizes all learning. Technology now enables educators and students who are miles apart to see one another, ask and answer questions, debate and discuss issues, and generally participate in a true, two-way communication process. Gone are the days when a university faculty member broadcast lessons without interaction with students. Sound educational methods and practices based on respected research data do not support the old view of teacher as pitcher and students as empty vessels waiting to be filled. Effective instructional techniques require two-way communication between teacher and learner and multifaceted interactions among learners, whether the teacher and students are in the same room or miles apart.

A VISION FOR TELECOMMUNICATIONS

The following model is offered as a vision for telecommunications in Nebraska learning communities.

Community Schools—Centers of Learning

The public school becomes the center for learning in Nebraska communities and neighborhoods. Each school district has access to satellite programs, telecomputing resources, and a regional network, which pull in a variety of educational opportunities originating from:

- other Nebraska communities,
- Nebraska postsecondary education institutions,
- state governmental agencies,
- the Nebraska Library Commission,
- the Nebraska Department of Education,
- the Nebraska Educational Telecommunications Commission,
- educational agencies outside of Nebraska, and, in some cases, international resources.

When appropriate courses are not available locally, elementary and secondary school-children receive instruction from teachers outside of their school district, either through satellite or regional and interactive television. In the evenings, housewives, farmers, doctors, business people, educators, and other community members use the facilities to take courses of interest, receive training, or keep up on the latest innovations in their profession.

Regional Pods

Communities in proximity can link their communities into an interactive fiber optic television network, or *pod*. The system enables a teacher in one community to deliver a class to students in others nearby. Using this system, both teacher and students can see and hear one another. Each pod can link into statewide and nationwide satellite systems through a satellite dish located in one of the pod communities. Telecomputing resources enable quick exchange of documents and provide access to vast research and conferencing resources. The system allows communities to create their own programs or to purchase those provided by others, depending on their specific needs.

Community Partnerships

The technologies described above are being utilized in several other states; however, these technologies are not presently being used by any school districts in Nebraska. To provide demonstration sites, three regional interactive networks are being proposed. Each consists of K-12 school districts in partnership with one or more higher education institutions and their communities at large. One network will be in an urban area and two in rural areas. These projects have been selected because each has completed comprehensive feasibility studies supporting the utilization of these technologies to improve the educational opportunity for students in the districts involved. Funding is also being requested for the following purposes:

1. Matching funds for three additional regions to conduct feasibility studies.

2. Technical and instructional support to be provided by the Nebraska Department of Education and the Nebraska Educational Telecommunications Commission.

3. Resources for a Nebraska Educational Telecomputing Network.

4. Matching funds for 25 additional satellite downlinks for school districts.

1993 to 1995 Biennium and Beyond

Nebraska educators envision the unfolding of several network pods over the next 10 to 15 years. Three more regional course pods will be requested during the next biennium, along with satellite and telecomputing resources for all schools. A long-range funding plan will include the proposal of a video rental tax similar to that in Missouri to fund a series of such networks in all regions of Nebraska.

New Mexico
Formation of the Educational
Technology Planning Committee

INTRODUCTION

In September 1990, the New Mexico Commission on Higher Education and the state board of education set up the Educational Technology Planning Committee, a task force charged with creating a plan incorporating technology to achieve the state's long-range educational goals. One goal is to give children in New Mexico's rural schools the same opportunities available to those in larger districts. To help teachers manage student diversity, the committee will encourage use of software that can help prepare individual student learning plans, which will be based on input from the student's parents and will be continually updated. In addition to computer-assisted teaching, audiographics and distance learning approaches will be utilized. To foster collaboration, the state's national laboratories, library networks, and museums will also be used to help achieve national goals.

The Educational Technology Planning Committee comprises nineteen representatives from the business community, national laboratories, public schools, museums, libraries, and higher education. The committee expects to produce a plan by September 1, 1991, to be submitted to the governor and the legislature. A description of the committee's purpose, goals, and membership as defined in September 1990 follows.

NEW MEXICO COMMITTEE FOR EDUCATIONAL
TECHNOLOGY PLANNING

Authority

The New Mexico Educational Technology Planning Committee is being appointed and authorized subject to the authority of the state board of education and the Commission on Higher Education. It is intended to be an ad hoc committee designed to accomplish certain planning activities, after which it will be dissolved by the commission and board.

Purpose

The Educational Technology Planning Committee (ETPC) will propose a long-range plan for improving the use of educational technology to better facilitate learning by students and adults. This purpose assumes that improved opportunities for learning will occur if the numerous and disparate interests in educational technology are better coordinated and further assumes the value of educational technology as an essential tool for preparing students in the year 2000.

Background Issues and Questions

Given the vision for New Mexico's education system, the planning committee should be charged to answer the following questions, among others:

1. How can the Educational Technology Planning Committee identify specific ways of utilizing technology to assist at-risk youth? Since the reduction of the drop-out rate in New Mexico is a clear public policy goal, what should be the role of the community, teachers, and university personnel in using technology to accomplish such goals? How should educational technology be managed?

2. To what end will the range of technologies be used? Are we primarily concerned with providing learning experiences that fit each individual's learning style and present level of ability? Are we concerned with providing tools to improve management of individualized learning? Are we concerned with providing opportunities for independent learning? Which of these objectives has primacy?

3. What is the range of technologies available in the marketplace? To schools in New Mexico's districts? (Technologies range from pencil and chalk through print materials, discovery kits, radio and audiotape to interactive TV, computers, videodiscs, and beyond.)

4. What is the ideal technology for each school? How much access to training, software, and equipment is needed for school staff?

5. Who should be end-users? Teachers? Students? Parents? Community members no longer in school? What should priorities be for access to materials and equipment?

6. What are useful considerations for a retraining schedule or replacement schedules for software and equipment? What entity should assume responsibility for coordinating technical issues such as specifications necessary for intertechnology communication?

Membership

It is proposed that this committee represent diverse interests related to educational technology. By October 15, 1990, the Executive Committee of the State Board of Education and the Executive Committee of the Commission on Higher Education should concur on individuals to fill the following positions:

- two business or industry representatives (one selected by the SBE and one by CHE)
- two public school representatives (to be recommended by the SBE)
- two postsecondary/higher education representatives (to be recommended by the CHE)

- one parent of a student enrolled in the education system
- one representative from an adult literacy organization
- governor's designate
- chairperson, Statewide Instructional Television Network Committee
- Legislative Finance Committee chairman or member (invited)
- Legislative Education Study Committee chairman or member (invited)
- Sandia National Laboratories education liaison
- Los Alamos National Laboratories education liaison
- state librarian
- museum system educational liaison

Timelines

The Educational Technology Planning Committee should be appointed by the joint Executive Committees by October 15, 1990, and expected to produce a proposed plan by September 1, 1991, or earlier.

North Dakota
Establishing a
Telecommunications Network

North Dakota is a rural state with a small population (637,000 people). The state is trying to ensure equality for students in every school, regardless of size, and telecommunications are vital to this endeavor. To address the need for educational technology, the North Dakota legislature allocated $2.9 million in grant funds during its last legislative session for the establishment of the North Dakota Educational Telecommunications Council. The council has been charged with developing a comprehensive, statewide telecommunications plan that would expand and enhance the voice, video, and data communications capacity of North Dakota's public education system, government, and other entities to conduct and provide education, training, and information services and activites. The council is also charged with studying the resources and facilities that are available or may be required to establish this plan throughout the state. The telecommunications network, which will serve the state's K-12 and higher education systems; state, school, county, and city governments; nonprofit organizations; and business and industry, has tremendous potential in the areas of educational equality, excellence, and accessibility; expanded instructional programming; expanded training and retraining opportunities for business, government, and social agencies; and economic and professional development.

The mission statement for the council follows:

Goal 1: To use telecommunications to improve quality of education for all students.

>*Priority A:* Support and expand the K-12 school curriculum for accreditation standards.

>*Priority B:* Provide opportunities for continuing education for K-12 school staff.

>*Priority C:* Support higher education's efforts in sharing services and improving access to course offerings.

Goal 2: Provide access to facilities and/or services to meet the needs of agriculture, industry, government, health, labor, business, and other interested groups.

The Educational Telecommunications Council assessed the unmet needs of education, training, and information in North Dakota. Specific needs that were identified include:

- more extensive curriculum offerings in schools
- more in-service training for teachers

- easier, equitable access to higher education institutions and educational services
- better opportunities for individuals with special learning needs
- easier, equitable access to libraries and databases
- easier access to information sources

North Dakota's statewide network will need to be a mix of technologies—satellite, microwave, Instructional Television Fixed Services (ITFS), fiber optics, computer, telephone, cable and broadcast television, and other means to provide video, voice, and data services to the entire state. This infrastructure will make use of technologies that already exist and add new technology to create full broadcast video, compressed video, and high-speed data transmission. The network model will eventually include a series of primary and secondary hubs capable of transmitting and receiving audio, video, and data signals. Voice and data will be transmitted between many communities in the state. This mode calls for a threshold level of one-way video, two-way audio, and two-way data transmission for any participant on the network on a statewide basis. Intercluster interactivity would allow two-way video and two-way audio transmissions.

The council completed its statewide plan with the assistance of Federal Engineering, Inc., a consulting firm. From that report, the council has decided that the following will be the stages, based on biennial funding, for implementation of a statewide plan:

1. *Regional planning.* Grants up to $10,000 per region, up to eight regions, will be awarded for regional technology planning. These grants are based on the Guidelines for Regional Planning Grants. Total: $80,000.

   In addition, $10,000 will be set aside for the representatives from each planning region to combine activities where possible, meet and discuss progress, and eliminate duplication throughout their respective regions and the state.

2. *Funding clusters.* Funding will be available for new technology clusters already in the beginning stages of implementation, up-and-coming clusters, clusters evolving out of regional planning, and existing clusters in need of expansion. Each cluster will be granted up to 75 percent of the total project cost, up to $50,000 per school. Total: $1.1 million.

3. *Pilot project for data network.* Approximately 12 schools, both small and large, in a general area should demonstrate the uses of a data network. Emphasis should equally address academic and administrative uses. Administrative uses should make administration more efficient. The Department of Public Instruction, Information Services Division, Higher Education, and HECN will select a region and find volunteers to begin this project. A region close to Bismarck would assure the greatest access to necessary resources, but other regions will be considered, including HB1507 regions. This project will also serve as a role model for possible federal grant monies pursued by higher education. Total: $200,000.

4. *Contingency.* There will be a sum left for contingency purposes. Contingency funds will cover any unexpected costs. Total: $100,000.

5. *Broadcasting of foreign language.* Prairie Public Broadcasting will begin developing a foreign language program in cooperation with the Division of Independent Studies and the Department of Public Instruction. Total: $352,000.

6. *Regional nodes*. Volume of intercluster activity will dictate location and start-up of regional nodes. Clusters will have to express need for interconnectivity to start up regional nodes. This will probably be the last connection and will be an evolutionary process.

7. *Statewide network*. North Dakota Education/Rural Health two-way interactive video system will connect ten colleges/universities in the state.

Past legislation provided grant monies to establish pilot projects in various long-distance learning applications: audiographics, interactive television (both analog and digital), and satellite delivery systems. North Dakota has used these projects to evaluate the feasibility and applicability of each long-distance application.

Various sites around the state continue to use satellite teaching. Approximately eight schools are involved in SERC from South Carolina, two schools are involved with TI-IN from Texas, and five schools are involved with Oklahoma State University. The Missouri Valley Tele-Learning Center teaches Spanish and probability and statistics using the audiographics system. Century High in Bismarck, North Dakota, plus five schools north of Bismarck are involved in this program.

During the 1989 fall semester, the West River Interactive System, a two-way, fully interactive television system, went on the air. The classes being taught during the 1989-90 school year included U.S. History, German 1 (two sessions), Anatomy, Accounting II, and Parenting and Child Development. There were approximately 127 students involved in this four-school project. Lastly, in January 1991, the Souris Loop Interactive System began teaching Spanish 1, Accounting III, Shorthand and Speed Writing, Fundamentals of Art, and Advanced English to approximately 68 students.

Many North Dakota schools are involved in many different types of technology projects, including the development of "Where in North Dakota is Carmen Sandiego?" software, a project undertaken in cooperation with the software company Broderbund. We have bulletin boards, standardized IEP systems, state library and higher education database access, the T1 Higher Education System that links 12 colleges and universities by interactive television across the state, networking in schools, and accreditation standards forcing computer literacy in the curriculum.

Ohio
State Technology Planning Process

The Ohio Department of Education is developing a statewide plan for the use of technology in schools and all other educational enterprises. This plan will include instructional uses of technology and will address administrative uses of technology, including the mandated Education Management Information System. Department of Education staff members began work on the plan in the summer of 1990. In the spring of 1991 the state board of education appointed an advisory council. This council has been given the following philosophical statement and charge:

> Technology should empower educators and students to more efficiently and effectively manage and create productive learning environments.
>
> Technology, appropriately applied, can improve information and data management for decision making related to the educational enterprise; enhance students' learning; enhance teacher efficiency and creativity; facilitate involvement and communication between and among administrators, teachers, students, parents and the community; accommodate individual student learning styles and needs; and interact with and change the content of the curriculum.

This philosophical statement is intended to guide the work of the advisory council. The council will provide guidance on a variety of issues pertaining to the development of a statewide plan for technology. Because it is anticipated that a model plan for implementing technology will be developed, a particular responsibility of the council will be to help define components of that model and present substantive issues to be addressed in the model. The work of the advisory council will contribute toward the creation of a coherent vision of appropriate education in the last decade of the twentieth century. It is axiomatic that such an education will include the institutionalization of technology into all appropriate aspects of administration and instruction. The work of the council will be structured around the areas to be addressed in the long- and short-range plans of districts:

- delineation of objectives regarding the nature and application of technology in educational settings
- identification of necessary resources to implement the plan
- articulation of a plan for staff development supporting the effective and efficient implementation of the technology plans
- establishment of criteria for assessing and measuring the impact of the applied technology on instruction, learning, and education operations

In short, this group's task is to develop a list of tenets, activities, and goals that will guide the preparation of the state model plan for implementing technology and generally inform the state board of education in the area of educational uses of technology.

Additionally, staff members of the Ohio Department of Education are developing a leadership document designed to help school districts in the planning process and in the implementation of programs which effectively use technology in education.

Texas
Long-Range Plan for Technology
of the Texas State Board of Education
1988-2000

INTRODUCTION

The *Long-Range Plan for Technology of the Texas State Board of Education* was developed during 1987 and 1988 under the direction of the board in response to pressing economic, legislative, and educational needs. The Commissioner's Advisory Committee on the Long-Range Plan for Technology and state and national experts in the applications of technology to education contributed critical technical and instructional guidance. Their varied perspectives enriched the planning process and immeasurably strengthened the plan.

The technologies encompassed in the plan are computer-based systems, devices for storage and retrieval of massive amounts of information, telecommunications for audio, video, and information sharing, and other electronic media devised by the year 2000 that can help meet the instructional and productivity needs of public education. This plan focuses on four priorities:

- classroom instruction
- instructional management
- distance learning
- communications

The long-range plan is based on principles to which the state board of education is committed regarding education and technology. These principles include the following:

- Technology must be infused into instruction: technology is, by definition, a tool.
- Technology is one of many vehicles that must work in concert with one another to improve education.
- Districts and campuses must be accorded flexibility in selecting technologies and applications to meet local needs while being held accountable for continual improvement in achievement and productivity.
- State and local governments must provide incentives for technology acquisition and implementation.
- Teachers are essential for high-quality education.
- Staff training is critical to successful integration of technology.

- Future decisions must be based on the results of research.

- Technology changes rapidly and unpredictably, and technology changes the settings into which it is incorporated. The plan, therefore, is flexible in the long term, able to incorporate a variety of technologies and to take advantage of the multivendor environment. The education system must also be flexible, able to revise assumptions as technology contributes to changing the current educational environment.

In keeping with the priorities and these principles, the purposes of this long-range plan for technology are to:

- improve learning and teaching and the ability to meet individual students' needs in order to increase student achievement,

- improve curriculum delivery in order to help meet the needs for educational equity across the state,

- improve inservice delivery,

- improve the efficiency and productivity of administrators, and

- encourage development by the private sector and acquisition by districts of technologies and applications appropriate for education.

PLAN SUMMARY

The *Long-Range Plan for Technology of the Texas State Board of Education* plots the course for meeting educational needs through technology and for implementing concomitant changes in education from 1988 to 2000. Both technology and the field of education are fluid; applying advances in the former to the practice of the latter can help achieve a vision of education that has been as yet unattainable. This plan complements the *Texas Education Agency Information Systems Long-Range Plan* that addressed the automation requirements for the agency from 1988 through 1993.

The vision. The education system that the state board of education envisions is one in which:

- no student would be denied, by virtue of district sparseness or teacher shortage, course work necessary for employment or higher education,

- teachers can have both the responsibility and the technical resources to guide the instruction of their students in the most appropriate and efficient ways,

- performance, not processes, can determine advancement,

- performance and socioeconomic status are unrelated, and

- adults can continually enhance their job and life skills.

The needs. Multiple needs support the implementation of this long-range plan for educational uses of technology. These needs are expressed in

- the demands of the state's economy,

- legislative mandates, and

- the *Long-Range Plan of the State Board of Education for Texas Public School Education, 1986-1990.*

The traditional sectors on which the Texas economy has relied—oil and gas production, manufacturing, and agriculture—are shriveling in comparison to expansion in the service sector:

- Between 1982 and 1987, employment in the first of these areas fell more than 40 percent.
- The service sector is projected to generate nearly 70 percent of total job growth by 2,000; a 44 percent increase is projected in computer and data-processing services alone.

These employment shifts have profound implications for education, for the jobs of the future will belong to the educated. Insufficient education and resources threaten quality of life, individual earning power, and the state's fiscal health producing multiple social and economic repercussions.

Legislative mandates include:

- Chapter 14 of the *Texas Education Code*, which stipulates action regarding software approval and access and a long-range plan for instructional uses of technology,
- *Texas Education Code* Section 11.33(b)(1), which requires financial assistance for computer services offered by regional education service centers, and
- *Vernon's Texas Civil Statutes* Article 4413(32h), Section 2.08, which authorizes the Information Systems Long-Range Plan.

Finally, the mission of quality, equity, and accountability of the state board of education as stated in its long-range plan and actions stipulated in that plan necessitate technology. Although narrowing, a gap in achievement exists between minority and non-minority students and between performance of Texas students and their counterparts nationwide. In addition, as illustrated by a drop between 1982-83 and 1986-87 of 41 percent in the number of initial teacher certificates issued by the state, teacher shortages are potentially severe. These problems indicate the need to address quality in the education system.

The attainment of equity also is compromised through the imbalance in course offerings across the state:

- While the largest districts in the state offer an average of more than 200 courses each, the smallest offer approximately one-quarter as many.
- Districts with a low percentage of low-income students offer an average of 20 percent more courses than do those with a high percentage of low-income students.

With technology, population density need not determine curriculum richness.

Technology can also improve accountability through increasing information sharing while reducing paperwork burdens:

- Up to 50 percent of teachers' time is spent on nonteaching tasks.
- More than 60 percent of teachers report that time-consuming paperwork tasks have increased in the past five years.

Successes of technology. Although no single solution can meet all of these needs, technology has been shown to contribute significantly to overcoming them. Research shows that:

- instructional television can increase student achievement,
- computer-assisted instruction (CAI) can improve basic skills acquisition by approximately 10 percentile points,
- CAI has contributed to a rise in higher-order thinking skills of at-risk students of up to 25 percentile points,
- adaptive/assistive devices can increase attention span, retention, and problem-solving skills of special education students,
- distance learning is a proven means for providing effective instruction and inservice, and
- a fully implemented statewide telecommunications system can save a projected $2 million annually.

Applications of technology. With the application of current and emerging technologies to education, students can work at their own pace, following the learning style most appropriate to their needs and skills and accessing libraries of information. Teachers' workstations can be multimedia productivity centers from which teachers can present visual and sound demonstrations, monitor individual student progress, and complete formerly tedious paperwork automatically. Administrators can review and aggregate data on achievement, teacher assessments, expenditures, and inventories and communicate rapidly with other education institutions. Entire communities can be served by campus learning centers where adults can improve their literacy and job skills.

Actors and actions. In order to realize the vision and meet economic, legislative, and educational needs, coordinated effort is necessary—by all levels of the public education system, by developers and vendors of current and emerging technologies and of the software and courseware that make them useful, by researchers who investigate and report on successes and inefficiencies, by institutions of higher education that prepare teachers for tomorrow's classrooms, and by communities and the state that must support and will benefit from citizens who are skilled and self-reliant. This plan helps coordinate the necessary actions by these participants.

The calendar for implementing the plan is divided into three phases of four years each. Key actions by the state during phase I (1988-89 through 1991-92) include:

- authorizing expenditures and other legislative changes for implementation of the plan,
- establishing a technology equipment allotment within the Foundation School Program of at least $50 per student per year on an equalized basis for district hardware and courseware and facility modification,
- reinstating support for instructional television,
- establishing a statewide electronic information transfer system,
- establishing a research and development consortium and demonstration programs,
- expanding distance learning by building on available services, including public broadcasting and other providers,

- assisting districts with selecting and acquiring equipment through revising arrangements with the State Purchasing and General Services Commission,

- incorporating courseware adoption into the textbook adoption process,

- revising curriculum rules,

- supporting teacher and administrator training in and by technology, and

- establishing quality, technical, functional, security, service, and other standards for equipment, courseware, and training through a Texas State Board of Education Advisory Committee on Technology Standards.

Key actions by regional education service centers emphasize:

- establishing technology preview centers,

- including in core services training and other assistance to districts in technology selection and use, and

- employing at least one full-time equivalent at each regional education service center to perform these functions.

Key actions by districts during phase 1 include:

- preparing annual district and campus plans for technology,

- providing training to staff in appropriate uses of technology,

- providing incentives for staff to use technology,

- procuring and integrating hardware and software according to local plans and state board of education equipment targets,

- using integrated telecommunications systems for instruction, inservice, and information sharing, and

- participating in demonstration programs.

Institutions of higher education are called on to incorporate technology in undergraduate and graduate instruction and training and to conduct and disseminate research in educational uses of technology. The consortium will, during phase 1, initiate research projects for value-added development and marketing by member companies of educational applications of technology. Actions by these entities during the subsequent two phases pursue those initiated in the first phase to reach the following cumulative outcomes. Interim outcomes of actions are stated in the calendar.

Cumulative outcomes. Procedural and interim outcomes will take place during the early phases. By 2000, the cumulative outcomes are expected to include:

- Technology and its applications in education will be distributed equitably and sufficiently throughout Texas.

- Statewide integrated telecommunications systems will be established.

- Professional staff employed in and entering public education will be skilled in using technology for instruction and management.

- Effective integration of technology in education will continually increase.

- Applications for education of emerging technology that meet state standards will be developed and marketed at competitive prices.

- A long-range plan for technology for the first decade of the twenty-first century will be prepared for implementation.

The budget 1990-91 biennium. The appropriation requested to initiate implementation of the plan during the first biennium is $16.65 million.

Virginia
Six-Year Technology Plan
for Virginia

FOREWORD

The *Six-Year Technology Plan for Virginia* is based on recommendations made in 1986 by the Governor's Commission on Excellence in Education. The commission identified disparity in educational opportunities as one of the major obstacles that Virginia must overcome if it is to have one of the best public school systems in the nation. A major goal of the *Six-Year Technology Plan for Virginia* is to reduce disparity in educational programs in public schools in the commonwealth.

The plan presented here can be achieved through the cooperation of the state and the school divisions and through the development of partnerships with business and industry. Some schools have already accomplished many of the 72 recommendations included in the plan. It is vitally important that all schools and school divisions carry out the recommendations presented in this plan and reap the benefits of educational technology.

Virginia has made a substantial financial commitment to provide school divisions with the equipment and programs students need in this age of technology. This commitment reflects agreement with the statement by the Commission on Excellence that educational technology "must take a central place in public school education."

The Six-Year Technology Planning Committee, which developed this plan, is to be commended for its hard work and its vision and insight into the needs of the public schools and the important role that technology must play in public education. The plan reflects a thoughtful and thorough study of educational technology and how it can be used to meet the needs of students in the commonwealth. The plan sets the course toward excellence and equity in public education for the present and the future and is designed to be responsive to changes in technology and its use in the public schools.

S. John Davis
Superintendent of Public Instruction

INTRODUCTION

The report of the Governor's Commission on Excellence in Education in 1986 recommended a number of steps to be taken to give Virginia one of the best programs of public education in the nation. One of the major recommendations was that the department of education develop a five-year plan to make educational technology an integral part of public education in Virginia. To meet the commission's challenge, the department of education seeks to initiate change by expanding present programs and services in addition to using new technologies in education.

Although the commission proposed a five-year plan for educational technology, the plan recommended in this report covers a period of six years. The longer period of time is proposed to conform to planning programs required of school divisions by the Standards of Quality for Public Schools in Virginia.

As caretakers of information technology in public schools, educators must provide educational systems, knowledge, and opportunities for learning to prepare students for life in the twenty-first century. Public trust and the mission of education will be compromised if we fail to give our youth adequate tools to help them fulfill their dreams and ambitions. Technology can promote educational excellence, aid instruction, and be used in evaluating instruction. Balance and growth in the quality and scope of educational programs throughout the state can also be enhanced by the use of technology.

Although satellites, computers, video technologies, networks, and traditional audiovisual media are referred to in the following report, the primary concerns of the committee that developed the six-year technology plan for the board of education are shared by all educators: academic excellence, development of critical-thinking and problem-solving skills, equality of educational opportunity, staff development, and research in the use of technology in teaching and learning. Technology is the tool and conduit for delivering educational programs. Technology can make education more productive, more relevant, more accessible, and more responsive to learning needs.

Depending upon the student's power to discover, control, and create, learning can be highly individualized through technology. The potential impact of technology upon learning styles may necessitate redefining and restructuring the way that teachers teach and the environments in which students learn. The need for such changes, however, will depend upon the involvement of Virginia's educators in using educational technology.

The ultimate success of technology as an educational tool will depend upon decisions affecting funding, personnel, and training opportunities at state and local levels. Untapped sources of funding may be found in partnerships with business, industry, and educational foundations. While it is true that technology is costly and subject to rapid changes, can we afford not to invest in technology if Virginia is to have one of the best educational programs in the nation?

In developing this report, the Six-Year Technology Plan Committee was assisted by the Communications Automation Transition System (CATS) subcommittee and an industry subcommittee. Before writing the plan, the committee solicited comments about the use of technology in public schools from professional organizations, teachers, local school consultants, Department of Education staff, the board of education, state officials, and community groups. Many of those responses have been included in the plan. A foundation study for the entire plan was the statewide technology assessment conducted by Virginia Tech. The committee hopes that the six-year technology plan will serve as a blueprint for future state initiatives in technology and for educational technology programs in public schools throughout Virginia.

This report contains recommendations that are directed at three major issues in public education: equity in access to education, excellence in the quality of teaching and learning, and connections to link learners in Virginia, the nation, and the world.

RECOMMENDATIONS

Equity

Disparity and illiteracy were cited by the Commission on Excellence as two major impediments to public education in Virginia. Technology initiatives, currently under way, address four potential solutions to those problems.

The first is distance learning. Distance learning, or the Electronic Classroom in Virginia, refers to one-way video, two-way audio course instruction sent via satellite and open broadcast from a central location to students in other schools. Distance learning via the Electronic Classroom can promote equitable access to education in all schools throughout the commonwealth, ensure that small rural school divisions can provide educational opportunities equal to those provided by large suburban and urban school divisions, and address instructional needs, including at-risk and potential drop-out school populations. Teacher shortages, small numbers of qualifying students within a school, inconveniences relating to travel to colleges and universities, and scheduling conflicts are reasons given by students and school administrators for Electronic Classroom program participation.

The second solution is instructional computing. The instructional computing program involves equitable distribution of state-funded equipment and software, and opportunities for teacher training. The initial focus of the instructional computing program is remediation in reading, writing, and mathematics for grade 6 to meet the needs of at-risk students and potential dropouts. The software and teacher training components will directly relate to the primary focus of the program. Schools will be able to use the computers for other purposes, including the teaching of writing across the curriculum, after-school and weekend programs, keyboarding, and teacher productivity.

The third solution is interactive teleconferences produced to provide current information to all teachers and students. Interactive teleconferencing in Virginia refers to one-way video, two-way audio instruction and information sent via satellite and open broadcast from a program origination classroom to classrooms in other locations across the state. Teleconferences are currently being scheduled by the Department of Education in one-hour slots twice weekly. The Department of Education Hour (DOE Hour), as it is called, provides an opportunity for equality in training and for program updates.

The fourth solution is automation. Automated, standardized databases, under development, will address statewide disparity in the management of student information, school finance, instructional personnel data, libraries, and other aspects of school administration. Electronic networks with automated, standardized databases provide interactive links between school divisions with abundant resources and school divisions lacking adequate resources. These networks also can provide access to information by students through a vast array of media formats designed to promote inquiry, critical thinking, and lifelong learning.

The establishment of foundation levels and standards for electronic hardware and software in classrooms and library media centers can also reduce disparity. Each student throughout the commonwealth should have access to computers, videodiscs, distance learning/electronic classrooms, interactive video technologies, communication networks, and online reference service and catalogs, as well as traditional media programs such as instructional television.

It should be emphasized, however, that the provision of technology alone does not reduce disparity. Access to technology will be futile and equipment will lie idle without the guidance of competent, trained teachers. The establishment of foundation levels and standards for inservice and preservice technology training for teachers is essential. Because technology is applicable to all areas of education, continuing programs of staff development that reflect teacher/administrator commitment will foster educational equity.

Through effective implementation, educational technology can expedite and provide equal access to teaching and learning throughout the commonwealth.

Excellence

The information revolution places new demands on individuals and on the knowledge and skills that they must possess to work and participate fully in society. Persons who do not adapt to technological changes may pay an enormous price, socially and economically. To avoid this it will be necessary to develop skills directed toward combining knowledge from a variety of fields. Knowledge gained is demonstrated in learning new techniques, in the ability to think critically, analyze and organize systems to solve problems, respond to changes, and exert initiative, and in the student's ability to communicate effectively. Application of this knowledge will constantly change, as the skills and information bases needed for employment will rarely be those needed for the same job a few years later. Relearning and retraining will become the expected norm for many people throughout their lives.

Continuing education programs can be a vital component in adult education through video technologies, using interactive television as well as more traditional modes of broadcasting. Home reception, for example, gives learners of all ages access to instruction via video and audio technology. Additionally, the production of smaller, cheaper, portable computers makes learning accessible to a variety of students. Homebound learners, who may be handicapped or chronically ill, can remain intellectually active through the use of computers and other new communication technologies.

Accessibility to education without constraints of time, schedule, and place can become a reality for all learners through the use of appropriate technology. Learning environments can be created to allow students and teachers to pace instruction according to individual learning styles. An increased sense of control over their own learning experiences results when students become active in determining what and how they learn. Technology, specifically the microcomputer, provides that sense of control.

Teachers should become as familiar with the use of educational technology as they are with the chalkboard in their classrooms. Skilled master teachers who have received special training in the use of technology can assist with staff development for their colleagues. Adequate staff training at the local level is essential to the successful use of educational technology. Technology is most effective in teaching and learning when it is used as a tool to aid instruction and to deliver information, not as a separate program added to the curriculum.

The full potential for achieving excellence in education in the future will depend upon adequate funding for the use of technology in public schools today.

Connections

Providing a method for linking learners in the state to each other and to students across the nation and around the world promotes equity and excellence in education. Online communication systems provide instantaneous access to information through modems, computers, and telephone lines. This access can be enhanced through video technologies. Information databases stored in computers can be retrieved quickly in geographical locations far removed from storage sites. Electronic mail and bulletin board systems provide worldwide connections through subscriptions and identification codes.

A vital part of the Communications Automation Transition System (CATS) is a communications network to connect electronically the Department of Education and all school divisions. This shared network is known as Virginia Net (VA.NET). Automated, standardized databases within this network will provide school administrators with student information, financial management data, and personnel information. A number of school libraries in Virginia are already linked through electronic networks with public libraries to share cataloging of materials and publications and to collect information. SpecialNet links state educators of handicapped students through electronic mail. Networks extended to Virginia also provide a variety of programs and services of interest to schools. Satellite programs developed in cooperation with other states offer courses in various subjects to consortium members on a national and international basis. The Satellite Educational Resources Consortium (SERC), a national satellite consortium, for example, offers courses to 18 states, including Virginia, and transmits Virginia-produced science seminars from the Thomas Jefferson High School for Science and Technology in Fairfax County to the 18 member states. Virginia has been a member of the Minnesota Educational Computing Corporation (MECC) for a number of years. The membership allows school divisions the option to purchase associate memberships under the state's institutional membership. The KIDS NETWORK (KIDS NET) is an example of a network students are beginning to use to communicate with students in other schools, states, and countries. University-based electronic networks are used by some teachers and college professors to maintain an information exchange program.

Hierarchical networks must be integrated and compatible to promote accessibility and to provide optimal learning opportunities to all users. Standardization provides a framework for merging a number of networks into single entities and increasing access for large numbers of students and programs.

However, full network usage requires trained users. Foundation levels for technology training should be established for staff support to assure maximum linkage at minimum cost. Staff development is a necessary component for network usability. Networks can be used to link students and teachers to schools and businesses and to offer mutually beneficial relationships to employees and schools. Through electronic networks and shared databases, consortia of schools, businesses, and higher education are provided instant access to vital research information.

Alternative models for delivering instruction to students with special learning needs can be provided through electronic networks. Handicapped, gifted, or homebound students can be linked to their peers and continue their learning in a variety of environments. Students who do not benefit from traditional classroom instruction can discover new avenues to learning through networks and technology.

The benefits of linking learners to information must be documented. Research is continually needed to guide educational decisions. Questions concerning the cost/benefit/learning ratio of technology-aided instruction to more traditional methods of instruction must be addressed on an ongoing basis. Further research and pilot programs will provide answers to many of these questions. National and state research literature has verified that increased learning occurs when technology is used. Virginia needs more research studies, however, to provide answers to legislators who are responsible for appropriating funds for technology and to educational administrators and teachers who decide how to use the funds. Informed decisions based upon valid, reliable research will promote public confidence in and support for educational technology.

BIBLIOGRAPHY

Alberta Education. Student Programs and Evaluation Division. Technology in Education Committee. *Visions 2000: A Vision of Educational Technology in Alberta by the Year 2000*. Alberta, Canada: Alberta Education, 1987.

American Association of School Librarians and Association for Educational Communications and Technology. *Information Power: Guidelines for School Library Media Programs*. Chicago: American Library Association, 1988.

American Association of School Librarians and Association for Educational Communications and Technology. *Media Programs: District and School*. Chicago: American Library Association, 1975.

Bangert-Drowns, R. L., James A. Kulik, and Chen-Lin C. Kulik. "Effectiveness of Computer-Based Education in Secondary Schools." *Journal of Computer-Based Education* 12 (1985): 59-68.

Barker, Bruce O. *Live via Satellite: Interactive Distant Learning in America's Rural Schools*. Alexandria, Va.: ERIC Document Reproduction Service, ED 272 340, 1986.

Batey, Anne, and Richard N. Cowell. *Distance Education: An Overview*. Alexandria, Va.: ERIC Document Reproduction Service, ED 278 519, 1986.

Becker, Henry Jay. *The Impact of Computer Use on Children's Learning: What Research Has Shown and What It Has Not*. Alexandria, Va.: ERIC Document Reproduction Service, ED 287 458, 1988.

Becker, Henry Jay. "A Year-Long Nationwide Field Experiment on the Effectiveness of Computer Use in Grade 5-8 Mathematics Classes." Paper delivered at the National Education Computing Conference, Boston, Mass., June 1988.

Bond, Elden A. "Diversity of Microcomputer Implementations: A Process Perspective." *Journal of Research on Computing in Education* 20 (Summer 1988): 321-30.

Brandt, Ronald S., ed. "Empowering Students and Teachers through Technology." (Special Issue). *Educational Leadership* 43, no. 6 (March 1986).

Carmichael, Hilda W., et al. *Computers, Children, and Classrooms: A Multisite Evaluation of the Creative Use of Micro-computers by Elementary School Children*. Alexandria, Va.: ERIC Document Reproduction Service, ED 268 994, 1986.

Colorado, Rafael J. "Computer-Assisted Instruction Research: A Critical Assessment." *Journal of Research on Computing in Education* 20, no. 3 (Spring 1988): 226-31.

Craver, Kathleen W. "The Changing Instructional Role of the High School Library Media Specialist: 1950-84; A Survey of Professional Literature, Standards, and Research Studies." *School Library Media Quarterly* 14, no. 4 (Summer 1986): 183-91.

Emery, Mary. *Some Potentials and Limitations of Technology in Serving Rural Post-secondary Learners*. Alexandria, Va.: ERIC Document Reproduction Service, ED 296 854, 1986.

Falsone, Anne M. *Distance Learning: A Practical Solution for Small or Low-Budget Schools to Meet the Needs of Every Student*. Huxton, Colo. Highlighter, 1986.

Fisher, Joseph L., and Richard T. Mayer. *Virginia Alternatives for the 1990s: Selected Issues in Public Policy*. Fairfax, Va.: George Mason University Press, 1987.

Hawley, David E., J. Dexter Fletcher, and Philip K. Piele. *Costs, Effects, and Utility of Microcomputer-Assisted Instruction*. Eugene: Center for Advanced Technology in Education, University of Oregon, 1986.

Hill, Franklin. *Tomorrow's Learning Environment: Planning for Technology: The Basics*. Alexandria, Va.: National School Boards Association, 1988.

Hinson, Stephanie, Michael S. Caldwell, and Mary Landrum. "Characteristics of Effective Staff Development Programs." *Journal of Staff Development* 10, no. 2 (Spring 1989): 48-52.

Hobbs, Daryl. *Bridging, Linking, Networking the Gap: Uses of Instructional Technology in Small Rural Schools*. Alexandria, Va.: ERIC Document Reproduction Service, ED 258 785, 1985.

Hobbs, Vicki. *Planning Guide and Implementation Manual for Satellite Instructional Programs*. Stillwater: Oklahoma State University, 1986.

Hudson, Heather E., and Charles H. Boyd. *Distance Learning: A Review for Educators*. Alexandria, Va.: ERIC Document Reproduction Service, ED 246 872, 1984.

Kitchen, Karen, and Will Kitchen. *Two-way Interactive Television for Distance Learning: A Primer*. Alexandria, Va.: National School Boards Association, 1988.

Kulik, James A. *Consistencies in Findings on Computer-Based Education*. Alexandria, Va.: ERIC Document Reproduction Service, ED 263 880, 1986.

Kulik, James A., Robert L. Bangert, and G. W. Williams. "Effects of Computer-Based Teaching on Secondary School Students." *Journal of Educational Psychology* 75, no. 1 (February 1983): 19-26.

Kulik, James A., and Chen-Lin C. Kulik. *Computer-Based Instruction: What 200 Evaluations Say*. Alexandria, Va.: ERIC Document Reproduction Service, ED 285 521, 1987.

Kulik, James A., Chen-Lin C. Kulik, and B. J. Schwalb. "Effectiveness of Computer-Based Education in Elementary Schools." *Computers in Human Behavior* 1, no. 1 (1985): 59-74.

Martinez, Michael E., and Nancy A. Mead. *Computer Competence: The First National Assessment*. Princeton, N.J.: Educational Testing Service, 1988.

Minnesota Educational Media Organization. *Philosophical Statement of the Role of Technology in the Library/Media Program*. St. Paul: Minnesota Educational Media Organization, 1984.

Minnesota State Department of Education. *Minnesota Technology Demonstration Sites*. St. Paul, Minn.: State Department of Education, 1986.

Moore, David M. *1988 Virginia Local Education Agency (LEA) Technology Assessment*. (A report prepared under contract for the Virginia Department of Education by the College of Education, Virginia Tech.) 2 vols. Blacksburg: Virginia Tech, 1988.

Naylor, Michele. *Distance Education: Overview. ERIC Digest* no. 44. Alexandria, Va.: ERIC Document Reproduction Service, ED 259 214, 1985.

New York Senate Education Committee. *Satellite-Based Education: A Preliminary Review of the Feasibility of Satellite-Based Educational Communications Technology*. Albany: New York State Senate, 1985.

O'Connor, Bridget, and Cynthia Levinson. "TI-IN Network: Evaluating the Diffusion and Adoption of an Interactive Instructional Satellite System." In *Teleconferencing and Electronic Communication: Vol. 5*. L. Parker and C. Olgren, eds. Madison: University of Wisconsin, 1986.

Perelman, Lewis J. *Technology and Transformation of Schools*. Report from Institute for the Transfer of Technology to Education. Alexandria, Va.: National School Boards Association, 1987.

Ridley, William J., and McAllister H. Hull. *Transforming American Education: Reducing the Risk to the Nation*. A Report to the Secretary of Education, U.S. Department of Education, by the National Task Force on Educational Technology. Alexandria, Va.: ERIC Document Reproduction Service, ED 269 012, 1986.

Roblyer, M. D. "The Effectiveness of Microcomputers in Education: A Review of the Research from 1980-1987." *T.H.E. Technological Horizons in Education Journal* 16, no. 2 (September 1988): 85-89.

Sununu, John H. Report of the Task Force on Technology. Supporting Works. *Time for Results: The Governors' 1991 Report on Education*. Washington, D.C.: National Governors' Association, 1986.

U.S. Congress. Office of Technology Assessment. *Informational Technology and Its Impact on American Education*. Washington, D.C.: Government Printing Office, 1982.

U.S. Congress. Office of Technology Assessment. *Power On! New Tools for Teaching and Learning*. (OTA-SET-379). Washington, D.C.: Government Printing Office, 1988.

U.S. Department of Education. Office of Educational Research and Improvement. Center for Education Statistics. *Statistics of Public and Private School Library Media Centers, 1985-86*. (Report OE-300-84-0262). Washington, D.C.: Government Printing Office, 1987.

Virginia Department of Education and Department of Information Technology. *Communications/Automation Transition Plan*. Richmond, Va.: Department of Education, 1986.

Virginia Department of Information Technology. *Organizational Study of Management Information Services, Department of Education*. Richmond, Va.: Department of Information Technology, 1986.

Virginia Governor's Commission on Excellence in Education. *Excellence in Education: A Plan for Virginia's Future*. Richmond, Va.: Department of Education, 1986.

Virginia Governor's Commission on Virginia's Future. *Toward a New Dominion: Choices for Virginians*. Charlottesville: University of Virginia, Institute of Government, 1984.

Wall, Milan. *Information Technologies: Alternative Delivery Systems for Rural Schools*. Alexandria, Va.: ERIC Document Reproduction Service, ED 270 253, 1985.

Wisconsin
Distance Education for
Elementary/Secondary Schools

CHARGE TO THE COUNCIL ON INSTRUCTIONAL TELECOMMUNICATIONS

On November 4, 1987, Herbert J. Grover, state superintendent of public instruction, requested that the Council on Instructional Telecommunications (CIT) study the concept of distance learning as it pertains to elementary and secondary education in Wisconsin and make recommendations to him regarding its use. The Council on Instructional Telecommunications consists of fifteen members appointed by the state superintendent of public instruction for four-year terms. Twelve members represent each of the twelve cooperative educational service agencies and are nominated by the boards of control of those agencies. Two members are appointed to represent private and secondary educational institutions. One member represents the Regional Service Unit directors. The council advises the superintendent of public instruction and the Educational Communications Board on matters relating to instructional telecommunications for the elementary and secondary schools.

DISTANCE EDUCATION BACKGROUND

For the purpose of this study, the term *distance education* rather than *distance learning* has been used. The intent is to broaden the focus from one dealing only with the learning aspect of education to one encompassing the entire educational process, which includes acquiring learning, thinking, communications, decision-making, information-and-data-retrieval, analysis, and usage skills. Consequently, *distance education* is defined as "education conducted via communication media (teleconferences, computers, correspondence, radio, television, and other technologies) with little face-to-face contact between students and the teacher of the course."

Essentially, distance education is a means of extending instruction beyond the boundaries of a single classroom. By means of various technologies, instruction may stretch between school and home, between schools in a district, between districts, between secondary and postsecondary institutions, between states, and even between countries. All indications are that the concept of distance education will be of increased interest to Wisconsin educators as they seek to expand instructional opportunities for students.

Historical Background

In the past 10 years a number of Wisconsin school districts have considered various distance education delivery systems to expand course offerings. There has been a general concern for quality education and a desire on the part of many districts to retain the concept of the "comprehensive high school." Examples of the distance education delivery systems used for direct instruction of students follow:

- Students in a number of Cooperative Educational Service Agency (CESA) #4 (La Crosse) schools have shared instruction in foreign language delivered by the CESA Teleconferencing Network (CTN), which is a two-way interactive audio system using special teleconferencing telephone lines. Courses available on this network include German 1 and 2; Spanish 1, 2, and 3; and French 1.

- Trempealeau County's Project Circuit offers the opportunity for students in eight small, rural school districts to share instruction using an interactive two-way video and audio system provided by the county's cable television system. Courses made available over this system include Spanish 1, 2, and 3; German 1 and 2; French 1 and 2; Shorthand; Digital Electronics; Advanced Mathematics; and Advanced Computers.

- Several suburban Milwaukee area schools provide Latin instruction for students by sharing instruction over a two-way interactive cable television link.

- Four high schools are receiving live interactive instruction via satellite in Japanese and in Probability and Statistics, as well as participating in a science enrichment seminar as members of the pilot semester of the Satellite Educational Resources Consortium (SERC). These schools are also participating in staff development programs offered through SERC.

Due to the installation of ITFS towers (Instructional Television Fixed Service) by the Educational Communications Board, districts within a certain range are beginning to explore sharing instruction via the television signal broadcast from the tower. Combined with a telephone teleconferencing system, students can have instruction delivered by one-way video and two-way interactive audio. These systems offer instructional opportunities to students that would not be available in their own school setting due to limited enrollment. By sharing teachers and instructional resources, districts can offer a course to enough students to make instruction cost-effective and eliminate the need for students to commute from one school district to another to share classes.

State Standards

In recent years there has been a great deal of interest in Wisconsin in distance education as an alternative method of providing direct instruction to students and staff development opportunities to educators. Attention has been focused on the need to provide equal access of educational opportunity to students throughout the state and the need to provide a variety of opportunities for Wisconsin educators to upgrade their skills to meet better the needs of today's students. To meet these needs, a series of 20 state educational standards have been developed. The Wisconsin Educational Standards (Wisconsin Statute 121.02[1]), one-half enacted in 1973 and the other half in 1985, reinforce the concerns of educators for quality education throughout the state and fulfill a state constitutional requirement that the legislature create school districts that are "as nearly uniform as possible."

The 20 standards focus on children, assuring that all Wisconsin students, regardless of where they reside, have increased opportunities for and equal access to quality education. The standards are based on current educational literature and on research about effective schools. They have a direct relationship to one or more of the seven key elements all schools must address if all students are to learn:

- A clear school mission and accompanying instruction program
- Strong instructional leadership
- High pupil expectations
- An orderly learning environment
- Ample opportunity for students to learn
- Frequent monitoring of pupil progress
- A high degree of parent and community involvement in the schools.

Several standards, which are cited below, relate directly to potential telecommunication activities on the part of Wisconsin school districts. More information on these standards is available from the Wisconsin Department of Public Instruction. The 20 standards are identified by letters of the alphabet.

Standard (l)
Regular Instruction. Each school board shall:

1. In the elementary grades, provide regular instruction in reading, language arts, social studies, mathematics, science, health, physical education, art, and music.

2. In grades 5 to 8, provide regular instruction in language arts, social studies, mathematics, science, health, physical education, art, and music. The board shall also provide pupils with an introduction to career exploration and planning.

3. In grades 9 to 12, provide access to an educational program that enables pupils each year to study English, social studies, mathematics, science, vocational education, foreign language, physical education, art and music. In this subdivision, "access" means an opportunity to study through school district course offerings, independent study, cooperative educational service agencies or cooperative arrangements between school boards and postsecondary institutions.

Standard (p)
High School Graduation. Each school board shall:

Comply with high school graduation standards under s.118.33(1). Administrative Rule PI 18.03 identifies the following course requirements as meeting this standard:

1. Course Requirements. Beginning September 1, 1988, a board may not grant a high school diploma to any pupil unless the pupil has:

   A. Earned a minimum of 12.5 credits in grades 9 to 12 as follows:
   - 4 credits of English
   - 3 credits of social studies

- 2 credits of mathematics
- 2 credits of science
- 1.5 credits of physical education

B. Earned in grades 7 to 12 at least 0.5 credit of health education.

2. Additional credits. In addition to the minimum course requirements outlined above, the state superintendent encourages boards to require a minimum of 8.5 additional credits in vocational education, foreign languages, fine arts, and other courses.

Standard (t)

Gifted and Talented Pupils. Each school board shall provide access to an appropriate program for pupils identified as gifted and talented.

Standard (b)

Staff Development. Each school board shall annually establish with school board employees a professional staff development plan designed to meet the needs of individuals or curriculum areas in each school.

Standard (m)

Education for Employment. Each school board shall provide access to an education for employment program that has been approved by the state superintendent.

Standard (n)

Children at Risk. Each school board shall develop a plan for children at risk under s.118.153.

State Agencies

Several state-level agencies and councils provide state leadership and/or coordination of instructional telecommunications activities, whether these activities employ distance learning or not.

The Educational Communications Board (ECB) is charged by Wisconsin statute (c.39s.1) to plan and, working with the educational institutions of the state, coordinate educational radio and television for the state. The board is composed of 16 members, including representatives of state, local, and private educational institutions; the governor; and four members of the legislature and makes policy decisions for public radio and television and the use of those systems for education in Wisconsin.

A structure of Regional Service Units (RSUs) that service all areas of the state is maintained with funding from local school districts. These RSUs are located in six CESAs and assist school districts in the selection of educational programs and in the successful use of that programming in the local school districts. The RSU director is responsible for working with ECB, the DPI telecommunications consultant, and local districts in accomplishing these goals.

The Department of Public Instruction (DPI) has placed primary responsibility for instructional telecommunications in its Bureau for Instructional Media and Technology (BIMT). The bureau includes an instructional telecommunications consultant who works for the effective use of telecommunications in K-12 schools. The consultant works closely with the RSU directors and maintains a close working relationship with ECB staff. During the past year the consultant has been codirector with an ECB staff member of the Rural Education Project, a federally funded project that uses telecommunications technology to improve reading instruction in rural areas of the state. Another major activity of the telecommunications consultant is working with CESAs to do needs assessment studies for their regions. A needs assessment instrument developed by the consultant and the CESAs has been used in three regions and will be used in others to gather curriculum and hardware data.

The BIMT also has responsibility for the Council on Instructional Telecommunications. CIT members are appointed by the state superintendent and include one member from each of the 12 CESA areas, two members representing private education and one member representing the RSU directors. These fifteen council members are selected from a broad range of K-12 educators, including administrators, teachers, media directors, directors of instruction and principals. In November 1987, State Superintendent Grover charged the council with the responsibility of examining the use of distance education in K-12 schools in Wisconsin. The director of the Bureau for Instructional Media and Technology is the DPI liaison to CIT.

DPI is a member of the Satellite Educational Resources Consortium. This interstate consortium of 18 states, formed in 1988, pools the expertise and resources of state departments of education, state broadcast entities, local school districts, individual public broadcasting stations, and institutions of higher education. SERC is involved in two major initiatives. It submitted a successful application for Star Schools Funding and conducted a pilot semester that delivered three direct teaching courses and several teacher inservice teleconferences and courses during the spring of 1989.

The Cooperative Education Service Agencies (CESAs) have played various roles in the telecommunications area. As already noted, they have housed the RSU directors and acted as fiscal agent for them. In the late 1960s four administrative data processing centers (ADPs) were established in CESAs 1, 5, 7, and 10. These centers were to ensure that all school districts had access to data processing services, consultation, and support. The ADPs have worked primarily in the area of financial reporting for the school districts. In terms of distance education, CESAs 3, 4, and 12 operate CESA Telephone Networks (CTNs), which are used for teleconference meetings and sharing instructors. Several CESAs are experimenting with ITFS for similar purposes. As mentioned previously, three CESA areas (CESAs 8, 9, and 10) have completed telecommunication needs assessment studies. Other CESAs plan to undertake the same type of study.

The Vocational Technical and Adult Education (VTAE) colleges have been very active in the use of telecommunications for instruction. The VTAE system has a media consortium group that represents both teaching areas and technical expertise from each of the 18 districts. This consortium meets regularly to report on activities at the various campuses. The consortium is particularly active in the use of satellite-delivered teleconferences. The consortium belongs to the National University Teleconference Network (NUTN), which allows them to access a large number of teleconferences at a reduced rate for each site. The coordinator of this consortium informs members of teleconference opportunities and coordinates site use.

The University of Wisconsin (UW) system has perhaps the longest history of using technology to reach all parts of the state. The UW Extension developed the teleconference network ETN and the Meet Me Bridge at a time when such an idea was unique. It is looked upon as a leader in providing for outreach of the university. The ETN network is still maintained and used by the DPI as well as many other educational institutions in the state. An offshoot of this network, the CTN, or CESA Teleconference Network, is at work in some areas. The Meet Me Bridge, now called WisLine, is also used by a wide variety of state agencies to facilitate conference calls. During the past year the UW system has completed a major study of its telecommunications needs. The report produced during this study will provide direction for use of telecommunications by the 29 campuses and county extension agents. The DPI telecommunications consultant was an ad hoc member of the task force that produced this report.

The Department of Administration (DOA) is designing a new telephone network for major state agencies for the transfer of data. This network will allow sharing of electronic information between the major state agencies and then will be open to contract with other state agencies. This network is going to piggyback on the existing State Telephone System (STS).

Information sharing among ECB, DPI, CESAs, RSUs, VTAEs, and universities at the regional level has increased. Needs assessment studies that included these agencies have been completed in CESAs 8, 9, and 10. CESAs 11 and 12 and the Green Bay Consortium are planning similar needs assessments. As a result of these activities it has become apparent that many K-12 educators in Wisconsin are not knowledgeable about telecommunications technologies, current telecommunications projects, or human resources.

Emerging Activities

In the past several years there have been major developments in distance education concomitant with the increased interest of school districts in expanding their course offerings for students. In particular, several out-of-state programs for delivering instruction via satellite are being marketed in Wisconsin. Though each has the similarity of satellite delivery, each has a different approach to the instructional setting.

A Texas firm called the TI-IN Network sends live instruction via the GTE Spacenet II satellite into the classrooms of students in a 15-state area. The classes are conducted much like conventional classes, with a teacher who uses a camera instead of a blackboard and who controls camera movement, slides, and graphics at the broadcasting studio in Webster, Texas. At the receiving end, students watch the teacher on a television set and use a cordless phone to talk to the teacher. Each remote classroom is equipped with a computer and a printer so teachers can send tests and study materials to their students. Course offerings include Computer Math 1, Computer Science, Trigonometry, Elementary Analysis, Algebra 2, Honors Calculus, Research and Technical Writing, Creative Imaginative Writing, English IV Honors, Composition, British Literature, Physics 1, Spanish 1 and 2, French 1 and 2, German 1 and 2, Latin, Psychology, Sociology, and Art History and Appreciation.

The Arts and Sciences Teleconferencing Service (ASTS) of Oklahoma State University in Stillwater, Oklahoma, offers a variety of courses taught by university professors via satellite. Programming combines two or three 45-minute television programs each week with computer-assisted instruction for the remaining class periods. Students at the receiving site are assisted by a certified teacher who takes the course with the students and serves as a teaching partner. Course offerings include German 1 and 2, Physics, Trigonometry, and Advanced Placement Calculus.

The Utah State Board of Education, International Business Machines (IBM), and Bonneville International have joined forces to use an accelerated learning methodology, a satellite dissemination system, and computer technology to provide Spanish instruction to a large number of students in remote sites. Instruction, dramatizations, and cultural inserts are delivered via satellite. In the classroom sites students are led through elaboration and enrichment exercises, and computer activities by a classroom manager.

Conclusion

Distance education has a relatively long history in the state of Wisconsin, beginning with educational radio and television and continuing with the new and emerging technologies of telecommunications. Currently, several state- and regional-level agencies and councils provide state leadership and/or coordination of instructional telecommunications activities, not all of which are compatible with each other. And with the increase in use of distance education at all levels of education, the legislature, school boards and teachers unions have become active participants in the discussion over governance and allocation of scarce resources among numerous competing agencies and needs.

Part Three

Leadership Profiles in
Educational Media and Technology

Introduction

This year the editors continue the historical/biographical function of *EMTY* by providing biographical sketches of two significant leaders in educational technology. Both have been written by longtime associates of these leaders.

Jerrold E. Kemp

Jerrold E. Kemp

Stephanie N. Jones
Assistant Professor
San José State University

Jerrold E. Kemp was born on April 23, 1921, in New York City. He spent much of his youth in Westchester County, and after graduating from high school he moved to Miami with his family, where he continued his education at the University of Florida, majoring in chemistry, with a secondary education minor.

Jerrold's decision to minor in education was in part influenced by his experiences at summer camp. From the time he was five years old, Jerrold spent two months each summer at a camp in Connecticut. His experiences there have had a profound influence on both his personal and his professional life. The young campers all shared deep respect for their camp director, whose motto, "Strong at the Finish!", was ingrained into each youth. No matter how tired they were, campers would return from long hikes singing, and if there was ever a choice between walking on a path or in a stream, the campers were led through the stream. When he was 16, Jerrold became head counselor at the camp, cultivating his interest in working with young people. Minoring in education allowed Jerrold to further develop this interest.

In 1942, upon completion of his bachelor of science degree, Jerrold volunteered for service in the U.S. Army Air Force, serving as a weather officer and air traffic controller in the Aleutian Islands and, later, Europe during World War II.

After returning from military service in 1948, Jerrold began his teaching career as a junior high school science teacher in Dade County, Florida. During an interview for this position, the principal told Jerrold that there was a closet at the back of the science room with the school's science and audiovisual equipment and whoever taught in that room would also be the school's audiovisual coordinator and the AV Club advisor. Jerrold accepted the challenge. Intrigued with the educational potential of audiovisual materials, Jerrold enrolled in the only course in audiovisual teaching techniques that was offered at the University of Miami. The course was taught by F. Edgar Lane, audiovisual director of Dade County schools. Lane became an influential force in Jerrold's professional life. Jerrold went on to teach the course and finished his master's degree in secondary education at the University of Miami in 1952.

On December 24, 1949, Jerrold married Dorothy Gallow, a native Floridian whom he had met in Chicago. With encouragement from his wife, Jerrold began looking into audio-visual programs in the United States and was put in contact with L. C. Larson at Indiana University, where he spent the summer of 1952 studying. Jerrold described this as an exciting time, with Harvey Frye, Warren Stevens, Malcolm Fleming, Ledford Carter, and Dennis Pett on the faculty. He remarked that students and faculty members would go home for dinner at 5:00 and then return to campus to study or work on a project. It was a very stimulating environment. At the end of the summer, Jerrold returned to his teaching position in Florida.

To further his interest in audiovisual education, Jerrold applied for and received a high school teaching fellowship sponsored by the Ford Foundation. The purpose of the project was to give young teachers an opportunity to spend a year away from the classroom for travel and self-improvement. Jerrold spent one semester traveling to Yellowstone and Yosemite national parks and visiting audiovisual programs along the route. He spent the second semester studying at Indiana University and at the end of the year went back to Miami to teach.

In 1954, Jerrold returned to Indiana University as a graduate assistant and taught audiovisual production courses. Later, as an assistant professor and motion picture production supervisor, he produced a live television show and acted as moderator. Amid his other responsibilities, he also finished his doctoral dissertation, entitled "A Survey of Production Facilities in School Districts." This scholarly experience made him much more interested in production. Later, in 1978, Jerrold became the first recipient of the Outstanding Alumni Award from the Department of Instructional Systems Technology at Indiana University.

In 1956, Jerrold received his doctoral degree from Indiana University in audiovisual education and remained on staff at Indiana University until 1958, when Richard B. Lewis, director of the Instructional Resource Center at San José State University, offered him a position as assistant professor and as coordinator of Audiovisual Production and Instructional Development Services.

Jerrold found a very supportive environment at San José State University, where Richard B. Lewis and James W. Brown were his supervisors. Each had a strong audiovisual background and supported his work. During this period, Jerrold saw a need for a book on production and wrote *Planning, Producing, and Using Instructional Media*. This book, first published in 1963, is now in its sixth edition and is a standard in the field. In addition to writing the text and supervising the preparation of artwork and photographs, Jerrold has also done the entire layout for each edition of the book. Later he realized that there is more to planning with media than the media themselves, so he wrote *The Instructional Design Process*, now in its third edition.

Throughout the sixties and seventies, Jerrold made numerous presentations on how to use the new media. In 1965, he received funding from the National Defense Education Act for a three-year project that involved designing an extensive media kit with accompanying training materials explaining how to use new resources and methods of instruction. Five teams were established to demonstrate the media kit to groups, and these teams presented workshops throughout the United States.

Jerrold also participated in professional associations. In 1968, he served as president of the Audio Visual Education Association of California (AVEAC). He was cofounder of the Silicon Valley chapter of the National Society for Performance and Instruction (NSPI), and in 1972, Jerrold became president of the Association for Educational Communications and Technology (AECT). He represented a membership of approximately 12,000 during AECT's fiftieth anniversary year. During his tenure as president, he fostered the continued development of AECT divisions. In an AECT convention program, he wrote, "There is the potential for a very exciting future employing widespread applications of instructional technology with its ramifications for extending, humanizing, and personalizing education." Jerrold demonstrated this potential in his classrooms by leading his students through audiotutorials and self-paced instruction, which they enjoyed.

Jerrold has also been influential on an international level. He has served as a consultant and visiting professor at the University of Puerto Rico, Brisbane Teachers College in Australia, UNESCO in Paris, and the National Taiwan University.

Jerrold remains true to the motto he learned as a youth, "Strong at the Finish!" He retired from San José State University in 1988 but remains very active, engaging in periodic teaching and professional writing. One of his latest projects is developing a proposal based on educational technology to restructure public schools. His enthusiasm for the field remains strong, and he continues to make significant contributions.

Lawrence C. Larson

Lawrence C. Larson

Carolyn Guss
and
Mendel Sherman

For more than 30 years Lawrence C. Larson, professor of education and associate dean and director of the Audio-Visual Center, gave dedicated leadership to the development of the instructional systems technology field and to the conceptualization and implementation of an integrated program of teaching, research, and service at Indiana University. His influence was felt not only throughout the university but throughout the world. He has, indeed, been a pioneer in a growing field and brought great distinction to the university, to the program he developed, and to the field.

L. C. Larson and his wife, Evelyn, were born on the same date (February 15, 1907) in Nebraska, he in Wolback and she in Pilger. They were married on December 20, 1930. They have three children—Jon, born on November 14, 1936, and twins, Karen and Sharen, born on July 13, 1943. Jon is a city planner in Fairfax County, Virginia, and the twins are nurses in California. The Larsons' current address is 12751 Gateway Park, Unit 404, Poway, California 92064.

Mr. Larson received his bachelor's degree at the University of Nebraska in 1929. He served two years as a science teacher and three years as a high school principal in Woodbine, Iowa, and two years as an instructor in science and adult education in the training division of the Tennessee Valley Authority, where he had an opportunity to help develop an audiovisual program in fundamental education.

In 1938, Professor Larson was appointed director of the Motion Picture Project sponsored by the American Council on Education at the University of Minnesota. While he was at the university, he completed his doctorate in educational psychology. In addition to graduate work at the University of Minnesota, he also did graduate work at the University of Nebraska and Teachers College of Columbia University.

In June 1940, Professor Larson joined the faculty of the School of Education at Indiana University, where he developed an integrated audiovisual program for the university departments and organizations and for the state, covering distribution, utilization, production, training, and research. In September 1942, he was granted a partial leave of absence until June 15, 1944, to become an associate director of the American Film Center. In this position, Professor Larson devoted his time to the activities of the Educational Film Library Association, which he had founded during the 1942-43 school year. Following his return to the university in 1944, he gained the support of the university administration for a program of professional education and research in audiovisual communications that included a major for the doctoral degree. At the same time, he gained support expanding the program of services for campus departments and off-campus school and community groups involving the evaluation, selection, production, circulation, and use of all types of audiovisual materials.

When Professor Larson assumed the teaching-administrative position at Indiana University in 1940, he was the only faculty member in audiovisual education in the School of Education, and there was but a small collection of films and lantern slides in the Bureau of Audio-Visual Aids in the Extension Division. Upon his retirement the department had grown to 28 faculty members in the Division of Instructional Systems Technology in the School of Education, and more than 200 students have received their doctorates in that division. The Audio-Visual Center made available for on- and off-campus use one of the largest educational film libraries in the world, as well as a number of media production, distribution, evaluation, and diffusion services.

As a result of Professor Larson's leadership, the National Educational Television (NET) Film Service was created at Indiana University in 1954 to make available television materials for nonbroadcast use. Since 1954 approximately 30,000 prints of $1,300 titles have been placed in circulation, and the estimated aggregate audience exceeds 360 million.

Under Professor Larson's direction some 30 man-years of Indiana University contract services were provided to the Republic of Nigeria and to Sierra Leone, where 11 national and regional media centers were established. He was also influential overseas as a consultant to the governments of the Republic of Mali, Puerto Rico, and the U.S. Virgin Islands. More than 800 students from 63 countries came to know the Indiana University Audio-Visual Center as their home away from home. Many of them hold positions of leadership in the field of educational media; many others hold high governmental positions throughout the world.

Professor Larson has made significant contributions to professional organizations, of which he founded three: the Educational Film Library Association (EFLA), now known as AFVA (American Film and Video Association), the University Film Producers Association (with Lee Cochran of the University of Iowa), and the Audio-Visual Instruction Directors of Indiana (AVID), now known as AIME (Association of Indiana Media Educators). He is a past national president of the National Education Association Department of Audio-Visual Instruction, now known as AECT (Association for Educational Communications and Technology), and a past member of the United States National Commission for UNESCO, and in 1951 he served as a U.S. representative at a UNESCO meeting in Paris concerned with the contribution of educational films to fundamental education. He was an initial member of the Advisory Committee on Newer Educational Media under Title VII of the National Defense Education Act of 1958. He served on the boards and committees of the Film Council of America; the National Audio-Visual Association, now known as ICIA (International Communications Industries Association), the American Film Center; the National University Extension Association; and the Midwest Film Forum. He is a member of Phi Delta Kappa and a number of other educational organizations. He has received several awards for outstanding contributions to the field of instructional technology, among which is the Distinguished Service Award to Ole Larson (as he is affectionately called by many colleagues and friends) presented by EFLA (Educational Film Library Association) at its twenty-fifth anniversary convention.

Anne Walker Cook's *History of the Indiana University Audio-Visual Center 1913 to 1975* (1980) a 355-page Ph.D. dissertation completed at Indiana University, provides a detailed and accurate history of the first 62 years of the center's program and services. On the basis of hours of taped interviews with present and past staff members, Dr. Cook provides the history of the pre-Larson years (1913-1940), the Larson years, and three of the post-Larson years (1940-1975). Traveling from Bloomington, Indiana, to San Diego, Cook taped Ole's recollections and comments as he recounted the events of his 32 years at Indiana University. Larson related one of his most successful strategies to Cook: Upon hearing that university president Herman B. Wells was taking the train to a meeting in New

York, Larson wrangled a ticket for the seat next to the president. "I had my five-year plan [for the center] with me and asked Wells if he would be interested in our discussing it. As I discussed it segment by segment, he would say, 'That sounds good,' and I would say, 'Would you O.K. it?' He would sign each one 'O.K.' with his signature and the date. Subsequently I submitted the plan and it was approved!" The five-year plan with the president's approval was a powerful influence in the budget committee meetings that followed. The revenue it generated established a growing revolving fund for the film library and for assistantships that launched many distinguished careers.

Upon Mr. Larson's retirement in 1972, many congratulatory notes and letters were received. The following are representative of the appreciation and congratulations expressed:

> He has bi-focal vision.... To say that his Indiana Eye was a little stronger than the national eye is only to point out that he realized that what was done well at Indiana could be done well nationally.
>
> Edgar Dale
> Professor of Education
> Ohio State University

> Many times beyond the borders of Indiana and even beyond the seas when Indiana University has been mentioned the response has been "We know of the University's great Audio-Visual Center under Professor Larson."
>
> Herman B. Wells
> President
> Indiana University

> Rewards come in their abundance from others, from what they have made of themselves, from the greatness of their service.
>
> Charles Hoban
> Professor of Communication
> University of Pennsylvania

> I have a sneaking suspicion that if we hang around for the next fifteen years we'll see much more than we've ever seen.
>
> James Brown
> Dean, Graduate School
> San José State College

A faculty tribute to Larson presented upon his retirement concludes this brief account of Larson's contributions to education in general and instructional systems technology specifically:

> Excellence in teaching, research, and professional service has been the hallmark of the Larson years at Indiana University. As a faculty we hope to continue in the tradition you have established of intellectual inquiry, professional services to the improvement of learning, and the full sharing of knowledge and hunches.

Even though no one of us may ever wear the many hats you have worn or do the "imagineering" and the "sophisticated doodling" you have done, we will consider it our challenge to strive toward the goals you have explicitly and implicitly set for the instructional systems technology field and our program at Indiana University.

You and Evelyn have won our admiration and affection, we treasure your friendship, and we wish you Godspeed.

Part Four

Organizations and Associations in North America

Introduction

Brenda Branyan-Broadbent, Ph.D.
Associate Professor

Lois A. Ward
Staff Assistant II
Department of Instructional Technology
Utah State University, Logan

Part 4 of *EMTY* contains several hundred descriptions of media-related organizations and associations. They are organized into two general geographic areas: the United States and Canada.

The section on the United States includes a classified list with headings useful to professionals. This classification will be useful in finding subject leads to the alphabetical list. Such a classified list is not included for Canada. All organizations listed in part 4 were sent copies of the entry which appeared in *EMTY 1990* which described their organization. Respondents were invited to update and edit these entries. In most cases they responded; if they did not, the information included in *EMTY 1990* is repeated so that the organization or association is represented in this directory.

The reader is reminded that changes in communications and media are frequent and extensive and that information in this directory is as accurate as possible at the time of publication.

United States

This section of *EMTY 1991* includes annotated entries for several hundred associations and organizations headquartered in the United States whose interests are in some manner significant to the fields of instructional technology/educational media, library and information science, communications, computer technology, training/management in business/industry, publishing, and many others.

Readers who know only the acronym for some association or organization of interest to them may refer to the index to obtain its full name.

CLASSIFIED LIST

Adult, Continuing, Distance Education
Audio (Records, Audiocassettes and Tapes, Telephone, Radio); Listening
Audiovisual (General)
Censorship
Children-, Youth-Related Organizations
Communication
Community Resources
Computers, Computer Software, Computer Hardware
Copyright
Databases; Networks
Education (General)
Education (Higher)
Equipment (Manufacturing, Maintenance, Testing, Operating)
ERIC-Related
Films — Educational/Instructional/ Documentary
Films — Theatrical (Film Study, Criticism, Production)
Films — Training
Futures

Games, Toys, Drama, Play, Simulation, Puppetry
Graphics
Health-Related Organizations
Information Science
Instructional Technology/Design/Development
International Education
Libraries — Academic, Research
Libraries — Public
Libraries — Special
Libraries and Media Centers — General, School
Microforms; Micrographics
Museums; Archives
Photography
Print — Books
Production (Media)
Publishing
Religious Education
Research
Selection, Collections, Processing (Materials)
Special Education
Training
Video (Cassette, Broadcast, Cable, Satellite, Videodisc, Videotex)

Adult, Continuing, Distance Education
(ALA) Reference and Adult Services Division
(RASD)
Association for Continuing Higher Education
(ACHE)
Association for Educational Communications
and Technology (AECT)
ERIC Clearinghouse on Adult, Career, and
Vocational Education (CE)
National University Continuing Education
Association (NUCEA)
Network for Continuing Medical Education
(NCME)
Society of Manufacturing Engineers (SME)
Superintendent of Documents

**Audio (Records, Audiocassettes and Tapes,
Telephone, Radio); Listening**
American Radio Relay League, Inc. (ARRL)
American Shortwave Listener's Club (ASWLC)
American Women in Radio and Television
(AWRT)
Clearinghouse on Development Communication
Corporation for Public Broadcasting (CPB)
Federal Communications Commission (FCC)
International Tape/Disc Association (ITA)
National Association of Broadcasters (NAB)
National Association of Business and Educa-
tional Radio (NABER)
National Public Radio (NPR)
Oral History Association
Radio Free Europe/Radio Liberty (RFE-RL)
Recording for the Blind
Recording Industry Association of America,
Inc. (RIAA)

Audiovisual (General)
Association for Educational Communications
and Technology (AECT)
(AECT) Division of Educational Media
Management (DEMM)
(AECT) Division of School Media Specialists
(DSMS)
Association of Audio-Visual Technicians
HOPE Reports

Censorship
Freedom of Information Center (FOI)
Women's Institute for Freedom of the Press

Children- , Youth-Related Organizations
(ALA) Association for Library Service to
Children (ALSC)
(ALA) Young Adult Services Division (YASD)
Association for Childhood Education Inter-
national (ACEI)
Center for Children's Media (CCM)
Children's Television International, Inc.
Close Up Foundation
Council for Exceptional Children
ERIC Clearinghouse on Elementary and Early
Childhood Education (PS)

ERIC Clearinghouse on Handicapped and
Gifted Children (EC)
National Association for Creative Children and
Adults (NACCA)
National Association for the Education of
Young Children (NAEYC)
National PTA
Technology and Media Division of CEC
(TAM)

Communication
American Newspaper Publishers Association
Foundation (ANPA)
American Radio Relay League, Inc. (AARL)
East-West Institute of Culture and
Communication
ERIC Clearinghouse on Information Resources
(IR)
ERIC Clearinghouse on Languages and
Linguistics (FL)
ERIC Clearinghouse on Reading and Commu-
nication Skills (CS)
Freedom of Information Center (FOI)
International Association of Business Commu-
nicators (IABC)
International Communication Association
International Communications Industries
Association (ICIA)
National Council of the Churches of Christ—
Communication Commission
Speech Communication Association (SCA)
Women in Film (WIF)
World Pen Pals (WPP)

Community Resources
Teachers and Writers Collaborative (T&W)

**Computers, Computer Software, Computer
Hardware**
(AECT) Division of Interactive Systems and
Computers (DISC)
Association for Computer Educators (ACE)
Computer-Based Research Lab (CERL)
ISTE
Minnesota Educational Computing Corpora-
tion (MECC)
OCLC (Online Computer Library Center)
PLATO
Resources in Computer Education (RICE)
SOFTSWAP
SpecialNet

Copyright
Copyright Clearance Center
International Copyright Information Center
(INCINC)

Databases; Networks
ERIC (Educational Resources Information
Center) (See separate entries for the
various clearinghouses.)
ERIC Document Reproduction Service (EDRS)

ERIC Processing and Reference Facility
PLATO
RICE
SpecialNet

Education (General)
American Association of School Adminis-
    trators (AASA)
American Montessori Society (AMS)
American Society of Educators (ASE)
Association for Childhood Education
    International (ACEI)
(AECT) Minorities in Media (MIM)
Association for Experiential Education (AEE)
Association of Teacher Educators (ATE)
Center for Instructional Research and Curric-
    ulum Evaluation
Council for Basic Education
Education Development Center, Inc.
Environmental Quality Instructional
    Resources Center
ERIC Clearinghouse on Counseling and
    Personnel Services (CG)
ERIC Clearinghouse on Elementary and Early
    Childhood Education (PS)
ERIC Clearinghouse on Handicapped and
    Gifted Children (EC)
ERIC Clearinghouse on Rural Education and
    Small Schools (RC)
ERIC Clearinghouse on Science, Mathematics,
    and Environmental Education (SE)
ERIC Clearinghouse for Social Studies/Social
    Science Education (ERIC/ChESS)
ERIC Clearinghouse on Teacher Education
    (SP)
ERIC Clearinghouse on Urban Education (UD)
International Reading Association (IRA)
National Art Education Association (NAEA)
National Association for the Exchange of
    Industrial Resources (NAEIR)
National Association of Secondary School
    Principals (NASSP)
National Association of State Boards of
    Education (NASBE)
National Association of State Educational
    Media Professionals (NASTEMP)
National Association of State Textbook
    Administrators (NASTA)
National Center for Appropriate Technology
National Clearinghouse for Bilingual Education
National Council for Accreditation of Teacher
    Education (NCATE)
National Education Association (NEA)
National Endowment for the Arts (NEA)
National Endowment for the Humanities
    (NEH)
National Science Foundation (NSF)
National Science Teachers Association (NSTA)
Project in Distance Education
Project in Educational Technology
Social Science Education Consortium

Education (Higher)
American Association of Community and
    Junior Colleges (AACJC)
American Association of State Colleges and
    Universities
Association for Continuing Higher Education
    (ACHE)
(AECT) Community College Association for
    Instruction and Technology
(AECT) Northwest College and University
    Council for the Management of Educa-
    tional Technology
Association of American Colleges (AAC)
ERIC Clearinghouse on Higher Education
    (HE)
University and College Designers Association
    (UCDA)
University Film and Video Association (UFVA)

Equipment (Manufacturing, Maintenance, Testing, Operating)
(ALA) Library and Information Technology
    Association (LITA)
American National Standards Institute (ANSI)
Association of Audio-Visual Technicians
    (AAVT)
EPIE Institute
ERIC Clearinghouse on Tests, Measurement,
    and Evaluation (TM)
International Communications Industries
    Association (ICIA)
National School Supply and Equipment
    Association (NSSEA)
Society of Motion Picture and Television
    Engineers (SMPTE)

ERIC-Related
ERIC (Educational Resources Information
    Center)
ERIC Clearinghouse on Adult, Career, and
    Vocational Education (CE)
ERIC Clearinghouse on Counseling and
    Personnel Services (CG)
ERIC Clearinghouse on Elementary and Early
    Childhood Education (PS)
ERIC Clearinghouse on Handicapped and
    Gifted Children (EC)
ERIC Clearinghouse on Higher Education
    (HE)
ERIC Clearinghouse on Information Resources
    (IR)
ERIC Clearinghouse on Language and Lin-
    guistics (FL)
ERIC Clearinghouse on Reading and Commu-
    nication Skills (CS)
ERIC Clearinghouse on Rural Education and
    Small Schools (RC)
ERIC Clearinghouse on Science, Mathematics,
    and Environmental Education (SE)
ERIC Clearinghouse on Teacher Education
    (SP)

ERIC Clearinghouse on Urban Education (UD)
ERIC Document Reproduction Service
(EDRS)
ERIC Processing and Reference Facility

**Films — Educational/Instructional/
Documentary**
Anthropology Film Center (AFC)
Association of Independent Video and
Filmmakers and the Foundation for
Independent Video and Film
Children's Film and Television Center of
America (CFTCA)
CINE Information
Council on International Non-theatrical
Events
Film/Video Arts Inc.
Films Inc.
National Aeronautics and Space Adminis-
tration (NASA)
National Alliance of Media Arts Centers
(NAMAC)
National Audiovisual Center (NAC)
National Film Board of Canada (NFBC)
National Information Center for Educational
Media (NICEM)
Pacific Film Archive (PFA)
PCR: Films and Video in the Behavioral
Sciences
Women's Media Project (WMP)

**Films — Theatrical (Film Study, Criticism,
Production)**
Academy of Motion Picture Arts and Sciences
(AMPAS)
American Society of Cinematographers
Film Advisory Board (FAB)
Film Arts Foundation (FAF)
Hollywood Film Archive
International Film and TV Festival of New
York
National Film Information Service (NFIS)

Films — Training
American Film and Video Association (AFVA)
(AECT) Industrial Training and Education
Division (ITED)
Association of Independent Video and
Filmmakers and the Foundation for
Independent Video and Film
Council on International Non-theatrical
Events
Great Plains National ITV Library
National Audiovisual Center
National Film Board of Canada
Training Media Association

Futures
Institute for the Future
Office of Technology Assessment (OTA)
World Future Society (WFS)

**Games, Toys, Drama, Play, Simulation,
Puppetry**
North American Simulation and Gaming
Association (NASAGA)
Puppeteers of America
Society for Computer Simulation (SCS)

Graphics
International Graphic Arts Education Asso-
ciation (IGAEA)
Newspaper Features Council (NFC)

Health-Related Organizations
American Medical Writers Association
(AMWA)
American Society for Healthcare Education
and Training of the American Hospital
Association (ASHET)
Health Sciences Communications Association
(HeSCA)
Lister Hill National Center for Biomedical
Communications of the National Library
of Medicine
Medical Library Association (MLA)
National Association for Visually Handicapped
(NAVH)
National Library of Medicine
Network for Continuing Medical Education
(NCME)

Information Science
International Information Management
Congress (IMC)

Instructional Technology/Design/Development
Agency for Instructional Technology (AIT)
Association for Educational Communications
and Technology (AECT)
(AECT) Community College Association for
Instruction and Technology (CCAIT)
(AECT) Division of Educational Media
Management (DEMM)
(AECT) Division of Instructional Development
(DID)
National Society for Performance and Instruc-
tion (NSPI)
Office of Technology Assessment (OTA)
Professors of Instructional Design and Tech-
nology (PIDT)
Society for Applied Learning Technology
(SALT)

International Education
(AECT) International Division (ITNL)
(AECT) International Visual Literacy Asso-
ciation, Inc. (IVLA)
Council on International Educational Exchange
(CIEE)
East-West Institute of Culture and
Communication
Institute of International Education

International Friendship League (IFL)
Office for International Networks in Education
and Development (INET)
United Nations Department of Public
Information
U.S. Advisory Commission on Public
Diplomacy
World Pen Pals (WPP)

Libraries — Academic, Research
American Library Association (ALA)
(ALA) Association of College and Research
Libraries (ACRL)

Libraries — Public
American Library Association (ALA)
(ALA) Audiovisual Committee (of the Public
Library Association)
(ALA) Library Administration and Manage-
ment Association (LAMA)
(ALA) Library and Information Technology
Association (LITA)
(ALA) Public Library Association (PLA)
(ALA) Reference and Adult Services Division
(RASD)
(ALA) Resources and Technical Services
Division
(ALA) Young Adult Services Division (YASD)

Libraries — Special
American Library Association (ALA)
(ALA) Association for Library Service to
Children (ALSC)
(ALA) Association of Specialized and Coopera-
tive Library Agencies (ASCLA)
(ALA) Technology in Public Libraries
Committee
Social Libraries Association (SLA)
Theater Library Association (TLA)

Libraries and Media Centers — General, School
American Library Association (ALA)
American Library Trustee Association
(ALIA)
Association for Educational Communications
and Technology (AECT)
(AECT) Division of School Media Specialists
(DSMS)
(AECT) National Association of Regional
Media Centers (NARMC)
(AECT) Northwest College and University
Council for the Management of Educa-
tional Technology
Association for Library and Information
Science Education
Catholic Library Association
Consortium of College and University Media
Centers
Continuing Library Education Network and
Exchange
Council for the Management of Educational
Technology

Council of National Library and Information
Associations
International Association of School Librarian-
ship (IASL)
Library of Congress
National Alliance of Media Arts Centers
(NAMAC)
National Association of State Educational
Media Professionals (NASTEMP)
National Commission on Libraries and Infor-
mation Science (NCLIS)
National Council of Teachers of English
(NCTE) Commission on Media
On-Line Audiovisual Catalogers (OLAC)

Microforms; Micrographics
See ERIC-Related entries.

Museums; Archives
American Federation of Arts (AFA)
(AECT) Archives
Association of Systematics Collections
Computer Museum
Hollywood Film Archive
International Museum of Photography at
George Eastman House
Lawrence Hall of Science
Museum Computer Network, Inc.
Museum of Broadcasting (MB)
Museum of Holography
Museum of Modern Art
National Gallery of Art (NGA)
Smithsonian Institution

Photography
International Center of Photography (ICP)
International Museum of Photography at
George Eastman House
Museum of Holography
National Press Photographers Association,
Inc. (NPPA)
Photographic Society of America (PSA)
Society for Photographic Education (SPE)
Society of Photo Technologists (SPT)
SPSE: The Society for Imaging Science and
Technology

Print — Books
American Booksellers Association (ABA)

Production (Media)
American Society of Cinematographers
Association for Educational Communications
and Technology (AECT)
(AECT) Media Design and Production
Division (MDPD)
Association of Independent Video and
Filmmakers and the Foundation for
Independent Video and Film
Film Arts Foundation (FAF)
Women in Film (WIF)
Women's Media Project (WMP)

Publishing
American Booksellers Association (ABA)
Association of American Publishers (AAP)
Authors' League of America
Government Printing Office (US GPO)
Magazine Publishers of America (MPA)
National Association of State Textbook
  Administrators (NASTA)

Religious Education
Catholic Library Association
National Religious Broadcasters
  (NRB)

Research
American Educational Research Association
  (AERA)
(AECT) Research and Theory Division (RTD)
(AECT) ECT Foundation
Center for Advanced Visual Studies
Center for Instructional Research and Curric-
  ulum Evaluation
Center for Interactive Programs
Clearinghouse on Development Communication
Council for Educational Development and
  Research (CEDaR)
Education Development Center, Inc.
ERIC clearinghouses. See ERIC-Related
  entries.
Far West Laboratory for Educational Research
  and Development (FWL)
HOPE Reports
Institute for Development of Educational
  Activities (IDEA)
Institute for Research on Teaching
National Technical Information Service
  (NTIS)
National Technology Center
The NETWORK
Northwest Regional Educational Laboratory
  (NWREL)

Selection, Collections, Processing (Materials)
National Information Center for Educational
  Media (NICEM)

Special Education
Council for Exceptional Children
ERIC Clearinghouse on Handicapped and
  Gifted Children (EC)
National Association for Visually Handicapped
  (NAVH)

Training
American Management Association (AMA)
(AMA) Human Resources Division

American Society for Training and Develop-
  ment (ASTD)
Association for Educational Communications
  and Technology (AECT)
(AECT) Federal Educational Technology
  Association (FETA)
(AECT) Industrial Training and Education
  Division (ITED)
Bergwall Productions, Inc.
ERIC Clearinghouse on Adult, Career, and
  Vocational Education (CE)
Training Modules for Trainers (TMT)

**Video (Cassette, Broadcast, Cable, Satellite,
Videodisc, Videotex)**
Agency for Instructional Technology (AIT)
American Women in Radio and Television
Association for Educational Communications
  and Technology (AECT)
(AECT) Division of Telecommunications
  (DOT)
Association of Independent Video and
  Filmmakers and the Foundation for
  Independent Video and Film
Central Educational Network (CEN)
Children's Television International, Inc.
Close Up Foundation
Corporation for Public Broadcasting (CPB)
Federal Communications Commission (FCC)
Great Plains National ITV Library (GPN)
International Tape/Disc Association (ITA)
International Telecommunications Satellite
  Organization (INTELSAT)
International Teleconferencing Association
  (ITCA)
International Television Association (ITVA)
National Association for Better Broadcasting
  (NABB)
National Association of Broadcasters (NAB)
National Cable Television Institute (NCTI)
National Federation of Community Broad-
  casters (NFCB)
National Telemedia Council (NTC)
Nebraska Videodisc Design/Production Group
  (VD-PG)
PBS ENCORE
PBS VIDEO
Public Broadcasting Service (PBS)
Public Service Satellite Consortium (PSSC)
Society of Cable Television Engineers (SCTE)
Society of Motion Picture and Television
  Engineers (SMPTE)
Telecommunications Research and Action
  Center (TRAC)
Television Licensing Center (TLC)
Women in Film (WIF)

ALPHABETICAL LIST

Academy of Motion Picture Arts and Sciences (AMPAS). 8949 Wilshire Blvd., Beverly Hills, CA 90211. (213) 278-8990. An honorary organization composed of outstanding individuals in all phases of motion pictures. Seeks to advance the arts and sciences of motion picture technology and artistry. Presents annual film awards; offers artist-in-residence programs; operates reference library and National Film Information Service. *Publications: Annual Index to Motion Picture Credits* and *Academy Players Directory.*

Agency for Instructional Technology (AIT). Box A, Bloomington, IN 47402. (812) 339-2203; (800) 457-4509. Michael F. Sullivan, Exec. Dir. Established to strengthen education through technology. In cooperation with state and provincial agencies, AIT develops instructional materials using video, computers, and other emerging technologies. AIT also acquires and distributes a wide variety of video, computer, and related print materials for use as major learning resources. From April 1973 to July 1984, AIT was known as the Agency for Instructional Television. Its predecessor organization, National Instructional Television, was founded in 1962. *Publications: AIT Newsletter* and *AIT Catalog.*

American Association of Community and Junior Colleges (AACJC). One Dupont Circle NW, Suite 410, Washington, DC 20036-1176. (202) 728-0200. Dale Parnell, Pres. AACJC serves the nation's 1,211 community, technical, and junior colleges through advocacy, professional development, publications, and national networking. The annual convention draws more than 4,000 mid- and top-level administrators of two-year colleges. Staff and presidents offer expertise in all areas of education. Sixteen councils and six commissions address all areas of education. *Membership:* 1,110 inst., 150 int'l., 4 fdn., 75 corp., 103 educ. assn. *Dues:* Vary for institutions, corporations, foundations, and individuals. *Publications: Community, Technical and Junior College Journal* (bi-mo.); *AACJC Letter* (mo.); College Times; Community College Press (books, monographs, etc.); and publications program (directories, books, monographs, policy statements, etc.).

American Association of School Administrators (AASA). 1801 N. Moore St., Arlington, VA 22209. (703) 528-0700. Richard D. Miller, Exec. Dir. Represents professional administrators and managers in education in the United States and overseas, provides an extensive program of professional development through the National Academy for School Executives (NASE). Also produces publications and audiovisual programs to increase knowledge and skills of administrators. *Membership:* 19,000. *Dues:* $175. *Publications: The School Administrator; Leadership News;* and numerous books and video programs.

American Association of State Colleges and Universities. One Dupont Circle NW, Suite 700, Washington, DC 20036-1192. (202) 293-7070. Allan W. Ostar, Pres. Membership is open to any regionally accredited institution of higher education, and those in the process of securing accreditation, which offer programs leading to the degree of bachelor, master, or doctor, and which are wholly or partially state-supported and state-controlled. Organized and operated exclusively for educational, scientific, and literary purposes, its particular purposes shall be to improve higher education within its member institutions through cooperative planning, studies, and research on common educational problems, and the development of a more unified program of action among its members; and to provide other needed and worthwhile educational services to the colleges and universities it may represent. *Membership:* 375 institutions, 28 system, and 7 associate members. *Dues:* Based on current student enrollment at institution. *Publications: MEMO: To the President; The Center Associate; Office of Federal Program Reports; Office of Federal Program Deadlines.* (Catalogs of books and other publications available upon request.)

American Booksellers Association (ABA). 137 W. 25th St., New York, NY 10001. (212) 463-8450; outside NY (800) 637-0037. Bernard Rath, Exec. Dir. A trade organization of large and small firms engaged in retail book sales. *Membership* (as of April 30, 1990): 8,382 members; total stores and branches, 5,442. *Dues:* $125 initially, sliding scale renewal on sales volume. *Publications: ABA Book Buyers Handbook*; *A Manual on Bookselling*; *American Bookseller*; *ABA Newswire*; *ABA Sidelines Directory*, *ABA Bookbuyers Returns Handbook*; *ABA Sourcebook*; and *ABA Bookseller's Choice*.

American Educational Research Association (AERA). 1230 17th St. NW, Washington, DC 20036. (202) 223-9485. William J. Russell, Exec. Dir. A national professional organization of educators and behavioral scientists active and/or interested in educational research and its application to educational problems. Sponsors annual meetings featuring presentations of original research findings. *Membership:* 16,800. *Dues:* $45. *Publications: Educational Researcher*; *American Educational Research Journal*; *Journal of Educational Statistics*; *Educational Evaluation and Policy Analysis*; *Review of Research in Education*; and *Review of Educational Research*.

The American Federation of Arts (AFA). 41 E. 65th St., New York, NY 10021. (212) 988-7700. Fax (212) 861-2487. Myrna Smoot, Dir. National nonprofit museum service which organizes and circulates exhibition and film programs to museums, university art galleries, and art centers throughout the United States and abroad. It also provides special services to museums including reduced rate insurance, air and van transport for art, professional management training, and design awards. *Membership:* 600. *Newsletter: ART* (q.).

American Film and Video Association (AFVA). 920 Barnsdale Rd., Suite 152, La Grange Park, IL 60525. (708) 482-4000. Ron MacIntyre, Exec. Dir. Formerly the Educational Film Library Association, the AFVA is recognized as the authoritative organization in assembling data about the 16mm and video fields, in encouraging quality production and appreciation of film generally, and in guidance in the proper use of these media. Serves as a national clearinghouse of information about films, conducts workshops on a variety of media-related topics, and sponsors the annual American Film and Video Festival. *Membership:* 1,300. *Dues:* $45 indiv., $175 inst. *Publications: SightLines*; *AFVA Bulletin*; and *AFVA Evaluations*.

American Library Association (ALA). 50 E. Huron St., Chicago, IL 60611. (312) 944-6780. Linda F. Crismond, Exec. Dir. The ALA is the oldest and largest national library association. Its 50,000 members represent all types of libraries — state, public, school, and academic, as well as special libraries serving persons in government, commerce, the armed services, hospitals, prisons, and other institutions. Chief advocate of achievement and maintenance of high-quality library information services through protection of the right to read, educating librarians, improving services, and making information widely accessible. *Membership:* 47,000. *Dues:* Basic dues $38 first year, $75 renewing members. *Publications: American Libraries*.

   (ALA) American Association of School Librarians (AASL). 50 E. Huron St., Chicago, IL 60611. (312) 944-6780. Ann Carlson Weeks, Exec. Dir. Seeks general improvement and extension of school library/media services as a means of strengthening education. Gives special attention to evaluation, selection, interpretation, and use of library media. Activities and projects of the association are divided among 55 committees and three sections. *Membership:* 7,300. *Dues:* Membership in ALA plus $35, $105 renewing member, $34 student member. *Publications: School Library Media Quarterly* and others.

   (ALA) American Library Trustee Association (ALTA). 50 E. Huron St., Chicago, IL 60611. (312) 944-6780. Sharon L. Jordan, Exec. Dir. Interested in the development of effective library service for people in all types of communities and libraries. Members, as policymakers, are concerned with organizational patterns of service, the development of competent personnel, the provision of adequate financing, the passage of suitable legislation and the encouragement of citizen support for libraries. *Membership:* 1,700. *Dues:* Membership in ALA plus $40. *Publications: ALTA Newsletter* and *Trustee Digest*.

(ALA) Association for Library Collections and Technical Services (ALCTS). 50 E. Huron St., Chicago, IL 60611. (312) 944-6780. Karen Muller, Exec. Dir.; Ruth C. Carter, Pres. Dedicated to acquisition, identification, cataloging, classification, and preservation of library materials, the development and coordination of the country's library resources, and aspects of selection and evaluation involved in acquiring and developing library materials and resources. Sections include Cataloging and Classification, Preservation of Library Materials, Reproduction of Library Materials, Resources, and Serials. *Membership:* 6,039. *Dues:* Membership in ALA plus $35. *Publications: Library Resources & Technical Services* (q.); *ALCTS Newsletter* (8/yr.).

(ALA) Association for Library Service to Children (ALSC). 50 E. Huron St., Chicago, IL 60611. (312) 944-6780. Susan Roman, Exec. Dir. Interested in the improvement and extension of library services for children in all types of libraries, evaluation, and selection of book and nonbook library materials, and the improvement of techniques of library services for children from preschool through the eighth grade or junior high school age. Annual conference and midwinter meeting with the ALA. Committee membership open to ALSC members. *Membership:* 3,600. *Dues:* Membership in ALA plus $35. *Publications: Journal of Youth Services in Libraries*; and *ALSC Newsletter*.

(ALA) Association of College and Research Libraries (ACRL). 50 E. Huron St., Chicago, IL 60611-2795. (312) 944-6780. JoAn Segal, Exec. Dir. Represents librarians and promotes libraries of postsecondary, research, and specialized institutions. Has available library standards for colleges, universities, and two-year institutions. Publishes statistics on academic libraries. Committees include Academic Status, Audiovisual, Professional Education, Legislation, Publications, and Standards and Accreditation. Free list of materials available. *Membership:* 11,000. *Dues:* Membership in ALA plus $35. *Publications: College & Research Libraries*; *College & Research Libraries News*; *Rare Books and Manuscripts Librarianship*; 11 section newsletters; and *Choice*.

(ALA) Association of Specialized and Cooperative Library Agencies (ASCLA). 50 E. Huron St., Chicago, IL 60611. (312) 944-6780. Andrew Hansen, ALA Staff Liaison. Represents state library agencies, multitype library cooperatives, and libraries serving special clientele to promote the development of coordinated library services with equal access to information and material for all persons. The activities and programs of the association are carried out by 21 committees, three sections, and various discussion groups. Write for free checklist of materials. *Membership:* 1,400. *Dues:* Membership in ALA plus $30 personal members, $50 organizations, $500 state library agencies. *Publications: Interface*.

(ALA) Audiovisual Committee (of the Public Library Association). 50 E. Huron St., Chicago, IL 60611. (312) 280-5752. Promotes use of audiovisual materials in public libraries.

(ALA) Library Administration and Management Association (LAMA). 50 E. Huron St., Chicago, IL 60611. (312) 280-5038. Karen Muller, Exec. Dir.; Susanne Henderson, Pres. Provides an organizational framework for encouraging the study of administrative theory, for improving the practice of administration in libraries, and for identifying and fostering administrative skills. Toward these ends, the association is responsible for all elements of general administration which are common to more than one type of library. These may include: Buildings and Equipment Section (BES);

Fundraising and Financial Development Section (FRFDS); Library Organization and Management Section (LOMS); Personnel Administration Section (PAS); Public Relations Section (PRS); Systems and Services Section (SASS); Statistic Section (SS). *Membership:* 5,200. *Dues:* Membership in ALA plus $35. *Publications: Library Administration & Management* (q.).

(ALA) Library and Information Technology Association (LITA). 50 E. Huron St., Chicago, IL 60611. (312) 280-4270. Linda J. Knutson, Exec. Dir. Concerned with library automation, the information sciences, and the design, development, and implementation of automated systems in those fields, including systems development, electronic data processing, mechanized information retrieval, operations research, standards development, telecommunications, video communications, networks and collaborative efforts, management techniques, information technology, optical technology, artificial intelligence and expert systems, and other related aspects of audiovisual activities and hardware applications. *Membership:* 5,000. *Dues:* Membership in ALA plus $35. *Publications: Information Technology and Libraries* and *LITA Newsletter*.

(ALA) Public Library Association (PLA). 50 E. Huron St., Chicago, IL 60611. (312) 944-6780. Eleanor Jo Rodger, Exec. Dir.; Charles Brown, Pres. Concerned with the development, effectiveness, and financial support of public libraries. Speaks for the profession and seeks to enrich the professional competence and opportunities of public libraries. Sections include Adult Lifelong Learning, Armed Forces Library, Community Information, Metropolitan Libraries, Public Library System, Small and Medium-sized Libraries, and Marketing Public Library Services. *Membership:* 6,200. *Dues:* $35/yr., open to all ALA members. *Publications: Planning and Role Setting for Public Libraries: A Manual of Options and Procedures*; *Output Measures for Public Libraries: A Manual of Standardized Procedures, 2nd Edition*; *Public Library Data Service, Statistical Report '90.*

(ALA) Reference and Adult Services Division (RASD). 50 E. Huron St., Chicago, IL 60611. (312) 944-6780. Andrew M. Hansen, Exec. Dir. Responsible for stimulating and supporting in every type of library the delivery of reference information services to all groups and of general library services and materials to adults. *Membership:* 5,201. *Dues:* Membership in ALA plus $25. *Publications: RQ*; *RASD Update*; and others.

(ALA) Technology in Public Libraries Committee (of the Public Library Association). 50 E. Huron St., Chicago, IL 60611. (312) 944-6780. Collects and disseminates information on technology applications in public libraries.

(ALA) Young Adult Services Division (YASD). 50 E. Huron St., Chicago, IL 60611. (312) 944-6780. Susan B. Madden, Pres. Seeks to improve and extend library services to young people, assumes responsibility within the ALA to evaluate and select books and nonbook media and to interpret and make recommendations regarding their use with young adults. Committees include Audiovisual Producers and Distributors Liaison, Best Books for Young Adults, Recommended Books for the Reluctant Young Adult Reader, Media Selection and Usage, Publishers' Liaison, and Selected Films for Young Adults. *Membership:* 2,400. *Dues:* Membership in ALA plus $25. *Publications: Journal of Youth Services in Libraries* (formerly *Top of the News*); *Best Books*; and many others.

American Management Association (AMA). 135 W. 50th St., New York, NY 10020. (212) 586-8100. Thomas R. Horton, Chairman and CEO. AMA is an international educational organization, membership-based and not-for-profit, dedicated to broadening the management knowledge and skills of people and, by so doing, strengthening their organizations.

AMA operates management centers and offices in the United States and, through AMA/International, in Brussels, Belgium; São Paulo, Brazil; Toronto, Canada; and Mexico City, Mexico. AMA offers public meetings through the Center for Management Development, Presidents Association, AMA/International, AMA Planning Services, AMA On-Site, and Operation Enterprise where interchange of management information, ideas, and experience in each field is provided through large-scale national conferences, seminars, briefings, and workshops. Other services offered by AMA include the Extension Institute (a self-study program), AMA Video, AMA COM Books, The Management Information Service, and the AMA Library. *Membership:* Approx. 75,000. *Publications: Management Review* (membership periodical); *The President*; *Personnel*; *Organizational Dynamics*; *Service Savvy*; *Supervisory Management*; *Supervisory Sense*; *Compensation and Benefits Review*; *CompFlash*; *Workshop Trainer's*; and *International Executive*.

(AMA) Human Resources Division. 135 W. 50th St., New York, NY 10020. (212) 903-8234. Phyllis White, Div. Mgr. Offers conferences, courses, and briefings in such areas as compensation, employee relations, human resources administration, management and supervisory training and development, employee benefits, flexible benefits and organization development. Members of this AMA division are typically vice presidents for personnel, industrial relations managers, safety directors, strategic planning directors, training directors, and employee benefit professionals. *Publications: Management Review*; *Personnel*; and *Organizational Dynamics*.

American Medical Writers Association (AMWA). 9650 Rockville Pike, Bethesda, MD 20814. (301) 493-0003. Lillian Sablack, Exec. Dir. An international society whose members are engaged in all media of communication in medicine and allied professions. Founded in 1940, it is the largest association dedicated to the advancement of medical communication. Aims to offer guidance in the art and techniques of medical communication and to develop courses and workshops in the field. *Membership:* 3,200. *Dues:* $65. *Publications: AMWA Journal* and *Freelance Directory*.

American Montessori Society (AMS). 150 5th Ave., New York, NY 10011. (212) 924-3209. Bretta Weiss, Nat. Dir. Dedicated to promoting better education for all children through teaching strategies consistent with the Montessori system. Membership is composed of schools in the private and public sectors employing this method, as well as individuals. It serves as a resource center and clearinghouse for information and data on Montessori, affiliates teacher training programs in different parts of the country, and conducts a consultation service and accreditation program for school members. Sponsors two regional and one national educational conference per year and four professional development symposia under the auspices of the AMS Teachers' Section. *Dues:* Teachers, $31.50; parents, $25; inst., $202.13-$973.88. *Publications: AMS Montessori LIFE* (q.) and occasional papers.

American National Standards Institute (ANSI). 1430 Broadway, New York, NY 10018. (212) 354-3300. Fax (212) 302-1286. Manuel Peralta, Pres.; James N. Pearse, Chairman of the Board. ANSI is the coordinator of the U.S. voluntary standards system, approves American National Standards, and represents the United States in the International Organization for Standardization (ISO) and the International Electrotechnical Commission (IEC). The Institute does not write standards or codes but coordinates those developed through an open consensus process by more than 240 organizations, 1,000 businesses, and 20 government agencies that constitute its membership. *Publications: Catalog of Standards* (yearly), lists more than 8,000 standards of all topic areas; *ANSI Reporter* (mo.), newsletter of the national and international standards community; and *Standards Action* (biweekly), listing status of revisions on standards in the United States, Europe, and other foreign national bodies.

American Newspaper Publishers Association (ANPA) Foundation. Box 17407, Dulles Airport, Washington, DC 20041. (703) 648-1000. Rosalind G. Stark, V.P./Dir. Seeks to advance professionalism of the press, to foster public understanding of a free press, to cultivate increased numbers of future newspaper readers, and to enhance minority opportunities in newspapering. Administers a national Newspaper in Education Program, encouraging local newspapers and school systems to cooperate in using the newspaper for various fields of study. Also administers a Literacy Program, encouraging newspapers to work in their communities to combat illiteracy. Sponsors a Minority Opportunity Program to foster diversity in the newspaper business and supports numerous efforts encouraging freedom of the press. *Dues:* Payable to association by newspapers. *Publications:* Training materials for students and professionals.

American Radio Relay League, Inc. (ARRL). 225 Main St., Newington, CT 06111. (203) 666-1541. David Sumner, Exec. V.P. A noncommercial association of radio amateurs interested in radio communication, experimentation, and the relaying of messages for the advancement of the radio art and public welfare. *Membership:* 160,000. *Dues:* $30. *Publications:* Send for list.

American Shortwave Listeners' Club (ASWLC). 16182 Ballad Lane, Huntington Beach, CA 92649-2204. (714) 846-1685. Stewart H. MacKenzie, Pres. A hobbyist organization founded to advance shortwave listening on a worldwide basis. Research and educational programs include studies of radio signals from earth satellites, relay stations, frequency interference, radio astronomy, propagation monitoring, sunspot studies, and computer communications worldwide. *Membership:* 1,000. *Dues:* $18/yr. Sample copy of *SWL*, $1. *Publications: SWL*; *Equipment Survey*; and *Proper Reporting Guide*.

American Society for Healthcare Education and Training of the American Hospital Association (ASHET). 840 N. Lake Shore Dr., Chicago, IL 60611. (312) 280-6113. Alexandra Gekos, Dir. Members include directors of health education and training, health educators, patient education coordinators, education managers, human resource development coordinators, staff development coordinators, media specialists and organization development practitioners who conduct and manage education and training programs in all types of health care institutions, and wellness/health promotion coordinators. *Membership:* 1,600. *Dues:* $90. *Publications: Healthcare Education Dateline*; and *Journal of Healthcare Education and Training*.

American Society for Training and Development (ASTD). 1630 Duke St., Box 1443, Alexandria, VA 22313. (703) 683-8100. Curtis Plott, Exec. V.P. Leading professional organization for individuals engaged in employee training and education in business, industry, government, and related fields. Members include managers, program developers, instructors, consultants, counselors, suppliers, and academics. The purpose of its extensive professional publishing program is to build an essential body of knowledge for advancing the competence of training and development practitioners in the field. Many special interest subgroups relating to industries or job functions are included in the organization. *Membership:* 55,000 national plus chapter. *Dues:* $120/yr. indiv. (group discounts available). *Publications: Training and Development Journal*; *Info-Line*; *ASTD Video Directories*; *A Checklist for Technical Skills and Other Training and Development*; *Competency Analysis for Trainers: A Personal Planning Guide*; *ASTD Directory of Academic Programs in T&D/HRD*; *Evaluating Training Programs*; *Training and Development Handbook*; *National Report*; and others. Additions include: *Technical & Skills Training Magazine*; and the following newsletters; *Focus* (chapter newsletter); *Management Development Report*; and *Technical Trainer/Skills Trainer*. ASTD also has recognized professional areas, networks, and industry groups, most of which produce newsletters.

American Society of Cinematographers. 1782 N. Orange Dr., Hollywood, CA 90078. (213) 876-5080. Leonard South, Pres. *Membership:* 271. *Publications: American Cinematographers Magazine.*

American Society of Educators (ASE). 1429 Walnut St., Philadelphia, PA 19102. (215) 563-3501. A multifaceted professional organization that serves the nation's teachers by providing information and evaluation of media resources and technologies for effective classroom use. *Membership:* 41,000. *Dues:* $29/yr., $47/yr. foreign. *Publications: Media and Methods.*

American Women in Radio and Television (AWRT). 1101 Connecticut Ave. NW, Suite 700, Washington, DC 20036. (202) 429-5102. Susan Kudla Finn, Exec. Dir. Organization of professionals in the electronic media including owners, managers, administrators, and those in creative positions in broadcasting, satellite, cable, advertising, and public relations. The objectives are to work worldwide to improve the quality of radio and television; to promote the entry, development, and advancement of women in the electronic media and allied fields; to serve as a medium of communications and idea exchange; and to become involved in community concerns. Organized in 1951. Student memberships available. *Membership:* 52 chapters. *Dues:* $105/yr. *Publications: News and Views; Resource Directory;* and *Careers in the Electronic Media.*

Anthropology Film Center (AFC). Box 493-87504, 1626 Canyon Rd., Santa Fe, NM 87501. (505) 983-4127. Joan and Carroll Williams, Co-Dirs. Offers Documentary Film Program, a 34-week fulltime course in 16mm film production and theory, and summer workshops. Also provides consultation, research, 16mm film equipment sales and rental, facilities rental, joint M.A. degree with Temple University, occasional seminars and workshops, and a specialized library. *Publications: A Filmography for American Indian Education; An Ixil Calendrical Divination* (16mm color film); and *First Impressions of Ixil Culture* (16mm color film).

Association for Childhood Education International (ACEI). 11141 Georgia Ave., Suite 200, Wheaton, MD 20902. (301) 942-2443. Lucy Prete Martin, Ed. and Dir. of Publications. Concerned with children from infancy through early adolescence, ACEI publications reflect careful research, broadbased views, and consideration of a wide range of issues affecting children. Many are media-related in nature. The journal (*Childhood Education*) is essential for teachers, teachers-in-training, teacher educators, daycare workers, administrators, and parents. Articles focus on child development and emphasize practical application. Regular departments include book reviews (child and adult); reviews on films, pamphlets, and software; research, and classroom idea-sparkers. Articles address timely concerns; of the five issues published yearly, one is a theme issue devoted to critical concerns. *Membership:* 15,000. *Dues:* $38/yr. *Publications: Childhood Education* (official journal); *ACEI Exchange* (newsletter); and *Journal of Research in Childhood Education* (new).

Association for Computer Educators (ACE). College of Business, IDS, James Madison University, Harrisonburg, VA 22807. (703) 568-6189. Dr. Thomas Seymour, Pres. Membership for those who teach or have an interest in computers and information systems. *Membership:* 1,000 plus libraries. *Dues:* $35/yr. *Publications: The Journal of Computer Information Systems.*

Association for Continuing Higher Education (ACHE). Division of Continuing Studies, Indiana University, Purdue University at Indianapolis, Indianapolis, IN 46202. (317) 274-5032. Dr. Scott Evenbeck, Exec. V.P. An association of institutions and individuals having a commitment to providing opportunities in higher education for adults in traditional and nontraditional programs. *Membership:* 1,600 indiv. representing 585 institutions. *Dues:* $50/yr. professional, $225/yr. institutional. *Publications: 5 Minutes with ACHE; The Journal of Continuing Higher Education;* and *Proceedings.*

Association for Educational Communications and Technology (AECT). 1025 Vermont Ave. NW, Suite 820, Washington, DC 20005. (202) 347-7834. Fax (202) 347-7839. Stanley Zenor, Exec. Dir.; Roger Tipling, Pres. Concerned with learning and educational technology; established in 1923. AECT members include instructional technologists; media or library specialists; university professors and researchers; industrial/business training specialists; religious educators; government media personnel; school, school district, and state department of education media program administrators and specialists; educational/training media producers; and numerous others whose professional work requires improvement of media and technology in education and training. AECT members also work in the armed forces, in public libraries, in museums, and in other information agencies of many different kinds, including those related to the emerging fields of computer technology. AECT serves as a central clearinghouse and communications center for its members. The association maintains TechCentral, a national electronic mail network and bulletin board service. Through its various committees and task forces, it compiles data and prepares recommendations to form the basis of guidelines, standards, research and information summaries on numerous topics and problems of interest to the membership. AECT professional staff members report on government activities of concern to the membership and provide current data on laws and pending legislation relating to the educational media/technology field. AECT also maintains the ECT Foundation, through which it offers a limited number of financial grants to further the association's work. Archives (see entry) are also maintained at the University of Iowa. The AECT annual convention features the nation's largest instructional media exposition, INFOCOMM International Exposition, held jointly with the International Communications Industries Association (ICIA). *Membership:* 5,000, plus 9,000 additional subscribers, 9 divisions, 12 national affiliates, 46 state affiliates, Puerto Rico, Guam, and more than 30 national committees and task forces. *Dues:* $50/yr. regular, $20/yr. student and retired. *Publications: TechTrends* ($6/yr. with membership, $30/yr. nonmember); *Report to Members* (newsletter); *Educational Technology Research and Development* (4/yr., $30/yr. member, $20/yr. student and retired, $45/yr. nonmember); various division publications; and a number of books and videotapes, including the following recent titles: *Copyright and Instructional Technologies: A Guide to Fair Use and Permissions Procedures* (second edition 1989); *Doctoral Research in Instructional/Design and Technology: A Directory of Dissertations 1989; Information Power: Guidelines for School Library Media Programs 1988; Information Power Discussion Guide 1988; Masters Curricula in Educational Communications and Technology: A Descriptive Directory* (third edition) 1989; *Mediatoons* 1989; *Safety in the Library Media Program: A Handbook* 1987; *Standards for College and University Learning Resources Programs: Technology in Instruction* (second edition) 1989; *The Information Power Video* (videotape) 1988; *Introduction to HyperCard* (videotape) 1989; *Interactive Learning with HyperCard–Apple MacIntosh Computers* (videotape) 1989; and *Interactive Video Demonstration Tapes–Video Archive Volume 1, 2, 3.*

Because of similarity of interests, the following organizations have chosen to affiliate with the Association for Educational Communications and Technology. (As many as possible have been polled for inclusion in EMTY.)

- Association for Multi-Image (AMI)
- Association for Special Education Technology (ASET)
- Community College Association for Instruction and Technology (CCAIT)
- Consortium of University Film Centers (CUFC)
- Federal Educational Technology Association (FETA)
- Health Science Communications Association (HeSCA)
- International Visual Literacy Association (IVLA)
- Minorities in Media (MIM)

- National Association of Regional Media Centers (NARMC)
- New England Educational Media Association
- Northwest College and University Council for the Management of Educational Technology
- Southeastern Regional Media Leadership Council (SRMLC)
- State University of New York Educational Communications Center

Two additional organizations are also related to the Association for Educational Communications and Technology:

- AECT Archives
- AECT ECT Foundation

Association for Educational Communications and Technology (AECT) Divisions:

(AECT) Division of Educational Media Management (DEMM). 1025 Vermont Ave. NW, Suite 820, Washington, DC 20036. (202) 347-7834. Alan Evans, Pres. Seeks to develop an information exchange network and to share information about common problems, solutions, and program descriptions of educational media management. Develops programs that increase the effectiveness of media managers, initiates and implements a public relations program to educate the public and administrative bodies as to the use, value, and need for educational media management, and fosters programs that will help carry out media management responsibilities effectively. *Membership:* 1,024. *Dues:* One division membership included in the basic AECT membership; additional division memberships are $10/yr. *Publications: Media Management Journal.*

(AECT) Division of Instructional Development (DID). 1025 Vermont Ave. NW, Suite 820, Washington, DC 20036. (202) 347-7834. Ellen Wagner, Pres. DID is composed of individuals from business, government, and academic settings concerned with the systematic design of instruction and the development of solutions to performance problems. Members' interests include the study, evaluation, and refinement of design processes; the creation of new models of instructional development; the invention and improvement of techniques for managing the development of instruction; the development and application of professional ID competencies; the promotion of academic programs for preparation of ID professionals; and the dissemination of research and development work in ID. *Membership:* 765. *Dues:* One division membership included in the basic AECT membership; additional division memberships are $10/yr. *Publications: DID Newsletter* and Occasional Papers; and *Journal of Instructional Development* (published by AECT).

(AECT) Division of Interactive Systems and Computers (DISC). 1025 Vermont Ave. NW, Suite 820, Washington, DC 20036. (202) 347-7834. Carl Stafford, Pres. Concerned with the generation, access, organization, storage, and delivery of all forms of information used in the processes of education and training. The division promotes the networking of its members to facilitate sharing of expertise and interests. *Membership:* 512. *Dues:* One division membership included in the basic AECT membership; additional division memberships are $10/yr. *Publications: Newsletter.*

(AECT) Division of School Media Specialists (DSMS). 1025 Vermont Ave. NW, Suite 820, Washington, DC 20036. (202) 347-7834. Phyllis Joseph, Pres. DSMS promotes communication among school media personnel who share common concerns in the development, implementation, and evaluation of school media programs; and strives to increase learning and improve instruction in the school setting through the utilization of educational media and technology. *Membership:* 860. *Dues:* One division membership included in the basic AECT membership; additional division member-ships are $10/yr. *Publications: Newsletter.*

(AECT) Division of Telecommunications (DOT). 1025 Vermont Ave. NW, Suite 820, Washington, DC 20036. (202) 347-7834. Elaine Harbison, Pres. Seeks to improve education through use of television and radio, video and audio recordings, and auto-tutorial devices and media. Aims to improve the design, production, evaluation, and use of telecommunications materials and equipment; to upgrade competencies of personnel engaged in the field; to investigate and report promising innovative prac-tices and technological developments; to promote studies, experiments, and demon-strations; and to support research in telecommunications. Future plans call for working to establish a national entity representing instructional television. *Member-ship:* 695. *Dues:* One division membership included in the basic AECT membership; additional division memberships are $10/yr. *Publications: Newsletter.*

(AECT) Industrial Training and Education Division (ITED). 1025 Vermont Ave. NW, Suite 820, Washington, DC 20036. (202) 347-7834. Leonard Arychuk, Pres. Seeks to promote the sensitive and sensible use of media and techniques to improve the quality of education and training; to provide a professional program that demonstrates the state-of-the-art of educational technology as a part of the AECT convention; to improve communications to ensure the maximum use of educational techniques and media which can give demonstrable, objective evidence of effectiveness. *Membership:* 250. *Dues:* One division membership included in the basic AECT membership; addi-tional division memberships are $10/yr. *Publications: Newsletter.*

(AECT) International Division (INTL). 1025 Vermont Ave. NW, Suite 820, Wash-ington, DC 20036. (202) 347-7834. Victor Carr, Pres. Seeks to improve international communications concerning existing methods of design; to pretest, use, produce, evaluate, and establish an approach through which these methods may be improved and/or adapted for maximum use and effectiveness; to develop a roster of qualified international leaders with experience and competence in the varied geographic and technical areas; and to encourage research in the application of communication processes to support present and future international social and economic develop-ment. *Membership:* 200. *Dues:* One division membership included in the basic AECT membership; additional division memberships are $10/yr. *Publications: Newsletter.*

(AECT) Media Design and Production Division (MDPD). 1025 Vermont Ave. NW, Suite 820, Washington, DC 20036. (202) 347-7834. Robert Appleman, Pres. Seeks to provide formal organized procedures for promoting and facilitating interaction between commercial and noncommercial, nontheatrical filmmakers, and to provide a communications link for filmmakers with people of similar interests. Also seeks to provide a connecting link between creative and technical professionals of the audio-visual industry. Advances the informational film producer's profession by providing scholarships and apprenticeships to experimenters and students and by providing a forum for discussion of local, national, and universal issues. Recognizes and presents awards for outstanding films produced and for contributions to the state of the art. *Membership:* 300. *Dues:* One division membership included in the basic AECT membership; additional division memberships are $10/yr. *Publications: Newsletter.*

(AECT) Research and Theory Division (RTD). 1025 Vermont Ave. NW, Suite 820, Washington, DC 20036. (202) 347-7834. Gary Anglin, Pres. Seeks to improve the design, execution, utilization, and evaluation of audiovisual communications research; to improve the qualifications and effectiveness of personnel engaged in communications research; to advise the educational practitioner as to use of the results of research; to improve research design, techniques, evaluation, and dissemination; and to promote both applied and theoretical research on the systematic use of all forms of media in the improvement of instruction. *Membership:* 337. *Dues:* One division membership included in the basic AECT membership; additional division memberships are $10/yr. *Publications: Newsletter*.

Association for Educational Communications and Technology (AECT) Affiliate Organizations:

(AECT) Community College Association for Instruction and Technology (CCAIT). College of DuPage, Instructional Design, 22nd St. and Lambert Rd., Glen Ellyn, IL 60137. (312) 858-2800. Joe Barillari, Pres. A national association of community and junior college educators interested in the discovery and dissemination of information about problems and processes of teaching, media, and technology in community and junior colleges. Facilitates member exchange of data, reports, proceedings, personnel, and other resources; sponsors AECT convention sessions and social activities. *Membership:* 200. *Dues:* $10. *Publications: Newsletter* and irregular topical papers.

(AECT) Federal Educational Technology Association (FETA). Grumman Electronics Systems Div., 10 Orville Dr., Bohemia, NY 11716. (516) 563-6850. James R. Stonge, Pres. FETA is dedicated to the improvement of education and training through research, communication, and practice. It encourages and welcomes members from all government agencies, federal, state, and local; from business and industry; and from all educational institutions and organizations. FETA encourages interaction among members to improve the quality of education and training in any arena, but with specific emphasis on government-related applications.

(AECT) International Visual Literacy Association, Inc. (IVLA). Virginia Tech, Education Technologies Div., Learning Resources Center, Blacksburg, VA 24061-0232. (703) 231-8992. Mike Moore, Pres. Provides a multidisciplinary forum for the exploration of modes of visual communication and their application through the concept of visual literacy; promotes development of visual literacy and serves as a bond between the diverse organizations and groups working in that field. *Dues:* $40 regular, $20 student. *Publications: Journal of Visual Literacy*; Readings from Annual Conferences.

(AECT) Minorities in Media (MIM). University of South Alabama, 2206 De Kruif Ct., Mobile, AL 36617-2405. (205) 478-5525. Dr. Joaquin M. Holloway, Jr., Pres. Seeks to encourage the effective use of educational media in the teaching/learning process; provide leadership opportunities in advancing the use of technology as an integral part of the learning process; provide a vehicle through which minorities might influence the use of media in institutions; develop an information exchange network to share information common to minorities in media; study, evaluate, and refine the educational technology process as it relates to the education of minorities; and encourage and improve the production of materials for the education of minorities. *Membership:* 100. *Dues:* $10. *Publications:* Annual newsletter.

(AECT) National Association of Regional Media Centers (NARMC). L. A. County Office of Education, 9300 E. Imperial Highway, Downey, CA 90242-2890. (213) 922-6107. Don Lake, Pres. Seeks to foster the exchange of ideas and information among educational communications specialists responsible for the administration of regional media centers through workshops, seminars, and national meetings. Studies the feasibility of developing joint programs that could increase the effectiveness and efficiency of regional media services. Disseminates information on successful practices and research studies conducted by regional media centers. *Membership:* 268 regional centers, 70 corporations. *Dues:* $45. *Publications: étin* (q. newsletter); and *Annual Report*.

(AECT) Northwest College and University Council for the Management of Educational Technology. Instructional Media Center, Eastern Washington University, Cheney, WA 99004. Bill Odell, Dir. The first regional group representing institutions of higher education in Alberta, Alaska, British Columbia, Idaho, Montana, Oregon, and Washington to receive affiliate status in AECT. Membership is restricted to media managers with campuswide responsibilities for educational technical services, in the membership region. Corresponding membership is available to those who work outside the membership region. An annual conference and business meeting is held the last weekend of October each year, rotating throughout the region. Current issues under consideration include managing the emerging telecommunication technologies, copyright, accreditation, and certification. Organizational goals include identifying the unique status problems of media managers in higher education, and improving the quality of the major publication. *Membership:* Approx. 85. *Dues:* $35. *Publications: NW/MET Bulletin*.

Other AECT-Related Organizations:

(AECT) Archives. University of Iowa, c/o Barry D. Bratton, N. 304 Lindquist Center, Iowa City, IA 52242. (319) 335-5566. A collection of media, projection and reproduction equipment, photographic devices, manuscripts, and related materials representing important developments in visual and audiovisual education and in instructional/educational technology. Maintained by the University of Iowa in cooperation with AECT. Open only to researchers and scholars.

(AECT) ECT Foundation. 1126 16th St. NW, Washington, DC 20036. Robert E. de Kieffer, Chair. The ECT Foundation is a nonprofit organization whose purposes are charitable and educational in nature. Its operation is based on the conviction that improvement of instruction can be accomplished, in part, by the continued investigation and application of new systems for learning, and by periodic assessment of current techniques for the communication of information. In addition to awarding scholarships, internships, and fellowships, the foundation develops and conducts leadership training programs for emerging professional leaders.

Association for Experiential Education (AEE). University of Colorado, Campus Box 249, Boulder, CO 80309. (303) 492-1547. Daniel Garvey, Exec. Dir. AEE believes that the learner and the teacher should use the most powerful and effective means to interact with each other and their environments, and to deal with the tasks at hand. Experience-based education emphasizes direct experience to increase the quality of learning. AEE helps to advance, expand, conceptualize, and formalize this learning process. *Membership:* 1,200. *Dues:* $35-$50 indiv., $125 inst. *Publications: Jobs Clearinghouse* and *The Journal of Experiential Education*.

Association for Library and Information Science Education. c/o Ilse Moon, 5623 Palm Aire Drive, Sarasota, FL 34243. (813) 355-1795. Seeks to advance education for library and information science and produces annual *Library and Information Science Education Statistical Report*. Open to professional schools offering graduate programs in library and information science; personal memberships open to educators employed in such institutions; other memberships available to interested individuals. *Membership:* 650 indiv., 85 inst. *Dues:* inst.: $250 full, $150 assoc., $75 int'l.; personal: $40 full-time, $20 part-time, student, retired. *Publications: Journal of Education for Library and Information Science*; directory; and *Library and Information Science Education Statistical Report*.

Association of American Colleges (AAC). 1818 R St. NW, Washington, DC 20009. (202) 387-3760. Paula P. Brownlee, Pres. AAC, founded in 1915, is the national voice for liberal learning. Through programs, grants, publications, and workshops, AAC strives to enhance liberal education and secure its integration with professional programs and courses of study. Programs include the Project on the Status and Education of Women. *Membership:* 615. *Dues:* Based on FTE. *Publications: Liberal Education; On Campus with Women;* and monographs.

Association of American Publishers (AAP). 220 E. 23rd St., New York, NY 10010. (212) 689-8920. Ambassador Nicholas A. Veliotes, Pres. A group of approximately 250 companies whose members produce the majority of printed materials sold to U.S. schools, colleges, libraries, and bookstores, as well as to homes. Range of member interests is reflected in textbooks; religious, scientific, and media books; instructional systems; software; audio- and videotapes; records, cassettes, slides, transparencies, and tests. Provides its members with information concerning trade conditions, markets, copyrights, manufacturing processes, taxes, duties, postage, freight, censorship movements, government programs and other matters of importance. *Membership:* 250 companies. *Dues:* Vary. *Publications: AAP Monthly Report.*

Association of Audio-Visual Technicians (AAVT). 2378 S. Broadway, Denver, CO 80210. (303) 698-1820. Elsa C. Kaiser, Exec. Dir. Proposes to increase communication and to assist audiovisual technicians in their work; holds seminars in conjunction with most of the major audiovisual shows. Maintains a lending library of programs on audiovisual equipment or production. Also has a lending library of old manuals for rent by AAVT members. *Membership:* 1,200. *Dues:* $35 indiv., $65 inst. *Publications: Fast Forword.*

Association of Independent Video and Filmmakers and the Foundation for Independent Video and Film. 625 Broadway, 9th floor, New York, NY 10012. (212) 473-3400. Lawrence Sapadin, Exec. Dir. The national trade association for independent video and filmmakers, representing their needs and goals to industry, government, and the public. Programs include domestic and foreign festival liaison for independents, screenings and seminars, insurance for members, and groups, and information and referral services. Recent activities include monitoring status of independent work on public television, advocacy for cable access, and lobbying for modifications in copyright law. *Dues:* $45 indiv., $85 inst., $60 libs., $25 students. *Publications: The Independent.*

Association of Systematics Collections. 730 11th St. NW, 2nd floor, Washington, DC 20001. (202) 347-2850. K. Elaine Hoagland, Exec. Dir. Promotes the care, management, and improvement of biological collections, provides information on biological collections and biologists who offer taxonomic services, and publishes current information on government permit regulations regarding the scientific use of plants and animals. *Membership:* 80 inst., scientific societies. *Dues:* After election to membership. *Publications: Biogeography of the Tropical Pacific; Crocodilian, Tuatara, and Turtle Species of the World; Collections of Frozen Tissues, Controlled Wildlife I, II, III; Sources of Federal Funding in the Biological Sciences; Guidelines to the Acquisition and Management of Biological Specimens; ASC Newsletter; The Systematic Community; A Guide to Museum Pest Control; Systematics: Relevance, Resources, Services, and Management* (a bibliography); and *Foundations for a National Biological Survey.*

Association of Teacher Educators (ATE). 1900 Association Dr., Suite ATE, Reston, VA 22091. (703) 620-3110. Robert J. Stevenson, Exec. Dir. Annual conference, usually held in February, and annual summer workshops. *Membership:* 4,000. *Dues:* $50. *Publications: Action in Teacher Education; ATE Newsletter;* and other miscellaneous publications.

Authors' League of America, Inc. 234 W. 44th St., New York, NY 10036. (212) 391-9198. Garson Kanin, Pres. A professional organization of authors of books, magazine materials, and plays. *Membership:* 14,500. *Publications: Dramatists Guild Quarterly;* and *Authors Guild Bulletin.*

Bergwall Productions Inc. 106 Charles Lindbergh Blvd., Uniondale, NY 11553-3695. (800) 645-3565. Charles Bergwall, Pres. The nation's largest producer of audiovisuals for technical/vocational education. Catalog available.

Catholic Library Association. 461 W. Lancaster Ave., Haverford, PA 19041. (215) 649-5250. Natalie A. Logan, Exec. Dir. Seeks to improve libraries in general, and religion-oriented libraries in particular; promotes discriminating taste in literature and other communication media. Encourages compilation, publication, and use of religious reference tools, seeks to attract persons into librarianship through scholarships, fosters research and developments in librarianship and communication, and encourages cooperation with associations interested in the field. Produces continuing education programs on videotape. *Membership:* 3,000. *Dues:* $45-$500. *Publications: CLA Handbook and Membership Directory* (annual); *Catholic Library World* (6/yr.); and *Catholic Periodical and Literature Index* (6/yr.).

Center for Advanced Visual Studies. MIT Building W11, 40 Massachusetts Ave., Cambridge, MA 02139. (617) 253-4415. Otto Piene, Dir. Founded by Gyorgy Kepes in 1968, offers a unique situation in which artists explore and realize art work in collaboration with scientists and engineers. Has done significant work on lasers, holography, video, kinetics, environmental art, and sky art.

Center for Instructional Research and Curriculum Evaluation. 1310 S. 6th St., Champaign, IL 61820. (217) 333-3770. Robert E. Stake, Dir. A unit within the College of Education, University of Illinois, the Center is primarily active in conducting curriculum research in the United States, but has been of considerable interest to program evaluation specialists in foreign countries.

Central Educational Network (CEN). 1400 E. Touhy, Des Plaines, IL 60018. (312) 390-8700. James A. Fellows, Pres. Provides general audience, postsecondary programming, and ITV services. *Membership:* Public television stations and educational agencies.

Children's Film and Television Center of America (CFTCA). USC School of Cinema-Television, 850 W. 34th St., University Park, Los Angeles, CA 90089-2211. (213) 743-8632. Shanta Herzog, Exec. Dir.; Steven J. Weller, Program Coordinator. CFTCA is a nonprofit organization affiliated with the University of Southern California School of Cinema-Television, working with parents, children, teachers, librarians, entertainers, USC students, and film/TV producers and distributors to encourage and support excellence in children's media. CFTCA is the United States' representative in the International Centre of Films for Children and Young People (CIFEJ) in Paris, France. CFTCA activities include the world premieres of major motion pictures for children, programs of educational/ entertaining short films for library screenings in the greater Los Angeles area, basic film-making workshops for children and parents, minifestivals of USC Cinema-TV students' films made for children, special events in conjunction with Disney Educational Media, Reading Is Fundamental (RIF), and many others. CFTCA publishes a quarterly newsletter for parents, educators, and professionals in the field of children's media worldwide that provides reviews of children's films, TV shows, and home videos; updates on CFTCA events; and more. *Dues:* (tax-deductible) $25 indiv., $40 families.

Children's Television International, Inc. 8000 Forbes Pl., Suite 201, Springfield, VA 22151. (703) 321-8455. Ray Gladfelter, Pres.; Karen Shipman, Dir. of Customer Services. An educational organization that develops, produces, and distributes a wide variety of color television programming and television-related materials as a resource to aid children's social, cultural, and intellectual development. Program areas cover language arts, science, social studies, art, and business communications for home, school, and college viewing. *Publications: Teacher's Guides* that accompany instructional TV series.

CINE Information. 215 W. 90th St., New York, NY 10024. (212) 877-3999. Barbara Margolis, Exec. Dir. CINE Information is a nonprofit educational organization established to develop sound methods and tools for the more effective use of film by community groups and educational programmers. It produces and distributes materials about film and videotape use, and produces films on topics of social and cultural importance. Newest releases include Academy Award nominee for Best Documentary feature *Adam Clayton Powell*, which also was broadcast on PBS's "The American Experience" series, and American Film Festival winner *Are We Winning, Mommy? America and the Cold War*. *Mommy* was also featured at the Berlin, Toronto, Chicago, and Park City, Utah film festivals. *Publications: In Focus: A Guide to Using Films*, by Linda Blackaby, Dan Georgakas, and Barbara Margolis, is a complete step-by-step handbook for film and videotape users, with detailed discussions of how to use film and tape in educational, cultural, and fundraising activities.

Clearinghouse on Development Communication. 1815 N. Fort Meyer Dr., 6th floor, Arlington, VA 22209. (703) 527-5546. Michael Laflin, Dir. A center for materials and information on applications of communication technology to development problems. Operated by the Institute for International Research and funded by the Bureau for Science and Technology of the U.S. Agency for International Development. Visitors and written requests for information are welcome. *Dues:* Subscription, $10. *Publications: Development Communication Report* (q.).

Close Up Foundation. 44 Canal Center Plaza, Alexandria, VA 22314. (703) 892-5400; (800) 336-5479. Stephen A. Janger, Pres. An organization dealing with the involvement of citizens in government. Brings participants to Washington for a series of week-long, in-depth looks into the federal government. Produces several series of television programs telecast on the C-SPAN cable network for secondary school and home audiences. Conducts national citizenship competition for high school students. *Membership:* 24,000 participants annually. *Publications: Perspectives*; *Current Issues*; *Economic Choices*; *International Relations*; *The Citizen Bee Guide to American Studies*; and videotapes on current domestic and foreign policy issues.

Computer-Based Education Research Laboratory (CERL). University of Illinois, 252 Engineering Research Laboratory, 103 S. Mathews Ave., Urbana, IL 61801. (217) 333-6210. Dr. Edwin L. Goldwasser, Acting Dir. CERL is a research laboratory dedicated to research on and development of systems for the delivery of cost-effective, interactive, computer-based education. CERL is best known for its PLATO and NovaNET systems used by colleges and universities, businesses and government installations, and by public schools. (PLATO originated at the University of Illinois in 1960, NovaNET in 1986.) Both of these are large-scale, mainframe-based systems with thousands of users, but CERL has also worked on stand-alone and local-area CBE delivery. NovaNET, the newest development, uses a custom-designed low-cost mainframe and satellite communications for continent-wide availability. It is capable of simultaneously serving a mix of students, teachers, educational administrators, and courseware developers numbering several thousands. *Publications:* Department and professional journals. Publications available on request.

The Computer Museum. 300 Congress St., Boston, MA 02210. (617) 426-2800. Dr. Oliver Strimpel, Exec. Dir. The world's only computer museum occupies 55,000 square feet in a renovated historic building on Boston's waterfront. The museum presents the history of the information revolution, from mammoth vacuum tube computers to state-of-the-art technology, through 60 hands-on exhibits, including a giant walk-through computer, displays, films, and animation, recreations of vintage computer installations, and the most extensive collection of computers and robots ever assembled. *Membership:* 2,000. *Dues:* $30 indiv., $45 family. *Publications: The Computer Museum Annual* (annual journal); *The Computer Museum News* (bi-monthly newsletter); *Educational Group Tour Planner*; and *Educational Activities Kit*.

Consortium of College and University Media Centers (formerly Consortium of University Film Centers). 121 Pearson Hall-MRC, Iowa State University, Ames, IA 50011. (515) 294-8022. Don Rieck, Exec. Dir. A professional group of higher education media personnel whose purpose is to improve education and training through the effective use of educational media. Assists educational and training users in business in making films, video, and educational media more accessible. Fosters cooperative planning among university media centers. Gathers and disseminates information on improved procedures and new developments in educational media and media center management. *Membership:* 200. *Dues:* $125/yr. constituents; $25 active; $125 sustaining (commercial); $15 students; $20 assoc. *Publications: The Educational Film/Video Locator; The Leader* (member newsletter); and *16mm Film Maintenance Manual.*

Continuing Library Education Network and Exchange. Round Table of the American Library Association. 50 E. Huron St., Chicago, IL 60611. (312) 280-3213. Elaine Wingate, Pres.; Vee Friesner Carrington, V.P. Seeks to provide access to quality continuing education opportunities for librarians and information scientists and to create an awareness of the need for such education in helping individuals in the field to respond to societal and technological changes. *Membership:* 350. *Dues:* Open to all ALA members; $15 indiv., $50 inst. *Publications: CLENExchange* (q.), available to nonmembers by subscription — $20/yr. U.S. zip code, $25/yr. non-U.S. zip code.

Copyright Clearance Center (CCC). 27 Congress St., Salem, MA 01970. (508) 744-3350. Fax (508) 741-2318. Eamon T. Fennessy, Pres. An organization through which corporations, academic and research libraries, information brokers, government agencies, and other users of copyrighted information may obtain authorizations and pay royalties for photocopying these materials in excess of exemptions contained in the U.S. Copyright Act of 1976. In addition to offering a Transactional Reporting Service, CCC also operates an Annual Authorization Service, which is an annual license program serving photocopy permissions needs of large U.S. corporations. *Membership:* 2,500 users, approx. 8,000 foreign and domestic publishers, 915,000 publications. *Publications: CCC Report* (newsletter, q., $10/yr., $12 foreign); and *COPI: Catalog of Publisher Information* (4/yr., $35/issue, $115/yr.).

Corporation for Public Broadcasting (CPB). 901 E St. NW, Washington, DC 20004. (202) 879-9800. Donald E. Ledwig, Pres. and CEO. A private, nonprofit corporation authorized by the Public Broadcasting Act of 1967 to develop noncommercial television and radio services for the American people, while insulating public broadcasting from political pressure or influence. CPB supports station operations and funds radio and television programs for national distribution. CPB sets national policy that will most effectively make noncommercial radio and television and other telecommunications services available to all citizens. *Publications: CPB Report* (bi-wk., 3 yr. for $25); *Annual Report*; and *CPB Public Broadcasting Directory* ($10 plus $2 postage and handling).

Council for Basic Education. 725 15th St. NW, Washington, DC 20005. (202) 347-4171. A. Graham Down, Exec. Dir. A vocal force advocating a broadly defined curriculum in the liberal arts for all students in elementary and secondary schools. *Membership:* 4,000. *Dues:* $40 members; $25 subscribers. *Publications: Basic Education; Perspective* (q., 2 yr. for $75 members, $45 subscribers); and various reports and books.

Council for Educational Development and Research (CEDaR). 1201 16th St. NW, Suite 305, Washington, DC 20036. (202) 223-1593. Dena G. Stoner, Exec. Dir. Members are educational research and development institutions. Aims to advance the level of programmatic, institutionally based educational research and development and to demonstrate the importance of research and development in improving education. Provides a forum for professional personnel in member institutions. Coordinates national dissemination program. Other activities include research, development, evaluation, dissemination, and technical assistance on educational issues. *Membership:* 14. *Publications: R & D Preview*; and *Directory*.

Council for Exceptional Children (CEC). 1920 Association Dr., Reston, VA 22091. (703) 620-3660. Jeptha Greer, Exec. Dir. A membership organization providing information to teachers, administrators, and others concerned with the education of handicapped and gifted children. Maintains a library and database on literature on special education; prepares books, monographs, digests, films, filmstrips, cassettes, and journals; sponsors annual convention and conferences on special education; provides on-site and regional training on various topics and at varying levels; provides information and assistance to lawmakers on the education of the handicapped and gifted; coordinates Political Action Network on the rights of exceptional persons. *Membership:* 55,000. *Dues:* Professionals, $55-$63, depending on state of residence; students, $24-$24.50, depending on state of residence. *Publications: Exceptional Children*; *Teaching Exceptional Children*; *Exceptional Child Educational Resources*; and numerous other professional publications dealing with the education of handicapped and gifted children.

Council of National Library and Information Associations. St. John's University, Library Room 322, Grand Central & Utopia Parkways, Jamaica, NY 11439. (718) 990-6735. D. Sherman Clarke, Chair. The council is a forum for discussion of many issues of concern to library and information associations. Current committees at work are the Joint Committee on Association Cooperation and the Ad Hoc Committee on Copyright Implementation. *Membership:* 21 associations. *Dues:* Inquire.

Council on International Educational Exchange (CIEE). 205 E. 42nd St., New York, NY 10017. (212) 661-1414. Founded in 1947, CIEE is a private, nonprofit membership organization, incorporated in the United States, with international offices, affiliations, and representations. Council develops, facilitates, and administers international exchange programs throughout the world. Through its subsidiary companies, CIEE provides a wide range of services to facilitate youth travel. *Publications include: Student Travel Catalog*; *Work, Study, Travel Abroad: The Whole World Handbook*; and *Volunteer! The Comprehensive Guide to Voluntary Service in the U.S. and Abroad*.

Council on International Non-theatrical Events. 1001 Connecticut Ave. NW, Suite 1016, Washington, DC 20036. (202) 785-1136. Fax (202) 785-4114. Richard Calkins, Exec. Dir. Coordinates the selection and placement of U.S. documentary, television, short subject, and didactic films in more than 200 overseas film festivals annually. A Golden Eagle Certificate is awarded to each professional film considered most suitable to represent the United States in international competition. A CINE Eagle Certificate is awarded to winning adult amateur, youth, and university student-made films. Prizes and certificates won at overseas festivals are presented by embassy representatives at an annual awards luncheon. Deadlines for receipt of entry forms are 1 February and 1 August. *Publications: CINE Yearbook* and *Annual International U.S. Film Festival Directory*.

Education Development Center, Inc., 55 Chapel St., Newton, MA 02160. (617) 969-7100. Janet Whitla, Pres. Seeks to improve education at all levels, in the United States and abroad, through curriculum development, institutional development, and services to schools and the community. Produces filmstrips and videocassettes, primarily in connection with curriculum development and teacher training. *Publications: Annual Report* and occasional papers.

Environmental Quality Instructional Resources Center. Ohio State University, 1200 Chambers Rd., Room 310, Columbus, OH 43212. (614) 292-6717. Robert W. Howe, Dir. Emphasizes water quality education and training. Maintains IRIS (Instructional Resources Information System), an audiovisual library, and makes publications and audiovisual aids available. Publication lists and audiovisual lists are available. *Publications: EQ-IRC Bulletin; IRIS supplements*; and various monographs.

EPIE Institute (Educational Products Information Exchange). Box 839, Water Mill, NY 11976. (516) 283-4922. P. Kenneth Komoski, Exec. Dir. Involved primarily in assessing educational materials and providing product descriptions/citations of virtually all educational software. All of EPIE's services, including its Curriculum Alignment Services for Educators, are available to schools and state agencies, as well as individuals. *Publications: Parents Guide to Educational Software; The Educational Software Selector (T.E.S.S.);* and the *EPIE Report on Integrated Instructional Systems.*

ERIC (Educational Resources Information Center). U.S. Department of Education/ OERI. 555 New Jersey Ave. NW, Washington, DC 20208-5720. Robert Stonehill, Dir. ERIC is a nationwide information network that provides access to the English-language education literature. The ERIC system consists of 16 clearinghouses, a small number of adjunct clearinghouses, and system support components that include the ERIC Processing and Reference Facility, ACCESS ERIC, and the ERIC Document Reproduction Service (EDRS). ERIC actively solicits papers, conference proceedings, literature reviews, and curriculum materials from researchers, practitioners, educational associations and institutions, and federal, state, and local agencies. These materials, along with articles from nearly 800 different journals, are indexed and abstracted for entry into the ERIC database. The ERIC database—the largest education database in the world—now contains more than 700,000 records of documents and journal articles. Users can access the ERIC database online, on CD-ROM, or through print and microfiche indexes. ERIC microfiche collections—which contain the full text of most ERIC documents—are available for public use at nearly 900 locations worldwide. Reprints of ERIC documents, on microfiche or in paper copy, can also be ordered from EDRS. A list of the ERIC Clearinghouses, together with full addresses, telephone numbers, and brief scope notes describing the areas they cover, is provided below. *Dues:* None. *Publications: Resources in Education* and *Current Index to Journals in Education.*

ERIC Clearinghouse on Adult, Career, and Vocational Education (CE). Ohio State University, Center on Education and Training for Employment, 1900 Kenny Rd., Columbus, OH 43210-1090. (614) 292-4353; (800) 848-4815. All levels and settings of adult and continuing, career, and vocational/technical education. Adult education, from basic literacy training through professional skill upgrading. Career education, including career awareness, career decisionmaking, career development, career change, and experience-based education. Vocational and technical education, including new subprofessional fields, industrial arts, corrections education, employment and training programs, youth employment, work experience programs, education/ business partnerships, entrepreneurship, adult retraining, vocational rehabilitation for the handicapped, and workplace literacy.

ERIC Clearinghouse on Counseling and Personnel Services (CG). University of Michigan, School of Education, Room 2108, 610 E. University St., Ann Arbor, MI 48109-1259. (313) 764-9492. Preparation, practice, and supervision of counselors at all educational levels and in all settings; theoretical development of counseling and guidance; personnel procedures such as testing and interviewing and the analysis and dissemination of the resultant information; group work and case work; nature of pupil, student, and adult characteristics; personnel workers and their relation to career planning, family consultations, and student orientation activities.

ERIC Clearinghouse on Educational Management (EA). University of Oregon, 1787 Agate St., Eugene, OR 97403-5207. (346) 686-5043. The leadership, management, and structure of public and private educational organizations; practice and theory of administration; preservice and inservice preparation of administrators; tasks and processes of administration; methods and varieties of organization and organizational change; and the social context of educational organizations. Sites, buildings, and equipment for education; planning, financing, constructing, renovating, equipping, maintaining, operating, insuring, utilizing, and evaluating educational facilities.

ERIC Clearinghouse on Elementary and Early Childhood Education (PS). University of Illinois, College of Education, 805 W. Pennsylvania Ave., Urbana, IL 61801-4897. (217) 333-1386. The physical, cognitive, social, educational, and cultural development of children from birth through early adolescence; prenatal factors; parental behavior factors; learning theory research and practice related to the development of young children, including the preparation of teachers for this educational level; educational programs and community services for children; and theoretical and philosophical issues pertaining to children's development and education.

ERIC Clearinghouse on Handicapped and Gifted Children (EC). Council for Exceptional Children, 1920 Association Dr., Reston, VA 22091-1589. (703) 620-3660. All aspects of the education and development of the handicapped and gifted, including prevention, identification and assessment, intervention, and enrichment, both in special and in integrated settings.

ERIC Clearinghouse on Higher Education (HE). George Washington University, One Dupont Circle NW, Suite 630, Washington, DC 20036-1183. (202) 296-2597. Topics relating to college and university conditions, problems, programs, and students. Curricular and instructional programs, and institutional research at the college or university level. Federal programs, professional education (medicine, law, etc.), professional continuing education, collegiate computer-assisted learning and management, graduate education, university extension programs, teaching-learning, legal issues and legislation, planning, governance, finance, evaluation, inter-institutional arrangements, management of institutions of higher education, and business or industry educational programs leading to a degree.

ERIC Clearinghouse on Information Resources (IR). Syracuse University, Huntington Hall, Room 030, Syracuse, NY 13244-2340. (315) 443-3640. Educational technology and library and information science at all levels. Instructional design, development, and evaluation are the emphases within educational technology, along with the media of educational communication: computers and microcomputers, telecommunications (cable, broadcast, satellite), audio and video recordings, film and other audiovisual materials, as they pertain to teaching and learning. Within library and information science, the focus is on the operation and management of information services for education-related organizations. All aspects of information technology related to education are considered within the scope.

ERIC Clearinghouse for Junior Colleges (JC). University of California at Los Angeles (UCLA), Mathematical Sciences Building, Room 8118, 405 Hilgard Ave., Los Angeles, CA 90024-1564. (213) 825-3931. Development, administration, and evaluation of two-year public and private community and junior colleges, technical institutes, and two-year branch university campuses. Two-year college students, faculty, staff, curricula, programs, support services, libraries, and community services. Linkages between two-year colleges and business/industrial organizations. Articulation of two-year colleges with secondary and four-year postsecondary institutions.

ERIC Clearinghouse on Languages and Linguistics (FL). Center for Applied Linguistics, 1118 22nd St. NW, Washington, DC 20037-0037. (202) 429-9551. Languages and language sciences; theoretical and applied linguistics; all areas of foreign language, second language, and linguistics instruction, pedagogy, or methodology; psycho-linguistics and the psychology of language learning; cultural and intercultural context of languages; application of linguistics in language teaching; bilingualism and bilingual education; socio-linguistics; study abroad and international exchanges; teacher training and qualifications specific to the teaching of foreign languages and second languages; commonly and uncommonly taught languages, including English as a second language; related curriculum developments and problems.

ERIC Clearinghouse on Reading and Communication Skills (CS). Indiana University, Smith Research Center, 2805 E. 10th St., Suite 150, Bloomington, IN 47408-2698. (812) 855-5847. Reading, English, and communication skills (verbal and nonverbal), preschool through college, and adults working with their children. Includes family literacy. Research and instructional development in reading, writing, speaking, and listening; identification, diagnosis, and remediation of reading problems; speech communication (including forensics), mass communication, inter-personal and small group interaction, interpretation, rhetorical and communication theory, and theater and drama. Preparation of instructional staff and related personnel in these areas. Includes all aspects of reading behavior, with emphasis on physiology, psychology, and sociology; instructional materials, curricula, tests/measurements, and methodology; and the role of libraries and other agencies in fostering and guiding reading. To obtain a list of most recent publications, write to ERIC/RCS at address above.

ERIC Clearinghouse on Rural Education and Small Schools (RC). Appalachia Educational Laboratory, 1031 Quarrier St., P.O. Box 1348, Charleston, WV 25325-1348. (800) 624-9120. Economic, cultural, social, or other factors related to educational programs and practices for rural residents; Native Americans/Alaska Natives, Mexican Americans, and migrants; educational practices and programs in all small schools; outdoor education.

ERIC Clearinghouse for Science, Mathematics, and Environmental Education (SE). Ohio State University, 1200 Chambers Rd., Room 310, Columbus, OH 43212-1792. (614) 292-6717. Science, mathematics, environmental, and engineering education at all levels, and within these four broad subject areas, the following topics: development of curriculum and instructional materials; teachers and teacher education; learning theory/outcomes (including the impact of parameters such as interest level, intelligence, values, and concept development upon learning in these fields); educational programs; research and evaluative studies; media applications; computer applications.

ERIC Clearinghouse for Social Studies/Social Science Education (ERIC/ChESS). Indiana University, Social Studies Development Center, Suite 120, 2805 E. Tenth St., Bloomington, IN 47405-2373. (812) 855-3838. All levels of social studies/social science education; contents and contributions of the social science disciplines (anthropology, economics, geography, civics, sociology, social psychology, political science) and selected humanities disciplines (history, art, music); education as a social science; comparative education (K-12); content and curriculum materials on social topics such as law-related education, ethnic studies, bias and discrimination, aging, adoption, women's equity, and sex education.

ERIC Clearinghouse on Teacher Education (SP). American Association of Colleges for Teacher Education, One Dupont Circle NW, Suite 610, Washington, DC 20036-2412. (202) 293-2450. School personnel at all levels; teacher selection and training, preservice and inservice preparation, and retirement; the theory, philosophy, and practice of teaching; curricula and general education not specifically covered by other ERIC clearinghouses; all aspects of physical, health, recreation and dance education.

ERIC Clearinghouse on Tests, Measurement, and Evaluation (TM). American Institutes for Research (AIR), Washington Research Center, 3333 K St. NW, Washington, DC 20007-3893. (202) 342-5060. Tests and other measurement devices; methodology of measurement and evaluation; application of tests, measurement, or evaluation in educational projects or programs; research design and methodology in the area of testing and measurement/evaluation; learning theory in general.

ERIC Clearinghouse on Urban Education (UD). Teachers College, Columbia University, Institute for Urban and Minority Education, Main Hall, Room 303, Box 40, 525 W. 120th St., New York, NY 10027-9998. (212) 678-3433. Programs and practices in public, parochial, and private schools in urban areas and the education of particular children and youth of the various racial and ethnic groups in various settings—local, national, and international; the theory and practice of educational equity; urban and minority experiences; and urban and minority social institutions and services.

ERIC Document Reproduction Service (EDRS). Computer Microfilm Corporation, 3900 Wheeler Ave., Alexandria, VA 22304-6409. (703) 823-0500 in VA; (800) 227-ERIC (3742). Fax (703) 823-0505. Operates the document delivery arm of the ERIC system. Furnishes microfiche and/or paper copies of most ERIC documents. Address purchase orders to the above address. Fax order and delivery service available.

ERIC Processing and Reference Facility. ARC Professional Services Group, Information Systems Division, 2440 Research Blvd., Suite 400, Rockville, MD 20850-3238. (301) 258-5500. Ted Brandhorst, Dir. A centralized information processing facility serving all components of the ERIC network, under policy direction of central ERIC. Services provided include: acquisitions, editing, receiving and dispatch, document control and analysis, lexicography, computer processing, file maintenance, database management, and others. Receives and edits abstracts from 16 ERIC clearinghouses for publication in *Resources in Education* (*RIE*), updates and maintains the *ERIC Thesaurus*. Publications: *Resources in Education*; *ERIC Thesaurus*; *Source Directory*; *Report Number Index*; *Clearinghouse Number/ED Number Cross Reference Listing*; *Title Index*; *ERIC Processing Manual*; and numerous other listings and indexes.

Far West Laboratory for Educational Research and Development (FWL). 1855 Folsom St., San Francisco, CA 94103. (415) 565-3000. Dr. Dean Nafziger, Exec. Dir. Far West Laboratory for Educational Research and Development serves the four-state region of Arizona, California, Nevada, and Utah, working with educators at all levels to plan and carry out school improvements. The mission of FWL is to challenge and enable educational organizations and their communities to create and sustain improved learning and development opportunities for their children, youth, and adults. To accomplish its mission, FWL directs resources toward advancing knowledge; developing products and programs for teachers and learners; providing assistance to educational agencies; communicating with outside audiences to remain informed and to inform others about the results of research, development, and exemplary practice; and creating an environment where diverse educational and societal issues can be addressed and resolved. Far West Laboratory maintains a reference library with a complete ERIC microfiche collection and conducts information searches. *Publications:* Books, newsletters; handbooks, guides; research syntheses; reports; and training materials. *See also* Council for Educational Development and Research (CEDaR).

Federal Communications Commission (FCC). 1919 M St. NW, Washington, DC 20554. (202) 632-7000. Patti Grace Smith, Chief, Consumer Assistance and Small Business Div. An agency that regulates radio, television, telephone, and telegraph operations within the United States. Allocates frequencies and channels for different types of communications activities, issues amateur and commercial operators' licenses, and regulates rates of interstate communication services of many different kinds. *Publications:* Bulletins pertaining to educational broadcasting and general information about FCC regulated services.

Film Advisory Board (FAB). 1727-½ Sycamore, Hollywood, CA 90028. (213) 874-3644. Elayne Blythe, Pres. Previews and evaluates films and film-type presentations in all formats, makes recommendations for improved family entertainment fare, and presents awards of excellence to outstanding motion pictures and TV programs and for innovations in these industries. Technical awards are also presented, and awards for outstanding contributions to the entertainment industry and for the most promising newcomers. Awards of excellence are presented for videocassettes; the FAB Winner Seal is featured worldwide on many of the family and child videocassettes for Prisms, Vestron's Children's Video Library, and others. Supplies film list to many national organizations encouraging them to support FAB award-winning products. *Membership:* 450. *Dues:* $40/yr. *Publications:* Monthly film list distributed to studios, libraries, churches, PR firms, youth groups, PTAs, clubs, and colleges. Now rating home videos with FAB rating system.

Film Arts Foundation (FAF). 346 9th St., 2nd floor, San Francisco, CA 94103. (415) 552-8760. Gail Silva, Dir. Service organization designed to support and promote independent film and video production. Services include low-cost 16mm editing facility, skills file, festivals file, resource library, group legal plan, seminars, workshops, annual film and video festival, grants program, monthly publication, work-in-progress screenings, proposal and distribution consultation, nonprofit sponsorship of selected film and video projects, and advocacy for independent film and video. *Membership:* 1,600. *Dues:* $35. *Publications: Release Print.*

Film/Video Arts, Inc. 817 Broadway, New York, NY 10003. (212) 673-9361. Film/Video Arts is dedicated to the advancement of emerging and established media artists of diverse backgrounds. F/VA provides support services that include low-cost production equipment and facilities; education and training; exhibition, grant, and employment opportunities. F/VA offers scholarship assistance to women, African-Americans, Hispanics, Asians, and Native Americans, and administers the Film Bureau which provides film rental and speaker subsidies to New York State nonprofit community organizations. *Dues:* $35 indiv., $50 nonprofit organizations (Oct. 1 - Sept. 30).

Films Incorporated. 817 Broadway, New York, NY 10003. (212) 673-9361. Films Inc. sells videos, laserdiscs, and film documentaries and instructional programs on subjects including foreign language, social science, science, health and guidance, fine and performing arts, and humanities.

Freedom of Information Center (FOI). 20 Walter William Hall, University of Missouri, Columbia, MO 65211. (314) 882-4856. Kathleen Edwards, Center Mgr. Collects and indexes material on action by government, media, and society affecting the flow of information at international, national, state, and local levels. The center answers questions on the federal FOI Act, censorship issues, access to government at all levels, privacy, ethics, bar-press guidelines, and First Amendment issues. *Publications:* Back issues of FOI publications available for purchase.

Government Printing Office (US GPO). N. Capitol and H Sts. NW, Washington, DC 20401. (202) 783-3238. The GPO provides printing and binding services to Congress and the agencies of the federal government and distributes government publications through its Superintendent of Documents sales and depository library programs.

Great Plains National ITV Library (GPN). Box 80669, Lincoln, NE 68501. (402) 472-2007; (800) 228-4630. Lee Rockwell, Dir. Distributor of instructional television courses and videos produced by organizations across the country. Offers more than 100 videotapes (videocassette) courses and related teacher utilization materials. Users may lease or purchase. Also distributes instructional videodiscs. *Publications:* Quarterly newsletter; annual catalog; and occasional flyers and brochures.

Health Sciences Communications Association (HeSCA). 6105 Lindell Blvd., St. Louis, MO 63122. (314) 725-4722. Lionelle Elsesser, Exec. Dir. Draws together people with a wide variety of knowledge, professions, and experience in work toward the common goal of improved instructional design in all areas of the health sciences communications. Recognizes excellence in biocommunications through its media festivals and awards programs. *Membership:* 700. *Dues:* $100 indiv., $145 inst. (1st yr.), $1,000 sustaining, $35 students (without journal), $40 retired members. For additional categories, contact association office. *Publications: Patient Education Sourcebook; Feedback* (newsletter); *Journal of Biocommunications*; and directory of accredited institutions with programs in biomedical communications.

Hollywood Film Archive. 8344 Melrose Ave., Hollywood, CA 90069. (213) 933-3345. D. Richard Baer, Dir. Archival organization for information about feature films produced worldwide, from the early silents to the present. Offers comprehensive movie reference works for sale, including *Variety Film Reviews* (1907-1989), as well as copyright records. *Publications:* Reference books.

HOPE Reports. 1600 Lyell Ave., Rochester, NY 14606. (716) 458-4250. Thomas W. Hope, Pres. and Chair. Provides reports for the audiovisual/video communication field covering statistical and financial status, sales, salaries, trends, and predictions. Also provides calendar scheduling service of national/international events. Makes private surveys and has consulting service.

Institute for Development of Educational Activities, Inc. (IDEA). 259 Regency Ridge, Dayton, OH 45459. (513) 434-6969. Fax (513) 434-5203. Action-oriented research and development organization, originating from the Charles F. Kettering Foundation, established to assist the educational community in bridging the gap that separates research and innovation from actual practice in the schools. Goal is to design and test new responses to problems in education and to create arrangements for their extensive application. Main activities include developing new and improved processes, systems, and materials and providing information and services that facilitate use of improved methods and materials. Sponsors seminars.

Institute for Research on Teaching. College of Education, Michigan State University, East Lansing, MI 48824. (517) 353-6413. Penelope Peterson and Jere Brophy, Co-Dirs. Funded primarily by the U.S. Department of Education and Michigan State University; conducts research on the continuing problems of practice encountered by teaching professionals, the teaching of subject matter disciplines in elementary schools (through the Center for the Learning and Teaching of Elementary Subjects), and publishes numerous materials detailing this research. *Publications: Research Series*; occasional papers; newsletter; Elementary Subjects Center research series; and annual catalog.

Institute for the Future (IFTF). 2740 Sand Hill Rd., Menlo Park, CA 94025. (415) 854-6322. Roy Amara, Pres. Works with organizations to plan their long-term futures. Helps them to evaluate the external environment and take advantage of the opportunities offered by new technologies. Founded in 1968, IFTF has emerged as a leader in action-oriented research for business, industry, and governments, having worked with more than 300 organizations. Typical projects include environmental scanning, strategic planning assistance, policy analyses, and market outlooks for new products and next-generation technologies. The success of the organization is based on several unique strengths including a pragmatic futures orientation, studies of emerging technologies, networking of ideas and people, use of scenarios to identify and analyze issues and options, and tailoring projects to meet client needs. *Publications:* List available free of charge.

Institute of Culture and Communication. East-West Center, 1777 East-West Road, Honolulu, HI 96848. (808) 944-7666. Dr. Tu Weiming, Dir. A program of the East-West Center, which was established by the U.S. Congress "to promote better relations and understanding among the nations of Asia, the Pacific and the United States through cooperative study, training and research." Institute staff study the effect of modernization and rapid economic development on cultures and social values and investigate how communication processes affect cultural and economic change.

Institute of International Education. 809 United Nations Plaza, New York, NY 10017. (212) 883-8200. Richard Krasno, Pres. A private, nonprofit organization administering public and private grants to enable U.S. students to study abroad and foreign students to study at universities in this country. *Membership:* 650 U.S. universities. *Publications: Academic Year Abroad; Vacation Study Abroad; Open Doors: Report on International Educational Exchange; English Language and Orientation Programs in the United States;* and numerous publications and directories for foreign nationals interested in study in the United States and for U.S. nationals interested in studying abroad.

International Association of Business Communicators (IABC). One Hallidie Plaza, Suite 600, San Francisco, CA 94102. (415) 433-3400. Fax (415) 362-8762. Norman G. Leaper, Pres. IABC is the worldwide association for the communication and public relations profession. It is founded on the principle that the better an organization communicates with all its audiences, the more successful and effective it will be in meeting its objectives. IABC is dedicated to fostering communication excellence, contributing more effectively to organizations' goals worldwide, and being a model of communication effectiveness. *Membership:* Over 11,000. *Dues:* $180 in addition to local and regional dues. *Publications: Communication World.*

International Association of Magnetic and Optical Media Manufacturers and Related Industries (formerly ITA). 505 Eighth Ave., New York, NY 10018. (212) 643-0620. Henry Brief, Exec. V.P. ITA's primary goals include the collection and dissemination of research and information; operation of forums and seminars to encourage interaction and understanding of issues and trends; fostering the development of technical standardization relating to marketing and maintenance of product quality; and identification, monitoring, and response to public policies which impact the magnetic and optical media and related industries. *Membership:* 450+ companies worldwide. *Dues:* Based upon annual gross dollar volume in the audio/video/data area. *Publications: ITA Membership Newsletter: Seminar Proceedings;* and *ITA Source Directory.*

International Association of School Librarianship (IASL). Box 1486, Kalamazoo, MI 49005. (616) 343-5728. Jean E. Lowrie, Exec. Secy. Seeks to encourage development of school libraries and library programs throughout the world, to promote professional preparation of school librarians and continuing education programs, to achieve collaboration among school libraries of the world, and to facilitate loans and exchanges in the field. *Membership:* More than 900. *Dues:* $20 indiv. and inst., based on membership for associations. *Publications: IASL Newsletter; Annual Proceedings; Persons to Contact; Indicators of Quality for School Library Media Programs;* and occasional papers.

International Center of Photography (ICP). 1130 5th Ave., New York, NY 10128. (212) 860-1777; and ICP Midtown (Branch Gallery), 1131 Avenue of the Americas, New York, NY 10036, (212) 768-4680. Cornell Capa, Dir. A comprehensive photographic institution whose exhibitions, publications, collections, and educational programs embrace all aspects of photography from aesthetics to technique; from the eighteenth century to the present; from master photographers to newly emerging talents; from photojournalism to the avant-garde. Changing exhibitions, lectures, seminars and workshops, a museum shop, and a screening room make ICP a complete photographic resource. *Membership:* 6,000. *Dues:* $40 general membership, $100 supporting, $250 photography circle, $500 silver card,

$1,000 gold card; corporate memberships available. *Publications: Library of Photography* and *Encyclopedia of Photography—Master Photographs from PFA Collection.*

International Communication Association. Box 9589, Austin, TX 78766. (512) 454-8299. Fax (512) 454-4221. Robert L. Cox, Exec. Dir. Established to study human communication and to seek better understanding of the process of communication. Engages in systematic studies of communication theories, processes, and skills, and disseminates information. *Membership:* 2,200. *Dues:* $40-$1,450. *Publications: Human Communication Research; A Guide to Publishing in Scholarly Communication Journals; Communication Theory* (q.); and *Communication Yearbook.*

International Communications Industries Association (ICIA). 3150 Spring St., Fairfax, VA 22031. (703) 273-7200. Kenton Pattie, Exec. V.P. An international association of media hardware and software producers and manufacturers, dealers, representatives, and others involved with educational, communications, and information activities, services, and products. Maintains close liaison with Congress in matters pertaining to small business media legislation. Annual convention and exhibit (INFOCOMM International Exposition) each winter bringing together over 10,000 manufacturers, dealers, producers, and equipment users with over 90,000 square feet of communications products. *Publications: Equipment Directory of Audio-Visual, Computer and Video Products; Communications Industries Report;* and various market research studies in the video industry.

International Copyright Information Center (INCINC). c/o Association of American Publishers, 1718 Connecticut Ave. NW, 7th floor, Washington, DC 20009. (202) 232-3335. Carol A. Risher, Dir. Assists developing nations in their efforts to translate and/or reprint copyrighted works published in the United States.

International Film and TV Festival of New York. 780 King St., Chappaqua, NY 10514. (914) 238-4481. Gerald M. Goldberg, Pres. An annual competitive festival for industrial and educational film and video productions, filmstrips and slide programs, multiimage and multimedia presentations, and TV programs. Entry fees begin at $100. First entry deadline is August 1.

International Friendship League (IFL). P.O. Box 127, Boston, MA 02133. Erik M. Eames, Pres. Organized in 1948 in 129 countries, the IFL aims to promote a better understanding of the world among young people through regular exchanges of personal letters. The largest percentage of mail matched is with secondary school students, although students of college age as well as adults participate. Send envelope for complete details or name, address, age, and interests with membership fee and self-addressed stamped envelope for faster service. *Membership:* 1,256,390. *Dues:* $5 (to 18 yrs.), $10 (18 yrs. and older).

International Graphic Arts Education Association (IGAEA). 4615 Forbes Ave., Pittsburgh, PA 15213. (412) 682-5170. Virgil Pufahl, Pres. (The president's address is Department of Communication, University of Wisconsin, Platteville, WI 53818.) An organization of professionals in graphic arts education and industry, dedicated to promoting effective research and disseminating information concerning graphic arts, graphic communications, and related fields of printing. *Dues:* $15 regular, outside North America, add $2. *Publications: Visual Communications Journal* and *Research and Resource Reports.*

International Information Management Congress (IMC). 345 Woodcliff Dr., Fairport, NY 14450. (716) 383-8330. George D. Hoffman, Exec. Dir. An educational association supporting education in the information management field, exchange of information, and publications. Organizes yearly conferences and exhibits in different parts of the world. *Membership:* 30 associations, 100 sustaining company members. *Dues:* $90 affiliates; $200 assoc.; varies for sustaining members. *Publications: IMC Journal* (bi-mo.).

International Museum of Photography at George Eastman House. 900 East Ave., Rochester, NY 14607. (716) 271-3361. James L. Enyeart, Dir. World-renowned museum of photographic and cinematographic history established to preserve, collect, and exhibit photography, technology, and film materials and to understand and appreciate photographic art and imaging science. Services include archives, traveling exhibitions, library, regional center for the conservation of photographic materials, and photographic print service. Educational programs, films, symposia, and internship stipends offered. *Dues:* $35 libraries; $45 families; $35 indiv.; $25 student or senior citizen; $75 Contributor; $125 Sustainer; $250 Patron; $500 Benefactor. *Publications: IMAGE; Microfiche Index to Collections;* and *Newsletter.*

International Reading Association (IRA). 800 Barksdale Rd., Box 8139, Newark, DE 19714-8139. (302) 731-1600. Robert G. Jones, Acting Exec. Dir. Seeks to improve the quality of reading instruction at all levels, to develop awareness of the impact of reading, to sponsor conferences and meetings planned to implement the association's purposes, and to promote the development of reading proficiency commensurate with each individual's unique capacity. *Membership:* 95,000. *Dues:* $19 and up. *Publications: Reading Research Quarterly; Journal of Reading; The Reading Teacher;* and *Lectura y Vida.*

International Society for Technology in Education (ISTE) (formerly International Council for Computers in Education—ICCE). University of Oregon, 1787 Agate St., Eugene, OR 97403-9905. (503) 346-4414. David Moursand, CEO. *Membership:* 13,000. *Dues:* $36 U.S., $43 outside U.S. *Publications:* Publishes guides to the instructional use of computers in instruction at pre-college level and in teacher training. These guides include *The Computing Teacher: 1989-1990 Educational Software Preview Guide; The Computer Coordinator; Guide for Microcomputer-Based Instructional Packages; Introduction to Computers in Education for Elementary/Middle School Teachers; AppleWorks for Educators, a Beginning and Intermediate Workbook; Introduction to Programming in LOGO Using Logowriter;* and *Microsoft Works for Educators 2.0.*

International Telecommunications Satellite Organization (INTELSAT). 3400 International Dr. NW, Washington, DC 20008. (202) 944-6800. Public Relations 944-7500. Dean Burch, Dir. Gen. Dedicated to the design, development, construction, establishment, operation, and maintenance of the global, international telecommunications satellite system which currently provides two-thirds of the world's international overseas telecommunications links and virtually all live international television services. *Membership:* 119 countries.

International Teleconferencing Association (ITCA). 1150 Connecticut Ave. NW, Suite 1050, Washington, DC 20036. (202) 833-2549. Thomas C. Gibson, Exec. Dir. Seeks to provide a clearinghouse for the exchange of information among users, researchers, and providers in the field of teleconferencing. *Membership:* 800 + . *Dues:* $500 organizational; $100 individual; $250 small business; $1,000 sustaining; $2,000 Gold Sustaining; $30 student. *Publications: ITCA Insider Newsletter* (mo.).

International Television Association (ITVA). 6311 N. O'Connor Rd., Suite 230, LB 51. Irving, TX 75039. (214) 869-1112. Fred M. Wehrli, Exec. Dir. ITVA is the only organization dedicated to serving the needs of the professional video communicator in non-broadcast settings. It has more than 100 chapters in North America and there are 3,000 international affiliate members in 14 countries around the world. *Membership:* 9,000. *Dues:* $125/yr. indiv. *Publications: International Television News (ITN).*

Lawrence Hall of Science. University of California, Berkeley, CA 94720. (415) 642-3167. Linda Lipner, Dir. A center for research and public education. Its Math Education Project introduces visitors and teachers to computers through classes, workshops, exhibits, and the publication of software packages. *Publications: Teaching Basic Bit by Bit; Creative Play; What's in Your Lunch?;* and *Micros for Micros: Estimation, Numbers, Words, Music.*

Library of Congress. James Madison Bldg., 101 Independence Ave. SE, Washington, DC 20540. As the research arm of Congress and the national library, the library provides materials on interlibrary loan and prepares traveling exhibits of photographs. Cataloging data are available in card, book, and machine-readable formats. The American Folklife Center provides for the preservation and dissemination of folklife through research, performances, exhibits, publications, and recordings. The Copyright Office catalogs copyright entries. Many other divisions are of interest to media specialists. *Publications:* Listed in *Library of Congress Publications in Print*.

Lister Hill National Center for Biomedical Communications of the National Library of Medicine. Bldg. 38A, 8600 Rockville Pike, Bethesda, MD 20894. (301) 496-4441. Daniel R. Masys, M.D., Dir. The center conducts research and development programs in three major categories: computer and information science as applied to the problems of medical libraries, of biomedical research, and health care delivery; biomedical image engineering, including image acquisition, processing, storage retrieval, and communications; and use of new technologies for health professions education. It carries on research in the use of computer-assisted videodisc technology and has a Learning Center for Interactive Technology which demonstrates new applications for health sciences education.

Magazine Publishers of America (MPA). 575 Lexington Ave., Suite 540, New York, NY 10022. (212) 752-0055. Donald D. Kummerfeld, Pres. MPA is the trade association of the consumer magazine industry. MPA promotes the greater and more effective use of magazine advertising, with ad campaigns in the trade press and in MPA member magazines, presentations to advertisers and their ad agencies, and magazine days in cities around the United States. MPA runs educational seminars, conducts surveys of its members on a variety of topics, represents the magazine industry in Washington, DC, maintains an extensive library on magazine publishing, and carries on other activities. *Membership:* 230 publishers representing over 1,200 magazines. *Publications: Newsletter of Research*; *Newsletter of International Publishing*; and *Magazine*.

Medical Library Association (MLA). 6 N. Michigan Ave., Suite 300, Chicago, IL 60602. (312) 419-9094. Lucretia W. McClure, Pres.; Raymond A. Palmer, Exec. Dir. A group of professionals in the health sciences library field dedicated to fostering medical and allied scientific libraries, promoting educational and professional growth of health sciences librarians, and exchanging medical literature among members. *Membership:* 5,000. *Dues:* $95 indiv., $315 sustaining. *Publications: MLA News*; *Bulletin of the Medical Library Association*; and monographs.

Minnesota Educational Computing Corporation (MECC). 3490 Lexington Ave. North, St. Paul, MN 55126-8097. (612) 481-3500. Dale LaFrenz, Pres. Since its inception in 1973, MECC has remained committed to serving education by listening and responding to the diverse and changing needs of students and educators. MECC promotes effective learning by developing high-quality, curriculum-based software in all major subject areas and by making it affordable through a variety of purchase plans. Approximately one-third of the nation's school districts have joined MECC through Direct License memberships, permitting them to duplicate MECC software products on site. MECC products are also available through authorized dealers nationwide or can be ordered directly from the MECC catalog. In addition to software products, MECC offers instructional management, emerging technology products, teacher training and development, and conferences. An academic research partnership, the MECC/University of Minnesota Center for the Study of Educational Technology conducts a variety of studies on the impact of technology on education. MECC respects the challenges faced by modern educators and pledges to remain on the cutting edge of technology. *Membership:* Available: institutional memberships, MECC Club. *Publications: MECC Network Newsletter*.

Museum Computer Network, Inc. School of Information Studies, Syracuse University, Syracuse, NY 13244. (315) 443-5612. Deirdre C. Stam, Exec. Dir. A nonprofit service organization which works to improve museum collection documentation and facilitates the sharing of collection-related data among museums through effective use of modern data management technology. Explores and explains other computer applications appropriate to museums. Activities include annual conferences, regional workshops, technical advisory services, and publication of a quarterly newsletter. *Publications: Spectra* (newsletter).

Museum of Holography. 11 Mercer St., New York, NY 10013. (212) 925-0526. Martha Tomko, Dir. Housed in a landmark cast-iron building, the museum boasts the world's largest collection of holograms, three-dimensional images. Through its extensive exhibition and education programs, the museum shows the work of artists working in the medium, and explains how holograms are made, how they work, and how they have become useful tools in art, science, and technology. The museum also maintains a library, a collection of slides and photographs, and an artist-in-residence program. *Publications: Holosphere; Directory and Buyer's Guide: 1990; The International Directory of Holography*.

Museum of Modern Art, Circulating Film and Video Library. 11 W. 53rd St., New York, NY 10019. (212) 708-9530. William Sloan, Libr. Sponsors film study programs and provides film rentals and sales. *Publications: Circulating Film and Video Catalog*.

Museum of Television and Radio (formerly the Museum of Broadcasting). 25 W. 52nd St., New York, NY 10022. Office (212) 752-4690. Information Tape (212) 752-7684. William S. Paley, Founder; Dr. Robert M. Batscha, Pres. A unique nonprofit institution with two equally important responsibilities: to collect and preserve radio and television programs, and to explore and interpret our television and radio heritage through public exhibitions of the collection. The Museum houses 40,000 radio and television programs and 10,000 commercials that reflect more than 70 years of broadcasting history. The informative card catalog is used for selecting programs for individual listening and viewing at easy-to-use consoles. The Museum also presents major exhibitions and seminars that highlight various aspects of radio and television. Exhibitions focus on topics of social, historical, popular, or artistic interest; and seminars feature in-person discussions with writers, producers, directors, actors, and others who have created landmark programming. The Museum is supported by daily contributions, membership fees, and grants by individuals, corporations, foundations, and government agencies. *Publications:* Exhibition catalogs; screening schedules; seminar monographs; and flyers.

National Aeronautics and Space Administration (NASA). Washington, DC 20546. (202) 453-1110. NASA's mission is to advance science and technology in the disciplines appropriate to aeronautics and space activities; to develop applications of aerospace technology; to explore space; to develop and operate those systems necessary to furthering space science, technology, applications, and exploration; to seek cooperation with other nations and groups of nations in the peaceful application of space activities; and to develop the necessary human resources to support these efforts. NASA's activities include the dissemination of scientific information through a wide variety of educational programs. These programs are designed to capture students' interest in science, mathematics, and technology at an early age, and to maintain that interest throughout higher learning. At the high school and university level, these education programs seek to channel more students into engineering and science careers. NASA's educational programs also recognize the importance of upgrading the knowledge, skills, and experience of teachers and university faculty. This effort is carried out through the Educational Affairs Division at NASA Headquarters and counterpart offices at the nine NASA field centers.

National Alliance of Media Arts Centers (NAMAC). 8540 18th Ave. NW, Seattle, WA 98117. (206) 789-2997. Robin Reidy, Vice-Chair. A nonprofit organization dedicated to increasing public understanding of and support for the field of media arts in the United

States. Members include media arts centers and media artists, as well as other individuals and organizations providing services for production, education, exhibition, preservation, and distribution of video, film, audio, and intermedia. NAMAC's information services are available to the general public, arts and non-arts organizations, businesses, corporations, foundations, government agencies, schools, and universities. *Membership:* 150 organizations, 150 indiv. *Dues:* Inst. $50-$250/yr., depending on annual budget; $20/yr. indiv. *Publications: Media Arts.*

National Art Education Association (NAEA). 1916 Association Dr., Reston, VA 22091. (703) 860-8000. Thomas A. Hatfield, Exec. Dir. A professional association of art educators in elementary school through university and continuing education. Purpose is to improve and expand visual art education at all levels of instruction. *Membership:* 14,500. *Dues:* Contact the association. *Publications: Art Education; Studies in Art Education;* and *NAEA News.*

National Association for Better Broadcasting (NABB). 7918 Naylor Ave., Los Angeles, CA 90045. (213) 641-4903. Frank Orme, Pres. Promotes the public interest in broadcasting through the development of greater awareness of the public's rights and responsibilities in broadcasting. *Publications: Better Radio and Television* and *You Own More Than Your Set!*

National Association for Creative Children and Adults (NACCA). 8080 Springvalley Dr., Cincinnati, OH 45236. (513) 631-1777. Ann Fabe Isaacs, CEO. Seeks to encourage the development of creativity in the general public and especially among gifted persons. Sponsors workshops, inservice training, and a yearly national conference. *Publications: Its Happening* (newsletter free with membership); *Creative Child and Adult Quarterly* (included with membership); *Common Sense Creativity; NACCA Creativity Projects;* and others.

National Association for the Education of Young Children (NAEYC). 1834 Connecticut Ave. NW, Washington, DC 20009. (202) 232-8777; (800) 424-2460. Offers professional development opportunities to early childhood educators designed to improve the quality of services to children from birth through age eight, the critical years of development. *Membership:* 70,000 in 390 local and state affiliate groups. *Dues:* $25 regular, $50 comprehensive. *Publications: Young Children* (journal) and more than 60 books, posters, videos, and brochures.

National Association for the Exchange of Industrial Resources (NAEIR). 560 McClure St., Box 8076, Galesburg, IL 61402. (309) 343-0704. Gary Smith, Pres. The organization operates as a clearinghouse for excess materials gathered from industrial sources and donated to participating school and nonprofit members. The materials must be new. Membership is restricted to schools and charitable service organizations within the United States that qualify as nonprofit entities exempt from federal income tax under Section 501(C)(3) of the Internal Revenue Code of 1954. *Membership:* 8,000 schools and nonprofit organizations in 50 states. *Dues:* $545. *Publications: NAEIR News* and *The NAEIR Bulletin.*

National Association for Visually Handicapped (NAVH). 22 W. 21st St., New York, NY 10010. (212) 889-3141. Lorraine H. Marchi, Pres., 3201 Balboa St., San Francisco, CA 94121. (415) 221-3201. Contact person for 11 Western states, Alaska, and Hawaii is Debra Strom. Publishes and distributes newsletters at irregular intervals (*Seeing Clearly* for adults and *In Focus* for youth). Informational literature, most of which is in large print, is available to visually impaired individuals, their families, and the professionals and paraprofessionals who work with them. Maintains a loan library (free) by U.S. Postal Service of large-print books, and offers counsel and guidance to visually impaired adults and their families and to the parents of visually impaired children. *Membership:* 9,574. *Publications: Catalog of Large Print Materials; Selected List of LPM for Adults;* and *Loan Library List.*

National Association of Broadcasters (NAB). 1771 N St. NW, Washington, DC 20036-2891. (202) 429-5300. Edward O. Fritts, Pres. and CEO. A trade association that represents commercial broadcasters. Encourages development of broadcasting arts, and seeks to protect its members and to strengthen and maintain the industry so that it may best serve the public. *Membership:* Radio and television stations, and all the major networks. *Dues:* Based on station revenue for radio and on market size for television. *Publications: Telemedia*, a video journal for members; weekly newsletters *TV Today, Radio Week*; and industry monographs.

National Association of Business and Educational Radio (NABER). 1501 Duke St., Alexandria, VA 22314. (703) 739-0300; (800) 759-0300. John Sherlock, Dir., Membership/Communications. Represents individuals whose business and professional needs interest them in the uses of TV-shared UHF, and 800 Mhz channels for communication purposes. *Membership:* 5,000. *Publications: Business Radio*; *ShopTalk*; *TechTalk*; *SMR Letter*; and *Private Carrier Pages*.

National Association of Secondary School Principals (NASSP). 1904 Association Dr., Reston, VA 22091. (703) 860-0200. Thomas F. Koerner, Ed. and Dir. Provides a national voice for secondary education, supports promising and successful educational practices, conducts research, examines issues, and represents secondary education at the federal level. *Membership:* 40,000. *Publications: NASSP Bulletin*; *NASSP NewsLeader*; *Curiculum Report*; *Legal Memorandum*; *Schools in the Middle*; *TIPS for Principals*; *AP Special*; *Practitioner*; and *Leadership Magazine*.

National Association of State Boards of Education (NASBE). 1012 Cameron St., Alexandria, VA 22314. (703) 684-4000. Gene Wilhoit, Exec. Dir. The National Association of State Boards of Education is a nonprofit association that represents state and territorial boards of education. Studies problems and improves communication among members, exchanges information, provides educational programs and activities, and serves as a liaison with other educators' groups. *Membership:* 562. *Publications: The State Board Connection*.

National Association of State Educational Media Professionals (NASTEMP). New Mexico Department of Education, Education Bldg., Santa Fe, NM 87501-2786. (505) 827-6562. Mary Jane Vinella, Library Media Consultant. Primary objectives are to strengthen state leadership in education policymaking; promote excellence in the education of all students; advocate equality of access to educational opportunity; and assure responsible lay governance of public education. Membership is open to U.S. Department of Education and state and district agencies. *Membership:* 110. *Dues:* $10. *Publications: Aids to Media Selection for Students and Teachers* and *Quarterly Newsletter*.

National Association of State Textbook Administrators (NASTA). Division of Textbooks, P.O. Box 1075, Jackson, MS 39215-1075. (601) 359-2791. Bob Tom Johnson, Pres. Its purposes are to foster a spirit of mutual helpfulness in adoption, purchase, and distribution of textbooks; to arrange for study and review of textbook specifications; to authorize special surveys/tests/studies; and to initiate action leading to better quality textbooks. NASTA is unaffiliated with any parent organization. It works with the Association of American Publishers and the Book Manufacturers Institute. Services provided include a working knowledge of text construction, monitoring lowest prices, sharing adoption information, identifying trouble spots, and discussions in the industry. *Membership:* Approx. 22.

National Audiovisual Center (NAC). National Archives and Records Administration, 8700 Edgeworth Dr., Capitol Heights, MD 20743. (301) 763-1896. Linda N. Brown, Acting Dir. Central information and distribution source for more than 8,000 audiovisual programs produced by or for the U.S. government. Materials are made available for sale or rent on a self-sustaining basis at the lowest price possible. *Publications: Media Resource Catalog* (1986), listing 2,700 of the latest and most popular programs, is available free. Also available free are specific subject listings such as science, history, medicine, and safety and health.

National Cable Television Institute (NCTI). P.O. Box 27277, Denver, CO 80227. (303) 761-8554. Byron Leech, Pres. Provides technical educational materials and services for the upgrading of professional and technical competencies of cable television personnel. *Publications: Cable Technology.*

National Center for Appropriate Technology. P.O. Box 3838, Butte, MT 59702. (406) 494-4572. George Turman, Pres. A private, nonprofit organization whose mission is to promote energy conservation, renewable energy, and sustainable agriculture technologies, and whose do-it-yourself publications/projects may be of special interest as learning activities in science classes. *Publications:* Consumer and technical publications.

National Clearinghouse for Bilingual Education. 1118 22nd St. NW, Washington, DC 20037. (202) 467-0867; (800) 321-6223. Joe Gomez, Dir. National information center for the education of language minority students in grades K-12 and a producer of various publications related to the field of bilingual education. *Dues:* None. *Publications: FORUM* (bi-mo. newsletter).

National Commission on Libraries and Information Science (NCLIS). 1111 18th St. NW, Suite 310, Washington, DC 20036. (202) 254-3100. Dr. Susan K. Martin, Exec. Dir. An agency in the Executive Branch of the U.S. government charged with advising Congress and the President in the entire field of library and information services. The commission has four major roles: to advise the President and Congress on the implementation of national policy; to conduct studies and analyses of the library and information needs of the nation; to promote research and development activities which will improve the nation's library and information services; and to conduct the White House Conference on Library and Information Services.

National Council for Accreditation of Teacher Education (NCATE). 2029 K St. NW, Suite 500, Washington, DC 20006. (202) 466-7496. Arthur E. Wise, Pres. A consortium of professional organizations that establishes standards of quality and accredits professional education units in colleges and universities. Interested in the self-regulation and improvement of standards in the field of teacher education. *Membership:* 520 colleges and universities, 26 educational organizations. *Publications: Standards, Procedures and Policies for the Accreditation of Professional Education Units*; and *Annual List* of accredited programs/units.

National Council of Teachers of English (NCTE) Commission on Media. 1111 Kenyon Rd., Urbana, IL 61801. (217) 328-3870. Miles Myers, Exec. Dir. An advisory body which identifies key issues in teaching of media. Reviews current projects and recommends new directions and personnel to undertake them, monitors NCTE publications on media, and suggests program ideas for the annual convention. *Publications: English Journal*; *College English*; *Language Arts*; *English Education: Research in the Teaching of English*; and *Teaching English in the Two-Year College.*

National Council of the Churches of Christ—Communication Unit. 475 Riverside Dr., New York, NY 10115. (212) 870-2227. Rev. Dr. J. Martin Bailey, Acting Assoc. General Secy. for Communication. Ecumenical arena for cooperative work of Protestant and Orthodox denominations and agencies in broadcasting, film, cable, and print media. Offers advocacy to government and industry structures on media services. Services provided include liaison to network television and radio programming; film sales and rentals; distribution of information about syndicated religious programming; syndication of some programming; cable television and emerging technologies information services; news and information regarding work of the National Council of Churches, related denominations, and agencies. *Membership:* 32 denominations.

National Education Association (NEA). 1201 16th St. NW, Washington, DC 20036. (202) 833-4000. Kerth Geiger, Pres. The world's largest advocacy organization of teachers, other school employees, and college faculty. Seeks to improve American public education, conducts research on school problems and professional teacher welfare, maintains lobby relationships with the federal government, and informs the public about education and educational needs. *Membership:* 2 million. *Dues:* $75 active membership.

National Endowment for the Arts (NEA). 1100 Pennsylvania Ave. NW, Washington, DC 20506. The Arts in Education Program offers Special Project Grants which are available to a wide range of nonprofit arts and education organizations for projects of regional or national significance which advance progress toward the arts becoming a basic part of education, K-12. Funds are also used for Arts Endowment leadership initiatives to help improve arts education. For further information, contact the Arts in Education Program (202) 682-5426 or the Office of Public Information (202) 682-5400. *Publications: Guideline Booklet.*

National Endowment for the Humanities (NEH). 1100 Pennsylvania Ave. NW, Room 426, Washington, DC 20506. (202) 786-0278. James Dougherty, Asst. Dir. for Media. Offers limited support for the planning, scripting, and production of radio and television projects pertaining to the humanities. Grants are available for children's, as well as adult, programming. The program has two deadlines each year, in March and in September. For further information, contact Media Program, Division of General Program, NEH. *Publications: Guidelines for Applications.*

National Federation of Community Broadcasters (NFCB). 666 11th St. NW, Suite 805, Washington, DC 20001. (202) 393-2355. Lynn Chadwick, Pres. NFCB represents its members in public policy development at the national level, provides a wide range of practical services, and distributes programs to all noncommercial stations. *Membership:* 70 stations, 100 (assoc.) stations and production groups. *Dues:* Based on income, from $75 to $500 for assn.; $300 to $2,000 for participants. *Publications: Legal Handbook; Audio Craft* (1989 edition) and *Community Radio Monthly.*

National Film Board of Canada (NFBC). 1251 Avenue of the Americas, New York, NY 10020. (212) 586-5131. John Sirabella, Nontheatrical Rep. Established in 1939, the NFBC's main objective is to produce and distribute high-quality audiovisual materials for educational, cultural, and social purposes. *Publications: U.S. Film Resource Guide.*

National Film Information Service (NFIS). 8949 Wilshire Blvd., Beverly Hills, CA 90211. (213) 278-8990. Provides an information service on film. All inquiries must be accompanied by SASE.

National Gallery of Art (NGA). Department of Education Resources and Extension Programs, Washington, DC 20565. (202) 842-6273. Ruth R. Perlin, Head. This department of NGA is responsible for the production and distribution of educational audiovisual programs. Materials available (all loaned free to schools, community organizations, and individuals) including films, videocassettes, and color slide programs. A free catalog of programs is available upon request. A videodisc on the gallery and its collection is available for loan. *Publications: Catalogue of Programs.*

National Information Center for Educational Media (NICEM). P.O. Box 40130, Albuquerque, NM 87196. (505) 265-3591; (800) 468-3453. Marjorie M. K. Hlava, Pres. NICEM, in conjunction with the Library of Congress, is a centralized facility that collects, catalogs, and disseminates information about nonbook materials of many different kinds. Its mission is to build and expand the database to provide current and archival information about nonbook educational materials; to apply modern techniques of information dissemination that meet user needs; and to provide a comprehensive, centralized nonbook database used for catalogs, indexes, multimedia publications, special search services, machine-readable tapes, and online access. *Publications:* Indexes to AV educational materials.

National Library of Medicine. 8600 Rockville Pike, Bethesda, MD 20894. (301) 496-6308. Donald A. B. Lindberg, M.D., Dir. Collects, organizes, and distributes literature on biomedicine; seeks to apply modern technology to the flow of biomedical information to health professionals; and supports development of improved medical library resources for the country. Responsible for MEDLINE, SDILINE, CATLINE, SERLINE, CANCERLIT, AVLINE, and TOXLINE. Maintains a collection of 20,000 health science audiovisual materials and supervises the Lister Hill Center for Biomedical Communications and the National Center for Biotechnology Information. Maintains seven regional medical libraries. *Publications: National Library of Medicine Audiovisuals Catalog.*

National Press Photographers Association, Inc. (NPPA). 3200 Croasdaile Dr., Suite 306, Durham, NC 27705. (919) 383-7246. Charles Cooper, Exec. Dir. An organization of professional news photographers who participate in and promote photojournalism in publications, and through television and film. Sponsors workshops and contests, and maintains a tape library and collections of slides in the field. *Membership:* 10,000. *Dues:* $55 professional, $30 student. *Publications: News Photographer*; membership directory; and *Best of Photojournalism Books.*

National PTA. 700 N. Rush St., Chicago, IL 60611. (312) 787-0977. Ann Lynch, Pres. A child advocacy association dedicated to improving the lives of our country's children through the school, home, community, and place of worship. Strengthens laws for the care and protection of children and youth. *Membership:* 8 million. *Dues:* Vary, established by local units. *Sample Publications: Children and Television*; *What Parents Can Do*; *PTA Today Magazine*; *Kids with Keys, Parents with Jobs: Who's in Charge? (English and Spanish)*; *Home Helps for Learning: A Guide to Pre-School Development*; *How to Talk to Your Child about Sex*; *Drug Abuse and Your Teens: What Parents Should Know*; *Young Children and Drugs: What Parents Can Do*; and *What's Happening in Washington.*

National Public Radio (NPR). 2025 M St. NW, Washington, DC 20036. (202) 822-2300. Douglas J. Bennet, Pres. Through member stations in 48 states, Puerto Rico, and the District of Columbia, NPR reaches a broad segment of the population. Its award-winning programming, "All Things Considered," "Morning Edition," "Performance Today," "Car Talk," and "Blue Stage" has helped build an audience base of more than 12 million weekly listeners. With programs such as "Horizons," "Afropop Worldwide," "Crossroads," and "National Native News," NPR acknowledges the diversity in American society and provides programs that focus on minorities, the elderly, and the disabled. In addition to programming, NPR provides more than 400 member stations with distribution and representation support services.

National Religious Broadcasters (NRB). 299 Webro Rd., Suite 250, Parsippany, NJ 07054. E. Brandt Gustavson, Exec. Dir. Sponsors an annual Summer Institute of Communications and holds an annual national convention and seven regional conventions. *Membership:* 1,200 stations, individuals, and agencies. *Dues:* Based on income. *Publications: Religious Broadcasting Magazine*; *Annual Directory of Religious Broadcasting*; and *Religious Broadcasting Cassette Catalog.*

National School Supply and Equipment Association (NSSEA). 2020 N. 14th St., Suite 400, Arlington, VA 22201. (703) 524-8819. Tim Holt, Exec. V.P. A service organization of 800 manufacturers, distributors, retailers, and independent manufacturers' representatives of school supplies, equipment, and instructional materials. Seeks to maintain open communications between manufacturers and dealers in the school market, to find solutions to problems affecting schools, and to encourage the development of new ideas and products for educational progress. *Publications: Tidings*.

National Science Foundation (NSF). Washington, DC 20550. (202) 357-9498. Primary purposes are to increase the nation's base of scientific knowledge; encourage research in areas that can lead to improvements in economic growth, productivity, and environmental quality; promote international cooperation through science; and develop and help implement science education programs to aid the nation in meeting the challenges of contemporary life. Grants go chiefly to colleges and other research organizations. Applicants should refer to the *NSF Guide to Programs*. Scientific material and media reviews are available to help the public learn about NSF-supported programs.

National Science Teachers Association (NSTA). 1742 Connecticut Ave. NW, Washington, DC 20009. (202) 328-5800. Bill Aldridge, Exec. Dir. International nonprofit association of science teachers ranging from kindergarten through university level. *Membership:* 48,000. *Dues:* $40/yr. indiv. (includes one journal), $45/yr. inst. (includes one journal). *Publications: Science and Children; The Science Teacher; Journal of College Science Teaching; Science Scope;* and *Quantum*.

National Society for Performance and Instruction (NSPI). 1126 16th St. NW, Suite 102, Washington, DC 20036. (202) 861-0777. Paul Tremper, Exec. Dir. NSPI is the leading association dedicated to increasing productivity in the workplace through the application of performance and instructional technologies. Founded in 1962, its 5,000 members are located throughout the United States, Canada, and 28 other countries. The society offers an awards program recognizing excellence in the field. The Annual Conference and Expo is held in the spring. *Membership:* 5,000. *Dues:* $95. *Publications: Performance Instruction Journal:* member directory; *Introduction to Performance Technology* Vol. 1; *Performance Improvement Quarterly*.

National Technical Information Service (NTIS). NTIS is a self-supporting agency of the U.S. Department of Commerce that actively collects, organizes, and distributes technical information generated by the United States and foreign governments in all areas of science and technology. There are two million titles in the NTIS permanent archives, some of which date as far back as 1945, and in 1989 NTIS added 63,000 new titles to its collection. The entire collection is available at any time—whether a report dates from 20 years ago or last month. In addition, NTIS provides government-generated computer software and computerized data files on both tape and diskette through its Federal Computer Products Center. To keep pace with technology transfer activities, the NTIS Center for the Utilization of Federal Technology licenses federal inventions and makes them available to private industry, and prepares and issues a number of publications, catalogs, and directories announcing federal technologies and resources. In the area of foreign technology, NTIS has recently increased its holdings—up to a third of the reports entering the collection are now from foreign sources. To get a free 32-page catalog describing NTIS products and services, contact the NTIS Order Desk, Springfield, VA 22161, (703) 487-4650, and ask for PR827/NCB.

National Technology Center (NTC). American Foundation for the Blind, 15 W. 16th St. New York, NY 10011. (212) 620-2080. Eliot M. Schreier, Dir. The Center has three components: National Technology Information System, Evaluations Laboratory, and Research and Development Laboratory. Provides a resource for blind and visually impaired persons and professionals in education, rehabilitation, and employment, and their families, rehabilitation professionals, educators, researchers, manufacturers, and employers. The NTC also develops products to enhance education, employment, mobility, and independent living opportunities for blind and visually impaired people worldwide. Evaluations Laboratory: (212) 620-2051.

National Telemedia Council Inc. (NTC). 120 E. Wilson St., Madison, WI 53703. (608) 257-7712. Dr. Marti Tomas, Pres.; Marieli Rowe, Exec. Dir. An organization working to develop a better informed, more evaluative public through media literacy, working with teachers, parents, and others concerned with children. Sponsoring organization of KIDS-4, a Sun Prairie, WI cable television channel produced by and for children. Every fall, NTC conducts Project LOOK-LISTEN-THINK-RESPOND, a classroom television evaluation activity. Other NTC activities include conferences and workshops, the Teacher Idea Exchange (T.I.E.), Sponsor Recognition Awards for excellence in telemedia programming, the newsletters *Telemedium* and *Telemedium Update*, and special projects. *Dues:* $20 and up. *Publications: Telemedium*; *Telemedium UPDATE*; and the *Annual Report of Project LOOK-LISTEN-THINK-RESPOND.*

National University Continuing Education Association (NUCEA). One Dupont Circle NW, Suite 615, Washington, DC 20036. (202) 659-3130. Thomas Hatfield, Pres.; Kay J. Kohl, Exec. Dir. An association of public and private institutions concerned with making continuing education available to all population segments and to promoting excellence in the continuing higher education community. Many institutional members offer university and college film rental library services. *Membership:* 4,000 institutions; 2,000 professionals. *Dues:* Vary according to membership category. *Publications:* Monthly newsletter; quarterly occasional papers; scholarly journal; *Independent Study Catalog*; *Guide to Certificate Programs at American Colleges and Universities*; *Conferences and Facilities Directory*; the *NUCEA-ACE/Macmillan Continuing Higher Education* book series; and a variety of other publications relevant to the field.

Nebraska Videodisc Design/Production Group (VD-PG). KUON-TV, University of Nebraska, Box 83111, Lincoln, NE 68501. (402) 472-3611. Ron Nugent, Group Dir. A group of designers and producers concerned with the development and production of programs that exploit the unique capabilities of the videodisc. Annual symposium and workshops.

The NETWORK. 300 Brickstone Square, Suite 900, Andover, MA 01810. (508) 470-1080. D. Max McConkey, Dir. A research and service organization providing consultation, training, assistance, and materials to schools, other educational institutions, and private sector firms with educational interests. *Publications: Administering Writing Programs: A Training Package for the Coordination of Writing Programs*; *The Cumulative Writing Folder*; *Nutrition Education Curriculum*; *Sex Equity Curriculum*; *The Effective Writing Teacher*; *Eighteen Strategies*; *An Action Guide to School Improvement*; *People, Policies and Practices*; *Examining the Chain of School Improvement* Vols. 1-10. *See also* Council for Educational Development and Research.

Network for Continuing Medical Education (NCME). One Harmon Plaza, Secaucus, NJ 07094. (201) 867-3550; (800) 223-0272; in NJ (800) 624-2102. Jim Disque, Exec. Dir. Produces and distributes videocassettes to hospitals for physicians' continuing education. *Membership:* By subscription. *Dues:* Subscription fees: VHS $1,820; ¾" $2,020.

Newspaper Features Council Inc. (NFC). Ward Castle, Comly Ave., Rye Brook, NY 10573. (914) 939-3919. Jack Loftis, Pres. NFC is a professional organization. In order to join the organization, one must be a syndicated cartoonist, syndicated columnist, newspaper feature editor, newspaper editor, syndicate president, or printer of newspaper color comics. The mission of the Newspaper Features Council is to provide the only permanent forum for the mutual discussion of industry issues among editors, cartoonists, columnists, and syndicate executives and to undertake specific projects to increase awareness and readership of newspaper features. *Membership:* 130. *Dues:* Newspaper syndicates $1,250/yr.; newspapers (includes editors) $160/yr.; creators (syndicated columnists and syndicated cartoonists) $75/yr.; inquire about associate membership. *Publications: Career for You in the Comics* $2; *Cavalcade of American Comics* $1.50; *Comics in the Classroom*

$1; *Grapevine* (newsletter/members only). Tape order taken for tapes made at seminars about "How to Become Syndicated"; order form is free and lists prices of tapes.

North American Simulation and Gaming Association (NASAGA). c/o Community Systems Foundation, 1130 Hill St., Ann Arbor, MI 48104. (313) 761-1368. Fred Goodman, Exec. Dir. Provides a forum for the exchange of ideas, information, and resources among persons interested in simulation and games. Assists members in designing, testing, using, and evaluating simulations and/or games, and in using these as research tools. A computerized mailing list and cross-referencing service are available through national headquarters and University of North Carolina-Asheville. Sponsors various conferences. *Membership:* 800. *Dues:* $35 regular, $10 students. *Publications: Simulation and Games.*

Northwest Regional Educational Laboratory (NWREL). 101 SW Main St., Suite 500, Portland, OR 97204. (503) 275-9500. Robert R. Rath, Exec. Dir. Assists education, government, community agencies, and business and labor in bringing about improvement in educational programs and processes by developing and disseminating effective educational products and procedures, including applications of technology. Provides technical assistance and training in educational problem solving. Evaluates effectiveness of educational programs and processes. *Membership:* 817. *Dues:* None. *Publications: Northwest Report* (newsletter).

Office for International Networks in Education and Development (INET). College of Education, Michigan State University, 238 Erikson, East Lansing, MI 48824-1034. (517) 355-5522. Anne Schneller, Mgr. The INET office makes a number of publications available to development planners and practitioners working on behalf of persons in Africa, Asia, Latin America, and the Middle East. Such materials are distributed for sale or on an exchange basis; that is, the office sends publications in hopes that recipients will give the office further materials, especially those of a "fugitive" nature. Such materials may be in the form of books, working papers, surveys, occasional papers, annual reports, journals, or newsletters which are relevant to education and development. The INET office strongly encourages participants to continue this exchange of publications which has proved to be so important to low-cost dissemination of information throughout the Third World. INET is interested particularly in matters and materials related to formal and nonformal education for development. *Membership:* Free. *Dues:* None. *Publications: The INET Update;* annotated bibliographies; and occasional papers.

Office of Technology Assessment (OTA). U.S. Congress, Washington, DC 20510-8025. (202) 224-9241. John Gibbons, Dir. Established by Congress to study, report on, and assess the significance and probable impact of new technological developments upon U.S. society and to advise Congress on public policy implications and options. Recent assessments focusing on technology and education issues include *Elementary and Secondary Education for Science and Engineering, A Technical Memorandum, 1989*; *Higher Education for Science and Engineering, A Background Paper, 1989*; *Linking for Learning: A New Course for Education, 1989*; *Critical Connections: Communication for the Future 1990*; *Computer Software and Intellectual Property, A Background Paper, 1990*; and *Special Report on Technologies for Learning at a Distance.* In addition, the assessment, *Power On! New Tools for Teaching & Learning* (1988), includes an interim staff paper on "Trends and Status of Computers in Schools: Use in Chapter 1 Programs and Use with Limited English Proficient Students" (March 1987). *Publications:* For a list, contact publishing office (202) 224-8996.

On-line Audiovisual Catalogers (OLAC). 3604 Suffolk, Durham, NC 27707. (919) 684-6359. Catherine Leonardi, Treas. Formed as an outgrowth of the ALA conference, OLAC seeks to permit members to exchange ideas, computer files, and information and to interact with other agencies that influence audiovisual cataloging practices. *Membership:* 600. *Dues:* Available for single or multiple years, ranges from $7-$24 indiv., $13-$42 inst. *Publications: OLAC Newsletter.*

Online Computer Library Center (OCLC). 6565 Frantz Rd., Dublin, OH 43017. (614) 764-6000. A nonprofit membership organization which engages in computer library service and research and makes available computer-based processes, products, and services for libraries and other educational organizations, and library users. From its facility in Dublin, Ohio, OCLC operates an international computer network that libraries use to catalog books, order custom-printed catalog cards and machine-readable records for local catalogs, arrange interlibrary loans, and maintain location information on library materials. OCLC also provides online and offline reference products and services for the electronic delivery of information. More than 10,000 libraries contribute to and/or use information in the OCLC Online Union Catalog. *Publications: OCLC Newsletter* (6/yr.).

Oral History Association. 1093 Broxton Ave., Suite 720, Los Angeles, CA 90024. (213) 825-0597. Richard Candida Smith, Exec. Secy. Seeks to develop the use of oral history as primary source material and to disseminate oral history materials among scholars. *Membership:* 1,400. *Publications: Oral History Newsletter*; *Oral History Review*; *Evaluation Guidelines*; *Annual Report and Membership Directory*; *Oral History and the Law*; and *Oral History in Secondary Education*.

Pacific Film Archive (PFA). University Art Museum, 2625 Durant Ave., Berkeley, CA 94720. (415) 642-1437. Sponsors the exhibition, study, and preservation of classic, international, documentary, animated, and avant-garde films. Provides media research and a service to locate film sources, books, and addresses.

PBS ENCORE. 1320 Braddock Pl., Alexandria, VA 22314. (703) 739-5225. Michael Patterson, Assoc. Dir. Distributes PBS programs with extant broadcast rights to public television stations. *Publications: PBS Encore Catalog*; and *Monthly News & Update Memo*.

PBS VIDEO. 1320 Braddock Pl., Alexandria, VA 22314. (703) 739-5380; (800) 424-7963. Jon Cecil, Dir. Markets and distributes PBS television programs for sale on videocassette to colleges, public libraries, schools, government, and other organizations and institutions. Top-selling programs include "Moyers: The Power of the Word," "Middle Ages School Kit," "Thinking Your Way to Better SAT Scores," "American Experience II," "The Mind," "Eyes on the Prize II," and "The Civil War." *Publications: PBS VIDEO Program Catalog*; *PBS VIDEO Check It Out Catalog*; and *PBS Video News*.

PCR: Films and Video in the Behavioral Sciences. Special Services Bldg., Pennsylvania State University, University Park, PA 16802. (814) 863-3102; purchasing info. (800) 826-0132. Thomas McKenna, Mng. Ed. Collects and makes available to professionals 16mm films and video in the behavioral sciences judged to be useful for university teaching and research. A free catalog of the films in PCR is available. The PCR catalog now contains some 1,400 films in the behavioral sciences (psychology, psychiatry, anthropology, animal behavior, sociology, teaching and learning, and folklife). Some 7,000 professionals now use PCR services. Films and tapes are available on loan for a rental charge. Many films may also be purchased. Films may be submitted for international distribution. Contact the managing editor.

Photographic Society of America (PSA). 3000 United Founders Blvd., Suite 103, Oklahoma City, OK 73102. (405) 843-1437. Terry S. Stull, Operations Manager. A nonprofit organization for the development of the arts and sciences of photography and for the furtherance of public appreciation of photographic skills. Its members, largely amateurs, consist of individuals, camera clubs, and other photographic organizations. Divisions include color slide, motion picture, nature, photojournalism, travel, pictorial print, stereo, and techniques. Sponsors national, regional, and local meetings, clinics, and contests. *Dues:* Request information. *Publications: PSA Journal*.

Professors of Instructional Design and Technology (PIDT). Audiovisual Center. Indiana University, Bloomington, IN 47405-5901. (812) 855-2854. Dr. Tom Schwen, contact person. An organization designed to encourage and facilitate the exchange of information among members of the instructional design and technology academic and corporate communities. It also serves to promote excellence in academic programs in instructional design and technology and to encourage research and inquiry that will benefit the field while providing leadership in the public and private sectors in its application and practice. Membership consists of faculty employed in higher education institutions whose primary responsibilities are teaching and research in this area, their corporate counterparts, and other interested persons.

Project in Distance Education. One key component of the OAS Multinational Project on Secondary and Higher Education. Organization of American States, Department of Educational Affairs, 1889 F St. NW, Washington, DC 20006. (202) 458-3309. Arturo Garzon, contact person. Promotes development of distance education in Latin America and Caribbean countries through technical cooperation, planning, human resource and institution building, and research. Main projects in Argentina, Brazil, Colombia, Costa Rica, El Salvador, and Panama.

Project in Educational Technology. One key component of the OAS Multinational Project on Secondary and Higher Education. Organization of American States, Department of Educational Affairs, 1889 F St. NW, Washington, DC 20006. (202) 458-3309. Arturo Garzon, contact person. Maintains support, information, and personnel exchanges among educational technology centers in Brazil, Argentina, and Chile, with tie-ins to other Latin American countries. Emphasizes development of human resources through a variety of programs, seminars, short courses, on-site training, and technical cooperation. Also disseminates information through its journal. *Publications: Revista de Tecnología Educativa*.

Public Broadcasting Service (PBS). 1320 Braddock Pl., Alexandria, VA 22314. (703) 739-5000. Bruce Christensen, Pres. Serves as a distributor of national public television programming, obtaining all programs from the stations or independent producers; PBS is not a production facility. Owned and operated by the licensees through annual membership fees. Funding for technical distribution facilities in part by the Corporation for Public Broadcasting. PBS services include national promotion, program acquisition and scheduling, legal services, development and fundraising support, engineering and technical studies, and research. Of special interest are the Adult Learning Service, which offers telecourses through college/public television station partnerships, and PBS VIDEO, which offers PBS programs for rent/sale to educational institutions. PBS is governed by a board of directors elected by licensees for three-year terms. *Membership:* 172 licensees; 337 stations.

Public Service Satellite Consortium (PSSC). 600 Maryland Ave. SW, Suite 220, Washington, DC 20024. (202) 863-0890. Louis A. Bransford, Pres. Represents the telecommunication interests of nonprofit organizations; provides members with information, consultation, educational briefings, and representation to federal agencies and other organizations; assists members in contracting for operational functions such as systems engineering and networking; conducts workshops on new technologies and telecommunications issues. PSSC offers its members discounts on its in-house audio bridging service, Telecommunications Access Corp. (TEACCO). PSSC is also the headquarters of the National Center for Telecommunications Information Policy. *Membership:* 100. *Dues:* $500/yr. nonprofit, $1,000/yr. corporate. *Publications: Report to Members Newsletter*; and *Teleguide: A Handbook on Video-Teleconferencing*.

Puppeteers of America. 5 Cricklewood Path, Pasadena, CA 91107. (818) 797-5748. Gayle Schulter, Membership Chair. Founded in 1937 to promote and develop the art of puppetry.

It has a large collection of films and videotapes for rent in its audiovisual library and offers books, plays, and related items from the Puppetry Store. Puppeteers is a national resource center which offers regional festivals, workshops, exhibits, and a puppetry exchange. *Dues:* Various classes of membership which range from $15-$40. *Publications: Puppeteering Journal* (annual directory).

Radio Free Europe/Radio Liberty (RFE-RL, Inc.). 1201 Connecticut Ave. NW, Washington, DC 20036. (202) 457-6900. An independent radio broadcast service funded by federal grants, which broadcasts to the Soviet Union; Bulgaria, Czechoslovakia, Hungary, Poland, and Romania; the Baltic States; and Afghanistan.

Recording for the Blind. 20 Roszel Rd., Princeton, NJ 08540. (609) 452-0606. Supported by volunteers and contributions from individuals, corporations, and foundations. Supplies free recordings of educational books for visually, perceptually, and physically disabled students and professionals.

Recording Industry Association of America, Inc. (RIAA). 1020 19th St. NW, Suite 200, Washington, DC 20036. (202) 775-0101. Jason S. Berman, Pres. Compiles and disseminates U.S. industry shipment statistics by units and wholesale/retail dollar equivalents, establishes industry technical standards, conducts audits for certification of gold and platinum records and video awards, acts as the public information arm of the U.S. recording industry, provides antipiracy intelligence to law enforcement agencies, presents an RIAA cultural award for contributions to cultural activities in the United States, and acts as a resource center for recording industry research projects. *Membership:* 50 sound recording manufacturers. *Publications: Statistical Report*; *Industry Sourcebook*; newsletter; and press releases.

Smithsonian Institution. c/o Smithsonian Information, Smithsonian Institution, Washington, DC 20560. (202) 357-2700. Robert McCormick Adams, Secy. An independent trust instrumentality of the United States which conducts scientific and scholarly research, administers the national collections, and performs other educational public service functions, all supported by Congress, trusts, gifts, and grants. Includes the National Museum of Natural History/National Museum of Man, National Museum of American History, National Air and Space Museum, Freer Gallery of Art, National Museum of American Art, National Portrait Gallery, National Museum of African Art, Cooper-Hewitt National Museum of Design, Renwick Gallery, Hirshhorn Museum and Sculpture Garden, Arthur M. Sackler Gallery, Anacostia Museum, and others. Museums are free and open daily except Dec. 25. (Exception: Cooper-Hewitt in New York City has entrance fees.) *Membership:* Smithsonian assoc., resident, national, and Air and Space. *Dues:* Vary. *Publications: Smithsonian* and *Air & Space/Smithsonian.*

Social Science Education Consortium (SSEC). 3300 Mitchell Lane, Suite 240, Boulder, CO 80301-2272. (303) 492-8154. James R. Giese, Exec. Dir. The major goal of SSEC is to improve social studies institution at all levels—elementary, secondary, and college. The consortium disseminates information about social studies materials, instructional methods, and trends. It assists educators in identifying selecting, and using new ideas and methods in social studies and provides a forum for social scientists and educators to exchange ideas and views. A free catalog of publications and services is available on request. *Membership:* 140.

Society for Applied Learning Technology (SALT). 50 Culpeper St., Warrenton, VA 22186. (703) 347-0055. Raymond G. Fox, Pres. Seeks to advance the development of highest standards and practices in the application of technology to learning, to foster wide dissemination of understanding and knowledge in actual and potential uses of technology in learning, and to provide an effective educational channel among scientists, managers, and users of training and learning technology. *Membership:* 700. *Dues:* $30. *Publications:*

Journal of Educational Technology Systems; *Journal of Interactive Instructional Development*; send for list of books.

Society for Computer Simulation (SCS). P.O. Box 17900, San Diego, CA 92117-7900. (619) 277-3888. Fax (619) 277-3930. Chip G. Stockton, Exec. Dir. A technical society devoted to the art and science of modeling and simulation. Its purpose is to advance the understanding, appreciation, and use of all types of computer models for studying the behavior of actual or hypothesized systems of all kinds. Sponsors standards and local, regional, and national technical meetings and conferences such as Eastern & Western Simulation Multiconferences, Summer Computer Simulation Conference, Winter Simulation Conference National Educational Computing Conference, and others. *Membership:* 1,900. *Dues:* $50. *Publications: Simulation*; Simulation series; and *Transactions of SCS.* Additional office in Ghent, Belgium.

Society for Imaging Science and Technology (IS&T) (formerly SPSE). 7003 Kilworth Lane, Springfield, VA 22151. (703) 642-9090. Seeks to advance the science and engineering of imaging materials and equipment and to develop means for applying and using imaging techniques in all branches of engineering and science. *Membership:* 3,000; 17 chapters. *Publications: Journal of Imaging Science*; and *Journal of Imaging Technology*.

Society for Photographic Education (SPE). Campus Box 318, University of Colorado, Boulder, CO 80309. (303) 492-0588. Judith Thorpe, Exec. Dir. An association of college and university teachers of photography, museum photographic curators, writers, and publishers. It promotes higher standards of photographic education. *Membership:* 1,700. *Dues:* $50. *Publications: Exposure*; and newsletter.

Society of Cable Television Engineers (SCTE). 669 Exton Commons, Exton, PA 19341. (215) 363-6888. William W. Riker, Exec. V.P. SCTE is dedicated to the technical training and further education of members. A nonprofit membership organization for persons engaged in engineering, construction, installation, technical direction, management, or administration of cable television and broadband communication technologies. Also eligible for membership are students in communications, educators, government and regulatory agency employees, and affiliated trade associations. *Membership:* 7,000. *Dues:* $40/yr. *Publications: The "Interval"* located inside *Communications Technology Magazine.*

Society of Manufacturing Engineers (SME). 1 SME Dr., Box 930, Dearborn, MI 48121. (313) 271-1500. Steven R. Bollinger, Video Admin. A technical society which, among many other services, distribute videotapes for purchase. Covers a wide range of manufacturing technologies, and processes including quality improvement, just-in-time, CAD/CAM, material processing, simultaneous engineering, lasers, and more. *Publications:* Free catalog.

Society of Motion Picture and Television Engineers (SMPTE). 595 W. Hartsdale Ave., White Plains, NY 10607-1824. (914) 761-1100. Lynette Robinson, Exec. Dir. Fosters the advancement of engineering and technical aspects of motion pictures, television, and allied arts and sciences; disseminates scientific information in these areas; and sponsors lectures, exhibitions, classes, and conferences. Open to those with clearly defined interest in the field. *Membership:* 9,500. *Dues:* $50. *Publications:* Booklets and reports related to non-book media, such as *SMPTE Journal*; *Special Effects in Motion Pictures*; and test films.

Society of Photo Technologists (SPT). 6535 S. Dayton, Suite 2000, Englewood, CO 80111. (303) 799-0667. Karen A. Hone, contact person. An organization of photographic equipment repair technicians, which improves and maintains communications between manufacturers and independent repair technicians. *Membership:* 1,000. *Dues:* $60-$250. *Publications: SPT Journal*; *SPT Parts and Services Directory*; *SPT Newsletter*; and *SPT Manuals - Training and Manufacturer's Tours.*

SOFTSWAP. P.O. Box 271704, Concord, CA 94527-1704. (415) 685-7289. Hal Gibson, contact person. SOFTSWAP is an inexpensive, yet high-quality library of many teacher-developed and commercial educational programs for use with the Apple, IBM, and MAC computers. These copyrighted programs are organized onto disks which are sold for a nominal charge, with permission to copy. *Publications: Catalog; Newsletter*.

Special Libraries Association (SLA). 1700 18th St. NW, Washington, DC 20009. (202) 234-4700. David R. Bender, Exec. Dir. Members are librarians and information managers serving industry, business, research, educational and technical institutions, government, libraries, newspapers, museums, and other public and private organizations requiring or providing specialized information. SLA is an international professional association of individuals and organizations with educational, scientific, and technical interests in information management and technology. The association encourages its members to increase professional competencies and performance. Continuing education seminars keep members informed of new developments in the information field. *Membership:* 12,000. *Publications: Special Libraries; SpeciaList*; and a number of books.

SpecialNet. Part of the GTE Educational Service Network. 2021 K St. NW, Suite 215, Washington, DC 20006. (202) 835-7300; (800) 468-8550. Mike Norman, contact person. A computerized fee-charging information database emphasizing special education resources.

Speech Communication Association (SCA). 5105 Backlick Rd., Bldg. E, Annandale, VA 22003. (703) 750-0533. James L. Gaudino, Exec. Dir. A voluntary society organized to promote study, criticism, research, teaching, and application of principles of communication, particularly of speech communication. *Membership:* 6,000. *Dues:* $50. *Publications: Spectra Newsletter* (mo.); *Quarterly Journal of Speech; Communication Monographs; Communication Education; Critical Studies in Mass Communication; Speech Communication Teacher; Index to Journals in Communication Studies through 1985; Speech Communication Directory of SCA and the Regional Speech Communication Organizations* (CSSA, ECA, SSCA, WSCA). For additional publications request brochure.

Superintendent of Documents. U.S. Government Printing Office, Washington, DC 20402. (202) 783-3238. Functions as the principal sales agency for U.S. government publications. Has over 20,000 titles in its active sales inventory. For information on the scope of its publications, write for the free Subject Bibliography index listing of over 240 subject bibliographies on specific topics. Of particular interest is SB 258, *Grants and Awards*; SB 114, *Directories and Lists of Persons and Organizations*; and SB 73, *Motion Pictures, Films and Audiovisual Information*.

Teachers and Writers Collaborative (T&W). 5 Union Square West, New York, NY 10003. Nancy Larson Shapiro, Dir. Sends writers and other artists into New York public schools to conduct long-term projects with classroom teachers and students and publishes materials on how to teach creative writing based on these workshops. *Dues:* $35/yr., basic membership. *Publications: Teachers and Writers* magazine; *Journal of a Living Experiment: The First 10 Years of Teachers & Writers; The Whole Word Catalogue, Vols. 1 & 2; Personal Fiction Writing; The Writing Workshop, Vols. 1 & 2; The Teachers & Writers Handbook of Poetic Forms; The Art of Science Writing; Like It Was: A Complete Guide to Writing Oral History; Moving Windows: Evaluating the Poetry Children Write; Poetic Forms: 10 Audio Programs*; and *Origins*.

Technology and Media Division (TAM). Council for Exceptional Children. 1920 Association Dr., Reston, VA 22091. (703) 620-3660. The Technology and Media Division (TAM) of the Council for Exceptional Children (CEC) encourages the development of new applications, technologies, and medias for use as daily living tools by special populations. This information is disseminated through professional meetings, training programs, and publications. TAM members receive four issues annually of the *Journal of Special Education*

Technology containing articles on specific technology programs and applications, and five issues of the TAM newsletter, providing news of current research, developments and products, conferences, and special programs information. *Membership:* 1,500. *Dues:* $10 in addition to CEC membership.

Telecommunications Research and Action Center (TRAC). Box 12038, Washington, DC 20005. (202) 462-2520. Samuel Simon, counsel. Seeks to educate telecommunications consumers, to improve broadcasting, and to support local and national media reform groups and movements. *Dues:* $25/yr. *Publications: After Divestiture: What the AT&T Settlement Means for Business and Residential Telephone Service*; *Citizens' Media Directory*; *A Citizens' Primer on the Fairness Doctrine*; *Phonewriting: A Consumer's Guide to the New World of Electronic Information Services*.

Television Licensing Center (TLC). 5547 N. Ravenswood Ave., Chicago, IL 60640. (312) 878-2600; (800) 323-4222, ext. 43. Offers licensing services for duplicating television programs from PBS, CBS, NBC, and others.

Theater Library Association (TLA). 111 Amsterdam Ave., Room 513, New York, NY 10023. (212) 870-1670. Richard M. Buck, Secy./Treas. Seeks to further the interests of collecting, preserving, and using theater, cinema, and performing arts materials in libraries, museums, and private collections. *Membership:* 500. *Dues:* $20 indiv., $25 inst. *Publications: Broadside* (q.) and *Performing Arts Resources* (membership annual).

Training Media Association. 198 Thomas Johnson Dr., Suite 206, Frederick, MD 21701. (301) 662-4268. Robert A. Gehrke, Exec. Dir. An organization dedicated to the protection of film and videotape copyright and copyright education. *Membership:* 75. *Dues:* Based on number of employees. *Publications: The Monthly*.

Training Modules for Trainers (TMT). School of Education, University of Michigan, Ann Arbor, MI 48109. (313) 763-4668. Dr. Carl F. Berger, Dir. Funded by the Michigan Department of Education, the TMT project was conceived to provide materials for use by trainers in addressing the computing needs of the educational community. The materials consist of a set of modules, each containing an overview, goals, training leader prerequisites, competency list, issues narrative, references, activities, blackline masters, and a feedback form. In addition, there is a videotape and set of slides available to supplement certain modules. Module topics include training methods, district planning, instructional methods, applications concepts, software evaluation, hardware configuration, basic technical skills, instructional management, software design, computers in the curriculum, computer-mediated communication, administrative uses, future images, computers and media services, emerging technology, artificial intelligence, CD-ROM, distance education, and videodiscs. *Publications: Training Modules for Trainers: A Resource for Training Leaders in the Educational Use of Computers* (set of 19).

United Nations Department of Public Information, Dissemination Division. Secretariat Bldg., New York, NY 10017. (212) 963-6824. Produces and distributes films, radio and television programs, still pictures, charts, posters, and various publications about the United Nations. Distribution is worldwide and is accomplished in part through a network of approximately 105 United Nations information centers, as well as via distributors and direct from New York. Items are provided in a number of different languages, including English, French, Spanish, Chinese, Russian, and Arabic.

University and College Designers Association (UCDA). 2811 Mishawaka Ave., South Bend, IN 46615. (219) 288-UCDA. Jody Zamirowski, Pres. Composed of individuals and institutions interested in better visual design to improve higher education communication through graphics, photography, signage, films, and other related media. *Membership:* 1,000. *Dues:* Regular $75, inst. $325, assn. $110, student $30. *Publications: Designer* (q.).

University Film and Video Association (UFVA). c/o Loyola Marymount University, Communication Arts Dept., Los Angeles, CA 90045. (213) 338-3033. Donald J. Zirpola, Pres. Members are people involved in the arts and sciences of film and video. Promotes film and video production in educational institutions, fosters study of world cinema and video in scholarly resource centers, and serves as central source of information on film/video instruction, festivals, grants, jobs, production, and research. *Membership:* Approx. 800. *Dues:* Indiv. $35, student $15, inst. $75, commercial firms $150. *Publications: Journal of Film and Video*; *UFVA Digest*; and a membership directory.

U.S. Advisory Commission on Public Diplomacy. 301 4th St. SW, Room 600, Washington, DC 20547. (202) 485-2457. Dr. Edwin J. Feulner, Jr., Chair. Established by Congress in 1978 to advise the president, Congress, the secretary of state, and the director of the U.S. Information Agency on the formulation of U.S. Information Agency policies and programs concerning international educational and cultural activities and on the effectiveness with which those programs are conducted. Issues periodic reports. *Membership:* 7. *Publications: 1989 Annual Report*; recent reports of the United States Advisory Commission on Public Diplomacy; *Public Diplomacy in a New Europe*; *Proceedings of the United States Advisory Commission on Public Diplomacy's Meeting on Eastern Europe, Jan. 24, 1990*; *United States Public Diplomacy in China*; *1989 Annual Report of the United States Advisory Commission on Public Diplomacy*; *Public Diplomacy: Lessons from the Washington Summit*; *Public Diplomacy in the Information Age: Proceedings of the 40th Anniversary Conference of the United States Advisory Commission on Public Diplomacy*; *Soviet Advocacy and the U.S. Media*; and *Terrorism and Security: The Challenge for Public Diplomacy*.

Women in Film (WIF). 6464 Sunset Blvd., Suite 900, Hollywood, CA 90028. (213) 463-6040. Marcy Kelly, Pres. For women in film and television, a communications and support network, an education and advocacy resource, and a showcase for outstanding work being done by women directors, producers, and writers. The mission of Women in Film is to advance the employment, position, and depiction of women. WIF annually produces the Women in Film Festival (four days of premiere, documentary, video, and animation screenings, awards in 11 categories, special events, and seminars); The Crystal Awards (recognizing contributions in film and television which promote the organization's mission); a program of film-finishing grants and scholarships for women through the Women in Film Foundation; and a series of workshops on subjects related to improving the image and increasing the participation of women in the industry. Membership criteria: Three years' professional experience in film and television. *Dues:* $125/yr. *Publications: Newsletter* (mo.).

Women's Institute for Freedom of the Press. 3306 Ross Pl. NW, Washington, DC 20008. (202) 966-7783. Dr. Donna Allen, Pres.; Dr. Martha Leslie Allen, Dir. Conducts research and publishes reports on communications media and women, and booklets on restructuring the communications system and expanding communications for women nationally and internationally. *Membership:* Non-member assoc. structure. *Publications: Women in Media: A Documentary Source Book* and *Syllabus Sourcebook on Media and Women*.

Women's Media Project (WMP) (formerly Media Project). 1333 H St. NW, 11th floor, Washington, DC 20005. (202) 682-0940. Alisa Shapiro, Dir. A project of the NOW Legal Defense and Education Fund. Feminist activists united to eliminate sex role stereotyping of women and men in the media and to increase the participation of women and minorities in broadcasting. Purposes are to conduct public education campaigns with up-to-date information on issues that affect women; guide individuals and groups in developing effective dialogues with local broadcasters and publishers through community action campaigns; monitor compliance with equal employment legislation in the communications industry; and encourage development and distribution of quality television and radio programming that offers realistic and contemporary images of women. Identifies programming promoting equality between women and men. Conducts research in broadcast employment. *Publications: Women's Media Campaign Workbook* (annual); research reports.

World Future Society (WFS). 4916 St. Elmo Ave., Bethesda, MD 20814-6089. (301) 656-8274. Edward Cornish, Pres. Organization of individuals interested in the study of future trends and possibilities. *Membership:* 30,000. *Dues:* Send for information. *Publications: The Futurist: A Journal of Forecasts, Trends and Ideas about the Future*; *Futures Research Quarterly*; and *Future Survey*. The society's bookstore offers audio and video tapes, books, films, and other items.

World Pen Pals (WPP). 1694 Como Ave., St. Paul, MN 55108. (612) 647-0191. Christina Burkhouse, Coordinator. Cultivates appreciation of other cultures and customs through encouraging personal letter-writing activities. The service charge is $3 indiv., $2.50 for groups (minimum of six names). Include a self-addressed stamped envelope, age, and sex.

Canada

This section on Canada includes information on many Canadian organizations whose principal interests lie in the general fields of education, educational media, instructional technology, and library and information science. Organizations listed in the 1990 *EMTY* were contacted for updated information, and changes have been made accordingly.

ACCESS NETWORK. Alberta Educational Communications Corporation, 16930 114 Ave., Edmonton, AB T5M 3S2, Canada. (403) 451-7272. ACCESS NETWORK is the registered trade name of the Alberta Educational Communications Corporation. The Corporation was established October 17, 1973, to consolidate and upgrade a variety of educational media services developing at that time within the province. Access Network acquires, develops, produces, and distributes television and radio programs, microcomputer courseware, multimedia kits, and related printed support materials for educational purposes. Access Network CKUA AM-FM broadcasts through a province-wide AM and FM network. Access Network productions, intended primarily for use in Alberta, are now available for national and international distribution.

Association for Media and Technology in Education in Canada (AMTEC). Vancouver Community College, Instructional Media Services, Box 24700, Station C, Vancouver, BC V5T 4N4, Canada. (604) 875-8293. Bruce MacLean, Pres. Promotes applications of educational technology in improving education and the public welfare. Fosters cooperation and interaction; seeks to improve professional qualifications of media practitioners; organizes and conducts media and technology meetings, seminars, and annual conferences; stimulates and publishes research in media and technology. *Membership:* 550. *Publications: Canadian Journal of Educational Communication*; *Media News*; Membership Directory (with membership).

Canadian Association of Broadcasters/Association canadienne des radiodiffuseurs (CAB/ACR). Box 627, Station B, Ottawa, ON K1P 5S2, Canada. (613) 233-4035. Fax (613) 233-6961. A nonprofit trade association representing the majority of Canada's local-serving, advertising supported radio and television stations.

Canadian Book Publishers' Council (CBPC). 250 Merton St., Suite 203, Toronto, ON M4S 1B1, Canada. (416) 322-7011; (416) 322-6999. Jacqueline Hushion, Exec. Dir. CBPC members publish and distribute an extensive list of Canadian and imported materials to schools, universities, bookstores, and libraries. CBPC provides exhibits throughout the year and works through a number of subcommittees and groups within the organization to promote effective book publishing. *Membership:* 40 companies, educational institutions, or government agencies who publish books as an important facet of their work.

Canadian Broadcasting Corporation (CBC). 1500 Bronson Ave., Box 8478, Ottawa, ON K1G 3J5, Canada. (613) 724-1200. The CBC is a publicly owned corporation established in 1936 by an act of the Canadian Parliament to provide a national broadcasting service in Canada in the two official languages. The CBC is financed mainly by public funds voted annually by Parliament.

Canadian Education Association/Association canadienne d'éducation (CEA/ACE). 252 Bloor St. W., Suite 8-200, Toronto, ON M5S 1V5, Canada. (416) 924-7721. Robert E. Blair, Exec. Dir. The Canadian equivalent of the U.S. National Education Association. *Publications: CEA Handbook; Education Canada; CEA Newsletter; An Overview of Canadian Education; Women and Men in Education: A National Survey of Gender Distribution in School Systems; Marketing the School System; School Board Leave Policies; Dollars and Sense: How School Boards Save Money; Evaluation for Excellence: The Price of Quality; The Public Finance of Elementary and Secondary Education in Canada; Student Transportation in Canada: Facts and Figures; Federal Involvement in Public Education; and Canada and Citizenship Education.*

Canadian Film Institute (CFI). 2 Daly, Ottawa, ON K1N 6E2, Canada. (613) 232-6727. Fax (613) 232-6315. Frank Taylor, Exec. Dir. Established in 1935, the institute promotes the study of film and television as cultural and educational forces in Canada. It distributes over 6,000 films and videos on the sciences and the visual and performing arts through the Canadian Film Institute Film Library, LM Media Marketing Services Ltd., 115 Torbay Rd., Unit 9, Markham, ON L3R 2M9. (416) 475-3750. Fax (416) 475-3756. *Publications: The Guide to Film, Television, and Communications Studies in Canada 1990; Canadian Film series (monographs); Northern Lights: A Programmer's Guide to the Festival of Festivals Retrospective.*

Canadian Library Association. 200 Elgin St., Suite 602, Ottawa, ON K1P 5E3, Canada. Ernie Ingles, Pres.; Marnie Swanson, Pres.-elect (officers change July 1991); Karen Adams, Exec. Dir.

Canadian Museums Association/Association des musées canadiens (CMA/AMC). 280 Metcalf St., Suite 400, Ottawa, ON K2P 1R7, Canada. (613) 233-5653. John G. McAvity, Exec. Dir. Seeks to advance public museum service in Canada. *Membership:* 2,000. *Publications: Museogramme* (mo. newsletter); *Muse* (q. journal); *Directory of Canadian Museums* (listing all museums in Canada plus information on government departments, agencies, and provincial and regional museum associations); and *CMA Bibliography* (an extensive listing of published material on the subjects of museology, museography, and museum and art gallery administration). CMA offers a correspondence course that serves as an introduction to museum operations and philosophy through selected readings.

National Film Board of Canada (NFBC). 1251 Avenue of the Americas, New York, NY 10020. (212) 586-5131. John Sirabella, Nontheatrical Rep. Established in 1939, the NFBC's main objective is to produce and distribute high-quality audiovisual materials for educational, cultural, and social purposes. *Publications: U.S. Film Resource Guide.*

Ontario Film Association, Inc. 3-1750 The Queensway, Suite 1341, Etobicoke, ON M9C 5H5, Canada. A nonprofit organization whose primary objective is to promote the sharing of ideas and information about film and video through seminars, workshops, screenings, and publications. Sponsors the annual Grierson Documentary Seminar on film and video subjects, bringing together users, makers, and students interested in production and use. *Publications: Visual Media/Visuels Miedias.*

Part Five

Graduate Programs

Doctoral Programs in Instructional Technology

Brenda Branyan-Broadbent, Ph.D.
Associate Professor

Lois A. Ward
Staff Assistant II
Department of Instructional Technology
Utah State University
Logan, Utah

This directory presents data on 63 doctoral programs (Ph.D. and Ed.D.) in instructional technology, educational communications/technology, media services, and closely-allied programs currently being offered throughout the United States. Information in this section was obtained from, and updated by, the institutional deans, chairpersons, or their representatives, in response to an inquiry-questionnaire mailed to them during the summer of 1990. The survey conducted for *EMTY 1991* revealed that no new doctoral-level programs have been created. One doctoral program, East Texas State University, has been eliminated due to economic cutbacks.

Doctoral programs have experienced some changes in their administrative leadership. International student enrollments continue to increase and as would be expected, most graduates seek positions as teachers in colleges or as instructional designers/developers in business and industry. Continuous interest in seeking employment in "high technology" areas, or working with distance education technologies, was apparent in data provided by the respondents.

Entries provide the following data (1) name and address of the institution; (2) chairperson or other individual in charge of the doctoral program; (3) types of degrees offered and specializations, including information regarding positions for which candidates are prepared; (4) special features of the degree program; (5) admission requirements, including minimal grade point average; (6) information on faculty; (7) number of full-time and part-time students participating in the program; (8) details of available financial assistance; (9) doctoral program trends; and (10) the total number of men (m), total number of women (w), and the number of foreign nationals who graduated with doctorates during the one-year period between 1 July 1989 and 30 June 1990.

Directors of advanced professional programs for instructional technology/media specialists should find the information furnished in this directory useful as a means of comparing their own offerings and requirements with those of institutions offering comparable programs. Individuals seeking a school at which to pursue advanced graduate studies should be assisted by this listing to locate institutions that best suit their interests and requirements.

Additional information concerning listed programs, including instructions on applying for admission, may be obtained by contacting individual program coordinators.

General or graduate catalogs usually will be furnished for a minimal charge, while specific program information normally will be sent at no charge.

In endeavoring to provide complete listings, we are greatly indebted to those individuals who responded to our requests for information.

While considerable effort has been expended to ensure completeness of the listings, there may be institutions within the United States or its territories that now have programs or that have been omitted. Readers are encouraged to furnish new information to the publisher who, in turn, will follow up for the next edition of *EMTY*.

Institutions in this section are listed alphabetically by state.

ALABAMA

University of Alabama. School of Library and Information Services, Tuscaloosa, AL 35487. J. Gordon Coleman, Jr., Coord., Doctoral Program, School of Library and Information Services. *Specializations:* Ph.D. in Library and Information Science with specializations in school library media, youth services, library management, information studies, and historical studies. *Features:* Program is designed to fit the needs of the student using the resources of the entire university. Students may prepare for careers in teaching and research in colleges and universities or for innovative practice in the profession. *Admission Requirements:* Master's in library science, instructional technology or equivalent, Miller Analogies Test score of 55, Graduate Record Exam score of 1,650, 3.5 graduate GPA, three letters of recommendation, writing sample, curriculum vitae, and statement of purpose. *Faculty:* 12 full-time; 4 part-time. *Students:* 7 full-time, 3 part-time. *Assistance:* Six 20-hour assistantships paying $622/month with all tuition waived (in-state and out-of-state); some scholarships. *Doctoral Program Trends:* Doctoral program initiated in August 1988. *Doctorates Awarded 1989-90:* 0 (relatively new program).

ARIZONA

Arizona State University. College of Education, Tempe, AZ 85287-0611. Howard Sullivan, Prof., Div. of Psychology in Education, College of Education. *Specializations:* School offers program of study leading to the Ph.D. and Ed.D. degree in educational technology. Primary content focus of both programs is on instructional design and development, with strong research emphasis. Students may complement this focus with concentrated work in such areas as instructional media, computer-based education, training, etc. Preparation is for work as university faculty and instructional designers and trainers in business, industry, the military, and higher education. *Features:* Instructional development internships in higher education, or in business, industry, and the military. *Admission requirements:* Three months prior to enrollment: all university application forms, two transcripts from each institution in which previous academic work has been completed, three letters of reference, a score report for either the Miller Analogies Test (65 or higher) or the GRE (1200 or higher verbal plus quantitative), statement of professional goals, and undergraduate GPA of 3.0 or better. *Faculty:* 3 full-time. *Students:* 12 full-time, 12 part-time. *Assistance:* Graduate assistantships $2,750-$10,000 per academic year; summer assistantship opportunities; fellowships; scholarships; loans administered through the university financial aid office. *Doctoral Program Trends:* More than half of program graduates obtain university positions. *Doctorates Awarded 1989-90:* 2w.

CALIFORNIA

United States International University. School of Education, San Diego, CA 92131. *Specializations:* The Ed.D. Program is designed to attract students interested in a variety of emphases: computer literacy, teaching with or about computers, computer program coordination, instructional systems development, distance education, and microcomputer management. Prepares individuals to serve in a variety of positions: school district coordinators for instructional computing, specialists in designing learning strategies and training programs, university directors of learning resources, and change agents in industry and the military having teaching or training as a primary concern. *Features:* Program involves required core courses in human behavior and futuristics, concentration courses in leadership, cognitive theory, global education, statistics, and elective specialization courses including computer literacy, problem solving, microcomputer programming, microcomputer applications, issues in computer education, curriculum theory and design, and instructional systems development. The development of independent microcomputer use skills is emphasized. *Admission Requirements:* Admission to graduate program recommended by committee of faculty to the Dean of the School of Education. Evaluation of GRE or MAT test score, candidate's vita, three letters of recommendation, statement of purpose for study, and final committee interview. *Faculty:* 15 full-time, 5 part-time. *Students:* 40 full-time, 10 part-time. *Assistance:* A limited number of graduate assistantships offered in conjunction with research and development work undertaken at the university. *Doctoral Program Trends:* Increasing enrollment of international students from Taiwan interested in infusing computer technology into Taiwanese public schools. *Doctorates Awarded 1987-88:* 4m, 4w, including 4 foreign nationals.

University of California at Berkeley. School of Library and Information Studies, Berkeley, CA 94720. Robert Harlan, Prof., Coord., School of Library and Information Studies. *Specializations:* School offers two doctoral programs, Ph.D. and D.L.I.S. degrees in library and information studies. *Features:* Ph.D. requires original piece of research revealing high critical ability and powers of imagination and synthesis; the D.L.I.S. specifies candidate's command of a comprehensive knowledge and technical skills needed for initiating, organizing, and carrying out the investigation of significant problems in the field of library science. Both programs stress the need for familiarity with information processing technology, educational technology, database management systems, etc. *Admission Requirements:* Contingent upon admission to graduate standing including graduation from an accredited master's degree program with at least a B average. *Faculty:* 14 full-time. *Students:* Approximately 30. *Assistance:* Scholarships, fellowships, assistantships (research and teaching), and readerships. *Doctoral Program Trends:* Cognitive science now a Ph.D. subfield. *Doctorates Awarded 1989-90:* 4m, 5w.

University of California at Los Angeles. Department of Education, Los Angeles, CA 90024-1521. Aimee Dorr, Prof. of Education, Dir. of Educational Technology, Learning and Instruction Specialization, Div. of Educational Psychology, Dept. of Education. *Specializations:* Offers Ph.D. and Ed.D. programs. Ph.D. program prepares graduates for research, teaching educational technology, and consultancies in the development of instructional materials. Ed.D. program prepares graduates for leadership roles in the development of instructional materials and educational technologies. *Features:* The program addresses the design and utilization principles and processes underlying all effective applications of instructional technologies and their products. Television and microcomputer-based systems are encouraged. *Admission Requirements:* Superior academic record, combined GRE score of 1,000 or better. For the Ed.D. program, two or more years of relevant field experience is desirable. *Faculty:* 8 faculty participate in learning and instruction, of whom 2 teach full-time in instructional technology and the remaining 6 (all with full-time academic appointments) teach part-time in instructional technology and part-time in other areas in the department. *Students:* 9 full-time; 2 part-time. *Assistance:* Includes fellowships, tuition remission, and some paid research and teaching assistantships. *Doctoral Program Trends:* Doctoral applications from high-quality students have increased in recent years, and more students are interested in the instructional uses of computers in education. *Doctorates Awarded 1989-90:* 2m.

University of Southern California. School of Education, Los Angeles, CA 90089-0031. Edward J. Kazlauskas, Assoc. Prof., Prog. Chair, Instructional Technology.

Specializations: M.A., Ph.D., Ed.D. to prepare individuals to teach instructional technology; manage educational media/training programs in business or industry, research and development organizations, and higher education institutions; perform research in instructional technology and media; and deal with computer-driven interactive technology. *Features:* Special emphasis upon instructional design, systems analysis, and interactive video instruction. *Admission Requirements:* A bachelor's degree and satisfactory performance (combined score of 1,100) on the GRE aptitude test. *Faculty:* 4 cooperative faculty with joint appointments; 1 part-time. *Students:* 20 full-time; 75 part-time. *Assistance:* Part-time work available (instructional technology-related) in the Los Angeles area and on the university campus. *Doctoral Program Trends:* Enrollments of students seeking position placements in business/industry, instructional design/development, media production, and computer education.

COLORADO

University of Colorado at Denver. School of Education, Denver, CO 80204. David H. Jonassen, Prof., Chair of Instructional Technology Program, School of Education. *Specializations:* Ph.D. in instructional technology, in instructional development, and/or instructional computing for use in business/industry and higher education. *Features:* Courses in management and consulting, emphasizing instructional development, interactive video technologies, evaluation, and internship opportunities in a variety of agencies. *Admission Requirements:* Satisfactory GPA, GRE, writing/publication background, letters of recommendation, transcripts, and application form. *Faculty:* 5-½ full-time; 4 part-time. *Students:* 2 full-time, 10 part-time. *Assistance:* Corporate internships are available. *Doctoral Program Trends:* Preparation of students seeking position placements in business/industry, government agencies, computer-related fields, higher education, and/or university teaching. *Doctorates Awarded 1989-90:* 0 (relatively new program).

University of Northern Colorado. College of Education, Greeley, CO 80639. David H. Roat, Prof., Dir., Div. of Research, Evaluation and Development, College of Education. *Specializations:* Ed.D. program in interdisciplinary studies including educational technology/instructional development. *Features:* Program tracks on "process" issues of analysis, design, and evaluation of learning systems. Issues are supported by a foundation based upon learning theory, measurement, evaluation, and instructional delivery, including instructional computing and distance education methodologies. Graduates are prepared for careers as instructional technologists, course designers, trainers, instructional developers, media specialists, and human resource managers. *Admission Requirements:* GPA of 3.0 for master's program applicants, three letters of recommendation, congruency between applicant's statement of career goals and program goals, and GRE combined test score of 1,050. *Faculty:* 7 full-time; 2 part-time. *Students:* 20 doctoral; 61 M.A.; 31 graduate certification. *Assistance:* A limited number of Colorado Fellowships are available for full-time incoming students; graduate and research assistantships are available for full-time students. *Doctoral Program Trends:* Information not available. *Doctorates Awarded 1989-90:* 1m, 1w.

CONNECTICUT

University of Connecticut. Storrs, CT 06269-2001. Phillip Sleeman, Dir., University Center for Instructional Media and Technology, and Prof. of Education. *Specializations:* Ph.D., sixth year, and master's degree programs involving advanced instructional media and technology to prepare individuals in instructional technology positions of major responsibility in universities, colleges, community colleges, large school systems, state departments of education, government and industry, and other educational and media organizations of national scope. *Features:* The program seeks an optimum mix of competencies involved in solving instructional media and technology problems, with competencies in several fields of professional education (psychological foundations, social foundations, research and evaluation, business administration, curriculum and supervision, instructional media and technology, computers, videodiscs, teleconferencing, computer graphics, and data processing). *Admission Requirements:* Admission to graduate school; undergraduate GPA above 3.0; filing of Miller Analogies Test; evidence of scholarly attainments, interests, and potential for growth; the strength of validity of career motive, previous significant experience in the instructional media field; and at least five years of highly successful teaching experience (of which one or more years of administrative or supervisory experience would be desirable). *Faculty:* 3 full-time; 4 part-time. *Students:* Data not available. *Assistance:* A number of graduate assistantships, predoctoral fellowships, research fellowships, and federal and minority fellowships available competitively. *Doctoral Program Trends:* Interactive video, advanced learning theory, computer graphics, videodisc, and research. *Doctorates Awarded 1989-90:* 2m, 1w.

FLORIDA

Florida State University. College of Education, Tallahassee, FL 32306. John Keller, Prof. and Program Leader, Instructional Systems Program, Department of Educational Research, College of Education. *Specialization:* Ph.D. degree in instructional systems with specializations for persons planning to work in academia, business or industry, government, or the military. *Features:* Core courses include systems and materials development, analysis of media, project management, psychological foundations, current trends in instructional design, and research and statistics. Internships are also required. *Admission Requirements:* Total score of 1,000 on the verbal and quantitative sections of the GRE, or a GPA of 3.0 for the last two years of undergraduate study, 3.3 graduate GPA. International students must provide TOEFL scores. *Faculty:* 10. *Assistance:* University and college fellowships; grant and contract-funded assistantships. *Doctoral Program Trends:* Increased enrollments of students interested in position placements in business and industry. *Doctorates Awarded 1989-90:* 7m, 8w, including 4 foreign nationals.

Nova University. Fort Lauderdale, FL 33314. John Scigliano, Dean and Dir., Center for Computer-Based Learning. *Specializations:* Ed.D./CED, DAIS, D.A.T.L., and D.A.M.I.S. degrees designed for professionals concerned with educational use of microcomputers, networks, information management, and telecommunications. *Features:* Program enables individuals to advance in their professions through information handling, computer utilization, telecommunications, and learning theory. Emphases are placed on individual computer-based learning online (during evenings and weekends); interactive computer learning; teleconferences; seminars and field projects through a core curriculum of leadership; advanced programming; systems analysis; learning theory; educational research; and learning futures. *Admission Requirements:* Master's degree from an accredited university, appropriate work experience and related credentials, demonstrated computer literacy, and an aptitude for programming. *Faculty:* 7 full-time. *Students:* Full-time in each of the following programs: D.A. not reported; Computer Education, 110. *Assistance:* Guaranteed student loan program; some teaching assistantships. *Doctoral Program Trends:* Student attendance/participation at selected computing institutes; successful student participation in three practicums related to microcomputers and new technology. This new program is expanding rapidly and presently includes six foreign nationals as students. *Doctorates Awarded 1987-88:* 38.

University of Florida. College of Education, Gainesville, FL 32611. Lee Mullally, Assoc. Prof., Chair, Educational Media and Instructional Design Program, College of Education. *Specialization:* Ph.D. and Ed.D programs that stress theory, research, training, teaching, evaluation, and instructional development. *Admission Requirements:* A composite score of at least 1,100 on the GRE, an undergraduate GPA of 3.0 minimum and a graduate GPA of 3.5 minimum, and three letters of recommendation. *Faculty:* 2 full-time; 1 part-time. *Students:* 5 full-time; 10 part-time. *Assistance:* 2 graduate assistantships. *Doctoral Program Trends:* Increasing enrollments of students interested in position placements in business/industry, instructional design/development, and computer education. *Doctorates Awarded 1989-90:* 2.

GEORGIA

Georgia State University. University Plaza, Atlanta, GA 30303. Rosalind Miller, Prof. of Library Media. *Specializations:* Ph.D. in instructional technology, instructional development, media management in schools, special libraries, or business. *Admission Requirements:* Three letters of recommendation, handwritten and autobiographical sketch, admission tests, and acceptance by department. *Faculty:* 3.5 full-time equivalent. *Students:* 18 full- and part-time. *Assistance:* Graduate research assistantships. *Doctoral Program Trends:* Budget has remained about the same; facilities including space, hardware, and software have been upgraded while faculty and staff have decreased slightly. *Doctorates Awarded 1989-90:* 0.

University of Georgia. College of Education, Athens, GA 30602. Kent L. Gustafson, Chair, Dept. of Instructional Technology, College of Education. *Specializations:* M.Ed., Ed.S., and Ed.D. for leadership positions as specialists in instructional design and development. The program offers advanced study for individuals with previous preparation in instructional media and technology, as well as a preparation for personnel in other professional fields requiring a specialty in instructional systems/instructional technology. Representative career fields for graduates include designing/developing/evaluating new courses, tutorial programs, and instructional materials in a number of different settings; military/industrial training; medical/dental/nursing professional schools; allied health agencies; teacher education/staff development centers; state/local school systems; higher education/teaching/research; and publishers/producers of instructional products (textbooks, workbooks, films, etc.). *Features:* Minor areas of study available in a variety of other departments. Personalized programs are planned around a common core of courses; practica, internships, and/or clinical experiences. Research activities include special assignments, applied projects, and task forces, as well as thesis and dissertation studies. *Admission Requirements:* Application to graduate school, satisfactory GRE score, other criteria as outlined in *Graduate School Bulletin. Faculty:* 11 full-time. *Students:* 21 full-time. *Assistance:* Graduate assistantships available. *Doctoral Program Trends:* Increasing enrollments of students interested in position placements in business/industry. *Doctorates Awarded 1989-90:* 2m, 1w.

ILLINOIS

Northern Illinois University. College of Education, DeKalb, IL 60115. Dr. Gary L. McConeghy, Chair, Instructional Technology, College of Education—LEPS. *Specialization:* Ed.D. in instructional technology emphasizing instructional design and development, computer education, media administration, production, and preparation for careers in business, industry, and higher education. *Features:* Considerable flexibility in course selection, including advanced seminars, internships, individual study, and research. Program is highly individualized. A total of 60 courses offered by several departments, including Library Science, Radio/Television/Film, Art, Journalism, Educational Psychology, and Research and Evaluation. *Admission Requirements:* 2.75 undergraduate GPA, 3.5 M.S. GPA; combined score of 1,000 on GRE; a writing sample; and three references. *Faculty:* 5 full-time, with courses in other departments taught by several members of the graduate faculty; 3 part-time. *Students:* 55 part-time. *Assistance:* 9 assistantships available involving laboratory supervision, instruction, and instructional development activities on and off campus. Some additional fellowships and grants possible, especially for minority students. *Doctoral Program Trends:* Increasing enrollments of students interested in positions in business/industry, health, instructional design/development, and computer education. *Doctorates Awarded 1989-90:* 2m, 1w.

Southern Illinois University. College of Education, Carbondale, IL 62901. Billy G. Dixon, Prof., Chair, Dept. of Curriculum and Instruction, College of Education. *Specializations:* Ph.D. and M.S. in education with specialty areas in instructional technology, instructional development, computer-based education, and school library media. *Features:* All specializations are oriented to multiple education settings. *Admission Requirements:* M.S., 2.7 GPA or better; Ph.D., 3.25 GPA or better; MAT or GRE score; letters of recommendation; and writing sample. *Faculty:* 5 full-time; 5 part-time. *Students:* Approximately 140 current graduate students in these specialty areas. *Assistance:* Six graduate scholarships available plus university fellowship program. *Doctoral Program Trends:* Graduate student enrollment has continued to increase. *Doctorates Awarded 1989-90:* 4m, 3w.

Southern Illinois University. School of Education, Edwardsville, IL 62026. Gene D. Allsup, Prof., Chair, Dept. of Educational Leadership, School of Education. *Specialization:* Ed.D. (all-school degree) in instructional processes emphasizing theory and research, teaching, evaluation, and instructional systems design and development. *Admission Requirements:* GRE, undergraduate GPA of B+. *Faculty:* 6 full-time; 1 part-time. *Students:* 4 full-time; 10 part-time. *Assistance:* 4 graduate assistantships, 2 fellowships. *Doctoral Program Trends:* Increasing enrollments of students interested in position placements in business/industry, health, government, instructional design/development, and computer education. *Doctorates Awarded 1989-90:* 5m, including 1 foreign national.

University of Illinois at Urbana-Champaign. College of Education, Champaign, IL 61820. J. Richard Dennis, Assoc. Prof., Dept. of Curriculum and Instruction, College of Education. *Specializations:* Ph.D., Ed.D. programs (including advanced certificate program) with emphasis in the following areas: preparation of university research faculty, materials/training designers, computer resources managers, and continuing professional teacher training. *Features:* Programs designed to accommodate individuals with diverse background preparations. *Admission Requirements:* Master's degree, 4.0 out of 5.0 GPA, GRE submitted, a sample of scholarly writing in English, TOEFL scores including scores on Test of Written English for non-English-speaking students. *Faculty:* 8 full-time. *Students:* 60 full-time and part-time including 20 foreign nationals. *Assistance:* Limited fellowships available; some assistantships; non-English applicants for assistantships must also submit TOEFL Test of Spoken English scores; tuition waiver support available for highly qualified applicants. *Doctoral Program Trends:* Increasing emphasis on application of artificial intelligence and the design of intelligence tutoring systems. *Doctorates Awarded 1989-90:* 3m, 2w, including 1 foreign national.

University of Illinois at Urbana-Champaign. Department of Educational Psychology, 220 A Ed., 1310 S. 6th St., Champaign, IL 61820. Charles K. West, Prof., Div. of Learning and Instruction, Dept. of Educational Psychology. *Specialization:* Ph.D. in educational psychology with emphasis in educational computing. *Features:* Individually tailored program. Strongly research-oriented with emphasis on applications of cognitive science to instruction. *Admission Requirements:* Flexible: good academic record, high GRE scores, and strong letters of recommendation. *Faculty:* 16. *Students:* 35. *Assistance:* Scholarships, research assistantships, and teaching assistantships available. *Doctoral Program Trends:* Data not available. *Doctorates Awarded 1989-90:* 5.

INDIANA

Indiana University. School of Education, Bloomington, IN 47405. Michael Molenda, Assoc. Prof., Chair, Dept. of Instructional Systems Technology, School of Education. *Features:* Three major emphasis areas—instructional design and development, message design and production, and organizational change. Students draw on all areas when planning their academic programs. Virtually all students are full-time residents. Many opportunities for students to combine practice with study by working in the AV center and other appropriate agencies on and off campus. *Admission Requirements:* Satisfactory

GPA, verbal, quantitative, and analytical sections of the GRE. *Faculty:* 10 full-time, equivalent. *Students:* 83 Master's students. *Assistance:* Graduate assistantships, associate instructorships, fellowships, scholarships, and fee remissions. *Doctoral Program Trends:* Increasing enrollments of students interested in position placements in business/industry, instructional design/development, and computer education. *Doctorates Awarded 1988-89:* 5m, 3w, including 3 foreign nationals.

Purdue University. School of Education, West Lafayette, IN 47907. James D. Russell, Prof. of Education, Dept. of Curriculum and Instruction. *Specialization:* Ph.D. programs to prepare individuals to direct instructional development in school districts, health, business, government, and industry. *Admission Requirements:* GPA of 3.0 or better, three recommendations, scores of at least 1,000 on the GRE, statement by the applicant concerning his or her proposed goals and time schedule, and acceptance by the Department of Curriculum and Instruction. *Faculty:* 6 full-time. *Students:* 22 full-time. *Assistance:* Graduate teaching assistantships and graduate laboratory assistantships. *Doctoral Program Trends:* Increasing enrollments of students interested in position placements in business/industry, health, instructional design/development, and computer education. *Doctorates Awarded 1989-90:* 4m, 4w.

IOWA

Iowa State University. College of Education, Ames, IA 50011. Michael Simonson, Prof., Secondary Education, College of Education. *Specializations:* Master's or Ph.D. in education with an emphasis on media, computers, curriculum and instruction for public school and private corporate training, college and university supervision of media use, operation of an instructional materials center, and instructional development; higher education research and teaching, and teacher education programs; and positions in business, industry, or public and private agencies concerned with communications and teaching processes. *Features:* Practicum experiences related to professional objectives, supervised study and research projects tied to long-term studies within the program, development and implementation of new techniques, teaching strategies, and operational procedures in instructional resources centers, and four computer labs. *Admission Requirements:* Admission to graduate school, top half of undergraduate class. *Faculty:* 5 full-time. *Students:* 20 full-time; 20 part-time. *Assistance:* Graduate assistantships. *Doctoral Program Trends:* Increasing enrollments of students interested in positions in business/industry and computer education. *Doctorates Awarded 1989-90:* 3m, 2w.

University of Iowa. College of Education, Iowa City, IA 52242. Leonard S. Feldt, Prof., Psychological and Quantitative Foundations, College of Education. *Specializations:* Computer applications, instructional development, training, and human resource development. *Features:* Flexibility in planning to fit individual needs, backgrounds, and career goals. The program is interdisciplinary involving courses within divisions of the College of Education, as well as in the schools of Business, Library Science, Radio and Television, Linguistics, and Psychology. *Admission Requirements:* A composite score of at least 1,000 on GRE (verbal and quantitative) and a 3.2 GPA on all previous graduate work for regular admission. (Conditional admission may be granted.) Teaching or relevant experience may be helpful. *Faculty:* 4 full-time; 3 part-time. *Students:* 40 full-time and part-time. *Assistance:* Special assistantships (in the College of Education) for which students in any College of Education program may compete. Application deadlines for the special assistantships is 1 February. *Doctoral Program Trends:* Increasing enrollments of students interested in position placements in business/industry, instructional design/development, and computer education. *Doctorates Awarded 1989-90:* 3w.

KANSAS

Kansas State University. College of Education, Manhattan, KS 66506-5301. Jackson Byars, Prof., Dept. of Educational Media and Technology, College of Education. *Specializations:* Ph.D. and Ed.D. program. This program is offered on a semester basis and requires 90 credit hours including 60 in media and technology, one year of residency, and a dissertation. *Faculty:* 4 full-time; 6 part-time. *Students:* 26. *Doctoral Program Trends:* Increasing enrollments of students interested in position placements in business/industry, health, college teaching, instructional design/development, and computer education. *Doctorates Awarded 1987-88:* 4m, 4w.

University of Kansas. Instructional Technology Center, Lawrence, KS 66045. Ronald Aust, Asst. Prof., Curriculum and Instruction, Dir., Instructional Technology Center. *Specializations:* Ph.D., Ed.D., Ed.S., and M.S. to prepare instructional technologists to serve in leadership roles in a variety of educational settings. Emphasis is on the use of research-based data to guide decision making in the various roles required of instructional technologists. Special attention is given to the principles and procedures for designing instruction with computers, video, interactive video, and for distance learning applications. *Features:* The Instructional Technology Center provides a laboratory setting to assist in research projects and in the acquisition of production, instructional development, and media management skills. The department's microcomputer laboratories provide access to current equipment and software. Students are encouraged to work with faculty on appropriate projects. In addition to a common core, flexibility is built into the program so students may pursue their own interests. *Admission Requirements:* Regular admission, 3.5 GPA and 900 GRE; Provisional, 3.25 GPA and 900 GRE or 3.5 GPA with less than 900 GRE. *Faculty:* 3. *Students:* 5 full-time; 12 part-time. *Assistance:* 4 graduate teaching assistantships (apply by 1 March). *Doctoral Program Trends:* Increasing enrollment of students interested in position placements in college teaching, in business and industry training, and computer education. *Doctorates Awarded 1988-89:* 2m, 1w.

KENTUCKY

University of Kentucky. College of Education, Lexington, KY 40506. Gary Anglin, Assoc. Prof., Dept. of Curriculum and Instruction, College of Education. *Specialization:* Ed.D. program emphasizing instructional design/instructional technology, research, and teaching. *Features:* Data not available. *Admission Requirements:* A minimum composite score (verbal and quantitative) of 1,000 on the GRE, minimum undergraduate GPA of 2.5, minimum graduate GPA of 3.4. Concurrent applications to the Graduate School and Department are required, including letters of recommendation. *Faculty:* 2 full-time. *Students:* 12. *Assistance:* A limited number of teaching associateships and research assistantships are awarded on a competitive basis. Applicants for available minority fellowships are encouraged. Financial assistance package includes tuition remission. *Doctoral Program Trends:* Increasing enrollments of students interested in positions in business/industry, college teaching, instructional design/development, and computer education. *Doctorates Awarded 1988-89:* 0.

MARYLAND

The Johns Hopkins University. School of Continuing Studies, Baltimore, MD 21218. Joyce Steeves, Prof., Div. of Education, School of Continuing Studies. *Specializations:* Ed.D. in human communications and its disorders—a dual-major degree in technology and one of the following areas: mild-moderate handicapped and severely/profoundly handicapped. The program requires 99 semester hours beyond the baccalaureate including 12 hours of dissertation research and 27 hours in computers and related rehabilitation educational technology. (A master's level program is also offered.) *Features:* Computer courses including but not limited to assistive technology, authoring programs, and systems, LOGO, interactive videodisc, hardware and adaptive devices, software selection/evaluation, expert systems, robotics, networking, and computerized information and data management in special education. Internships and practicum opportunities in special education and rehabilitation settings. *Admission Requirements:* Master's or doctorate from an accredited institution. *Faculty:* 3 full-time; 12 part-time. *Students:* 30 full-time and part-time. *Assistance:* Information available through Joyce Steeves, Center for Technology and Human Disabilities, 2301 Argonne Street, Baltimore, MD 21218. *Doctoral Program Trends:* Emphasis on applications of microcomputers and related technology. *Doctorates Awarded 1989-90:* 1.

University of Maryland. College of Library and Information Services, College Park, MD 20742. Claude E. Watson, Prof. and Dean, College of Library and Information Services. *Specializations:* Ph.D. in Library Science and Educational Technology/Instructional Communication. *Features:* Program is broadly conceived and interdisciplinary in nature, using the resources of the entire campus. The student and the advisor design a program of study and research to fit the student's background, interests, and professional objectives. Students prepare for careers in teaching and research in information science and librarianship and elect concentrations including educational technology/instructional communication. *Admission Requirements:* Baccalaureate degree (the majority enter with master's degrees in library science, educational technology, or other relevant disciplines), GRE general tests, three letters of recommendation, and a statement of purpose. Interviews required when feasible. *Faculty:* 15-½ with doctorates and 16 part-time. *Students:* 22 full-time. *Assistance:* Some fellowships starting at $8,800, with remission of tuition; some assistantships also available. *Doctorates Awarded 1988-89:* 3.

MASSACHUSETTS

Boston University. School of Education, Boston, MA 02215. Gaylen B. Kelley, Prof., Chair, Program in Educational Media and Technology, School of Education. *Specializations:* Ed.D. for developing and teaching academic programs in instructional technology in community colleges and universities; or specialization in such application areas as business and industrial training, biomedical communication, or international development projects. Program specializations in instructional development, media production and design, and instructional facilities design for media and technology. Students participate in mandatory research sequence and may elect courses in other university schools and colleges. *Features:* Doctoral students have a great deal of flexibility in program planning and are encouraged to plan programs that build on prior education and experience and that lead to specific career goals; there is strong faculty participation in this process. *Admission Requirements:* Three letters of recommendation, Miller Analogies Test score, copies of undergraduate and graduate transcripts, complete application form with statement of goals, and a personal interview with the department chair (may be waived). Minimum GPA is 2.7 with MAT score of 50. *Faculty:* 3 full-time; 13 part-time. *Students:* 10 full-time; 57 part-time. *Assistance:* A number of assistantships and part-time instructor positions. *Doctoral Program Trends:* Increasing enrollments of students interested in position placements in business/industry, health, government, program administration, instructional design/development, media production, and computer education. *Doctorates Awarded 1989-90:* 4m, 2w, including 3 foreign nationals.

MICHIGAN

Michigan State University. College of Education, East Lansing, MI 48824. Leighton A. Price, Prof., Coord. of the Educational Systems Development Program, Department of Counseling, Educational Psychology and Special Education. *Program Basis:* Quarter. *Specializations:* Ph.D. and Ed.D. to prepare individuals to improve the quality and effectiveness of instructional delivery systems, to improve learning at all educational and training levels, and to serve as instructional developers and highly qualified training personnel. Emphasis is given to systems design and analysis, to selection and evaluation of instructional computing and other educational technologies, to design and validation of instructional materials, and to research on attributes of teaching strategies and supporting technologies. *Features:* Individually designed doctoral programs, guided field experience in instructional design projects, and cognitive work in areas such as communication, higher education, or instructional resource management. *Admission Requirements:* Master's degree with an acceptable academic record, transcripts, teaching credentials (preferred), three letters of recommendation, acceptable verbal and quantitative GRE scores, statement describing professional goals and ways that the doctoral program may contribute to their achievement, and a personal interview. *Faculty:* 9 full-time; 1 part-time. *Students:* 15 Ph.D. candidates. *Assistance:* Some fellowship and graduate assistantship opportunities in instructional development and technology are available for qualified applicants. *Doctoral Program Trends:* The program is responding to rapid developments in the field of educational technology. *Doctorates Awarded 1987-88:* 2m, 1w, including 1 foreign national.

University of Michigan. Department of Educational Studies, Ann Arbor, MI 48109-1259. Patricia Baggett, Assoc. Prof., Chair, Computers and Education. *Specializations:* M.A., Ed.D. and joint M.A. and Ph.D. with the Computer Science Department. *Minimum Degree Requirements:* 30 credit hours for master's, 60 for doctorate. *Faculty:* 2 full-time; several partial appointments. *Graduate students:* Approximately 15.

Wayne State University. College of Education, Detroit, MI 48202. Rita C. Richey, Coord., Instructional Technology Progrms, Div. of Administrative and Organizational Studies, College of Education. *Specializations:* Ed.D. and Ph.D. programs to prepare individuals for leadership in business, industry, health care, and the K-12 school setting as instructional development specialists, media or learning resources managers or consultants, specialists in instructional video, and computer-assisted specialists. *Features:* Guided field experience and participation in instructional development activities in business and industry. *Admission Requirements:* Master's, GPA of 3.5, strong professional recommendations, and an interview. *Faculty:* 4 full-time; 5 part-time. *Students:* 135 full-time and part-time. *Assistance:* Contract industrial internships. *Doctoral Program Trends:* Increased enrollments of students seeking position placements in college teaching, instructional design/development, and computer education. *Doctorates Awarded 1989-90:* 2m, 2w.

MINNESOTA

University of Minnesota. College of Education, Minneapolis, MN 55455. Gregory C. Sales, Assoc. Prof., Curriculum and Instructional Systems, College of Education. *Specializations:* M.A., M.Ed., and Ph.D. in education are offered through the graduate school. Areas of study include instructional design and technology, computer-based instruction, and curriculum systems and instruction research. *Features:* Internships and special field experiences. *Admission Requirements:* General requirements for admission. *Faculty:* 5 full-time; 5 associate. *Students:* 140 full- and part-time. *Assistance:* Teaching fellowships, research, project assistantships, and internships are available. *Doctoral Program Trends:* Increasing enrollments of students interested in position placements in college teaching, business/industry, instructional design/development, and computer education. *Doctorates Awarded 1989-90:* 1m, 4w.

MISSOURI

University of Missouri—Columbia. College of Education, Columbia, MO 65211. John F. Wedman, Assoc. Prof., Educational Technology Program, Curriculum and Instruction Dept., College of Education. *Specializations:* Ph.D. and Ed.D. programs to prepare individuals for positions in higher education and instructional development positions in both industry and the military. *Features:* Program deals with educational computing, instructional design, and media development. Support areas, such as communications and management, are integrated with educational technology courses to form a degree plan that is both focused and broadbased. An internship experience, in a setting consistent with the career goals of the student, is also included. *Admission Requirements:* Graduate GPA above 3.5 and a combined score of 1,350 or better on the GRE or a graduate GPA of 3.2 and a combined score of 1,500 or better on the GRE. Minimum of two years of appropriate professional experience, letters of recommendation, and statement of purpose. A TOEFL score of 550 or better is required for students whose native language is not English. *Faculty:* 3 full-time; 3 part-time; plus selected faculty in interdisciplinary fields. *Students:* 14 students are currently active in the doctoral program. *Assistance:* Scholarships and fellowships, ranging from $200 to $8,000, available from several sources. Teaching and research assistantships available to qualified individuals. Special financial support available for minority and foreign national students. *Doctoral Program Trends:* Research and development activities related to distance learning technologies used in various educational settings. *Doctorates Awarded 1989-90:* 2m (foreign nationals).

NEBRASKA

University of Nebraska. Teachers College, Lincoln, NE 68588-0515. Gordon F. Culver, Prof., Teachers College. *Specializations and Features:* Ph.D. and Ed.D. programs are in administration, curriculum, and instruction with an emphasis in instructional technology. Students in these programs demonstrate competencies for professions in instructional design, research in instructional technology, and training by developing appropriate portfolios. Within the context of a balanced graduate experience in instructional technology, extensive experiences in the use of videodisc technologies are possible. *Admission Requirements:* Admission standards are set by the graduate college. *Faculty:* 3 full-time faculty teach in the instructional technology program; 5 are involved in videodisc design and production. *Assistance:* Scholarship and externally-based funding support available. *Doctoral Program Trends:* Program emphasizes "design and theory" in the area of instructional technology. *Doctorates Awarded 1989-90:* 1.

NEW JERSEY

Rutgers – The State University of New Jersey. The Graduate School, New Brunswick, NJ 08903. Brent D. Ruben, Prof., and Dir., Ph.D. Program, School of Communication, Information and Library Studies, The Graduate School. *Specializations:* Ph.D. programs in communication; information and communication in management and organizational processes; information systems, structures and users; information and communication policy and technology; and library and information services. *Features:* Program provides doctoral-level coursework for students seeking theoretical and research skills for scholarly and professional leadership in the information and communication fields. *Admission Requirements:* Typically, students should have completed a master's degree in information studies, communication, library science, or related field. The undergraduate GPA should be 3.0 or better. The GRE is required; TOEFL is also required for foreign applicants whose native language is not English. *Faculty:* 36 full-time. *Students:* 82 full-time and part-time. *Assistance:* Approximately 16 teaching assistantships and one Title II-B Fellowship available per year for full-time students. Research assistantships and other work opportunities are also available. *Doctoral Program Trends:* Increasing emphasis on relationship between communication and information, and the impact of both on human behavior. *Doctorates Awarded 1989-90:* 3m, 5w.

NEW YORK

Columbia University. Teachers College, New York, NY 10027. John B. Black, Prof. and Chair. *Specialization:* Ed.D. for individuals seeking careers in instructional technology; programs in instructional technology (in a department that also includes communication and computing in education). *Features:* Part-time employment is available and encouraged as part of the coursework of 90 semester hours (in addition to the dissertation). Programs are individually planned, interdisciplinary, and based on prior and present interests and anticipated future developments in instructional technology. Up to 45 credits of relevant coursework may be transferred. *Admission Requirements:* A record of outstanding capability, potential for leadership, and creativity as indicated from academic records, recommendations, score on the GRE, statement of expressed interest and future plans. *Faculty:* 5 full-time; 2 part-time. *Students:* 12 full-time; 32 part-time. *Assistance:* Limited scholarships (applications must be received before 1 January for the following September semester) and work-study financial aid for qualified applicants. *Doctoral Program Trends:* Increasing enrollments of students interested in position placements in business/industry, instructional design/development, and computer education. *Doctorates Awarded 1987-88:* 3w.

New York University. New York, NY 10003. Donald T. Payne, Assoc. Prof., Dir., Educational Communication and Technology Program. *Specializations:* Preparation of individuals to perform as instructional media designers, developers, and producers in education, business and industry, health and medicine, community services, government, and other fields; to coordinate media communications programs in educational television centers, museums, schools, corporations; health and medicine, and community organizations; to serve as directors and supervisors in audiovisual programs in all settings listed; and to teach in educational communications and instructional technology programs in higher education. *Features:* Emphasizes theoretical foundations, in particular a cognitive perspective of learning and instruction and their implications for designing media-based learning environments; participation in special research and production projects in multi-image, television, microcomputers, and computer-based interactive multimedia systems. *Admission Requirements:* Combined score of 1,000 minimum on GRE, interview related to academic and/or professional preparation and career goals. *Faculty:* 2 full-time; 7 part-time. *Students:* 100. *Assistance:* Some financial aid and work-study programs. *Doctoral Program Trends:* Increasing enrollments of students interested in position placements in business, industry, health, instructional design/development, media production, and computer education. *Doctorates Awarded 1989-90:* 1m, 1w; *Master of Arts Awarded 1989-90:* 1m, 9w.

State University of New York at Buffalo. Graduate School of Education, Buffalo, NY 14214. T. A. Razik, Prof. of Education, Dept. of Educational Organization, Administration and Policy. *Specializations:* Ph.D., Ed.D., and Ed.M. to educate graduate students in the theories, resources, and dynamics of instructional design and management. Emphasis is on the systems approach, communication, computer-assisted instruction, and model building, with a specific focus on the efficient implementation of media in instruction. *Features:* The program is geared to instructional development, systems analysis, systems design and management in educational and non-educational organizations; research is oriented to the analysis of communication and information theory. Laboratories are available to facilitate student and faculty research projects in educational and/or training settings. Specifically, the knowledges and skills are categorized as follows: planning and designing; delivery systems and managing; and evaluating. *Admission Requirements:* Satisfactory scores on the Miller Analogies Test and/or GRE, master's degree or equivalent in field of specialization, and minimum 3.0 GPA. *Faculty:* 3 full-time; 3 part-time. *Students:* 20 full-time; 33 part-time. *Assistance:* 3 graduate assistantships (apply by 10 March). *Doctoral Program Trends:* Increasing enrollments of students interested in position placements in business/industry, health, university teaching, instruction design/development, and computer application. *Doctorates Awarded 1989-90:* 5m, 2w, including 2 foreign nationals.

Syracuse University. School of Education, Syracuse, NY 13244-2340. Donald Ely, Prof., Chair, Instructional Design, Development, and Evaluation Program, School of Education. *Specializations:* Ph.D., Ed.D., and M.S. degree programs for instructional design of programs and materials, educational evaluation, human issues in instructional development, media production including computers and videodisc, and educational research and theory (learning theory, application of theory, and educational and media research). Graduates are prepared to serve as curriculum developers, instructional developers, program and product evaluators, researchers, resource center administrators, communications coordinators, trainers in human resource development, and instructors in education in higher education. *Features:* Field work and internships, special topics and special issues seminar, student- and faculty-initiated minicourses, seminars and guest lecturers, faculty-student formulation of department policies, and multiple international perspectives. *Admission Requirements:* A bachelor's degree from an accredited institution. *Faculty:* 7 full-time; 4 part-time. *Students:* 55 full-time; 45 part-time. *Assistance:* Some fellowships (competitive); and graduate assistantships entailing either research or administrative duties in instructional technology. *Doctoral Program Trends:* Increasing enrollments of students interested in position placements in business/industry, program administration, instructional design/development, and computer education. *Doctorates Awarded 1989-90:* 3m, 2w, including 4 foreign nationals.

OHIO

Kent State University. Instructional Technology Program, White Hall 405, KSU, Kent, OH 44242. Dr. Drew Tiene, Program Coordinator. *Specializations:* Ph.D. in educational psychology with courses in research methods, new technologies, instructional design, production and evaluation of media programming, change strategies, etc. *Features:* Program encourages students to take elective courses in relevant departments in the College of Education and across the university, for example in communications, psychology, technology, etc. *Admission Requirements:* Obtain a doctoral program application packet from the Graduate School of Education, White Hall 306. Send two completed copies of the application, a $10 application fee, transcripts, 5 letters of recommendation (at least 2 from previous instructors), score on one of the following: Miller Analogies Test, Terman Concept Mastery Test, or Graduate Record Exam. *Assistance:* Graduate assistantships and teaching assistantships available. *Faculty:* 4.

Ohio State University. College of Education, Columbus, OH 43210. Marjorie Cambre, Assoc. Prof., Contact Person, Instructional Design and Technology Program, College of Education. *Specializations:* Ph.D. in instructional design and technology for preparation of individuals to perform research and to teach in higher education, administer comprehensive media services, or engage in research, production and development leadership functions in higher education and related educational agencies. *Features:* Interdisciplinary work in other departments (photography, journalism, communications, radio and television, computer and information science); individual design of doctoral programs according to candidate's background, experience, and goals; internships provided on campus, in business and industries, and in schools; integrated school media laboratory, microcomputer, and videodisc laboratory. *Admission Requirements:* Admission to graduate school and specific program area in the College of Education, GRE general test, minimum 2.7 GPA, and satisfactory academic and professional recommendations. *Faculty:* Regular faculty—8 full-time in education. *Students:* 21 full-time; 14 part-time. *Assistance:* Graduate fellowships and scholarships are often available, as well as departmental teaching and research assistantships and assistantship opportunities in media facilities on campus. *Doctoral Program Trends:* Increasing enrollments of students interested in position placements in business/industry, instructional design/development, and computer education. *Doctorates Awarded 1987-88:* 6m, 1w, including 1 foreign national.

University of Toledo. College of Education and Allied Professions, Toledo, OH 43606. Amos C. Patterson, Prof., Chair, Dept. of Curriculum and Educational Technology, College of Education and Allied Professions. *Features:* Research and theory in the areas of instructional design, development, evaluation, computers, video, and training and human resources. Emphasis is in the empirical study of systematic processes and procedures in instructional technology, 135 quarter hours beyond the baccalaureate degree or 90 quarter hours beyond the master's degree, including tool skill courses and dissertation credit. Residency requirement of one year or three full-time summer quarters depending on Ph.D. or Ed.D. option. Option of one or two minor areas of study to be included in total program hours. *Admission Requirements:* Miller Analogies Test at or above 50th percentile, three letters of recommendation, official transcripts of undergraduate and graduate work, and autobiographic sketch. *Tuition and Fees:* $62.30 per quarter hour. *Faculty:* 11 full-time, 1 part-time. *Assistance:* Graduate assistantships require 20 hours of work per week. Basic stipend for assistantships of $4,800 with full tuition remission. *Doctoral Program Trends:* Increasing enrollments of students seeking position placements in business/industry, health, government, college teaching, program administration, instructional design/development, media production, and computer education. *Doctorates Awarded 1987-88:* 3m, 1w, including 3 foreign nationals.

OKLAHOMA

Oklahoma State University. College of Education, Stillwater, OK 74078. Douglas B. Aichele, Head, Dept. of Curriculum and Instruction, College of Education. *Specializations:* M.S. and Ed.D. programs in educational technology (microcomputers), media management/administration, materials production, utilization/application, theory and research, selection, college teaching, evaluation, instructional systems design, instructional development, curriculum foundations, and learning theory. *Admission Requirements:* Minimum of 3.0 GPA on undergraduate work (master's), Miller Analogies Test and minimum of one year teaching experience (doctorate). *Faculty:* 3 full-time; 2 part-time. *Students:* 14 full-time, 18 part-time M.S. candidates; 8 full-time, 12 part-time Ed.D. candidates. *Assistance:* 9 graduate assistantships. *Doctoral Program Trends:* Increasing enrollments of students interested in position placements in business/industry, college teaching, program administration, and instructional design/development. *Doctorates Awarded 1988-89:* 2m.

University of Oklahoma. College of Education, Norman, OK 73069. Tillman J. Ragan, Prof., Head, Dept. of Educational Psychology, Educational Technology Program Area, College of Education. *Specializations:* Ph.D. and Ed.D. leading to specializations for research, teaching, management, and consulting in instructional technology (including preparation in instructional design and development, computer, video, computer-assisted video instruction, and preparation in management of instructional systems and programs). *Features:* Programs are designed through the vehicle of an advisory conference in which the student's background and goals are translated into a program of study and research proficiencies; a practicum is included to provide experiences resembling those related to the individual's career objectives. Computer emphasis area now available. *Admission Requirements:* Evidence of potential for contribution to the field, satisfactory performance on the GRE aptitude test, satisfactory performance on advisory conference in second semester of post-master's work. *Faculty:* 3 full-time; 3 part-time. *Assistance:* Graduate assistantships involving teaching and service or research are available. *Doctoral Program Trends:* Increasing interest in instructional psychology, management and change, interactive multimedia, and instructional design. *Doctorates Awarded 1989-90:* 3m, 2w.

OREGON

University of Oregon. Division of Teacher Education, Eugene, OR 97401. Judith Grosenick, Assoc. Dean, Division of Teacher Education. *Specializations:* Ph.D. or Ed.D. in Curriculum and Instruction leading to public school, junior college, college, and university supervision of media use and instructional development; higher education research and teaching; and positions in business, industry, and public and private agencies concerned with instructional development, computers-in-education, product development, and training. *Features:* A flexible program designed to meet a specific student's needs. *Admission Requirements:* Master's degree. *Faculty:* 2 full-time; 4 part-time. *Assistance:* Graduate assistantships available: 8. *Doctoral Program Trends:* Increasing enrollments of students interested in computers-in-education, and in locating positions in nontraditional learning environments such as business and industry. *Doctorates Awarded 1988-89:* 4m, 2w.

PENNSYLVANIA

Pennsylvania State University. Division of Curriculum and Instruction, University Park, PA 16802. Paul W. Welliver, Div. of Curriculum and Instruction. *Specializations:* Ph.D. and Ed.D. for individuals seeking professional pursuits in instructional systems design, development, management, evaluation, and research in instructional endeavors within business, industrial, medical, health, religious, higher education, and public school settings. Present research emphases are on instructional development, dissemination, implementation, and management; interactive video; computer-based education; and visual learning. *Features:* A common thread throughout all programs is that candidates have basic competencies in the understanding of human learning, curriculum, instructional design development, evaluation, and research procedures. Practical experience is available in mediated independent learning, research, instructional development, computer-based education, and dissemination projects. *Admission Requirements:* GRE or MAT and acceptance as a prospective candidate by a graduate faculty member. *Faculty:* 6 full-time. *Students:* 48 full-time; 52 part-time. *Assistance:* Graduate assistantships in managing mediated independent study courses, operating media facilities, assisting in research projects, and participating in university instructional development projects and computer-based education. *Doctoral Program Trends:* Increasing enrollments of students interested in position placements in business/industry, program administration, instructional design/development, interactive video, and computer education. *Doctorates Awarded 1989-90:* 1m, 3w.

Temple University. Educational Media Program, Dept. of Curriculum, Instruction and Technology, College of Education, Philadelphia, PA 19122. Elton Robertson, Prof., Dept. of Educational Media. *Specializations:* Ed.D. in Curriculum, Instruction and Technology with emphasis in educational media for proficiency in employing instructional technology to enhance learning and teaching at elementary, secondary, and university levels, as well as in industrial training situations. *Features:* The program is designed to take into account the candidate's personal and professional goals. Practical experience is provided for those wishing to teach media-related courses, apply the newer interactive technology to enhance the instructional development process, and function in various administrative roles in support of learning resource and instructional resource centers. *Admission Requirements:* Bachelor's degree, master's degree or 24 credits in educational media, admission to the graduate school, media experience, and a satisfactory interview with the faculty. *Faculty:* 2 full-time. *Students:* 3 full-time; 27 part-time. *Assistance:* 4 departmental assistantships, fellowships. *Doctoral Program Trends:* Increasing enrollments of students interested in position placements in business/industry, government, instructional design/development, media production, and computer education. *Doctorates Awarded 1989-90:* 1m, 3w.

University of Pittsburgh. School of Education, Pittsburgh, PA 15260. Barbara Seels, Assoc. Prof., Prog. Coord., Program in Instructional Design and Technology, Dept. of Instruction and Learning, School of Education. *Specializations:* Ed.D. and M.Ed. programs for the preparation of generalists with skills in production, selection, use, instructional design, and CBI; certification programs for instructional technologists. Program prepares people for positions in which they can effect educational change through instructional technology. Program includes three competency areas: instructional design, technological delivery systems, and communications research. *Admission Requirements:* Submission of written statement of applicant's professional goals, three letters of recommendation, demonstration of English proficiency, satisfactory GPA, sample of professional writing, GRE, and personal interviews. *Faculty:* 4 full-time; 2 part-time. *Students:* 20 full-time; 80 part-time, of which approximately 16 are foreign nationals. *Assistance:* Tuition scholarships and assistantships may be available. *Doctoral Program Trends:* Increasing enrollments of students interested in instructional design. *Doctorates Awarded 1988-89:* 5m, 4w, including 2 foreign nationals.

TENNESSEE

Memphis State University. College of Education, Memphis, TN 38152. Thomas Rakes, Prof., Chair, Dept. of Curriculum and Instruction, College of Education. *Specializations:* Ed.D. offered in instructional design with career emphasis in schools, health care, and business and industry. *Features:* Internship, special projects, and research opportunities. *Admission Requirements:* Master's degree or equivalent and acceptable GRE. *Faculty:* 3 full-time; 2 part-time. *Assistance:* Assistantships. *Doctoral Program Trends:* Applied instructional design research and applied CBI research. *Doctorates Awarded 1989-90:* 2m, 5w.

University of Tennessee. College of Education, Dept. of Curriculum and Instruction, Knoxville, TN 37996-3400. Dr. Al Grant, Coord., Instructional Media and Technology Program, College of Education. *Specializations:* M.S. in Ed. and Ed.S. in the Department of Curriculum and Instruction, concentration in Instructional Media and Technology; Ph.D. in the College of Education, concentration in Instructional Media and Technology; Ed.D. in Curriculum and Instruction, concentration in Instructional Media and Technology. *Features:* Coursework in media management, advanced software production, utilization, research, theory, psychology, instructional computing, television, and instructional development. Coursework will also meet some of the requirements for state certification as Instructional Materials Supervisor in the public schools of Tennessee. *Admission Requirements:* Send for the Graduate Catalog, The University of Tennessee. *Faculty:* 1 full-time, with additional assistance from Curriculum and Instruction and university faculty. *Doctoral Program Trends:* Graduate students are seeking professional media positions in medicine/health, corporations, and higher education. *Doctorates Awarded 1989-90:* 0.

TEXAS

East Texas State University. Dept. of Secondary and Higher Education, Commerce, TX 75428. Robert G. Munday, Prof. and Head, Dept. of Secondary and Higher Education. *Specializations:* Ed.D. is offered for individuals interested in emphasizing educational technology within the broad area of supervision, curriculum, and instruction; master's degree with majors in educational technology or library science is offered. Programs are designed to prepare professionals in instructional design, production of instructional materials, and teaching and leadership in public schools and higher education. *Features:* Programs are designed to meet professional goals of individuals. Opportunities are provided for practical applications through internships, practicums, and assistantships. *Admission Requirements:* Satisfactory GPA and GRE score, evidence of literary and expository skills and aptitudes, and recommendations. *Faculty:* 8 full-time; 2 part-time.

Texas A&M University. College of Education, College Station, TX 77843. Ronald D. Zellner, Assoc. Prof., Coord., Educational Technology Program, College of Education. *Specializations:* Ph.D. and Ed.D. programs to prepare individuals to teach college and university courses in educational technology, manage learning resource centers, and apply educational technology skills and knowledges in various settings related to communication and instructional processes in higher education, public education, business and industry, and public and private agencies. *Features:* The doctoral programs are flexible and inter-disciplinary; degrees are established and granted in conjunction with other departments in the College of Education; specialization areas include computer applications (CAI, CMI, interactive video), media, and video production; program provides laboratories, equip-ment, and a PBS television station. *Admission Requirements:* A bachelor's degree, admission to graduate college which includes satisfactory performance on the GRE; some requirements may vary with respect to the particular program in which the degree is housed. *Faculty:* 6 full-time; 1 part-time. *Students:* 3 full-time; 98 part-time. *Assistance:* Several graduate assistantships (teaching and project) and a limited number of fellowships; part-time employment on campus, in local school districts, and in surrounding commu-nities. *Doctoral Program Trends:* Increasing emphasis on placement in government, industry, and computer education settings. *Doctorates Awarded 1989-90:* 1m, 1w.

The University of Texas. College of Education, Austin, TX 78712. DeLayne Hudspeth, Assoc. Prof., Area Coord. at Austin, Instructional Technology, Dept. of Curriculum and Instruction, College of Education. *Specializations:* Ph.D. program emphasizes research, design, and development of instructional systems and communications technology. *Features:* The program is interdisciplinary in nature, although certain competencies are required of all students. Programs of study and dissertation research are based on individ-ual needs and career goals. Learning resources include a model LRC, computer labs and classrooms, a color television studio, interactive multimedia lab, and access to a photo and graphics lab. *Admission Requirements:* Minimum 3.0 GPA and a score of at least 1,100 on the GRE. *Faculty:* 3 full-time; 2 part-time. Many courses are offered cooperatively by other departments, including Radio-TV Film, Computer Science, and Educational Psy-chology. *Students:* 20. *Assistance:* Assistantships are available in planning and developing instructional materials, teaching undergraduate computer literacy, and assisting with research in instructional technology; there are also some paid internships. *Doctoral Pro-gram Trends:* Increasing enrollments of students seeking positions in business/industry, health, program administration, instructional design/development, and computer educa-tion. *Doctorates Awarded 1989-90:* 4.

UTAH

Brigham Young University. Department of Instructional Science, Provo, UT 84602. Paul F. Merrill, Prof., Chair. *Specializations:* M.S. and Ph.D. degrees are offered in instruc-tional science and technology. In the M.S. program students may specialize in instructional design and production, computers in education, or research and evaluation. In the Ph.D. program students may specialize in instructional design, instructional psychology, or research and evaluation. *Features:* Course offerings include principles of learning, instruc-tional design, assessing learning outcomes, evaluation in education, empirical inquiry in education, project and instructional resource management, quantitative reasoning, micro-computer materials production, naturalistic inquiry, and more. Students are required to participate in internships and projects related to development, evaluation, measurement, and research. *Admission Requirements:* For further information, write to Dr. Paul F. Merrill at the above address. *Faculty:* 10 full-time. *Students:* 20 M.S.; 40 Ph.D. *Doctoral Program Trends:* Increasing enrollments of students interested in position placements in business/industry, health, college teaching, instructional design/development, and computer education. *Doctorates Awarded 1989-90:* 6.

Utah State University. College of Education, Logan, UT 84322-2830. Don C. Smellie, Prof., Chair, Dept. of Instructional Technology, College of Education. *Specializations:* Ph.D. in educational technology. Offered for individuals seeking to become professionally involved in instructional development and administration of media programs in public schools, community colleges, and universities. Teaching and research in higher education is another career avenue for graduates of the program. *Features:* A relatively small program allowing individual attention. The doctoral program is built on a strong master's and specialist's program in instructional technology. All doctoral students complete a core with the remainder of the course selection individualized, based upon career goals. *Admission Requirements:* 3.0 GPA, successful teaching experience or its equivalent, satisfactory performance on the GRE, written recommendations, and a personal interview. *Faculty:* 8 full-time; 7 part-time. *Students:* 97 M.S./M.Ed. candidates; 6 Ed.S. candidates; 24 Ph.D. candidates. *Assistance:* Approximately 18 to 26 assistantships (apply by 1 June). *Doctoral Program Trends:* Increasing enrollments of students seeking position placements in business/industry, college teaching, instructional design/development, and computer education. *Doctorates Awarded 1989-90:* 3m.

VIRGINIA

University of Virginia. Curry School of Education, Charlottesville, VA 22903. John B. Bunch, Assoc. Prof. of Education, Dept. of Educational Studies, School of Education. *Specializations:* Ed.D. or Ph.D. program for well-qualified students seeking professional training in the design, production, and evaluation of instructional programs and materials in school or nonschool settings. Students may also work with faculty to conduct research on the effective uses of technology for instruction or information exchange. Graduates are placed as instructional developers or media specialists in education, as training developers in business, industry, or government agencies, or as university faculty. *Features:* A relatively small program that enables the department to tailor programs to the needs and goals of individual students (including options of minor area concentrations in other professional schools). Specializations are available in interactive technologies (a multimedia approach employing computer, compact disc, and videodisc-based materials), or media production (including video and photography). *Admission Requirements:* Satisfactory performance on GRE, written recommendations, and a personal interview. *Faculty:* 3 full-time. *Students:* 15 full-time; 25 part-time. *Assistance:* A number of graduate assistantships are available as well as a limited number of fellowships (application must be made prior to 1 April). *Doctoral Program Trends:* Increasing enrollments of students seeking positions in business/industry, health, college teaching, instructional design/development, media production, and computer education. *Doctorates Awarded 1989-90:* 2.

Virginia Polytechnic Institute and State University (Virginia Tech). College of Education, Blacksburg, VA 24061. John K. Burton, Prof., Program Area Leader, Instructional Systems Development, Curriculum and Instruction. *Specializations:* M.A., M.S., and Ed.D. programs in instructional technology. Preparation for education, business, and industry. *Features:* Areas of emphasis are instructional design, educational computing, evaluation, and media management. Psychology is the disciplinary theory/research perspective. The Instructional Systems Development Program houses the Self-Instructional Curriculum Lab (SICL) and the Education Microcomputer Lab (EML) which contains some 70 microcomputers (Apple, IBM, and Macintosh) including interactive video and speech synthesis capabilities. The program is also affiliated with the university's Learning Resources Center (LRC) which houses production services for graphics and video as well as satellite communications. Doctoral students are expected to intern either on campus (e.g., LRC) or off campus (e.g., Arthur Andersen Associates, AT&T, etc.) or both. *Admission Requirements:* 3.3 GPA for master's degree, three letters of recommendation, all transcripts. Experience in education recommended but not required. *Faculty:* 10 full-time; 2

split; 4 adjunct. *Students:* 10 full-time; 12 part-time. *Assistance:* Seven graduate assistantships; three tuition waivers; two to four additional graduate assistantships usually available due to contracts and grants. *Doctoral Program Trends:* Increasing use of computers for most production. Increasing liaison with private sector although most doctorates still take academic positions. Continued emphasis on graduate student research and publication presentation. *Doctorates Awarded 1989-90:* 4m, 3w.

WASHINGTON

University of Washington. College of Education, Seattle, WA 98195. William D. Winn, Prof. of Education, College of Education. *Specializations:* Ph.D. and Ed.D. for individuals in business, industry, higher education, public schools, and organizations concerned with education or communication (broadly defined). *Features:* Emphasis on instructional design as a process of making decisions about the shape of instruction; additional focus on research and development in such areas as message design (especially graphics and diagrams); electronic information systems; interactive instruction via videodisc, videotex, and computers. *Admission Requirements:* GRE scores, letters of reference, transcripts, personal statement, master's degree or equivalent in field appropriate to the specialization, 3.5 GPA in master's program, two years of successful professional experience and/or experience related to program goals. *Faculty:* 2 full-time; 3 part-time. *Students:* 12 full-time; 32 part-time. *Assistance:* Assistantships awarded competitively and on basis of program needs; other assistantships available depending on grant activity in any given year. *Doctoral Program Trends:* Students increasingly interested in applying ID principles to interactive instructional environments. *Doctorates Awarded 1989-90:* 3.

WEST VIRGINIA

West Virginia University. College of Human Resources and Education, Morgantown, WV 26506. David McCrory, Prof., Chair, Technology Education, Communication and Information Systems Sequence of Study, College of Human Resources and Education. *Specializations:* M.A. and Ed.D. degree programs in history of technical development, research, college teaching, instructional systems design, instructional development, and communication and information systems. *Admission Requirements:* GRE and Miller Analogies Test, minimum GPA 3.0. *Faculty:* 4 full-time; 2 part-time. *Students:* 10 full-time; 6 part-time. *Assistance:* Two teaching assistantships, three research assistantships. *Doctoral Program Trends:* Increasing enrollments of students seeking position placements in business/industry, government, program management, educational delivery systems, and computer education. *Doctorates Awarded 1988-89:* 2m.

WISCONSIN

University of Wisconsin. School of Education, Madison, WI 53706. Ann De Vaney, Prof., Dept. of Curriculum and Instruction, School of Education. *Specializations:* Ph.D. programs to prepare college and university faculty and staff, and instructional developers. *Features:* The program is coordinated with media operations of the university. Traditional instructional technology courses are processed through a social, cultural, and historical frame of reference. Current curriculum emphasizes communication, perception, and cognitive theories, critical cultural studies, and theories of textual analysis and instructional development. Strength in small-format video production and computers. *Admission Requirements:* Previous experience in instructional technology preferred, previous teaching experience, minimum 2.75 GPA on all undergraduate work completed, acceptable scores on either the Miller Analogies Test or the GRE test, and a minimum 3.0 GPA on all graduate work. (Note: Exceptions may be made on some of these requirements if all others are acceptable.) *Faculty:* 5 full-time; 2 part-time. *Students:* 25 Ph.D.; 35 M.S. *Assistance:*

A few stipends of approximately $1,000 a month for 20 hours of work per week; and other media jobs are also available. *Doctoral Program Trends:* Preparation of academics with strengths in social/cultural aspects of educational technology and the role of media in education. *Doctorates Awarded 1988-89:* 5m, 4w.

WYOMING

University of Wyoming. College of Education, Box 3374, Laramie, WY 82071. Landra L. Rezabek, Prog. Area Coordinator, Instructional Technology. *Specializations:* The College of Education offers both the Ed.D. and the Ph.D. programs. Students select areas of specialization and Instructional Technology is one option. *Faculty:* 6 full-time. *Doctorates Awarded 1989-90:* 0. For additional information, contact Dr. Landra L. Rezabek and see the university's master's degree programs.

Master's Degree and Six-Year Programs
in Instructional Technology

Brenda Branyan-Broadbent, Ph.D.
Associate Professor

Lois A. Ward
Staff Assistant II
Department of Instructional Technology
Utah State University
Logan, Utah

Program data for this yearbook were updated by program chairpersons or their representatives in response to an inquiry-questionnaire submitted to them during the summer of 1990.

Six-year specialist/certificate programs in instructional technology and related media are included in this directory, as was the case in 1990. Each of these specialist/certificate programs is identified by an asterisk and follows information about the institution's master's degree program.

Institutions of learning that offer master's and/or six-year specialist certificate programs have remained fairly constant in terms of enrollment, program offerings, and graduates. Regrettably, full programs have been deleted from this year's directory at the request of the respondents.

The M.Ed. program in Computers in Education at the University of North Carolina-Greensboro and the University of Maryland have been terminated. The master's programs at Queens College, Jersey City State College, and University of Missouri-Kansas City have either been discontinued or are not accepting new students. The University of Delaware reported that its master's program in educational studies is being phased out but will be replaced by an expanded program in educational technology. Although economic restrictions generally were reported as the catalysts for eliminating programs, it is interesting to note that staff changes, such as retirements, untimely deaths, and relocations also appeared as the principal reasons for the termination of programs.

As was true in 1990, foreign nationals continue to represent a small but significant part of the enrollment. Slightly more than 3 out of every 20 instructional technology program graduates are foreign nationals. Presently, a small number of foreign nationals are coming from Europe, the Middle East, Africa, and South America. Most foreign nationals, however, are coming from the Pacific Rim (Taiwan, Southeast Asia, Korea, the Philippines, and China).

Each entry in the directory contains the following information: (1) name and mailing address of the institution; (2) name, academic rank, and title of program head; (3) name of the administrative unit offering the program; (4) the basis on which the program is offered, i.e., semester, quarter, or trimester; (5) minimum degree requirements; (6) faculty information (male full-time faculty, female full-time faculty and equivalent part-time faculty);

(7) the number of men (m) and the number of women (w) who graduated with master's degrees from the program during the one-year period between 1 July 1989 and 30 June 1990; and (8) identification of those institutions offering six-year specialist degree programs in instructional technology. Several institutions have been listed twice because their computer technology programs are offered separately from their educational/instructional technology programs.

In endeavoring to update and make complete the listings that follow, we are greatly indebted to the staff members of the Association of Educational Communications and Technology (AECT) and the American Library Association (ALA); the state departments of education throughout the nation; and especially the instructional technology, educational communications, and media representatives of the participating colleges and universities in the United States. A special word of thanks is also due to those college/university secretaries who rendered special assistance.

To ensure completeness of this directory, considerable effort has been expended. However, readers who may know of either new programs or omissions are encouraged to provide information to the publisher who, in turn, will follow up on them for the next edition of *EMTY*. In those instances where repeated appeals for updated information were not responded to, the entry that appeared in *EMTY 1990* is included in order to have the program represented. Individuals who are interested in any of these graduate programs are encouraged to make direct contact with the head of the program to ensure that the most recent information available is acquired.

Institutions in this section are arranged alphabetically by state.

ALABAMA

Alabama State University. Library Education Media, School of Education, Montgomery, AL 36195. Katie R. Bell, Prof., Coord., Library Education Media, School of Education. *Program Basis:* Semester. *Minimum Degree Requirements:* 36 credit hours including 18 in media; thesis optional. *Faculty:* 2, 1, 0. *Graduates:* 3m, 31w.

*School also offers a six-year specialist degree program in instructional technology and library media. This 36-42 semester program includes 18 semester hours in an instructional support area, 12 hours in education including statistics on human development and behavior, and 3 hours in a research project. *Graduates:* Data not available.

Auburn University. Educational Foundations, Leadership, and Technology, Auburn, AL 36849. Jeffrey Gorrell, Prof., Dept. Head. *Program Basis:* Quarter. *Minimum Degree Requirements:* 48 credit hours including 36 in media. *Faculty:* 24, 14, 10. *Graduates:* 1m, 3w.

*School also offers a six-year specialist degree program in instructional technology. Program is offered as either a degree or a nondegree option. The program serves either to improve the certification of school media specialists or to provide higher level study in instructional design and/or the application of computers in the learning environment.

Jacksonville State University. Instructional Media Division, Jacksonville, AL 36265. Stanley Easton, Dept. Head, Dept. of Educational Resources, Instructional Media Division. *Program Basis:* Semester. *Minimum Degree Requirements:* 33 credit hours including 18 in media; thesis optional. *Faculty:* 2. *Graduates:* 10w.

University of Alabama. School of Library and Information Studies, Tuscaloosa, AL 35487-0252. Philip M. Turner, Prof., Dean. *Program Basis:* Semester. *Minimum Degree Requirements:* 36 credits including 21 in media. *Faculty:* 13, 6, 0. *Graduates:* 6m, 40w, including 2 foreign nationals.

*School also offers a six-year specialist degree program in instructional technology which is highly flexible and tailored to the students' educational needs. The program, leading to an Ed.S. degree, consists of 30 semester hours of coursework, does not require a thesis, and requires 12 of the 30 hours be taken in library media. *Graduates:* 1m, 1w.

University of South Alabama. College of Education, Mobile, AL 36688. John G. Baylor, Assoc. Prof., Dept. of Behavioral Studies and Educational Technology, College of Education. *Program Basis:* Quarter. *Minimum Degree Requirements:* 48 credit hours including 38 in media; thesis optional. M.Ed. program in educational media is for state school library media certification; M.S. program in instructional design is for employment in business, industry, the military, etc.; the Ed.S. in educational media leads to higher certification in library media. *Faculty:* 8, 1, 0. *Graduates:* 13m, 5w.

*School also offers a six-year specialist degree program in instructional technology for the improvement of teaching. The specific course offerings relating to the specialty field of educational media add to and complement the common core of the program and provide additional information and skills the media specialist needs to support the classroom teacher's efforts. *Admission to Candidacy:* Refer to the College of Education general section of the school's *Bulletin* for specific requirements for admission. *Ed.S. Graduates:* 1w.

ARIZONA

Arizona State University. College of Education, Tempe, AZ 85287-0611. Howard E. Sattler, Prof., Coord., Learning and Instructional Technology, Division of Psychology in Education, College of Education. *Program Basis:* Semester. *Minimum Degree Requirements:* 30 credit hours; thesis optional. *Faculty:* 4.5, 0. *Graduates:* M.A. degree: 6m, 4w; M.Ed. degree: 5m, 11w.

University of Arizona. Graduate Library School, 1515 East First Street, Tucson, AZ 85719. C. D. Hurt, Prof. and Dir., Graduate Library School. *Program Basis:* Semester. *Minimum Degree Requirements:* 38 graduate credit hours including 12 hours of core courses and a computer proficiency requirement; comprehensive required. *Faculty:* 9, 0, 0. *Graduates:* 25m, 71w, including 6 foreign nationals (1989 calendar year).

ARKANSAS

Arkansas Tech University. Department of Instructional Technology, Russellville, AR 72801. Dr. Elizabeth Salmeri, Head, Dept. of Secondary Education, School of Education. *Program Basis:* Semester. *Minimum Degree Requirements:* 36 credit hours including 24 in media and related courses; thesis optional. *Faculty:* 1, 1, 1. *Graduates:* 2m, 2w.

University of Arkansas. College of Education, Graduate Education Bldg., Room 339, Fayetteville, AR 72701. Donald E. Bumpass, Prof., Prog. Coordinator for Educational Technology. *Minimum Degree Requirements:* M.Ed., 33 credit hours, 18 in educational technology. *Faculty:* 3. *Graduates:* 8m, 12w.

University of Central Arkansas. Library Science Department, Conway, AR 73032. Selvin W. Royal, Prof., Chair, Educational Media/Library Science Dept. *Program Basis:* Semester: *Minimum Degree Requirements:* 36 credit hours. *Faculty:* 5, 3, 2. *Graduates:* 5m, 22w.

CALIFORNIA

California State University—Chico. College of Communications, Chico, CA 95929-0504. John Ittelson, Prof., Advisor, Instructional Technology Program and Communication Design, College of Communication. *Program Basis:* Semester. *Minimum Degree*

Requirements: 30 credit hours; thesis or project required. *Faculty:* 6, 0, 0. *Graduates:* 2m, 5w, including 1 foreign national.

California State University—Dominguez Hills. School of Education, Carson, CA 90747. Peter Desberg, Prof., Coord., Computer-Based Education, Graduate Education Department. *Program Basis:* Semester. *Minimum Degree Requirements:* 30 credit hours including 9 hours of educational common core units and 21 units of educational technology/computers; thesis optional. *Faculty:* 6, 1, 1. *Graduates:* 30m, 38w, including 7 foreign nationals.

California State University—Long Beach. Instructional Media, Long Beach, CA 90840. Richard J. Johnson, Prof., Chair, Dept. of Instructional Systems Technology. *Program Basis:* Semester. *Minimum Degree Requirements:* 30 credit hours including 21 in media; thesis optional. *Faculty:* 5, 1, 2 quarter-time. *Graduates:* 7m, 12w, including 2 foreign nationals.

California State University—Los Angeles. School of Education, Los Angeles, CA 90032. James H. Wiebe, Prof., Div. of Educational Foundations, School of Education. *Program Basis:* Quarter. *Minimum Degree Requirements:* 45 credit hours including 33 in media, including 2 options in the M.A. degree program: (1) computer education, and (2) instructional media and design. *Faculty:* 6, 1, 13. *Graduates:* 12m, 13w, including 2 foreign nationals.

California State University—Northridge. School of Communication, Health and Human Services, Northridge, CA 91330. Judith Marlane, Prof., Chair, Dept. of Radio-TV-Film. Master's program is in mass communication, offered jointly with Dept. of Journalism, R-TV-F Prog. Coord., John Allyn, Prof. Emphasis on theory and criticism and instructional media available within the mass communication program. *Program Basis:* Semester. *Minimum Degree Requirements:* 30 credit hours, plus needed prerequisites for students lacking needed undergraduate preparation. Seven 3-unit instructional media-oriented course offerings available to students. *Faculty:* 10, 4, 2. *Graduates:* 1m, 2w.

California State University—San Bernardino. Television Center, San Bernardino, CA 92407. R. A. Senour, Prof., Dir., Audiovisual and Instructional Television Center. *Program Basis:* Quarter. *Minimum Degree Requirements:* 45 credit hours including 20 in media; plus 8 video production and 8 computer-based education; program in media required. *Faculty:* 1, 2, 3. *Graduates:* 4.
*School also offers technical certificate programs in computer education and educational technology.

National University. School of Education, Vista, CA 92083. James R. Brown, Dir., Dept. of Instructional Technology, School of Education. *Program Basis:* Monthly. *Minimum Degree Requirements:* The equivalent of 60 quarter hours with media courses tailored to meet student needs; project required. *Faculty:* 7, 0, 2. *Graduates:* 26m, 11w.

Pepperdine University. Graduate School of Education and Psychology, Culver City, CA 90230. Terence R. Cannings, Prof., Graduate School of Education and Psychology. *Program Basis:* Trimester. *Minimum Degree Requirements:* 30 unit hours in educational computing. *Faculty:* 5, 0, 0. *Graduates:* 14m, 27w, including 2 foreign nationals.

San Diego State University. Educational Technology, San Diego, CA 92182. Patrick Harrison, Prof., Chair, Dept. of Educational Technology. *Program Basis:* Semester. *Minimum Degree Requirements:* 30 credit hours including 27 in educational technology, instructional design, and training. *Faculty:* 8, 1, 0. *Graduates:* 20m, 30w, including 5 foreign nationals.

San Francisco State University. Center for Educational Technology, San Francisco, CA 94132. Eugene Michaels, Coord. and Prof. *Program Basis:* Semester. *Minimum Degree Requirements:* 30 credit hours, specializations in instructional systems, instructional computing, and instructional video. Field study thesis or project required. *Faculty:* 5, 7, 3. *Graduates:* 10m, 12w.

*School also offers 18-unit Graduate Certificate in Training Systems Development which can be incorporated into the Master's program.

San Jose State University. Instructional Technology Program, School of Education, San Jose, CA 95192-0076. Robert Stephens, Assoc. Prof., Dir., Instructional Technology Program, Educational Leadership and Development Div., School of Education. *Program Basis:* Semester. *Minimum Degree Requirements:* 30 credit hours including 20 in media; thesis program. *Faculty:* 9, 2, 0. *Graduates:* 11m, 29w, including 8 foreign nationals.

United States International University. School of Education, San Diego, CA 92131. Dr. Maria T. Fernandez-Wilson, Acting Prog. Coord. and Asst. Prof., School of Education. *Program Basis:* Quarter. *Minimum Degree Requirements:* 45 quarter hours and nine-course M.A. in Computer Education tailored to meet computer literacy, problem-solving, software applications, curriculum development, and integrating microcomputers into instructional needs of classroom teachers, curriculum coordinators, and district-level specialists from the United States and a number of international countries. (International Summer 3-3-3 Master's Program available for candidates who wish to study abroad for one or two summers with a one-course per quarter load during the academic year.) *Faculty:* 4, 2, 2. *Graduates:* 10m, 24w, including 5 foreign nationals.

University of California–Berkeley. School of Library and Information Studies, Berkeley, CA 94720. Charlotte Nolan, Assoc. Dean, Library and Information Studies, School of Library and Information Studies. *Program Basis:* Semester. *Minimum Degree Requirements:* 28 credit hours in library science, computer science, and related. *Faculty:* 12, 6, 2. *Graduates:* 31m, 60w, including 8 foreign nationals.

*School also offers six-year specialist degree certificate program, 20 semester credit hours are required for each of the following four certificate programs: library and information studies; bibliography; library automation and information science; and library management. Students are expected to carry out an independent research or design project. There are no language requirements, qualifying examinations, or final comprehensive examinations to be met or passed in any of the programs. Each program of studies is drawn up by individual students in consultation with a faculty counselor. *Graduates:* 1m, 1w.

University of California–Los Angeles. Graduate School of Education, Los Angeles, CA 90024-1521. Aimee Dorr, Prof., Learning and Instruction Specialization, Div. of Educational Psychology, Graduate School of Education. *Program Basis:* Quarter. *Minimum Degree Requirements:* 36 credit hours with emphasis on all media of communication and instruction. *Faculty:* 2, 0, 6. *Graduates:* 1m, 3w.

University of California–Santa Barbara. Department of Education, Santa Barbara, CA 93106. Willis D. Copeland, Prof., Program Leader, Instruction, Dept. of Education. *Program Basis:* Quarter. *Minimum Degree Requirements:* 40 credit hours including 28 required and 12 elective; thesis required. *Faculty:* 2, 4, 0. *Graduates:* 8m, 8w, including 3 foreign nationals.

University of Southern California. Instructional Technology, Div. of Curriculum and Instruction, Los Angeles, CA 90007-0031. Ed Williams, Prof., Chair, Dept. of Educational Psychology and Technology, School of Education. *Program Basis:* Semester. *Minimum Degree Requirements:* 31 credit hours including 12 hours in media; thesis optional. *Faculty:* 5, 11, 2. *Graduates:* 11m, 13w, including 8 foreign nationals.

COLORADO

University of Colorado — Denver. Instructional Technology Program, School of Education, Denver, CO 80204. David H. Jonassen, Prof. and Chair, Instructional Technology Program, School of Education. *Program Basis:* Semester. *Minimum Degree Requirements:* For several tracks—instructional computing; corporate training and development, library/media and instructional technology, 36 credit hours including comprehensive; project or internship required. *Faculty:* 5, 2, 0. *Graduates:* 3m, 10w.

University of Northern Colorado. College of Education, Greeley, CO 80639. David H. Roat, Prof., Dir., Div. of Research, Evaluation and Development, College of Education. *Program Basis:* Semester. *Minimum Degree Requirements:* For M.A. degrees in educational media, instructional development, and educational computing, 30 credit hours with media credit varying with M.A. emphasis; comprehensive required; thesis optional. *Faculty:* 7, 2 adj. *Graduates:* 13m, 24w.

CONNECTICUT

Central Connecticut State University. Department of Educational Technology and Media, New Britain, CT 06050. Mary Ann Pellerin, Assoc. Prof., Chair, Dept. of Educational Technology and Media. *Program Basis:* Semester. *Minimum Degree Requirements:* 30 credit hours of which the number taken in media varies. *Faculty:* 3, 6. *Graduates:* 3m, 6w, M.S.; 2m, 4w, Certified Library Media Specialists; 2w, Elementary Education with Specialization in Educational Technology; 1w, M.S. without certification.
   *School offers 5th- and 6th-year planned programs in educational media.

Southern Connecticut State University. School of Library Science and Instructional Technology, New Haven, CT 06515. Emanuel T. Prostano, Dean and Prof., School of Library Science and Instructional Technology. *Program Basis:* Semester. *Minimum Degree Requirements:* For instructional technology only, 30 credit hours including 21 in media with comprehensive examination; 36 hours without examination. *Faculty:* 1, 2, 1. *Graduates:* 4m.

University of Connecticut. Center for Instructional Media, Storrs, CT 06268. Phillip J. Sleeman, Prof., Dir., Univ. Center for Instructional Media and Technology. *Program Basis:* Semester. *Minimum Degree Requirements:* 24 credit hours including 15 in media; thesis optional. *Faculty:* 3, 1, 4. *Graduates:* 6m, 5w, including 4 foreign nationals. Program for school certification is being discontinued.

DISTRICT OF COLUMBIA

Gallaudet University. School of Education, Washington, DC 20002. Ronald Nomeland, Prof., Chair, Dept. of Educational Technology, School of Education and Human Services. *Program Basis:* Semester. *Minimum Degree Requirements:* 36 credit hours including 26 in educational media and a related practicum. *Faculty:* 3, 0, 2. *Graduates:* 5w.

Howard University. School of Education, Washington, DC 20059. John W. Greene. Prof., Chair, Dept. of Educational Leadership and Community Services, School of Education, and Coord., Educational Technology Prog. *Program Basis:* Semester. *Minimum Degree Requirements:* 36 credit hours for M.Ed., including introduction to educational technology; computer-assisted instruction; individualized instruction; and instructional systems development; thesis required for M.A. degree. *Faculty:* 3, 3, 5. *Graduates:* 6m, 7w, including 1 foreign national.
   *School also offers a certificate of advanced graduate study usually totaling 30 credit hours of which 12-20 hours are in educational technology. Foundation courses in philosophy, sociology, and human learning are also required.

University of the District of Columbia. College of Education and Human Ecology, 4200 Connecticut Ave. NW, Washington, DC 20008. Leo Pickett, Assoc. Prof. and Chair, Dept. of Media/Library and Instructional Systems, College of Education and Human Ecology. *Program Basis:* Semester. *Minimum Degree Requirements:* For M.S. Degree in Instructional Systems, 30 hours of required courses and six hours of electives; for M.S. Degree in Library and Information Science, 30 hours of required courses and six hours of electives. *Faculty:* 6, 0, 2. *Graduates:* 11m, 10w, including 6 foreign nationals.

FLORIDA

Barry University. School of Education, Miami Shores, FL 33161. Sister Evelyn Picne, Dean, School of Education and Joel S. Levine, Prof., and Dir. of Computer Education Programs. *Program Basis:* Four nine-week cycles plus two intensive three-week and one two-week summer cycle. *Minimum Degree Requirements:* 36 semester credit hours including 6 credits in one of the following: practicum, internship, or thesis. *Faculty:* 6, 0, 0. *Graduates:* 15m, 20w, including 4 foreign nationals.

*School also offers 36 credit hours above the master's degree leading to a specialist degree in computer education. This program, while adhering to the master's program description, emphasizes in-depth studies in the area of specialized technology and related applications. *Graduates:* 6m, 4w.

Florida Atlantic University. College of Education, Boca Raton, FL 33431. Dan Kauffman, Prof., Cognitive Science and Artificial Intelligence, College of Education. *Program Basis:* Semester. *Minimum Degree Requirements:* 33 credit hours with emphasis on cognitive science and educational technology; thesis optional, but recommended. Graduates must demonstrate competence in learning theory, research methodology, future technologies, hypertext/hypermedia, computer applications, chaos theory, and two computer languages. *Faculty:* 3, 0, 0. *Graduates:* 8w.

Florida State University. College of Education, Tallahassee, FL 32306. Walter Wager, Prof. and Prog. Leader, Instructional Systems Prog., Dept. of Educational Research, College of Education. *Program Basis:* Semester. *Minimum Degree Requirements:* 36 hours; no thesis required. *Faculty:* 10, 0, 0. *Graduates:* 6m, 5w, including 2 foreign nationals.

Jacksonville University. Division of Education, Jacksonville, FL 32211. Daryle C. May, Prof. and Dir. of Teaching Prog. in Computer Education, Div. of Education. *Program Basis:* Semester. *Minimum Degree Requirements:* 36 credit hours including 18 in computer-related major. *Faculty:* 4, 3, 0. *Graduates:* 8m, 9w.

Nova University. Center for Advancement of Education, 3301 College Avenue, Fort Lauderdale, FL 33314. Donald Stanier, Dir. of the GEM Programs. M.S. and Ed.S. in Educational Media. *Program Basis:* Modules. *Minimum Degree Requirements:* 39 credit hours all in media; practicum required instead of thesis. *Faculty:* 5, 2, 2. *Graduates:* 3m, 22w, including 15 foreign nationals. (Please refer to Nova's doctoral program listing.)

University of Central Florida. College of Education, Orlando, FL 32816. Donna Baumbach, Assoc. Prof., Dept. of Educational Services, Educational Media/Instructional Technology Programs, College of Education. *Program Basis:* Semester. *Minimum Degree Requirements:* 39-45 semester hours including 30 in technology/media; thesis, project, or research options required. *Faculty:* 4, 4, 5. *Graduates:* 10m, 18w.

University of Florida. Educational Media and Instructional Design, Gainesville, FL 32611. Lee J. Mullally, Assoc. Prof., Educational Media and Instructional Design, Prog. Leader. *Program Basis:* Semester. *Minimum Degree Requirements:* 36 credit hours including 24 in educational media and instructional design; thesis optional. *Faculty:* 2, 0. *Graduates:* 1m, 4w.

*The Education Specialist Program is an advanced degree program and has the same requirements for admission as the Ph.D. and Ed.D. Programs. A special research and/or development project is required for the Ed.S. It also requires 72 semester hours beyond the B.E.

University of Miami. School of Education and Allied Professions, Coral Gables, FL 33124. Charles E. Hannemann, Assoc. Prof., Area Coord. for Educational Technology, Dept. of Teaching and Learning, School of Education. *Program Basis:* Semester. *Minimum Degree Requirements:* 30 credit hours including 12 hours in media for M.S. Ed. in organizational training; 30 credit hours including 15 hours in media for M.S. Ed. in instructional design; no thesis required but comprehensive written exam required. *Faculty:* 7, 4, 3. *Graduates:* 6m, 5w.

University of South Florida. School of Library and Information Science, Tampa, FL 33620. Robert J. Grover, Prof., Dir., School of Library and Information Science. *Program Basis:* Semester. *Minimum Degree Requirements:* 36 hours; thesis optional. *Faculty:* 7, 3, 0. *Graduates:* 12m, 67w, including 2 foreign nationals.

*The sixth-year specialist program allows students to specialize in areas such as services for special clientele and library management. Students pursue work in the School of Library and Information Science and in other departments depending on the student's particular needs and interests, e.g., communications, aging studies, guidance, and public administration. The 36 hours include 9 hours for a thesis or project. Application procedures are similar to those for the master's program. Admission requirements are (1) an undergraduate grade point average of 3.0, a minimum grade of B on the last half of the baccalaureate degree, or minimum GRE aptitude score of 1,000 (quantitative and verbal), (2) three letters of recommendation, and (3) a master's degree from an ALA-accredited library school.

GEORGIA

Georgia Southern University. School of Education, Statersboro, GA 30460. Jack A. Bennett, Assoc. Prof., Dept. of Educational Leadership, Technology, and Research. *Program Basis:* Quarter. *Minimum Degree Requirements:* 60 quarter-credit hours including a varying number of hours of media for individual students. *Faculty:* 3, 0, 0. *Graduates:* M.Ed., 6w.

*School also offers a six-year specialist degree program. The six-year specialist program is designed to extend the leadership preparation of school media specialists through a combination of courses in administration, supervision, and advanced media processes. *Graduates:* 4w.

Georgia State University. School of Education, Atlanta, GA 30303. Rosalind Miller, Prof., Coord., Library, Media and Technology, Dept. of Curriculum and Instruction, School of Education. *Program Basis:* Quarter. *Minimum Degree Requirements:* 60 credit hours including 45 hours in media; thesis optional. *Faculty:* 3, 3, 0. *Graduates:* 14w.

*School also offers a 50-hour six-year specialist degree program in educational media. Program is designed for practicing media specialists who have a master's degree. Research, education, content courses, and a research paper are required. *Graduates:* 5m, 7w.

University of Georgia. College of Education, Athens, GA 30602. Kent L. Gustafson. Prof., Chair., Dept. of Instructional Technology, College of Education. *Program Basis:* Quarter. *Minimum Degree Requirements:* 60 credit hours including 25 in media; thesis optional. *Faculty:* 11, 0, 0. *Graduates:* 6m, 23w, including 6 foreign nationals.

*School also offers a 45-hour six-year specialist degree program in instructional technology and a doctoral program. Master's program designed to meet certification requirements for those seeking to work in Georgia schools. Coursework includes educational psychology, curriculum design, instructional design, production, media center management, and an applied project. *Graduates:* 2m, 9w, including 2 foreign nationals.

West Georgia College. Dept. of Media Education, Education Center, Carrollton, GA 30118. Price Michael, Prof., Chair, Media Education Dept. *Program Basis:* Quarter. *Minimum Degree Requirements:* 60 credit hours. *Faculty:* 3 full-time. *Graduates:* 7w.

*School also offers a six-year specialist degree program. This program is designed to develop advanced competencies in such areas as curriculum design, information retrieval, development of instructional systems, design of media programs and facilities, skills in media research, and management. *Graduates:* 0 (new program).

HAWAII

University of Hawaii-Manoa. Educational Technology Department, 1776 University Ave., Honolulu, HI 96822. Geoffrey Z. Kucera, Prof., Chair, Educational Technology Dept. (808) 956-7671 or 956-3910. In fall 1990, 18 students enrolled. *Program Basis:* Semester. *Minimum Degree Requirements:* 39 credit hours, including 33 in educational technology; thesis and non-thesis available. *Faculty:* 4, 3, 0. *Graduates:* 2w.

IDAHO

Boise State University. College of Technology, Boise, ID 83725. Dean Spitzer, Assoc. Prof., Dir., Instructional/Performance Technology Program, College of Technology. *Program Basis:* Semester. *Minimum Degree Requirements:* 33 credit hours in instructional/performance technology and related coursework; project or thesis required (included in 33 credit hours). Program is also delivered through computer-mediated conferencing to students located anywhere in North America. *Faculty:* 2, 2, 0. *Graduates:* 8 (relatively new program).

ILLINOIS

Chicago State University. Department of Library Science and Communications Media, Chicago, IL 60628. Harry Liebler, Prof., Chair, Dept. of Library Science and Communications Media. *Program Basis:* Semester. *Minimum Degree Requirements:* 36 credit hours; thesis optional. *Faculty:* 4, 0, 0. *Graduates:* 7m, 41w, including 1 foreign national.

Eastern Illinois University. Secondary Education Department, Charleston, IL 61920. John T. North, Prof., Chair, Secondary Education and Foundations Dept. *Program Basis:* Semester. *Minimum Degree Requirements:* 32 credit hours including 24 in library/media; thesis optional. *Faculty:* 2, 2, 1. *Graduates:* 3m, 7w, including 1 foreign national.

Governors State University. College of Arts and Sciences, University Park, IL 60466. Michael Stelnicki, Prof., Instructional and Training Technology, College of Arts and Sciences. *Program Basis:* Trimester. *Minimum Degree Requirements:* 36 credit hours, all in instructional and performance technology. *Faculty:* 2, 2, 0. *Graduates:* 4m, 7w.

Illinois State University. Department of Communication, Normal, IL 61761. Vincent Hazelton, Prof., Chair, Dept. of Communication. *Program Basis:* Semester. *Minimum Degree Requirements:* 32 credit hours including 18 in media; thesis optional. *Faculty:* 2, 0, 0. *Graduates:* 4m, 6w.

Northeastern Illinois University. Instructional Media, Chicago, IL 60625. Christine Swarm, Prof., Asst. Chair. of Curriculum and Instruction, Coord. of Instructional Media, Coord. of Secondary Education. *Program Basis:* Semester. *Minimum Degree Requirements:* 33 credit hours including 21 in media; thesis optional. *Faculty:* 2, 2, 0. *Graduates:* 10m, 52w, including 2 foreign nationals.

Northern Illinois University. College of Education, DeKalb, IL 60115. Dr. Gary L. McConeghy, Chair, Instructional Technology, College of Education–LEPS. *Program Basis:* Semester. *Minimum Degree Requirements:* 39 credits including 30 in instructional technology; thesis optional. *Faculty:* 5, 3, 3. *Graduates:* 4m, 11w.

Rosary College. Graduate School of Library and Information Science, River Forest, IL 60305. Michael E. D. Koenig, Dean. *Program Basis:* Semester. *Minimum Degree Requirements:* 36 credit hours including media; nonthesis; required entrance examinations may include GRE and TOEFL. *Faculty:* 9, 15, 0. *Graduates:* 18m, 71w.

*School also offers certificate programs in law librarianship, library administration, and technical services and several joint-degree programs.

Southern Illinois University–Carbondale. College of Education, Carbondale, IL 62901. Sharon Shrock, Assoc. Prof., Coord., Instructional Development, Computer-Based Instruction, and School Library Media Programs, Div. of Curriculum and Instruction, College of Education. *Program Basis:* Semester. *Minimum Degree Requirements:* 32 credit hours plus thesis or 36 credit hours without thesis. *Faculty:* 7, 1, 2. *Graduates:* 8m, 12w.

Southern Illinois University–Edwardsville. School of Education, Edwardsville, IL 62026. Gene D. Allsup, Prof., Chair, Dept. of Educational Administration and Instructional Technology, School of Education. *Program Basis:* Quarter. *Minimum Degree Requirements:* 52 degree credit hours including 36 in instructional technology; thesis optional. *Faculty:* 5, 5, 0. *Graduates:* 12m, 17w, including 2 foreign nationals.

University of Illinois at Urbana-Champaign. College of Education, Champaign, IL 61820. J. Richard Dennis, Assoc. Prof., Dept. of Curriculum and Instruction, College of Education. *Program Basis:* Semester. *Minimum Degree Requirements:* 32 credit hours with emphasis on theory and design of interactive instructional systems, educational psychology, and educational policy studies; 4.0 (out of 5.0) minimum GPA required; TOEFL scores for non-English-speaking students; including scores for Test of Written English; and GRE submitted. *Faculty:* 9, 5, 0. *Graduates:* 6m, 15w, including 12 foreign nationals.

*School also offers a six-year specialist degree program in instructional technology. Program requires two years of demonstrated professional service and admission requirements comparable to those required for the master's degree. This program also requires 32 credit hours beyond the master's, of which 16 are at the most advanced graduate level. *Graduates:* 1m.

University of Illinois at Urbana-Champaign. Department of Educational Psychology, Champaign, IL 61820. Charles K. West, Prof., Div. of Learning and Instruction, Dept. of Educational Psychology. *Program Basis:* Semester. *Minimum Degree Requirements:* 8 units of credit, at least 3 of which must be in 400-level courses, 2 in the major field (graduate courses are offered for 1 or ½ unit each); thesis required. *Faculty:* 17.

Western Illinois University. Department of Media and Educational Technology, Macomb, IL 61455. Don Crawford, Prof., Chair, Dept. of Media and Educational Technology. (Offered in cooperation with Dept. of Educational Administration.) *Program Basis:* Semester. *Minimum Degree Requirements:* 32-36 credit hours including 18 in media; thesis optional. *Faculty:* 10, 5. Note: Faculty includes individuals also teaching undergraduate courses (our basic mission). We offer graduate courses in library/media and educational computing for support in other programs. *Graduates:* 2m, 4w.

INDIANA

Indiana State University. Media Technology, Terre Haute, IN 47809. James E. Thompson, Prof., Chair, Dept. of Educational Foundations and Media Technology. *Program*

Basis: Semester. *Minimum Degree Requirements:* 32 credit hours including 18 in media; thesis optional. *Faculty:* 9, 8, 1. *Graduates:* 5m, 10w, including 6 foreign nationals.

*School also offers a six-year specialist degree program in instructional technology.

Indiana University. School of Education, Bloomington, IN 47405. Michael Molenda, Assoc. Prof., Chair, Dept. of Instructional Systems Technology (IST), School of Education. *Program Basis:* Semester. *Minimum Degree Requirements:* 37 credit hours including 19 in IST; thesis optional. *Faculty:* 10, 2, 2. *Graduates:* 20m, 26w, including 16 foreign nationals.

*School also offers a specialist degree program in instructional systems technology. The description of this program is the same as the school's doctoral program in instructional systems technology except for the *Doctoral Program Trends* and *Doctorates Awarded* sections. *Graduates:* 3m, 3w, including 2 foreign nationals.

Purdue University. School of Education, West Lafayette, IN 47907. James Russell, Prof., Educational Computing and Instructional Development, Dept. of Curriculum and Instruction. *Program Basis:* Semester. *Minimum Degree Requirements:* 30 credit hours including 20 in instructional research and development; thesis optional. *Faculty:* 6, 0, 0. *Graduates:* 5m, 6w, including 2 foreign nationals.

*School also offers a six-year specialist degree program in instructional technology and related fields with emphasis in instructional research and development. Admission to the program requires prior completion of a master's degree. In addition to 30 hours of coursework, each student conducts a research project. At least one unit of residence credit for this degree must be earned on campus. The degree is a terminal degree and is not an intermediate step between the master's and doctoral degrees. *Graduates:* 1w.

Purdue University—Calumet. Department of Education, Hammond, IN 46323. John R. Billard, Assoc. Prof., Coord., Educational Media Prog., Dept. of Education. *Program Basis:* Semester. *Minimum Degree Requirements:* 33 credit hours including 24 in media; thesis optional. *Faculty:* 2, 2, 2. *Graduates:* 3m, 5w.

IOWA

Clarke College. Computers in Education, Dubuque, IA 52001. Judith Decker, Prof., Coord. *Program Basis:* Semester. *Minimum Degree Requirements:* 20-22 credit hours in computers, 9 hours in education, and 2-7 of electives. *Faculty:* 2.25, 1, 3. *Graduates:* 3m, 1w.

Iowa State University. College of Education, Ames, IA 50011. Michael Simonson and Roger Volker, Profs. and Coords., Curriculum and Instructional Technology (including media and computers), College of Education. *Program Basis:* Semester. *Minimum Degree Requirements:* 30 credit hours including 15 in media; thesis. *Faculty:* 5, 6, 1. *Graduates:* 6m, 7w.

Marycrest College. Graduate and Adult Programs, 1607 W. 12th St., Davenport, IA 52804. Thomas Faquet, Dean, Graduate and Adult Programs. *Program Basis:* Semester. *Minimum Degree Requirements:* For MA in Education: Computer Applications, 30 hours; For MS in Computer Science, 33 hours with thesis, 36 hours nonthesis. *Faculty:* 4, 0, 0. *Graduates:* 9m, 6w.

University of Iowa. College of Education, Iowa City, IA 52242. Leonard S. Feldt, Prof., Chair, Psychological and Quantitative Foundations, College of Education. *Program Basis:* Semester. *Minimum Degree Requirements:* 35 semester hours with or without thesis. *Faculty:* 4, 4, 0. *Graduates:* 9m, 15w, including 9 foreign nationals.

University of Northern Iowa. Department of Curriculum and Instruction, Cedar Falls, IA 50614. Robert R. Hardman, Prof. and Dir., Educational Media, Dept. of Curriculum and Instruction. *Program Basis:* Semester. *Minimum Degree Requirements:* For the educational media degree, 38 credit hours including 34 in media; thesis optional. For the communications and training technology degree, 38 credit hours including 32 in media; thesis optional. For the computers applications in education degree, 30 credit hours including 18 in computers; thesis optional. *Faculty:* 9, 4, 0. *Graduates:* 3m, 1w in educational media; 6m, 8w in communications and training technology.

KANSAS

Emporia State University. School of Library and Information Management, Emporia, KS 66801. Martha L. Hale, Dean, School of Library and Information Management. *Program Basis:* Semester. *Minimum Degree Requirements:* The ALA-accredited MLS requires 42 credit hours; the School Library Media Certificate Program requires approximately 27 hours and a teaching certificate. Media technology is a component of both programs. *Faculty:* 10, 0, 0. *Graduates:* 5m, 14w, including 3 foreign nationals.

*School also offers a school library certification program which includes 27 hours of the MLS program plus technologies mainstreamed into other courses. Computer theory and use is integrated into practically every course. In addition, the program offers three 2-hour computer courses and one 3-hour course which are combination theory and hands-on. Program is also available in Colorado and other out-of-state sites. Video courses are being developed.

Kansas State University. College of Education, Manhattan, KS 66506. John A. Hortin, Prof., Dept. of Curriculum and Instruction, College of Education. *Program Basis:* Semester. *Minimum Degree Requirements:* 30 credit hours including 21 in media; thesis optional. *Faculty:* 4, 6, 0. *Graduates:* 7m, 24w.

*School also offers a supervisory certification program in instructional technology. *Graduates:* 2m, 12w.

University of Kansas. School of Education, Lawrence, KS 66045. Ronald Aust, Asst. Prof., Dir., Instructional Technology Center, School of Education. *Program Basis:* Semester. *Minimum Degree Requirements:* 30 credit hours including 10 in media; thesis optional. *Faculty:* 1, 1, 1. *Graduates:* 2m, 3w, including 1 foreign national.

KENTUCKY

University of Kentucky. College of Education, Lexington, KY 40506. Gary Anglin, Assoc. Prof., Instructional Design, Dept. of Curriculum and Instruction, College of Education. *Program Basis:* Semester. *Minimum Degree Requirements:* 36 credit hours including 24 in instructional design and technology; no thesis required. *Faculty:* 2, 2, 1. *Graduates:* 8m, 18w, including 1 foreign national.

*School also offers six-year specialist and doctoral degree programs in instructional technology. Admission requirements include a minimum GPA of 3.4 for all graduate work and 30 credit hours of work completed in education. Program requires a minimum of 30 hours beyond the master's degree including 15 hours of advanced graduate level courses.

University of Louisville. School of Education, Louisville, KY 40292. Carolyn Rude-Parkins (M.Ed., Occupational Education), Instructional Technology Concentration, School of Education. *Program Basis:* Semester. *Minimum Degree Requirements:* M.Ed. 30 credit hours; thesis optional. *Faculty:* 5 professors in 3 departments contribute to this concentration. *Graduates:* 2m, 2w. Note: Media utilization instruction is "mainstreamed" within education courses. The collaborative Technology Project with Jefferson County Public Schools supports courses in computer technology applications.

Western Kentucky University. Department of Teacher Education, Bowling Green, KY 42101. Robert C. Smith, Assoc. Prof., LME Coord., Dept. of Teacher Education. *Program Basis:* Semester. *Minimum Degree Requirements:* 33 credit hours including 21 in media; thesis optional. *Faculty:* 4, 3, 2. *Graduates:* 3m, 6w.

LOUISIANA

Louisiana State University. School of Library and Information Science, Baton Rouge, LA 70803. Bert R. Boyce, Dean, Prof., School of Library and Information Science. *Program Basis:* Semester. *Minimum Degree Requirements:* 37 credit hours including comprehensive; residence student on full-time basis for semester or summer; and completion of degree program in five years. *Faculty:* 9, 0, 0. *Graduates:* 11m, 45w, including 2 foreign nationals.

McNeese State University. Department of Administration and Educational Technology, Lake Charles, LA 70609. Joe Savoie, Head, Dept. of Administration and Educational Technology. *Program Basis:* Semester. *Minimum Degree Requirements:* 30 credit hours including 15 in media; thesis not required. *Faculty:* 2, 1, 1. *Graduates:* 5m, 6w.

Southern University. College of Arts and Humanities, Baton Rouge, LA 70813. Henry Wiggins, Prof., Chair, Dept. of Mass Communications, College of Arts and Humanities. *Program Basis:* Semester. *Minimum Degree Requirements:* 30 credit hours including 21 in mass communications and instructional technology; thesis optional. *Faculty:* 4, 3, 4. *Graduates:* 19m, 13w, including 1 foreign national.

MARYLAND

The Johns Hopkins University. Division of Education, Baltimore, MD 21218. Dianne Tobin, Coord., M.S. Technology for Educators, Ed.D. Technology for Special Education, Div. of Education. *Program Basis:* Semester. *Minimum Degree Requirements:* 33 credit hours, 8 required courses in computer-related technology and media with remaining courses being electives in several broad areas. *Faculty:* 4, 0, 1. *Graduates:* 5m, 15w, including 1 foreign national.

Towson State University. College of Education, Baltimore, MD 21204. Paul Jones, Assoc. Prof., Instructional Technology Program, General Education Department. *Program Basis:* Semester. *Faculty:* 5, 4, 1. *Graduates:* 1m, 6w, including 1 foreign national. Concentrations available in Instructional Design and School Library Media.

University of Maryland. College of Library and Information Services, College Park, MD 20742. Claude E. Walston, Dean and Prof., College of Library and Information Services. *Program Basis:* Semester. *Minimum Degree Requirements:* 36 credit hours including majors in library media; no thesis required. *Faculty:* 15, 0, 0. *Graduates:* 2m, 22w.

University of Maryland. Department of Education, Catonsville, MD 21228. David B. Young, Assoc. Prof., Coord., Instructional Systems Development Master's Degree Prog., Dept. of Education. *Program Basis:* Semester. *Minimum Degree Requirements:* 36 credit hours including 18 in systems development for each of three programs: (1) Training Systems, (2) English as a Second Language, and (3) School Instructional Systems and Post-Baccalaureate Teacher Certification. *Faculty:* 4, 4, 5. *Graduates:* 1m, 6w.

Western Maryland College. Department of Education, Westminster, MD 21157. Margaret W. Denman-West, Assoc. Prof., Coord., Media/Library Science, Dept. of Education. *Program Basis:* Semester. *Minimum Degree Requirements:* 33 credit hours including 18 in media; thesis optional. *Faculty:* 2, 2, 2. *Graduates:* 3m, 18w.

MASSACHUSETTS

Boston College. Department of Education, Chestnut Hill, MA 02167. Walter M. Haney, Assoc. Prof., Dir., Educational Technology Prog., 523 McGuinn Hall, Dept. of Education, Graduate School of Arts and Sciences. *Program Basis:* Semester. *Minimum Degree Requirements:* 36 credit hours including 30 in media; practicum; thesis optional. *Faculty:* 4, 3, 1. *Graduates:* 4m, 5w.

    *School also offers a certificate of advanced education studies degree (30 credit hours) beyond M.Ed. and a special fifth-year M.Ed. program in instructional technology for Boston College undergraduates.

Boston University. School of Education, Boston, MA 02215. Gaylen B. Kelley, Prof., Prog. Dir. of Educational Media and Technology, Div. of Instructional Development, School of Education. *Program Basis:* Semester. *Minimum Degree Requirements:* 32 credit hours; thesis optional. *Faculty:* 3, 0, 13. *Graduates:* 1m, 12w, including 2 foreign nationals.

    *School also offers a six-year specialist degree program Certificate of Advanced Graduate Specialization (C.A.G.S.) in instructional technology and a corporate training program. This program is offered to those wishing to update their skills in instructional technology or those who wish to concentrate in a particular subdiscipline of the field. Concentrations are available in instructional television, facilities design for communications technology, instructional design, computer-based instruction, and library and information science. Program also provides a vehicle for those who wish to certify as Supervisors/Directors of Unified Media Programs for the Massachusetts Public Schools. Program requires 30 credit hours of course work for program completion. Students entering the program must have completed a master's degree. *Graduates:* 1m, 1w.

Bridgewater State College. Department of Media and Librarianship, Bridgewater, MA 02324. Alan Lander, Prof., Chair., Dept. of Media and Librarianship. *Program Basis:* Semester. *Minimum Degree Requirements:* 33 credit hours including 27 in media; thesis optional. *Faculty:* 4, 4, 0. *Graduates:* 9w.

    *School also offers a unified media specialist certification program which provides preparation and background in both print and nonprint resources and services. Enrollment is required in a master's degree program in instructional media, library science, or graduate school certification program to be eligible for this certification program.

Fitchburg State College. Communications/Media Department, Fitchburg, MA 01420. Lee DeNike, David Ryder, Profs., Communications/Media Dept. *Program Basis:* Semester. *Minimum Degree Requirements:* 36 credit hours in communications/media management including a required thesis. *Faculty:* 5, 0, 0. *Graduates:* 5m, 1w.

Harvard University. Graduate School of Education, Cambridge, MA 02138. David N. Perkins, Senior Research Assoc., Coord., Technology in Education, Graduate School of Education. *Program Basis:* Semester. *Minimum Degree Requirements:* Semester courses including emphasis in technology and educational theory and practice. *Faculty:* 6, 0, 0. *Graduates:* 11m, 14w, including 6 foreign nationals.

Lesley College. Division of Education and Special Education, Graduate School, Cambridge, MA 02138-2790. Nancy Roberts, Prof., Dir., Computers in Education Prog., Div. of Education and Special Education, Graduate School. *Program Basis:* Semester. *Minimum Degree Requirements:* 33 credit hours including 18 in computers. *Faculty:* 5, 3, 4. *Graduates:* 3m, 15w, including 2 foreign nationals.

Simmons College. Graduate School of Library and Information Science, Boston, MA 02115. Robert D. Stueart, Dean, Graduate School of Library and Information Science. *Program Basis:* Semester. *Minimum Degree Requirements:* 36 credit hours including 36 in library science and instructional technology. *Faculty:* 14, 17, 0. *Graduates:* 28m, 131w, including 18 foreign nationals.

MICHIGAN

Eastern Michigan University. Teacher Education Department, Ypsilanti, MI 48197. Dr. Bert Greene, Prof., Coord., Educational Technology Concentration, Teacher Education Dept. *Program Basis:* Semester. *Minimum Degree Requirements:* 30 credit hours including 18 in educational technology. *Faculty:* 8, 2, 0. *Graduates:* 7m, 8w, including 8 foreign nationals.

Michigan State University. College of Education, East Lansing, MI 48824. Leighton A. Price, Prof., Coord., Educational Systems Development Program in the Department of Counseling, Educational Psychology and Special Education. *Program Basis:* Quarter. *Admission Requirements:* At least a 3.0 GPA during the last two years of undergraduate study. *Minimum Degree Requirements:* 45 credit hours with emphasis in instructional design or in educational technology and instructional computing applications; no thesis required. *Faculty:* 9, 0, 4. *Graduates:* 9m, 6w, including 1 foreign national.

*School also offers a six-year specialist degree program in instructional technology. The Educational Specialist Degree provides opportunities for advanced work in specialized aspects of educational systems development (e.g., instructional design and development, computer-based education, instructional program administration) as well as opportunities to broaden foundations in education, communication, applied educational technologies, and other cognate fields. *Minimum Degree Requirements:* 45 credit hours beyond the master's, written comprehensive examination, demonstrated competence in statistics where appropriate, no dissertation required.

University of Michigan. Curriculum, Teaching and Psychological Studies, Ann Arbor, MI 48109. Robert B. Kozma, Assoc. Prof., Chair, Instructional Technology Committee, Dept. of Curriculum, Teaching and Psychological Studies. *Program Basis:* Trimester. *Minimum Degree Requirements:* 30 credit hours including project. *Faculty:* 1, 0, 3. *Graduates:* 3m, 1w, including 3 foreign nationals.

Wayne State University. College of Education, Detroit, MI 48202. Rita C. Richey, Prof., Instructional Technology Prog. Coord., Div. of Administrative and Organizational Studies, College of Education. *Program Basis:* Semester. *Minimum Degree Requirements:* 6 credit hours including required project internship recommended. *Faculty:* 4, 0, 10. *Graduates:* 7m, 20w.

*School also offers a six-year specialist degree program in instructional technology. This 36-credit hour program includes required work in instructional design and evaluation with a core of additional work in the specialty area of concentration. Internships encouraged. *Graduates:* 1m, 3w.

MINNESOTA

Mankato State University. Library Media Education, Mankato, MN 56002. Frank Birmingham, Prof., Chair, Library Media Education. *Program Basis:* Quarter. *Minimum Degree Requirements:* 51 credit hours including 27 in media. *Faculty:* 4, 2, 0. *Graduates:* 20w.

*School also offers a six-year specialist degree program in the instructional technology/media field. The library media specialist degree prepares individuals as media administrators managing the human and material resources of the media program. An individual's program seeks an in-depth knowledge in a specific area, e.g., administration, materials, production. Program may or may not lead to additional certification or licensure. The 45-quarter-credit-hour program includes a research course involving library automation; 21 hours in library media education, including library/media colloquium, or educational administration or curriculum and instruction; internship; 6 hours of elective coursework outside the College of Education; thesis/field study; 6 hours of elective courses in area of media specialization; and an oral examination, a comprehensive examination, and an oral thesis defense.

St. Cloud State University. College of Education, St. Cloud, MN 56301-4498. John Berling, Prof., Dir., Center for Information Media, College of Education. *Program Basis:* Quarter. *Minimum Degree Requirements:* 48 credit hours/thesis, 51 credit hours/ research paper; 54 credit hours/portfolio. *Faculty:* 7, 0, 0. *Graduates:* 1m, 13w, including 1 foreign national.

*School also offers a 45-quarter-credit six-year specialist degree program in information media. This program is available to those who have completed a master's degree in media, another field, or comparable field. The program is designed to develop competencies for media supervisor licensure, and administrative positions in public, academic, or school district media programs. Most students are required to take the GRE. A minimum grade point average on all graduate work is 3.0. References required. *Graduates:* 0.

University of Minnesota. Curriculum and Instructional Systems, 130 Peik Hall, 159 Pillsbury Drive S.E., Minneapolis, MN 55455. Gregory C. Sales, Prof., Chair, Curriculum and Instructional Systems. *Program Basis:* Quarter. *Minimum Degree Requirements:* 44 credit hours including 22 in instructional systems. *Faculty:* 5, 5, associates. *Graduates:* 4m, 5w, including 3 foreign nationals.

MISSISSIPPI

Jackson State University. School of Education, Jackson, MS 39217-0175. William Rush, Prof., Chair, Dept. of Educational Foundations and Leadership, School of Education. *Program Basis:* Semester. *Minimum Degree Requirements:* 36 credit hours including 24 in media; thesis and field practicum optional. *Faculty:* 3. *Graduates:* 1m, 1w, including 1 foreign national. Two programs are available: B.S.Ed. and M.S.Ed. in Educational Technology.

University of Southern Mississippi. School of Library Science, Hattiesburg, MS 39406-5146. Jeannine Laughlin, Assoc. Prof., Dir., School of Library Science. *Program Basis:* Semester. *Minimum Degree Requirements:* 41 credit hours, comprehensive required. *Faculty:* 9. *Graduates:* 12m, 29w, including 2 foreign nationals.

MISSOURI

Central Missouri State University. Department of Special Services and Instructional Technology, Warrensburg, MO 64093. Kenneth Brookens, Assoc. Prof., Coord., Instructional Technology. *Program Basis:* Semester. *Minimum Degree Requirements:* M.S.E., 32 credit hours in curriculum and instruction with emphasis on instructional technology. *Faculty:* 1, 1, 0. *Graduates:* 1m, 2w.

*School also offers a certification program in learning resources by arrangement. Inquiries about the status of this program should be directed to the Chair of the Department of Special Services.

Northwest Missouri State University. Department of Computer Science, Maryville, MO 64468. Phillip J. Heeler, Prof., Dir., School Computer Studies Prog., Dept. of Computer Science. *Program Basis:* Semester. *Minimum Degree Requirements:* 32 credit hours for each of three master's degree programs: (1) M.S. in school computer studies includes 26 credit hours of core computer courses; (2) M.S.Ed. in educational uses of computers includes 14 credit hours of core computer courses and 12 hours of educational courses; and (3) a M.S.Ed. in using computers in specific disciplines requires 7 hours of core computer courses, 12 hours of education courses, and 7 hours in technology-related areas. *Faculty:* 3, 1, 1. *Graduates:* 8m, 10w, including 6 foreign nationals.

University of Missouri – Columbia. College of Education, Columbia, MO 65211. John F. Wedman, Assoc. Prof., Coord., Educational Technology Program, Curriculum and Instruction Dept., College of Education. *Program Basis:* Semester. *Minimum Degree Requirements:* 32 credit hours including 16 hours of upper level graduate work. *Faculty:* 3, 0, 0. *Graduates:* 3m, 4w, including 2 foreign nationals.

*School also offers a six-year specialist degree program in instructional technology. Program consists of 30 semester hours beyond the master's degree and includes 15 hours of upper level graduate work, a research course, a statistics course, and 12 hours of educational technology involving internship or equivalent (new program).

University of Missouri – St. Louis. School of Education, St. Louis, MO 63121. Donald R. Greer, Assoc, Prof., Coord. of Educational Technology, Dept. of Educational Studies, School of Education. *Program Basis:* Semester. *Minimum Degree Requirements:* 32 credit hours including 18 in media. *Faculty:* 1, 1, ⅓. *Graduates:* 2m, 3w.

Webster University. Instructional Technology, St. Louis, MO 63119. Paul Steinmann, Assoc. Dean and Dir., Graduate Studies and Instructional Technology. *Program Basis:* Semester. *Minimum Degree Requirements:* 33 credit hours including 24 in media; internship required. *Faculty:* 3, 1, 0. *Graduates:* 3m, 12w.

MONTANA

University of Montana. School of Education, Missoula, MT 59812. Geneva Van Horne, Prof. of Library/Media, School of Education. *Program Basis:* Quarter. *Minimum Degree Requirements:* 54 credit hours including 32 in media; thesis optional. *Faculty:* 2, 1, 0. *Graduates:* 3m, 12w.

*School also has an endorsement program in addition to the master's program.

NEBRASKA

Kearney State College. Department of Educational Administration, Kearney, NE 68849. Daniel W. McPherson, Assoc. Prof., Supervisor of Educational Media, Dept. of Educational Administration. *Program Basis:* Semester. *Minimum Degree Requirements:* 36 credit hours including 15 in media; thesis optional. Since this is a cooperative program, Kansas State University provides the 15 hours required for media and computer course work, and the supporting faculty. *Graduates:* 4 (relatively new program).

University of Nebraska – Lincoln. Instructional Technology, Teachers College, Lincoln, NE 68588. David W. Brooks, Prof., Coord., Instructional Technology, Teachers College. *Program Basis:* Semester. *Minimum Degree Requirements:* 36 credit hours including 24 in media; thesis optional. *Faculty:* 1, 1.5, 0. *Graduates:* 2m, 2w.

University of Nebraska – Omaha. Omaha, NE 68182. Verne Haselwood, Prof., Educational Media Program in Teacher Education. *Program Basis:* Semester. *Minimum Degree Requirements:* 36 credit hours including 27 in media; thesis optional. *Faculty:* 2, 0, 3. *Graduates:* 3m, 14w.

NEVADA

University of Nevada – Reno. College of Education, Reno, NV 89557. Thomas W. Sawyer, Dir. of the Learning and Resource Center, Curriculum and Instruction Dept., College of Education. *Program Basis:* Semester. *Minimum Degree Requirements:* 36 credit hours including 16 or more in (a) computer education — media or (b) library — media; thesis optional. *Faculty:* 22, 15, 7. *Graduates:* 2w.

*School also offers a six-year specialist degree program in curriculum and instruction with an emphasis in (a) or (b) above. A minor is also offered in media/library science.

NEW JERSEY

Glassboro State College. School and Public Librarianship, Glassboro, NJ 08028. Rinehart S. Potts, Graduate Advisor and Program Coord. for School and Public Librarianship. *Program Basis:* Semester. *Minimum Degree Requirements:* 39 credit hours including required thesis project. *Faculty:* 1, 4, 0. *Graduates:* 3m, 9w, including 1 foreign national.

Montclair State College. Department of Reading and Educational Media, Upper Montclair, NJ 07043. Robert R. Ruezinsky, Dir. of Media and Technology. *Program Basis:* Semester. No degree program exists. Two certification programs, AMS and EMS, exist on the graduate level. Eighteen to 20 credit hours of media and technology are required for the AMS program and 30-33 hours for the EMS program. *Faculty:* Includes 5 administrators and 1 adj., teaching on an overload basis.

Rutgers — The State University of New Jersey. School of Communication, Information and Library Studies, New Brunswick, NJ 08903. Betty J. Turock, Chair, Dept. of Library and Information Studies, School of Communication, Information and Library Studies. *Program Basis:* Semester. *Minimum Degree Requirements:* 36 credit hours in which the hours for media vary for individual students. *Faculty:* 18. *Graduates:* 23m, 112w, including 14 foreign nationals.

*School also offers a six-year specialist certificate program. This 24 credit-hour program must be completed within a three-year period. Some courses may be taken in library/information, an advanced curriculum that includes one or more doctoral seminars and a project culminating in a thesis, survey, film, etc. Other courses may be taken in related fields. Admission criteria include a master's degree; at least a B average and distinction in proposed area of advanced study; a minimum of two years of successful demonstrated experience; a description of applicant's area of interest; a proposed independent study project; and two letters of recommendation.

Saint Peter's College. Computer Education, Jersey City, NJ 07306. Henry F. Harty, Dir., Graduate Prog. in Computer Education. *Program Basis:* Semester. *Minimum Degree Requirements:* 39 credit hours including 27 in computers. *Faculty:* 9, 0, 0. *Graduates:* 12m, 33w.

Seton Hall University. Division of Educational Media, College of Education and Human Services, South Orange, NJ 07079. Rosemary W. Skeele, Asst. Prof., Dir., Graduate Prog. in Educational Media, Div. of Educational Media, College of Education and Human Services. *Program Basis:* Semester. *Minimum Degree Requirements:* 36 credit hours including 24 in media; mediated project instead of thesis. *Faculty:* 3, 1, 0. *Graduates:* 1m, 4w.

*School also offers an educational specialist certificate; 36 credits may lead to state certification as media specialist.

William Paterson College. School of Education, Wayne, NJ 07470. Amy Job, Librarian, Assoc. Prof., Coord., Prog. in Library/Media, Curriculum and Instruction Dept. *Program Basis:* Semester. *Minimum Degree Requirements:* 30 credit hours in media including research. *Faculty:* 1, 0, 0. *Graduates:* 4w.

NEW MEXICO

University of New Mexico. College of Education, Albuquerque, NM 87131. Dr. Frank Field, Chair, or Guy A. Watson, Assoc. Prof., Training and Learning Technologies, College of Education. *Program Basis:* Semester. *Minimum Degree Requirements:* Master's: 36 credit hours in learning technologies; Ed.D., 72 hours minimum; Ph.D., 78 hours. *Faculty:* 11, 0, 3. *Graduates:* 18m, 22w (1988-89).

NEW YORK

Fordham University. Communications Department, Bronx, NY 10458. Donald C. Matthews, S.J., Chair; James A. Capo, Assoc. Prof., Chair, Director of Graduate Studies, Communications Dept. *Program Basis:* Semester. *Minimum Degree Requirements:* 30 credit hours; internship or thesis required. *Faculty:* 9. *Graduates:* 4m, 5w, including 1 foreign national.

Ithaca College. School of Communications, Ithaca, NY 14850. Diane M. Gayeski, Assoc. Prof., Chair, Graduate Corporate Communications; Roy H. Park, School of Communications. *Program Basis:* Semester. *Minimum Degree Requirements:* 36 credit hours including 30 in communications; thesis optional. *Faculty:* 8, 0, 0. *Graduates:* 4m, 17w.

New School for Social Research. Media Studies Program, New York, NY 10011. Mark Schulman, Dir., Media Studies Program. *Program Basis:* Semester. *Minimum Degree Requirements:* 36 credit hours in media; thesis encouraged. *Faculty:* 6, 1, 2. *Graduates:* 69m, 111w, including 33 foreign nationals.

New York Institute of Technology. Graduate Communication Arts, Old Westbury, NY 11568 (also in NYC). Adrienne O'Brien, Dean, School of Media and Arts. *Program Basis:* Semester. *Minimum Degree Requirements:* 32/34 credit hours with one specialization in television, film, electronic journalism, advertising/public relations, computer graphics, studio arts, or media generalists; thesis optional. *Faculty:* 18, 0, 21. *Graduates:* 41m, 48w, including 15 foreign nationals.

New York Institute of Technology. Graduate Programs in Training and Learning Technology, School of Media and Arts, Old Westbury, NY 11568 (also in NYC). Dr. Angus Reynolds, School of Media and Arts. *Program Basis:* Semester. *Minimum Degree Requirements:* 37 credits with a specialization in management of training, computer applications, or instructional media; required thesis project in an instructional system. *Faculty:* 4, 0, 2. *Graduates:* 12m, 14w, including 6 foreign nationals.

New York University. School of Education, Health, Nursing and Arts Professions, New York, NY 10003. Donald T. Payne, Assoc. Prof. and Dir., Program in Educational Communication and Technology, School of Education, Health, Nursing and Arts Professions. *Program Basis:* Semester. *Minimum Degree Requirements:* 36 credit hours including 24 in media; terminal experience required; thesis optional. *Faculty:* 2, 0, 6. *Graduates:* 1m, 9w, including 3 foreign nationals.
    *School also offers an 18-credit-hour certificate and a 30-credit-hour, six-year specialist program in educational communication and technology. Specializations for the six-year program are located in the school's doctoral program description. Admissions requirements include a master's degree with a 3.0 cumulative average. Students work closely with master's and doctoral program students who are in the same courses. *Faculty:* 2, 0, 6. *Graduates:* 0.

New York University – Tisch School of the Arts. Interactive Telecommunications Program, 721 Broadway, New York, NY 10003. Red Burns, Prof., Chair, The Interactive Telecommunications Program/Institute of Film and Television. *Program Basis:* Semester.

Minimum Degree Requirements: 60 credit hours (15 courses at 4 credit hours each; program is two years for full-time students) including 56 required courses and thesis. *Faculty:* 3, 1, 4. *Graduates:* 20m, 20w, including 2 foreign nationals.

Rochester Institute of Technology. Information Technology, Rochester, NY 14623-0887. Clint Wallington, Prof., Dir. of the Dept. of Information Technology, College of Applied Science and Technology. *Program Basis:* Quarter. *Minimum Degree Requirements:* 48 credit hours including an instructional development project (noncredit). *Faculty:* 4, 3, 1. *Graduates:* 8m, 11w.

St. John's University. Library and Information Science, Jamaica, NY 11439. Emmett Corry, Assoc. Prof., Dir., Div. of Library and Information Science. *Program Basis:* Semester. *Minimum Degree Requirements:* 36 credit hours including 21 in media; no thesis required. *Faculty:* 7, 4, 3. *Graduates:* 11m, 18w, including 11 foreign nationals.

*School also offers a six-year specialist program, which is a 24-credit-hour, advanced certificate program that can be tailored to the student's individual needs.

State University College of Arts and Science. School of Professional Studies, Potsdam, NY 13676. Norman Licht, Prof., Coord., Instructional Technology and Media Management, Center for Mathematics, Science and Technology, School of Professional Studies. *Program Basis:* Semester. *Minimum Degree Requirements:* 33 credit hours including emphasis in instructional technology, media, and computer education; thesis optional. *Faculty:* 5, 5, 0. *Graduates:* 9m, 28w, including 67 foreign nationals.

State University of New York at Albany. Department of Program Development and Evaluation, Albany, NY 12222. Instructional Design and Technology Program, Dept. of Program Development and Evaluation. *Program Basis:* Semester. *Minimum Degree Requirements:* 30 credit hours including 15 in instructional design and technology; thesis optional. *Faculty:* 2, 3, 0. *Graduates:* 6m, 3w, including 2 foreign nationals.

State University of New York at Buffalo. Graduate School of Education, Buffalo, NY 14260. Taher Razik, Prof., Instructional Design and Management, Dept. of Education, Organization, and Policy, Faculty of Educational Studies. *Program Basis:* Semester. *Minimum Degree Requirements:* 33 credit hours including 21 hours in instructional design and management; thesis or project required; comprehensive examination. *Faculty:* 3, 0, 3. *Graduates:* 1m, 2w, including 1 foreign national.

*School also offers a certificate program in instructional technology.

State University of New York at Buffalo. School of Information and Library Studies, Buffalo, NY 14260. George S. Bobinski, Dean, School of Information and Library Studies. *Program Basis:* Semester. *Minimum Degree Requirements:* 36 credit hours including 15 in media; thesis optional. *Faculty:* 9, 6, 0. *Graduates:* 22m, 71w, including 5 foreign nationals.

*School also offers a sixth-year, 30-credit-hour certificate program in instructional technology.

State University of New York at Stony Brook. College of Engineering and Applied Sciences, Stony Brook, NY 11794-2250. Thomas T. Liao, Prof., Chair, Dept. of Technology and Society, College of Engineering and Applied Sciences. *Program Basis:* Semester. *Minimum Degree Requirements:* 30 credit hours with emphasis in technological systems, industrial, management, educational computing, and environmental and waste management. *Faculty:* 8, 4, 4. *Graduates:* 29m, 21w, including 15 foreign nationals.

Syracuse University. School of Education, Syracuse, NY 13244-2340. Donald P. Ely, Prof., Chair, Instructional Design, Development and Evaluation Prog., School of Education, *Program Basis:* Semester. *Minimum Degree Requirements:* 30 credit hours. *Faculty:* 6, 1, 1. *Graduates:* 3m, 7w.

Teachers College, Columbia University. Program in Communication, New York, NY 10027. John B. Black, Prof., Chair, Dept. of Communication, Computing and Technology in Education. *Program Basis:* Semester. *Minimum Degree Requirements:* M.A., 32 credit hours including 18 in media, core courses in communication and computing, thesis optional; M.A. media specialist (certification), 36 credit hours, core in School of Library Service, internship, research paper. *Faculty:* 5, 2, 1. *Graduates:* 3m, 7w, including 3 foreign nationals.

NORTH CAROLINA

Appalachian State University. College of Education, Boone, NC 28608. Ken McEwin, Prof., Coord., Dept. of Curriculum and Instruction, Library/Media Studies, College of Education. *Program Basis:* Semester. *Minimum Degree Requirements:* 42 credit hours including selected sources in media; thesis optional. *Faculty:* 6, 0, 0. *Graduates:* 8m, 17w.

Appalachian State University. Department of Library Science and Educational Foundations, Boone, NC 28608. John H. Tashner, Prof., Coord., Department of Library Science and Educational Foundations, College of Education. *Program Basis:* Semester. *Minimum Degree Requirements:* 36 credit hours including 15 in computer education; thesis optional. *Faculty:* 4, 1, 0. *Graduates:* 1 (new program).

East Carolina University. Department of Library and Information Studies, Greenville, NC 27858. Lawrence Auld, Assoc. Prof., Chair, Dept. of Library and Information Studies. *Program Basis:* Semester. *Minimum Degree Requirements:* 44 credit hours in library service and media. *Faculty:* 3, 5, 0. *Graduates:* 5m, 21w.

North Carolina Central University. School of Education, Durham, NC 27707. Marvin E. Duncan, Prof., Dir., Learning Resources Center, School of Education. *Program Basis:* Semester. *Minimum Degree Requirements:* 33 credit hours including 21 in media; thesis or project required. *Faculty:* 4, 1, 0. *Graduates:* 4m, 6w.

University of North Carolina. School of Education, Chapel Hill, NC 27514. Ralph E. Wileman, Prof., Chair, Educational Media and Instructional Design, School of Education. *Program Basis:* Semester. *Minimum Degree Requirements:* 36 credit hours including 21 in media and comprehensive examination. *Faculty:* 2.5, 0, 0. *Graduates:* 1m, 9w.

Western Carolina University. Department of Administration, Curriculum and Instruction, Cullowhee, NC 28723. John W. McFadden, Prof., Coord., Dept. of Administration, Curriculum and Instruction. *Program Basis:* Semester. *Minimum Degree Requirements:* 30 credit hours including 18 in media. *Faculty:* 5, 4, 0. *Graduates:* 1m, 5w, including 1 foreign national. (Program on inactive status.)

OHIO

Kent State University. Instructional Technology Program, White Hall 405, KSU, Kent, OH 44242. (216) 672-2294. Dr. Drew Tiene, Prog. Coordinator. *Program Basis:* Semester. *Minimum Degree Requirements:* 34 credit hours including 14-20 hours of instructional technology coursework, depending upon certification sought. *Faculty:* 4. *Graduates:* Approx. 10-15 per year.

Miami University. School of Education and Allied Professions, Oxford, OH 45056. Joe Waggener, Assoc. Prof., Coord., Instructional Technology Program, School of Education and Allied Professions. *Program Basis:* Semester. *Minimum Degree Requirements:* 30 credit hours, thesis optional. *Faculty:* 5, 4, 1. *Graduates:* Data not available.

Ohio State University. 236 Ramseyer Hall, 29 W. Woodruff Avenue, Columbus, OH 43210-1177. Dr. Richard Howell, Assoc. Prof. Since 1980, the school offers M.A. and Ph.D. in Instructional Systems Design, including concentrations in instructional and interactive technologies, within the program area of Instructional Design and Technology. *Minimum Degree Requirements:* M.A. 50 credit hours with a minimum of 18 hours core, 6 hours foundations, 3 hours multicultural courses; Ph.D. is 135 hours post-bachelor's, general examination (written and oral), dissertation. *Outside Funding for the Department:* No. *Summer Session:* 3, 5, 8, and 10 weeks. A master's degree, or its equivalent, is also required. *Faculty:* 8 full-time; 4 part-time; graduate faculty members. *Students:* 78 students in the master's program and 35 students in the doctoral program. Quarter credit basis.

Ohio University. College of Education, McCracken Hall, Athens, OH 45701-2979. Seldon D. Strother, Prof., Dir. of Educational Media, College of Education. *Program Basis:* Quarter. *Minimum Degree Requirements:* 52 credit hours including 26 in media; thesis optional. *Faculty:* 4, 2, 0. *Graduates:* 1m, 2w.

University of Toledo. Department of Educational Technology, Toledo, OH 43606. Mary Jo Henning, Prof., Chair, Dept. of Curriculum and Educational Technology. *Program Basis:* Quarter. *Minimum Degree Requirements:* 48 credit hours including 36 in media; master's project. *Faculty:* 6, 5, 1. *Graduates:* 12m, 10w.

*School also offers a six-year specialist degree program in educational technology requiring 45 credit hours, including 5-credit-hour supervised internship. *Graduates:* 2m, 2w.

Wright State University. 244 Millett Hall, Dayton, OH 45435. Bonnie Mathies, Assoc. Prof., Chair, Dept. of Educational Technology, Vocational Education and Allied Programs, College of Education and Human Services. *Program Basis:* Quarter. *Minimum Degree Requirements:* 48 credit hours; thesis optional. *Faculty:* 4. *Graduates:* 1m, 12w.

Xavier University. Department of Education, Cincinnati, OH 45207. John Pohlman, Asst. Prof., Dir., Graduate Programs in Educational Media, Dept. of Education. *Program Basis:* Semester. *Minimum Degree Requirements:* 30 credit hours including 18 in media; nonthesis but field practicum required. *Faculty:* 2, 1, 0. *Graduates:* 1m, 15w.

OKLAHOMA

Central State University. College of Education, Edmond, OK 73034-0193. Frances Alsworth, Assoc. Prof., Library Media Education, Dept. of Curriculum and Instruction, College of Education. *Program Basis:* Semester. *Minimum Degree Requirements:* 32 credit hours including 17 in media. *Faculty:* 2, 0, 1. *Graduates:* 4w.

Oklahoma State University. Curriculum and Instructional Department, Stillwater, OK 74078. Douglas B. Aichele, Prof., Head, Curriculum and Instruction Dept. *Program Basis:* Semester. *Minimum Degree Requirements:* 30 credit hours including 18 in media; thesis optional. *Faculty:* 3, 4, teaching assistants. *Graduates:* 4m, 4w.

Southwestern State University. School of Education, Weatherford, OK 73096. Lessley Price, Asst. Prof., Coord. of Library/Media Prog., School of Education. *Program Basis:* Semester. *Minimum Degree Requirements:* 32 credit hours including 24 in media; thesis optional. *Faculty:* 2, 2, 0. *Graduates:* 1m, 6w.

University of Oklahoma. Educational Technology, Norman, OK 73019. Tillman J. Ragan, Prof., Area Head, Educational Technology Prog. Area, Dept. of Educational Psychology. *Program Basis:* Semester. *Minimum Degree Requirements:* 32 credit hours including 21 in educational technology; no thesis required. *Faculty:* 3, 3, 4. *Graduates:* 4m, 9w.

OREGON

Portland State University. School of Education, P.O. Box 751, Portland, OR 97207. Joyce Petrie, Prof., Coord., Educational Media, School of Education. *Program Basis:* Quarter. *Minimum Degree Requirements:* 45 credit hours including 42 in media; thesis optional. *Faculty:* 6, 2, 4. *Graduates:* 14m, 23w.

University of Oregon. Division of Teacher Education, 1787 Agate St., Eugene, OR 97403. Gary W. Ferrington, Program Head. *Program Basis:* Quarter. *Minimum Degree Requirements:* 45-48 credit hours including 30 in instructional technology or computers-in-education; thesis, synthesis paper, or field study. *Faculty:* 2, 4, 0. *Graduates:* 6m, 5w, including 5 foreign nationals. Master's degree in Curriculum and Instruction with a specialization in Instructional Systems Technology.

Western Oregon State College. School of Education, Monmouth, OR 97361. Richard Forcier, Prof. and Dir., Information Technology. *Program Basis:* Quarter. *Minimum Degree Requirements:* 45 credit hours including 36 in media; thesis optional. *Specialization:* Computer education; instructional systems. *Features:* Offers advanced courses in media management, media production, instructional systems, instructional development, and computer technology. Some specialization in "distance delivery" of instruction and computer-interactive video instruction. *Admission Requirements:* Bachelor's degree, minimum 2.75 GPA in undergraduate program, interview, satisfactory performance on GRE or Miller Analogies Test. *Faculty:* 6, 5, 1. *Graduates:* 8m, 12w, including 3 foreign nationals.

PENNSYLVANIA

Clarion University of Pennsylvania. Department of Communication, Clarion, PA 16214. Carmen S. Felicetti, Prof., Chair, Dept. of Communication. *Program Basis:* Semester. *Minimum Degree Requirements:* 36 credit hours. Emphasis on training and development. Required courses in design, production, research, electives include interactive video, multi-image. Thesis optional. *Faculty:* 11, 6, 0. *Graduates:* 14m, 14w, including 12 foreign nationals.

Drexel University. College of Information Studies, Philadelphia, PA 19104. Richard H. Lytle, Prof. and Dean, College of Information Studies. *Program Basis:* Quarter. *Minimum Degree Requirements:* M.S. degree program of 48 credit hours comprised primarily of five functional groupings: organization and retrieval information; information technology; resources and their use; information services; and management and evaluation. Nonthesis. *Faculty:* 18, 11, 7. *Graduates:* 15m, 54w, including 3 foreign nationals.

Indiana University of Pennsylvania. Department of Communications, Indiana, PA 15701. Kurt P. Dudt, Assoc. Prof., Chair, Dept. of Communications Media. *Program Basis:* Semester. *Minimum Degree Requirements:* 36 credit hours including 21 in media; thesis optional. *Faculty:* 10, 2, 0. *Graduates:* 15m, 8w, including 7 foreign nationals.

Lehigh University. Lehigh University School of Education, Bethlehem, PA 18105. Leroy J. Tuscher, Prof., Dir., Educational Technology Center, School of Education. *Program Basis:* Semester. *Minimum Degree Requirements:* 30 credit hours including 15 in media; thesis optional. *Faculty:* 4, 2, 3. *Graduates:* 5m, 9w, including 3 foreign nationals.

Pennsylvania State University. Division of Curriculum and Instruction, University Park, PA 16802. Paul W. Welliver, Prof., contact person, Instructional Systems Prog., Div. of Curriculum and Instruction. *Program Basis:* Semester. *Minimum Degree Requirements:* 30 credit hours including either a thesis or project paper. *Faculty:* 5, 0, 0. *Graduates:* 5m, 6w, including 2 foreign nationals.

Shippensburg University. Department of Communications and Journalism, Shippensburg, PA 17257. Dr. Pat Waltermyer, Chair, Dept. of Communication and Journalism, College of Arts and Sciences. *Program Basis:* Semester. *Minimum Degree Requirements:* 30 credit hours in media/communications studies; thesis optional. (Program stresses mass communications.)

Temple University. Educational Media Program, Philadelphia, PA 19122. Elton Robertson, Prof., Chair, Educational Media Program. *Program Basis:* Semester. *Minimum Degree Requirements:* 33 credit hours including 24 in media; thesis optional. *Faculty:* 2, 2, 5. *Graduates:* 11m, 9w, including 3 foreign nationals.

University of Pittsburgh. Instructional Design and Technology, School of Education, Pittsburgh, PA 15260. Barbara Seels, Assoc. Prof., Prog. Coord., Instructional Design and Technology, Dept. of Instruction and Learning, School of Education. *Program Basis:* Trimester. *Minimum Degree Requirements:* 36 credit hours including 18 in instructional technology, 9 in core courses and 9 in electives; comprehensive examination. *Faculty:* 3, 0, 0. *Graduates:* 3m, 3w.

*School also offers a six-year specialist certification program. This instructional design and technology program offers a sequence of courses leading to Pennsylvania state certification as an instructional technologist. This option provides for study of media design and production, design of inservice programs, application of instructional technology to the curriculum, curriculum development, group processes, leadership skills, selection and utilization of materials with consideration for a multicultural society, evaluation strategies, and administration of media programs. The certification program can be taken concurrently with a master's degree sequence.

West Chester University. School of Education. West Chester, PA 19380. Joseph Spiecker, Prof., Chair., Instructional Media Dept., School of Education. *Program Basis:* Semester. *Minimum Degree Requirements:* 34 credit hours including 28 in media; thesis optional. *Faculty:* 5, 1, 1. *Graduates:* 10m, 4w, including 1 foreign national.

RHODE ISLAND

Rhode Island College. Department of Leadership Foundations and Technology, Providence, RI 02908. James E. Davis, Assoc. Prof., Chair, Dept. of Leadership Foundations and Technology. *Program Basis:* Semester. *Minimum Degree Requirements:* 30 credit hours including 21 in media; thesis optional. *Faculty:* 3, 2, 0. *Graduates:* 5m, 5w.

The University of Rhode Island. Graduate School of Library and Information Studies, College of Arts and Sciences, Kingston, RI 02881-0815. Elizabeth Futas, Prof., Dir., Graduate School of Library and Information Studies. *Program Basis:* Semester. *Minimum Degree Requirements:* 36 credit hours including specializations in areas such as media programs, information services, technical services, and bibliography. *Faculty:* 8, 12, 3. *Graduates:* 8m, 37w.

SOUTH CAROLINA

University of South Carolina. Educational Psychology Department, Columbia, SC 29208. J. C. Rotter, Prof., Chair, Educational Psychology Dept. *Program Basis:* Semester. *Minimum Degree Requirements:* 33 credit hours including 3 each in administration, curriculum, and research, 9 in production, and 3 in instructional theory; no thesis required. *Faculty:* 3, 1, 2. *Graduates:* 1m, 3w, including 1 foreign national.

Winthrop College. School of Education, Rock Hill, SC 29733. George Robinson, Assoc. Prof., Educational Media Coord., School of Education. *Program Basis:* Semester. *Minimum Degree Requirements:* 36-42 credit hours including 15-33 in media depending on media courses a student has had prior to this program; nonthesis. *Faculty:* 2, 0, 2. *Graduates:* 13w.

TENNESSEE

East Tennessee State University. College of Education, Johnson City, TN 37614-0002. Rudy Miller, Assoc. Prof. of Instructional Communication, College of Education. *Program Basis:* Semester. *Minimum Degree Requirements:* 36 credit hours including 18 in instructional technology; thesis optional. *Faculty:* 1, 1, 3. *Graduates:* 5w.

Memphis State University. College of Education, Memphis, TN 38152. Thomas A. Rakes, Prof., Chair, Dept. of Curriculum and Instruction, College of Education. *Program Basis:* Semester. *Minimum Degree Requirements:* 33 credit hours including 15 in instructional design and technology; thesis optional. *Faculty:* 2, 1, 0. *Graduates:* 3m, 12w.
    *School also offers a six-year specialist degree program in instructional technology. Program comprised of 66 credit hours including 36 in major, 3 hours in educational research, 21 hours of supportive collateral, and 2 years of teaching experience or equivalent.

Middle Tennessee State University. Department of Youth Education and School Personnel Services, Murfreesboro, TN 37132. Ralph L. White, Prof. and Chair, Dept. of Youth Education and School Personnel Services. *Program Basis:* Semester. *Minimum Degree Requirements:* 33 credit hours including 15 in media; no thesis required. *Faculty:* 2, 1, 0. *Graduates:* 9m, 26w.

University of Tennessee. College of Education, Knoxville, TN 37906-3400. Dr. Al D. Grant, Coord., Graduate Media Program, Dept. of Curriculum and Instruction. *Program Basis:* Semester. *Minimum Degree Requirements:* M.S. in Education, concentration in Instructional Media and Technology 24 hours, 6 semester hours thesis; 33 hours, nonthesis. *Faculty:* 1. *Graduates:* 2m.
    *Department of Curriculum and Instruction also offers a six-year specialist degree program in Curriculum and Instruction with a concentration in instructional media and technology. This new program has 24 semester hours beyond the M.S. and a seminar paper, 6 semester hours, for a total of 30 hours.

TEXAS

East Texas State University. Dept. of Secondary and Higher Education, Commerce, TX 75428. Robert S. Munday, Prof., Head, Dept. of Secondary and Higher Education. *Program Basis:* Semester. *Minimum Degree Requirements:* 30 credit hours with thesis; 36 nonthesis, including 18 in media. *Faculty:* 7, 3, 1. *Graduates:* 8m, 19w, including 12 foreign nationals.

North Texas State University. College of Education, Denton, TX 76203-3857. J. L. Poirot, Prof., Prog. Coord., Computer Educatiuon and Cognitive Systems, College of Education. *Program Basis:* Semester. *Minimum Degree Requirements:* 36 hours including 27 hours in instructional technology and computer education; nonthesis. *Faculty:* 7, 1, 0. *Graduates:* 5m, 8w, including 10 foreign nationals.

Prairie View A&M University. Department of School Services, Prairie View, TX 77446. Marion Henry, Prof., Dir., Educational Media and Technology Program. *Program Basis:* Semester. *Minimum Degree Requirements:* 36 credit hours, 21 in media; no thesis required. *Faculty:* 6, 2, 0. *Graduates:* 10w.

Texas A&M University. College of Education, College Station, TX 77843. Ronald D. Zellner, Assoc. Prof., Coord., Educational Technology Prog., College of Education.

Program Basis: Semester. *Minimum Degree Requirements:* 37 credit hours including 19 in educational technology; nonthesis. *Faculty:* 6, 5, 1. *Graduates:* 6m, 6w, including 3 foreign nationals.

Texas Tech University. College of Education, Box 4560, Lubbock, TX 79409. Robert Price, Assoc. Prof., Dir., Instructional Technology Program, College of Education. *Program Basis:* Semester. *Minimum Degree Requirements:* 39 credit hours; nonthesis. *Faculty:* 3, 3, 0. *Graduates:* 9m, 8w, including 1 foreign national.

University of Texas. College of Education, Austin, TX 78712. De Layne Hudspeth, Assoc. Prof., Coord., Area of Instructional Technology, Dept. of Curriculum and Instruction, College of Education. *Program Basis:* Semester. *Minimum Degree Requirements:* 36 credit hours including 18 in instructional technology plus research course; thesis optional. A six-hour minor is required outside the department. *Faculty:* 6, 0, 0. *Graduates:* 12w, including 4 foreign nationals.

The University of Texas Southwestern Medical Center at Dallas. Biomedical Communications Department, Dallas, TX 75235. James B. Battles, Ph.D., Chair, Media Development Progs., Biomedical Communications Dept. *Program Basis:* Semester. *Minimum Degree Requirements:* 36 credit hours including 24 in media; thesis required. *Faculty:* 7, 5, 1. *Graduates:* 9m, 18w, including 3 foreign nationals.

UTAH

Brigham Young University. Instructional Science Department, Provo, UT 84602. Paul F. Merrill, Prof., Chair. *Program Basis:* Semester. *Minimum Degree Requirements:* 36 credit hours including 13 in core; thesis required. *Faculty:* 10, 0, 0. *Graduates:* 4m, 3w.

Utah State University. Department of Instructional Technology, Logan, UT 84322-2830. Don C. Smellie, Prof., Head, Department of Instructional Technology. *Program Basis:* Quarter. *Minimum Degree Requirements:* 60 credit hours including 45 in media; thesis or practicum encouraged. Programs in school library media administration and master resource teacher/educational technology are also delivered via an electronic distance education system. *Faculty:* 8, 7, 1. *Graduates:* 17m, 15w, including 1 foreign national.
   *School also offers a six-year specialist degree program in instructional technology. Program prepares individuals in the design, development, and evaluation of learning programs and materials for use in education, industry, and government. Admission requires 3.2 GPA, 900 GRE or 46 MAT, master's degree, three letters of recommendation, and individual's written statement of goals and philosophy. Program includes minimum of 45 quarter hours emphasizing research, core, electives plus either a developmental practicum project or practicum internship. *Graduates:* 1w.

VIRGINIA

James Madison University. Dept. of Educational Resources, Harrisonburg, VA 22807. Alvin Pettus, Head, Dept. of Secondary Education, Library Science and Educational Leadership. *Program Basis:* Semester. *Minimum Degree Requirements:* 33 credit hours including 21 in media; thesis optional. *Faculty:* 2, 2, 1. *Graduates:* 4w.

Radford University. Educational Media, Radford, VA 24142. Gary Ellerman, Prof., Academic Advisor, Educational Media, Human Services. *Program Basis:* Semester. *Minimum Degree Requirements:* 33 credit hours; thesis optional. *Faculty:* 3, 1, 0. *Graduates:* 2m, 4w.

University of Virginia. Curry School of Education, Charlottesville, VA 22903. John Bunch, Assoc. Prof., Coord., Instructional Technology Prog., Dept. of Educational

Studies, Curry School of Education. *Program Basis:* Semester. *Minimum Degree Requirements:* 35 credit hours including 18 in media and computers. *Faculty:* 3, 2, 1. *Graduates:* 3m, 2w.

*School also offers a post-master's certificate program in instructional technology. Applicants for the Ed.S. degree must hold a master's degree; have earned a grade point average of B or better; submit an application for admission and official transcripts of all undergraduate and graduate work; be recommended by two persons qualified to judge his or her potential; submit basic aptitude test scores for the GRE; and submit a statement of professional goals. To earn the degree, a minimum of 30 credit hours is required in the student's program area and a written comprehensive exam of 8-10 hours is also required. *Graduates:* 2 Ph.D., 4 M.Ed. (1990).

Virginia Commonwealth University. Division of Teacher Education, Richmond, VA 23284. Sheary Johnson, Asst. Prof., Core Coord. of Instructional Technology, Div. of Teacher Education. *Program Basis:* Semester. *Minimum Degree Requirements:* 36 semester hours including 24 in media plus externships; thesis optional. *Faculty:* 2, 0, ⅓. *Graduates:* 6w.

Virginia Polytechnic Institute and State University (Virginia Tech). College of Education, Blacksburg, VA 24061-0313. John K. Burton, Assoc. Prof., Program Area Leader, Instructional Systems Development, Curriculum and Instruction. *Program Basis:* Semester. *Minimum Degree Requirements:* 30 credit hours including 15 in instructional technology; thesis optional. *Faculty:* 9, 0, 0. *Graduates:* 4m.

Virginia State University. School of Education, Petersburg, VA 23803. Vykuntapathi Thota, Coord., Educational Media. *Program Basis:* Semester. *Minimum Degree Requirements:* 30 credit hours plus thesis for master of science; 33 semester hours plus project for the master of education.

WASHINGTON

Eastern Washington University. College of Science, Mathematics and Technology, Cheney, WA 99004. Donald R. Horner, Prof., Computer Science, College of Science, Mathematics and Technology. *Program Basis:* Quarter. *Minimum Degree Requirements:* 48 credit hours with emphasis in computer science. *Faculty:* 11, 2, 4 TAs. *Graduates:* 18m, 6w.

University of Washington. Department of Education, Seattle, WA 98195. William D. Winn, Prof., Prog. in Educational Communication and Technology, School of Education. *Program Basis:* Quarter. *Minimum Degree Requirements:* 45 credit hours including 24 in media; thesis optional. *Faculty:* 2, 3, 0. *Graduates:* 3w, including 1 foreign national.

Western Washington University. Woodring College of Education, Bellingham, WA 98225. Tony Jongejan, Assist. Prof., Div. of Educational Technology, Dept. of Educational Administration and Foundations. *Program Basis:* Quarter. *Minimum Degree Requirements:* 45 credit hours including 22 in media; thesis optional. *Faculty:* 3, 3, 8. *Graduates:* 5w.

WEST VIRGINIA

Marshall University. Department of Instructional Technology and Library Science, Huntington, WV 25701. Virginia D. Plumley, Prof., Chair, Dept. of Instructional Technology and Library Science. *Program Basis:* Semester. *Minimum Degree Requirements:* 36 credit hours including 24 in media; thesis optional. *Faculty:* 2, 5, 0. *Graduates:* 1m, 3w, including 2 foreign nationals.

West Virginia University. Morgantown, WV 26506. David McCrory, Prof., Chair, Technology Education Program, Communication and Information Systems, College of Human Resources and Education. *Program Basis:* Semester. *Minimum Degree Requirements:* 36 credit hours including 15 hours in communication technology; thesis optional. *Faculty:* 2, 5, 0. *Graduates:* 3m, 1w, including 1 foreign national.

WISCONSIN

University of Wisconsin – La Crosse. La Crosse, WI 54601. Clyde L. Greve, Dir., Educational Media Program, College of Education. *Program Basis:* Semester. *Minimum Degree Requirements:* 30 credit hours including 15 in media; nonthesis. *Faculty:* 3, 0, 0. *Graduates:* 4m, 11w.

University of Wisconsin – Madison. School of Education, Madison, WI 53706. Ann DeVaney, Prof., Coord., Educational Communications and Technology, Dept. of Curriculum and Instruction, School of Education. *Program Basis:* Semester. *Minimum Degree Requirements:* 30 credit hours including 22 hours in media; thesis or project required. *Faculty:* 5, 3, 2. *Graduates:* 40m, 33w, including 14 foreign nationals.

University of Wisconsin – Oshkosh. Oshkosh, WI 54901. Richard R. Hammes, Prof., Coord., Dept. of Human Services and Professional Leadership, College of Education and Human Services. *Program Basis:* Semester. *Minimum Degree Requirements:* 36 credit hours including 15-21 in library, media, and technology. *Faculty:* 2, 0, 4. *Graduates:* 6m, 2w.

University of Wisconsin – Stout. Menomonie, WI 54751. Dr. Roger L. Hartz, Program Dir., Media Technology Program. *Program Basis:* Semester. *Minimum Degree Requirements:* 32 credit hours including 15 in media; thesis optional. *Faculty:* 4, 2, 4. *Graduates:* 5m, 4w, including 5 foreign nationals.

WYOMING

University of Wyoming. College of Education, Box 3374, Laramie, WY 82071. Dr. Landra Rezabek, Prog. Area Coord., Instructional Technology. *Program Basis:* Semester. *Minimum Degree Requirements:* 36 credit hours including 32 in instructional technology and 4 in thesis option, or 36 hours of coursework including project option. Degree offered is Master of Science in Instructional Technology; three tracks are available: Instructional Design, Computer-based Education, and Library/Media Management. *Faculty:* 6, 0, 0. *Graduates:* 4m, 11w. For additional information, contact Dr. Landra Rezabek.

Graduate Programs in
Educational Computing

Brenda Branyan-Broadbent, Ph.D.
Associate Professor

Lois A. Ward
Staff Assistant II
Department of Instructional Technology
Utah State University
Logan, Utah

When the directory of graduate programs in educational computing first appeared in the 1986 *EMTY*, there were only 50 programs. This year's listing consists of 82 such programs. The information in this section has been revised, and updates the information assembled in *EMTY 1990*. Individuals who are considering graduate study in educational computing should contact the institution of their choice for current information.

Data in this section include institution, degree offered, year the program began, number of full- and part-time faculty, number of students currently enrolled, academic credit information, degree requirements, information on outside funding for the department, availability of summer sessions, tuition, and contact person with phone number.

This section is arranged alphabetically by name of institution.

Appalachian State University. Department of Library Science and Educational Foundations, Boone, NC 28608. Department offers M.A. in Educational Media (Instructional Technology-Computers). Master's started in 1986. In fall 1989, had 2 full-time and 1 part-time faculty. Selective admissions. Semester credit basis. *Minimum Degree Requirements:* 36 semester hours; thesis optional; internship required. *Outside Funding for the Department:* No. *Summer Sessions:* Two 5-week terms. *Tuition:* $480 full-time, residents (in-state, 9 hours or more). Dr. John H. Tashner, (704) 262-2243.

Arizona State University. Educational Media and Computers. FMC Payne 146, Tempe, AZ 85287-0111. Department offers M.A. and Ph.D. in Educational Media and Computers. Master's started in 1971 and doctorate started in 1976. In fall 1989, had 9.5 full-time faculty members on the master's and doctoral levels; 25 male and 29 female students on the master's level, and 7 male and 6 female students on the doctoral level. Semester credit basis. *Minimum Degree Requirements:* Master's—33 hours (21 hours in educational media and computers, 9 hours in education, 3 hours outside education); thesis not required; internship required; practicum required. Doctorate—93 hours (24 hours in educational media and computers, 57 hours in education, 12 hours outside education); thesis required; internship required; practicum required. *Outside Funding for the Department:* Yes (various grants). *Summer Session:* 10 weeks. *Tuition Per Credit:* $67 residents (summer and 6 hours or less, $681 for 7 hours or more); $67 nonresidents (summer and 6 hours or less, cost varies for 7-11 hours, $2,742 for 12 hours or more). Dr. Gary Bitter, Coordinator, Educational Media and Computers, (602) 965-7192.

Buffalo State College. 1300 Elmwood Ave., Buffalo, NY 14222-1095. School offers M.S. in Ed. in Educational Computing. Master's started in 1988. In fall 1990, had 0 full-time and 10 part-time faculty members; 29 male and 39 female students. Semester credit basis. *Minimum Degree Requirements:* 33 hours (18 hours in computers, 12-15 hours in education, no hours outside education); thesis or project required; internship not required; practicum not required. *Outside Funding for the Department:* No. *Summer Session:* Three 3-week sessions, two 6-week sessions. *Tuition Per Credit:* $90 residents; $192 nonresidents. Mr. Anthony J. Nowakowski, Acting Coordinator of M.S. in Education in Educational Computing, (716) 878-4923.

Cardinal Stritch College. Department of Educational Computing, 6801 North Yates Road, Milwaukee, WI 53217. Department offers an M.E. in Educational Computing and M.S. in Computer Science Education. Master's program started in 1984. In fall 1990, had 3 full-time and 3 part-time faculty members in the master's program; 50 male and 54 female students. Semester credit basis. *Minimum Degree Requirements:* Master of Education – 30-32 hours (15-21 hours in computer, 6-15 hours in education, no hours outside education); degrees may be completed via coursework option or one of the culminating experiences: thesis, field experience, or software project. Master of Science – 30-32 hours (24-26 hours in computer, 3-6 in education, no hours outside education). *Outside Funding for the Department:* No. *Summer Session:* 6 weeks generally; although there are courses which span 1 week, 4 weeks. *Tuition Per Credit:* $190 on-campus (residents and nonresidents); $150 off-campus (residents and nonresidents). Dr. Jim Kasum, Chair, Department of Educational Computing, (414) 352-5400.

Central Missouri State University. Lovinger 300, Warrensburg, MO 64093. School offers M.S.E. in Curriculum and Instruction with an emphasis in Educational Computing. Master's started in 1986. In fall 1989, had 15 full-time and 2 part-time faculty members; 3 male students and 4 female students. Semester credit basis. *Minimum Degree Requirements:* 32 hours (15 hours in computers, 10 hours in education, 7 hours outside education). *Outside Funding for the Department:* Not specified. *Summer Session:* 8-12 weeks. *Tuition Per Credit Hour:* $75 residents; $136 nonresidents. Dr. Max McCulloch, Professor, (816) 429-4235.

Clarke College. Graduate Studies, 1550 Clarke Drive, Dubuque, IA 52001. Clarke offers an M.A. in Education: Computers in Education. Master's started in 1964, this program in 1980. Four regular Clarke faculty and occasional adjunct instructors teach the technology courses in the predominantly summer program. *Students, summer 1990:* 10 male, 15 female. *Minimum Degree Requirements:* 20-22 hours in computer courses, 9 in education, 2-7 hr. elective. Nonthesis program; internships or practica available but not required. *Outside Funding for the Program:* No. Summer courses vary in length, spreading over seven weeks. *Tuition* (summer 1990): $160 per semester hour. Dr. Marge Clark, BVM, Ed.D., Director, Graduate Studies, (319) 588-6331.

Concordia College. 7400 Augusta, River Forest, IL 60305-1499. School offers M.A. in Mathematic Computer Science Education. Master's started in 1987. In fall 1989, had 8 full-time and 3 part-time faculty members; 11 male and 19 female students. *Minimum Degree Requirements:* 48 quarter hours; no thesis, internship, practicum required. *Outside Funding for the Department:* No. *Summer Session:* 4 weeks each. *Tuition Per Credit:* $170 for all students. Dr. Paul T. Kreiss, Assoc. Dean, School of Graduate Studies, (708) 209-3010.

Eastern Michigan University. College of Education, Boone Hall, Ypsilanti, MI 48197. College offers M.A. in Educational Psychology with an Educational Technology area of concentration. Master's started in 1983. In fall 1989 had 5 full-time and 10 part-time faculty members; 55 male and 137 female students. Semester credit basis. *Minimum Degree Requirements:* 31 hours (22 hours in computers, 8 hours in education); thesis not specified; internship not specified; practicum not required. *Outside Funding for the Department:*

No. *Summer Session:* 6 weeks. Dr. Bert Greene, Professor, Department of Teacher Education, (313) 487-3260.

Eastern Washington University. Department of Mathematics and Computer Science, Cheney, WA 99004. Department offers M.Ed. in Computer Education (elementary), M.Ed. in Computer Education (secondary), and M.S. in Computer Education (interdisciplinary) and M.S.T. (interdisciplinary). Master's started in 1983. In fall 1990, had 11 full-time and 2 part-time faculty; total number of students is about 50, most are active in summers only. Quarter credit basis. *Minimum Degree Requirements:* Master of Science — 52 hours (30 hours in computers, 0 hours in education, 8 hours outside education — not specifically computer science; the hours do not total to 52 because of freedom to choose where Methods of Research is taken, where 12 credits of supporting courses are taken, and where additional electives are taken); thesis not required (a research project with formal report is required although it need not be a thesis in format); internship not required; practicum not required. M.S.T. — 52 hours divided between computer science and another science or mathematics; one area is primary and includes a research project; the second area generally requires fewer hours than the primary. Master of Education — 48 hours minimum (24 hours in computer science, 16 hours in education, 8 hours outside education). *Outside Funding for the Department:* No. *Summer Session:* 8 weeks. *Tuition Per Credit* (1990): $62 residents and nonresidents. Dr. Donald R. Horner, Professor of Computer Science, (509) 359-7092.

Edgewood College. Department of Education, 855 Woodrow Street, Madison, WI 53711. Department offers M.A. in Education with emphasis on Computer-based Education. Master's started in 1987. In fall 1990, had 2 full-time and 6 part-time faculty members; 15 male and 42 female students. Semester credit basis. *Minimum Degree Requirements:* 36 hours (18 hours in computers, 30 hours in education, 6 hours outside education); thesis not required; internship not required; practicum not required. *Outside Funding for the Department:* No. *Summer Session:* Yes (number of weeks not specified). *Tuition Per Credit:* $227 residents; $227 nonresidents. Dr. Joseph E. Schmiedicke, Chair, Department of Education, (608) 257-4861, ext. 2293.

Fitchburg State College. Graduate Program in Educational Technology, 160 Pearl Street, Fitchburg, MA 01420. Program offers M.Ed. in Computers in Education. Master's started in 1983. In fall 1989, had 9 full-time faculty members, 5 part-time faculty (adjunct status); 85 students (about 50 on campus and 35 off campus). Semester credit basis. *Minimum Degree Requirements:* 39 hours (30 hours in educational computers, 9 hours outside education; [electives]); thesis not required; internship not required; practicum not required. *Outside Funding for the Department:* Yes (students pay educational services fees — $15 per lab course — used for purchasing software). *Summer Session:* 4 weeks. *Tuition Per Credit:* $90 credit MA resident; $110 credit nonresident. Lab has been upgraded (networked): 2 MacPlus, 15 Apple IIgs, 5 Apple IIe. Dr. Sandy Miller-Jacobs, Chair, Graduate Program, (508) 345-2151, ext. 3308.

Florida Institute of Technology. Computer Education Department, 150 West University Boulevard, Melbourne, FL 32901-6988. Department offers M.S. in Computer Education. Master's started in 1984. In fall 1989 department had 5 full-time and 4 part-time faculty members; 10 male and 9 female students on the master's level. Quarter credit basis. *Minimum degree requirements:* 48 hours (18 in computer, 18 in education, 12 outside education); thesis and internship not required; practicum required. *Outside Funding for the Department:* No. *Summer Session:* 8 weeks. *Tuition Per Credit:* $205 nonresidents. Dr. Robert Fronk, Head of Computer Education Department, (407) 768-8000, ext. 8126.

Fontbonne College. 6800 Wydown Blvd., St. Louis, MO 63105. School offers M.S. in Computer Education. Master's program started in 1986. Thus far, 65 students have graduated from program, levels K-junior college teachers. Currently 55 students. Semester credit basis. *Minimum Degree Requirements:* 33 hours, thesis not required; internship not required; practicum not required. *Outside Funding for the Department:* Yes. *Summer Session:* 6 weeks. Fall and winter sessions. *Tuition Per Credit:* $220 per credit hour with 15 percent discount for full-time, currently employed educators. Dr. Mary K. Abkemeier, Master of Science in Computer Education, (314) 862-3456, ext. 365.

George Mason University. Center for Interactive Educational Technology, 4400 University Drive, Fairfax, VA 22030. Center offers M.Ed. in Curriculum and Instruction, specialization in Instructional Applications and Microcomputers (I.A.M.), Special Education Technology (S.E.T.), and D.A.Ed. specialization in Instructional Computing. Master's started in 1983 and doctorate in 1984. In fall 1990, had 4 full-time and 4 part-time faculty members on the master's level, and 5 full-time and 5 part-time faculty members on the doctoral level; 15 male and 45 female students on the master's level, and 5 male and 37 female students on the doctoral level. Semester credit basis. *Minimum Degree Requirements:* Master's school-based computer coordinator – 30 hours (12 hours in computers, 18 hours in education, 0 hours outside education); thesis an option; internship an option; practicum an option. Master's computer science educator – 30 hours (15 hours in computers [12 of 15 are the "outside education" hours], 15 in education, 12 outside education); thesis an option; internship an option; practicum an option. Master's special education technology (36-42 hours). Doctorate – 69 hours beyond Master's (12 hours in computers, 54 hours in education [12 of these are computer courses], 15 hours outside education); thesis required; internship required; practicum required. *Outside Funding for the Department:* Yes (various grants and contracts, generally federal and state). *Summer Session:* Yes (three 5-week sessions, one 8-week session). *Tuition Per Credit:* $102 residents; $233 nonresidents. Dr. Wayne P. Thomas, Center Director, (703) 764-6099; Dr. Charles S. White, I.A.M. Coordinator, (703) 764-6744; Dr. Michael M. Behrmann, S.E.T. Coordinator, (703) 323-4396.

George Washington University. 2201 G Street NW, Washington, DC 20052. School offers M.A. in Educational Technology Leadership. Master's started in 1988. In fall 1990, had 5 full-time and 0 part-time faculty members; number of students not specified. Semester credit basis. *Minimum Degree Requirements:* 36 hours (15 hours in computers, 9 hours in education, 12 hours electives inside or outside education); thesis required; internship not required; practicum not required. *Outside Funding for the Department:* No. *Summer Session:* Varying length sessions – normally 6-8 weeks. *Tuition Per Credit:* $445 residents and nonresidents. Mary Louise Ortenzo, Coordinator of Admissions, (202) 994-6163; or Dr. William Lynch, (202) 994-6862.

Georgia State University. Educational Foundations Department, Atlanta, GA 30303. Department offers M.A. and Ph.D. in Educational Psychology (emphasis option in Educational Computers). Master's and doctorate started in 1984. In fall 1990, had 2 full-time and 2 part-time faculty members on the master's and doctoral levels; 4 male and 21 female students on the master's level, and 5 male and 5 female students on the doctoral level. Quarter credit basis. *Minimum Degree Requirements:* Master's – 60 hours (25 hours in computers, 35 hours in education); thesis required; internship not required; practicum not required. Doctorate – 90 hours (35 hours in computers, 40 hours in education, 15 hours outside education); thesis required; internship not required; practicum not required. *Outside Funding for the Department:* No. *Summer Session:* 6 and 8 weeks. *Tuition Per Credit:* $22 residents; $74 nonresidents. Dr. Dave O'Neil, Associate Professor, (404) 651-2582.

Governors State University. College of Education, University Park, IL 60466. College offers M.A. in Education (with Computer Education as specialization). Master's started in 1986. In fall 1989, had 3 full-time and 5 part-time faculty members; 16 male and 30 female students. Semester credit basis. *Minimum Degree Requirements:* 36-39 hours (15 hours in computer, 21-24 hours in education, 0 hours outside education); thesis/project required; internship not required; practicum required. *Outside Funding for the Department:* No.

Summer Session: 8 weeks. *Tuition Per Credit:* $70 residents; $210 nonresidents. Dr. John Meyer, University Professor, (312) 534-5000, ext. 2273.

Grambling State University. College of Education, Grambling, LA 71245. College offers Ed.D. in Developmental Education with an Instructional Systems and Technology specialization. Doctoral program started in 1986. In fall 1990, had 10 full-time and 4-6 part-time faculty members; exact number of students not specified (45 admitted candidates, 120+ taking classes and applying for admission, mostly female, 45 percent white and 55 percent black). Semester credit basis. *Minimum Degree Requirements:* 90+ hours (6 hours CAI, 6 hours design, 6 hours educational psychology, 6 hours video, 6 hours theory, 36 hours minimum in education, 0 hours outside education [but encouraged as cognate]) dissertation required; internship required; practicum not required. *Outside Funding for the Department:* No. *Summer Session:* Yes (6-12 weeks). *Tuition Per Credit:* Residents, 1-3 units, $303; 12 units, $637; nonresidents, 1-3 units, $303; 12 units, $1,312. Dr. JoAnn Dauzat, Professor/Director of Doctoral Program, (318) 274-2656; Dr. Ben Lowery, Assistant Professor, (318) 274-2238.

Hampton University. School of Education, Hampton, VA 23668. School offers M.A. in Computer Education. Master's started in 1983. In spring 1990, had 0 full-time and 4 part-time faculty members; 8 male and 20 female students. Semester credit basis. *Minimum Degree Requirements:* 36 hours (21 hours in computers, 15 in education, 0 hours outside education); thesis not required; internship not required; practicum required. *Outside Funding for the Department:* No. *Summer Session:* 8 weeks. *Tuition Per Credit:* $115 residents and nonresidents. Dr. Carlton E. Brown, Dean, School of Education, (804) 727-5793.

Harvard University. Graduate School of Education, 111 Longfellow Hall, Cambridge, MA 02138. School offers Ed.M. and C.A.S. (certificate of advanced studies) with a concentration in Technology in Education. Master's started in 1983. In fall 1990, had 1 full-time and 4 part-time faculty members; number of students not specified (students do not have to declare a concentration until the beginning of their last semester). Semester credit basis. *Minimum Degree Requirements:* 32 hours (number of hours in computers, education, and outside education not specified); thesis not required; internship not required; practicum not required. *Outside Funding for the Department:* Not specified. *Summer Session:* No. *Tuition Per Credit:* $1,644/course (4 credit hours) residents and nonresidents. Ms. Carly Moreno, Director of Admissions, (617) 495-3414.

Iona College. New Rochelle, NY 10801. College offers M.S. in Educational Computing. Master's started in 1982. In fall 1990, had 5 full-time and 2 part-time faculty members; 50 male and 50 female students. Trimester credit basis. *Minimum Degree Requirements:* 36 hours ("all hours listed in educational computing"); thesis not required; internship not required; practicum not required. *Outside Funding for the Department:* No. *Summer Session:* Two 5-week sessions and 2-week institute. *Tuition Per Credit:* $270 residents and nonresidents. Dr. Catherine Ricardo, Coordinator and Associate Professor, Computer and Information Sciences, (914) 633-2578.

Iowa State University. College of Education, Ames, IA 50011. College offers Master's and Ph.D. in Curriculum and Instructional Technology with an emphasis in Instructional Computing. Master's and doctorate started in 1967. In fall 1989, had 4 full-time and 5 part-time faculty members on the master's and doctoral levels; 10 male and 24 female students on the master's level, and 10 female and 10 male students on the doctoral level. Semester credit basis. *Minimum Degree Requirements:* Master's—30 hours; thesis required; internship not required; practicum not required. Doctorate—78 hours, thesis required; internship not required; practicum not required. *Summer Session:* 4 or 8 weeks. Dr. Michael R. Simonson, Professor, (515) 294-6840.

Jacksonville University. Department of Education, 2800 University Boulevard North, Jacksonville, FL 32211. Department offers MAT in Computer Education. Master's program started in 1983. In fall 1989, had 5 full-time and 2 part-time faculty members; 7 male and 5 female students. Semester credit basis. *Minimum Degree Requirements:* 36 hours (21 hours in computer, 15 hours in education, 0 hours outside education); thesis not required; internship not required; practicum not required; comprehensive exam required. *Outside Funding for the Department:* No. *Summer Session:* 6 weeks. *Tuition Per Credit:* $250/semester hour, residents and nonresidents. Dr. Daryle C. May, Director, Teacher Education and MAT Program, (904) 744-3950.

Johns Hopkins University. Div. of Education, Rm. 101 Whitehead Hall, Baltimore, MD 21218. Division offers M.S. in Education, with concentration in Technology for Educators, and C.A.S.E. in Technology for Educators, and Ed.D. in Human Communication and Its Disorders – Technology and Special Education. Master's started in 1980 and doctorate in 1984. In fall 1990, had 3 full-time and 25 part-time faculty members on the master's and doctoral levels; number of students not specified. Semester credit basis. *Minimum Degree Requirements:* Master's – 33 hours (24 hours in computers, 9 hours in education [computer courses are all education related]); thesis not required; internship required; practicum required. Specialist's – 30 hours (30 hours in computers and education [computer courses are all education related]); thesis not required; internship required; practicum required. Doctorate – 99 hours (hours in computers and education vary); thesis required; internship required; practicum required. *Outside Funding for the Department:* Yes (for doctoral program only, sources not specified). *Summer Session:* Yes (number of weeks varies). Special summers only master's degree offered. *Tuition Per Credit:* $165 residents and nonresidents. Dr. Dianne Tobin, Assistant Professor, (301) 338-8273.

Kansas State University. Educational Technology and Computer Ed., 253 Bluemont Hall, Manhattan, KS 66506. Department offers M.S. in Elementary or Secondary Education with specialization in Computer-based Education, Ed.D. in Computer Education, and Ph.D. in Computer Education. Master's started in 1982; doctorate in 1984. In fall 1989, had 4 full-time and 3 part-time faculty members on the master's level, and 4 full-time and 0 part-time faculty members on the doctoral level; 10 male and 10 female students on the master's level, and 6 male and 3 female students on the doctoral level. Semester credit basis. *Minimum Degree Requirements:* Master's – 30 hours (minimum of 9 in computer education); thesis not required; internship not required; practicum not required (but these are possible). Doctorate – 90 hours (minimum of 18 in computer education, 12 hours outside education); thesis required; internship and practicum not required but encouraged. *Outside Funding for the Department:* Yes (WEEA grant, others pending). *Summer Session:* 8 weeks. *Tuition Per Credit:* Fall and spring – residents, part-time $37-$45, full-time $550-$600; nonresidents, part-time $118-$126, full-time $1,765-$1,885. Dr. Jackson A. Byars, Chair, Educational Technology and Computer Education, (913) 532-5556.

Kearney State College. Kearney, NE 68849. School offers M.S. in Educational Technology. Master's started in 1984. In fall 1990, had 3 full-time and 5 part-time faculty members; 21 male and 11 female students. Semester credit basis. *Minimum Degree Requirements:* 36 hours (18 hours in computers, 18 hours in education); internship not required; practicum not required. *Outside Funding for the Department:* No. *Summer Session:* 8 weeks. *Tuition Per Credit:* $40.50 residents; $64.50 nonresidents. Dr. Lynn Johnson, Chair, Professional Teacher Education, (308) 234-8513.

Kent State University. Educational Technology Program. 405 White Hall, KSU, Kent, OH 44242. Four faculty members. Semester credit basis. *Minimum Degree Requirements:* 34 credit hours (15-20 in computer studies, 12-17 in education). *Summer Session:* Two 5-week sessions. *Tuition Per Credit:* $117 in-state, $209 out-of-state. Dr. Drew Tiene, Program Coordinator, (216) 672-2294.

Lesley College. 29 Everett Street, Cambridge, MA 02238. College offers M.A. in Computers in Education and C.A.G.S. in Computers in Education. Master's started in 1980. In fall 1990, had 5 full-time and 12 part-time faculty members on the master's and specialist levels; 9 male and 28 female students on the master's level, and 2 male and 3 female students on the specialist level. Semester credit basis. *Minimum Degree Requirements:* Master's—33 hours in computers (number of hours in education and outside education not specified); thesis not required; internship not required; practicum not required. Specialist—36 hours (hours in computers, in education, and outside education not specified); thesis, internship, practicum not specified. *Outside Funding for the Department:* Yes (NSF grant). *Summer Session:* Two 3-week sessions. *Tuition Per Credit:* $285 residents and nonresidents. Dr. Nancy Roberts, Professor of Computer Education, (617) 868-9600.

Long Island University. C. W. Post, Brookville, NY 11548. School offers M.S. in Education, concentration in Computers in Education. Master's started in 1985. In fall 1989, had 4 full-time and 10 part-time faculty members; number of students not specified. Semester credit basis. *Minimum Degree Requirements:* 36 hours (27 hours in computers, 9 hours in education, 0 hours outside education); thesis required; internship not required; practicum not required. *Outside Funding for the Department:* No. *Summer Session:* 3 sessions, 5 weeks each. *Tuition Per Credit:* $260 per credit, $25 computer lab fee residents; same for nonresidents. Advisor of Educational Technology, (516) 299-2147.

Mankato State University. Education Technology M.S. Program, Box 20, Mankato, MN 56002. Program offers M.S. in Educational Technology (integrated interdisciplinary degree). Master's started in 1986. In fall 1990, had 8 full-time faculty members and 35 students. Quarter credit basis. *Minimum Degree Requirements:* 51 hours (6-15 hours in computers, 12-15 hours in education, 12-18 hours [optional] outside education); thesis not required; internship required; practicum not required. *Outside Funding for the Department:* No. *Summer Session:* Yes. *Tuition Per Credit:* $52.40 residents; $73.35 nonresidents. Kenneth C. Pengelly, Professor and Coordinator of Educational Technology M.S. Program, (507) 389-1965.

Minot State University. 500 Urn Avenue West, Minot, ND 58702. School offers M.S. in Audiology, M.S. in Education of the Deaf, M.S. in Elementary Education, M.S. in Learning Disabilities, M.S. in Special Education, M.S. in Speech-Language Pathology, MAT in Mathematics, M.S. in Criminal Justice. Master's program started in 1964. In fall 1990, had 40 full-time and 9 part-time faculty members; 12 male and 68 female students. Quarter credit basis. *Minimum Degree Requirements:* 45 hours (hours in computers, in education and outside education vary according to program). *Outside Funding for the Department:* Yes (federal grants in special education and speech-language pathology). *Summer Session:* 8 weeks. *Tuition:* Full-time students: $729 residents (Minnesota reciprocity $831); $1,851 nonresidents (contiguous states/provinces $831). Dr. James Croonquist, Dean, Graduate School, (701) 857-3822.

National College of Education. Department of Computer Education, 2840 Sheridan Road, Evanston, IL 60201. Department offers M.Ed., M.S., C.A.S. (certificate of advanced studies) in Computer Education, and Ed.D. in Instructional Leadership with minor concentration in Computer Education. Master's started in 1983, specialist in 1983, and doctorate in 1984. In fall 1989, had 2 full-time faculty and 4 part-time faculty members on the master's, specialist, and doctoral levels; 15 male and female students in the master's program, 31 male and female students in the specialist program, and 5 female students in the doctoral program (had 92 graduates). Semester credit basis. *Minimum Degree Requirements:* Master's—34 hours (18 hours in computers, 10 hours in education, and 0 hours outside education); thesis optional; internship not required, practicum not required. Specialist's, C.A.S.—30 hours (18 hours in computers, 4 hours in education, 0 hours outside education); thesis not required; internship not required; practicum not required.

Doctorate—63 hours (14 hours in computers, 37 hours in education, 0 hours outside education); thesis required; internship required; practicum not required; *Outside Funding for the Department:* No. *Summer Session:* 6 weeks. *Tuition Per Credit:* $215 per semester hour, residents; $215 per semester hour, nonresidents. Dr. Sandra V. Turner, Chair, Department of Computer Education, (708) 475-1100, ext. 2256.

North Carolina State University. Department of Curriculum and Instruction, P.O. Box 7801, Raleigh, NC 27695-7801. Department offers M.Ed. and M.S. in Instructional Technology—Computers (program track within one master's in Curriculum and Instruction). Master's started in 1986. In fall 1989, had 3 full-time faculty members; 18 male and female students. Semester credit basis. *Minimum Degree Requirements:* 36 hours; thesis optional; internship not required; practicum required. *Outside Funding for the Department:* No. *Summer Session:* Yes (number of weeks not specified). *Tuition Per Credit:* Not specified. Dr. Ellen Vasu, Associate Professor, Department of Curriculum and Instruction, (919) 737-3221.

Northern Illinois University. College of Education, DeKalb, IL 60115. College offers M.S.Ed. in Instructional Technology with a concentration in Microcomputers or Instructional Design in Education and Training. Master's started in 1968. In fall 1990, had 5 full-time and 0 part-time faculty members; number of students 87. Semester credit basis. *Minimum Degree Requirements:* 39 hours (27 hours in technology, 9 hours in education, 0 hours outside education); thesis not required; internship not required; practicum not required. *Outside Funding for the Department:* No. *Summer Session:* 8 weeks. *Tuition Per Credit:* Not specified. Dr. Gary L. McConeghy, Chair, Instructional Technology, (815) 753-0465.

Nova University. Ed.D./CED Program, Ft. Lauderdale, FL 33314. Program offers M.S., Ed.D., and Ed.S. in Computer Education. Master's started in 1985; specialist in 1984; doctorate in 1984. In fall 1989, had 2 full-time and 0 part-time faculty members on the master's level, and 8 full-time and 0 part-time faculty members on the doctoral level (specialist program is phasing out); 35 male and 35 female students on the master's level, 2 male and 3 female students on the specialist's level, and 55 male and 44 female students on the doctoral level. Semester credit basis. *Minimum Degree Requirements:* Master's—36 hours (24 hours in computer, 12 hours in education, 0 hours outside education); no thesis required; no internship required; practicum required. Doctorate—66 hours (33 hours in computer, 21 hours in education, 12 hours outside education); thesis required; internship not required; practicum required. *Outside Funding for the Department:* No. *Summer Session:* Number of weeks not specified. *Tuition Per Credit:* Master's, $190 residents and nonresidents; doctorate, $225 residents and nonresidents. Dr. John Kingsbury, Director of Marketing, (305) 475-7047, (800) 541-6682, ext. 7047.

Ohio State University. 225 Ramseyer Hall, 29 W. Woodruff Avenue, Columbus, OH 43210-1177. Since 1980, school offers M.A. and Ph.D. in Computers in Education in the program area of Instructional Design and Technology. In fall 1989, had 8 full-time and 4 part-time graduate faculty members: 34 students in the master's program and 29 students in the doctoral program. Quarter credit basis. *Minimum degree requirements:* M.A. 50 credit hours—18 hrs. core, 6 hrs. foundations, 3 hrs. multicultural—minimum: Ph.D. 135 hrs. post-bachelor's, general examination (written and oral), dissertation. *Outside Funding for the Department:* No. *Summer Session:* 3, 5, 8, and 10 weeks. *Tuition Per Credit:* 1 credit Ohio resident, $108, out-of-state, $144; 10 or more credits Ohio resident $867, out-of-state $2,230. Dr. Marjorie A. Cambre, Associate Professor, Ohio State University, (614) 292-4872.

Pace University. Department of Educational Administration, White Plains, NY 10606. Department offers M.S. in Curriculum and Instruction with a concentration in Computers. Master's started in 1986. In fall 1990, had 2 full-time and 15 part-time faculty members; 20

male and 33 female students. Semester credit basis. *Minimum Degree Requirements:* 33-34 hours (15 hours in computers, 15 hours in education); thesis not required; internship not required; practicum not required; comprehensive exam required. *Outside Funding for the Department:* No. *Summer Session:* 4 weeks. *Tuition Per Credit:* $300 residents and non-residents. Dr. Lawrence Roder, Chair, Department of Educational Administration, (914) 422-4198.

Pennsylvania State University. University Park, PA 16802. School offers M.S. in Instructional Systems, M.Ed. in Instructional Systems, Ph.D. in Instructional Systems, and D.Ed. in Instructional Systems. Master's started in 1970. In fall 1990, had 5 full-time and 3 part-time faculty members on the master's and doctoral levels; 14 male and 16 female students on the master's level, and 11 male and 17 female students on the doctoral level. Semester credit basis. *Minimum Degree Requirements:* Master's — 30 hours (15 hours in computers, 9 hours in education, 6 hours outside education); thesis not required; internship not required; practicum not required. Doctorate — 90 hours (27 hours in computers, 33 hours in education, 15 hours outside education); thesis required; internship not required; practicum not required. *Outside Funding for the Department:* Yes. *Summer Session:* 3-, 6-, and 8-week sessions. *Tuition Per Credit:* $176 residents; $349 nonresidents. Paul W. Welliver, Professor of Education, (814) 865-1500.

Purdue University. School of Education, West Lafayette, IN 47907. Department of Curriculum and Instruction offers M.S., Ed.S., and Ph.D. in Educational Computing and Instructional Development. Master's started in 1984 and specialist's and doctorate in 1980. In fall 1990, had 6 full-time and 0 part-time faculty members at all levels; 48 students on the master's level, and 22 students on the doctoral level. Semester credit basis. *Minimum Degree Requirements:* Master's — 36 hours (15 in computer or instructional development, 9 in education, 12 unspecified); thesis optional. Specialist — 60-65 hours (15-18 in computer or instructional development, 30-35 in education); thesis required; internship required; practicum required. Doctorate — 70-82 hours (15-18 in computer or instructional development, 42-45 in education); thesis required; internship required; practicum/project/report required. *Outside Funding for the Department:* No. *Summer Session:* 8 weeks. *Tuition Per Credit:* $77.50 residents; $222.50 nonresidents. Dr. James Russell, Chair, Educational Computing and Instructional Development, (317) 494-5673.

Saint Peter's College. Graduate Programs in Education, 2641 Kennedy Boulevard, Jersey City, NJ 07306. School offers M.A. in Education-Computer Science/Data Processing. Master's started in 1979. In fall 1989 had 9 full-time and 8 part-time faculty members; 12 male and 47 female students. Semester credit basis. *Minimum Degree Requirements:* 39 hours (27 hours in computers, 12 hours in education, 0 hours outside education); thesis not required; internship not specified; practicum not specified. *Outside Funding for the Department:* No. *Summer Session:* 5 weeks. *Tuition Per Credit:* $227 residents and non-residents. Dr. Henry F. Harty, Director, Graduate Programs in Education, (201) 915-9254.

San Diego State University. Department of Educational Technology, San Diego, CA 92182-0311. Department offers M.A. in Education with specializations in Educational Technology, and Educational Computing. In spring 1990, had 7 full-time and 3 part-time faculty members; 40 male and 75 female students. Semester credit basis. *Minimum Degree Requirements:* 36 hours (3 hours in education, hours in computers and outside education not specified); thesis not required; internship not required; practicum required. *Outside Funding for the Department:* Yes (local companies, gifts from Apple Computer, federal and state grants). *Summer Session:* 12 weeks. *Tuition Per Credit:* $70/unit residents and nonresidents (differs in summer). Dr. Pat Harrison, Chair, Department of Educational Technology, (619) 594-6718.

Southern Illinois University — Carbondale. Department of Curriculum and Instruction, Carbondale, IL 62901. Department offers M.S. in Curriculum and Instruction with a specialization in Computer-based Education and Ph.D. in Curriculum and Instruction with a specialization in Instructional Technology. Master's and doctorate started in 1983. In fall 1990, had 5 full-time and 5 part-time faculty members on the master's and doctoral levels; 11 male and 14 female students on the master's level, and 5 male and 4 female students on the doctoral level. Semester credit basis. *Minimum Degree Requirements:* Master's — 32 hours (specialty in computer-based education: 21 hours in computers, 9 hours in education, 2-6 outside education); thesis optional; internship not required; practicum not required. Doctorate — 64 hours (specialty in instructional technology: hours in computers vary, 17 hours in education, hours outside education vary); thesis required; internship not required; practicum not required. *Outside Funding for the Department:* $1,000,000+ in the areas of early childhood, science education, math education, and teacher education. *Summer Session:* 8 weeks. *Tuition Per Credit:* $65 residents; $195 nonresidents. Dr. Pierre Barrette, Coordinator, Department of Curriculum and Instruction, (618) 536-2441.

Southwest Baptist University. School of Education, 1601 South Springfield, Bolivar, MO 65613. School offers M.S. in Education with specialization in Computer Education. Master's started in 1982. In fall 1989, had 2 full-time and 3 part-time faculty members; 9 male and 19 female students. Semester credit basis. *Minimum Degree Requirements:* 36 hours (18 hours in computers, 18 hours in education, 0 hours outside education); thesis not required; internship not required; practicum required. *Outside Funding for the Department:* No. *Summer Session:* Two 4-week terms. *Tuition Per Credit:* $88 residents and nonresidents. Dr. Fred A. Teague, Dean, School of Education, (417) 326-1710.

Spalding University. Education Technology Program, 851 South Fourth Avenue, Louisville, KY 40203. Program offers Ed.S. in Technology in Education and M.A. in Education Technology. Master's program started in 1983; specialist in 1983. In fall 1989, had 1 full-time and 1 part-time faculty member; 11 students in the master of arts and 8 on the specialist's levels. Semester credit basis. *Minimum Degree Requirements:* Master's — 30-36 hours (21-27 in computers, 9 hours in education, 0 hours outside education); thesis not required; internship not required; practicum required (directed study and position paper). Specialist's — 30-36 hours (21-27 hours in computers, 9 hours in education, 0 hours outside education); thesis not required; internship not required; practicum required (directed study and position paper). Students may obtain Kentucky certificate endorsement (K-12) as specialist in Computerized Instruction (36 graduate semester hours) and Indiana certificate endorsement (K-12) as Computer Educator (15 graduate semester hours). *Outside Funding for the Department:* No. *Summer Session:* 2 sessions of 5 weeks each. *Tuition Per Credit:* $185 plus fees, residents and nonresidents; Ed.S. $195. Dr. Eileen Boyle Young, Director, Education Technology Program, (502) 585-9911, ext. 237.

State University of New York, College of Arts and Science at Potsdam. 204 Satterlee Hall, Potsdam, NY 13676. School offers M.S. in Education, Instructional Technology, and Media Management with Educational Computing concentration. Master's started in 1981. In spring 1990, had 65 full-time and 4 part-time faculty members; 52 male, 83 female students, and 10 foreign students (Taiwan). Semester credit basis. *Minimum Degree Requirements:* 33 hours (18 hours in computers, 15 hours in educaiton, 0 hours outside education); thesis not required; internship or practicum required. *Outside Funding for the Department:* No. *Summer Session:* 5 weeks (two sessions, early and regular). *Tuition Per Credit:* $90 residents; $156 nonresidents. Dr. Norman Licht, Professor of Education, (315) 267-2527.

State University of New York. Department of Technology and Society, Stonybrook, NY 11794. Department offers Master's in Technological Systems Management with a 15-credit concentration in Educational Computing. Master's started in 1979. In fall 1989 had 10 full-time and 4 part-time faculty members; 21 male and 18 female students. Semester credit basis. *Minimum Degree Requirements:* 30 hours (hours in computer, education, and outside education not specified); thesis required; internship not specified; practicum not specified. *Outside Funding for the Department:* Yes (source not specified). *Summer Session:* 6 weeks. *Tuition Per Credit:* $90 residents; $228 nonresidents. Dr. Thomas T. Liao, Professor and Chairperson, (516) 632-8767.

Texas A&M University. Department of Interdisciplinary Education, Educational Technology Program, College Station, TX 77843. Department offers M.Ed. in Educational Technology, emphasis in Computer Applications. Master's started in 1984. In fall 1990, had 6 full-time and 1 part-time faculty members; 8 male and 9 female students. Semester credit basis. *Minimum Degree Requirements:* 37 hours (12 hours in computers, 6 hours in education); thesis not required; internship or practicum required. *Outside Funding for the Department:* No. *Summer Session:* Two 6-week sessions. *Tuition Per Credit:* $16 residents; $122 nonresidents. Dr. Ronald Zellner, Coordinator, Educational Technology, (409) 845-7276.

Texas Christian University. P.O. Box 32925, Fort Worth, TX 76129. School offers Master of General Education with specialization in Computers in Education. Master's started in 1984. In fall 1989, had 1 full-time and 1 part-time faculty member; number of students not specified. Semester credit basis. *Minimum Degree Requirements:* 36 hours (18 hours in specialization, 6 hours in professional education, 6 hours thesis, 6 hours elective); thesis required; internship not required; practicum required. *Outside Funding for the Department:* No. *Summer Session:* One 3-week session, two 5-week sessions. *Tuition Per Credit:* Not specified (financial assistance is available). Dr. Sherrie Reynolds, Assistant Professor, (817) 921-7660.

Texas Tech University. College of Education, Box 4560, TTU, Lubbock, TX 79409. College offers M.Ed. and Ed.D. in Instructional Technology (educational computing). Master's started in 1981; doctorate in 1982. In fall 1989, had 3 full-time and 2 part-time faculty members on the master's and doctoral levels; 28 students on the master's level and 17 students on the doctoral level. Semester credit basis. *Minimum Degree Requirements:* Master's – 39 hours (24 hours in computing, 15 hours in education or outside education); thesis not required; internship not required; practicum required. Doctorate – 81 hours (33 hours in computers, 24 hours in education, 24 hours outside education); thesis not specified; internship not required; practicum required. *Outside Funding for the Department:* No. *Summer Session:* Two 6-week sessions. *Tuition Per Credit:* $16 residents; $120 nonresidents. Dr. Robert Price, Director, Instructional Technology, (806) 742-2362.

Texas Wesleyan University. School of Education, Fort Worth, TX 76105. School offers M.S. in Computers in Education. Master's started in 1982. In fall 1989, had 3 full-time and 1 part-time faculty members; 10 male and 19 female students. Semester credit basis. *Minimum Degree Requirements:* 36 hours (18 hours in computers, 18 hours in education, 0 hours outside education); thesis or practicum required; internship not required. *Outside Funding for the Department:* No. *Summer Session:* Two 5-week sessions. *Tuition Per Credit:* $180/hr. residents and nonresidents. Dr. Allen Henderson, Dean, School of Education, (817) 531-4940.

Texas Woman's University. Denton, TX 76204. School offers M.A. and M.Ed. major in Elementary Education. Master's program started in 1985. In fall 1989, had 3 full-time faculty members (all are partially involved); 4 female and 0 male students. Semester credit basis. *Minimum Degree Requirements:* 36 hours (6 hours in computer science, 30 hours in education [6-9 hours in computers in education]); thesis not specified; internship not specified; practicum not specified. *Outside Funding for the Department:* Not specified. *Summer Session:* 12 weeks. *Tuition Per Credit:* Varies for residents (minimum of $100 through 6 hours); $120 per hour for nonresidents. Vera T. Gershner, Professor, (817) 898-2256.

United States International University. School of Education, 10455 Pomerado Rd., San Diego, CA 92131. School offers M.A. in Computer Education and Ed.D. with specialization in Computer Education. Master's and doctorate started in 1983. In fall 1989, had 4 full-time and 4 part-time faculty members on the master's and doctoral levels; 40 male and 60 female students on the master's level, and 25 male and 25 female students on the doctoral level. Quarter credit basis. *Minimum Degree Requirements:* Master's—45 hours (30 hours in computers, 15 hours in education, 0 hours outside education); thesis not required; internship not required; practicum required. Doctorate—95 hours (60 hours in computers, 35 hours in education, 0 hours outside education); thesis required; internship required; practicum required. *Outside Funding for the Department:* No. *Summer Session:* 10 weeks. *Tuition Per Credit:* $195 residents and nonresidents. Dr. Maria T. Wilson, Associate Professor and Coordinator of Computer Education Programs, (619) 693-4721.

University of Colorado—Colorado Springs. School of Education, P.O. Box 7150, Colorado Springs, CO 80933-7150. School offers M.A. in Curriculum and Instruction with an emphasis in Educational Computing and Technology. Students reflect K-12 track for educators or CBT instructional design track for corporate trainers. Master's program started in 1983. In fall 1990, had 1 full-time and 6 part-time faculty members in the master's program; 15 male and 14 female students. Semester credit basis. *Minimum Degree Requirements:* 33 hours (27 hours required in educational technology; 6 hours in education; 0 hours outside education); no thesis required; no internship required; no practicum required. *Outside Funding for the Department:* No. *Summer Session:* 4-8 weeks. *Tuition Per Credit:* $77 residents; $227 nonresidents. Dr. Doris Carey, Graduate Faculty, (719) 593-3299.

University of Denver. School of Education, Denver, CO 80208. School offers M.A. in Curriculum and Instruction or in Educational Psychology. Master's started in 1984. In fall 1989, had 3 full-time and 3 part-time faculty members; 2 male and 2 female students. Quarter credit basis. *Minimum Degree Requirements:* 45 hours (20 hours in computers, 35 hours in education, 0-10 hours outside education); thesis not required; internship not required; practicum not required. *Outside Funding for the Department:* No. *Summer Session:* Yes (number of weeks not specified). *Tuition Per Credit:* $330 residents and nonresidents. Dr. Raymond Kluever, Coordinator, Graduate Study in Education, (303) 871-2508.

University of Florida. College of Education, G-518 Norman Hall, Gainesville, FL 32611. College offers Ed.S. and Ph.D. in Computers in Education. Specialist's program started in 1984 and doctorate in 1984. In fall 1989, had 2 full-time and 1 part-time faculty members on the specialist and doctoral levels; 2 male and 1 female students on the specialist level, and 3 male and 2 female students on the doctoral level. Semester credit basis. *Minimum Degree Requirements:* Specialist's—hours vary (dependent on student's background); a minor in computer science (not computers in education) is required; thesis not required; internship not required; practicum required. Doctorate—hours vary (dependent on student's background); a minor in computer science is required; thesis required; internship not required; practicum not required. *Outside Funding for the Department:* No. *Summer Session:* Two 6-week terms. *Tuition Per Credit:* Not specified. Dr. Roy Bolduc, Professor, (904) 392-5049.

University of Georgia. College of Education, Athens, GA 30602. College offers M.Ed. in Computer-based Education. Master's started in 1985. In fall 1990, had 3 full-time and 5 part-time faculty members; 14 students. Quarter credit basis. *Minimum Degree Requirements:* 60 hours (25 hours in computers, 10 hours in education, 25 hours not specified [55 hours with applied project]); thesis not required; internship and practicum optional. *Outside Funding for the Department:* No. *Summer Session:* Variable (4-9 weeks). *Tuition Per Credit:* $46 residents; $138 nonresidents. Dr. C. Hugh Gardner, Associate Professor of Instructional Technology, (404) 542-3810.

University of Hartford. Math Education and Educational Computing, 200 Bloomfield Avenue, West Hartford, CT 06117. School offers M.Ed. in Educational Computing. Master's started in 1985. In fall 1990, had 2 full-time and 24 part-time male and 1 female faculty members; 8 male and 27 female students. Semester credit basis. *Minimum Degree Requirements:* 30 hours (21 hours in computers, 9 hours in education); thesis not specified; internship not specified; practicum not specified. *Outside Funding for the Department:* Yes (NSF grant). *Summer Session:* 7 courses/1 week per course. *Tuition Per Credit:* $180 residents and nonresidents. Dr. Marilyn Schaffer, Associate Professor of Educational Computing, (203) 243-4277.

University of Hawaii. Educational Technology Department, 1776 University Avenue, Honolulu, HI 96822. Department offers Educational Computing as an area of concentration in Educational Technology, which began in 1983. In fall 1990, had 4 full-time employees (3m, 1w) and 3 part-time faculty; 3 male and 4 female students. Semester credit basis. *Minimum Degree Requirements:* 39 credit hours (27 in computing, 6 in instructional design, 6 electives); thesis available; practicum required, internship required. *Outside Funding for the Department:* No. *Summer Session:* 12 weeks. *Tuition Per Credit:* $61 residents; $183 nonresidents. Dr. Geoffrey Z. Kucera, Professor and Chair, Educational Technology Department, (808) 956-7671 or 956-3910.

University of Houston. University Park, College of Education, Houston, TX 77204-5872. College offers M.Ed. and Ed.D. in Curriculum and Instruction with emphasis in Instructional Technology, specialization in Computer Education. Master's started in 1981; doctorate in 1981. In fall 1989, had 3 full-time and 5 part-time faculty members on the master's and doctoral levels; about 50 students on the master's level, and about 12 students on the doctoral level. Semester credit basis. *Minimum Degree Requirements:* Master's—36 hours without thesis; internship not required; practicum not required. Doctorate—60 hours plus dissertation beyond Master's. *Outside Funding for the Department:* Yes (NSF, U.S. Dept. of Education, Texas Educational Agency, institutional grants). *Summer Session:* 12 weeks. *Tuition Per Credit:* $18 residents; $122 nonresidents. Department of Curriculum and Instruction, (713) 749-1685.

University of Kentucky. Department of Special Education, Lexington, KY 40506-0001. Department offers Ed.S. degree in Special Education Microcomputer Specialist Program. Specialist's program started in 1984. In fall 1989, had 0 full-time and 5 part-time faculty members; 3 male and 10 female students. Semester credit basis. *Minimum Degree Requirements:* 35 hours (35 hours in education [all courses offered in Special Education Department and focus on computer applications], 0 hours outside education); thesis required; internship not required; practicum required. *Outside Funding for the Department:* Yes (Office of Special Education Programs, U.S. Department of Education). *Summer Session:* 8 weeks. *Tuition Per Credit:* Under review. Dr. A. Edward Blackhurst, Professor, (606) 257-4713.

University of Lowell. College of Education, One University Avenue, Lowell, MA 01854. College offers M.Ed. in Curriculum and Instruction, C.A.G.S. in Curriculum and Instruction, Ed.D. in Leadership in Schooling. (Note: An option, called Technology and Learning Environments is offered within broader program streams at M.Ed., and C.A.G.S. levels). Master's, specialist's, doctorates started in 1984. In fall 1990, had 1 full-time (plus courses taught by other faculty) on the master's and specialist's levels; number of students not specified. Semester credit basis. *Minimum Degree Requirements:* Master's—33 hours (hours in computers, education, and outside education not specified); thesis not required; internship not required; practicum required. Doctorate—60 hours beyond master's plus dissertation (hours in computers, education, and outside education not specified); thesis required; internship not required; comprehensive exams required. *Outside Funding for the Department:* No. *Summer Session:* Yes (individual courses, schedule varies). *Tuition Per*

Credit: Residents, $61.50 plus fees; nonresidents, $195.95 plus fees. Dr. John LeBaron, Associate Professor, College of Education, (508) 934-4621.

University of Minnesota. Department of Curriculum and Instructional Systems, 130 Peik Hall, 159 Pillsbury Drive SE, Minneapolis, MN 55455. Department offers M.Ed., M.A., Ph.D. in Instructional Design and Technology. Master's and doctorate started in 1972. In fall 1990, had 5 full-time and 5 part-time faculty members on the master's and doctoral levels; 150 students in the master's program, and 50 students in the doctoral program. Quarter credit basis. *Minimum Degree Requirements:* Master's—45 hours (18 hours in technology, 45 hours in education, 0 hours outside education); M.A. thesis (4 credits) required; internship not required; practicum for M.Ed. required. Doctorate—136 hours; thesis (36 credits) required; internship not required; practicum not required. *Outside Funding for the Department:* Yes (assistantships with business). *Summer Session:* Two 5-week sessions. *Tuition Per Credit:* $64.25 residents (M.Ed.); $159.83 nonresidents (M.Ed.); varies for M.A. and Ph.D. (residents: one credit = $272.27, six credits = $694.36, 7-15 credits = $980.27; nonresidents: one credit = $544.54, six credits = $1,388.72, 7-15 credits = $1,960.54). Dr. Gregory Sales, Curriculum and Instructional Systems, (612) 624-2034.

University of Nevada—Reno. College of Education, Reno, NV 89557. College offers M.Ed. in Curriculum/Instruction. Master's started in 1986. In fall 1989, had 2 full-time and 2 part-time faculty members; 15 male and 20 female students. Semester credit basis. *Minimum Degree Requirements:* 36 hours (12 hours in computers, 24 in education); thesis optional; practicum required. *Outside Funding for the Department:* No. *Summer Session:* Two 5-week sessions. *Tuition Per Credit:* $40 residents; $1,100 nonresidents for 7 or more credits = $40 per credit. Dr. LaMont Johnson, Professor, Department of Curriculum and Instruction, (702) 784-4961.

University of North Carolina—Charlotte. College of Education, Charlotte, NC 28223. College offers M.Ed. in Curriculum and Instruction-Computer. Master's started in 1987. In fall 1989, had 0 full-time faculty and 6 part-time faculty members (full-time faculty devoting part of time to computer education program); 2 male and 18 female students. Semester credit basis. *Minimum Degree Requirements:* 36 hours (12 hours in computes, 15 hours in education, 9 hours outside education); thesis not required; internship required; practicum not required. *Outside Funding for the Department:* No. *Summer Session:* Two 5-week sessions. *Tuition Per Credit:* Residents, $190.38 per 3-semester-hour course; nonresidents, $1,323.25 per 3-semester-hour course. Dr. Clarence Smith, Professor of Education, (704) 547-4542.

University of North Texas. Department of Computer Education and Cognitive Systems, Box 5155, Denton, TX 76203. Department offers M.S. in Computer Education and Cognitive Systems. Master's started in 1987. In fall 1989, had 7 full-time and 3 part-time faculty members; 30 male and 50 female students. Semester credit basis. *Minimum Degree Requirements:* 36 hours (33 in computers, 6 in education); thesis not specified; internship not specified; practicum not specified. *Outside Funding for the Department:* Yes (computer grant for equipment). *Summer Session:* Two 5-week terms. *Tuition Per Credit:* $16 residents; $120 nonresidents. Dr. J. L. Poirot, Chair, (817) 565-3790.

The University of Oklahoma. Educational Technology Graduate Program, Norman, OK 73019. Program offers M.Ed. in Educational and Technology with a Computer emphasis option. Master's started in 1982. In fall 1990, had 3 full-time and 2 part-time faculty members; 10 male and 16 female students. Semester credit basis. *Minimum Degree Requirements:* 32 hours (12 hours in computers, 21 hours in education [including above 12]); thesis not required; internship required; practicum not required. *Outside Funding for the Department:* Yes (Special Educational Technology Grant—Office of Education). *Summer Session:* 8 weeks. *Tuition Per Credit:* Residents $61.50 as of 6/90; nonresidents, $190.40 as of 6/90. Dr. Tillman J. Ragan, Professor and Area Head, (405) 325-1521.

University of Oregon. ISTE, Eugene, OR 97403. College offers M.S., M.A., M.Ed., and D.Ed./Ph.D. in Curriculum and Instruction with specialization in Computers in Education. Master's started in 1970 and doctorate in 1971. Number of faculty members not specified; 38 students on the master's level, and 36 students on the doctoral level. Quarter credit basis. *Minimum Degree Requirements:* Master's—45-48 hours; thesis optional. Doctoral programs are individualized, but include a residency requirement. *Outside Funding for the Department:* Not specified. *Summer Session:* 8 weeks. *Tuition Per Credit:* Academic year: 9-16 hours (resident $854, nonresident $1,388). Dr. David Moursund, Professor, ISTE, (503) 346-4414.

University of Texas—Austin. College of Education, Austin, TX 78712. College offers M.Ed. and M.A. in a specialization in Instructional Technology. Master's programs started in 1984. In fall 1989, had 3 full-time and 2 part-time faculty on the master's levels; about 40 students. Master's awarded 1989-90: 9. Semester quarter basis. *Minimum Degree Requirements:* 12-18 hours in computers, 18-24 hours in education, 6 hours outside education; thesis and internship optional. *Outside Funding for the Department:* Yes (source not specified). *Summer Session:* Two 6-week sessions. *Tuition Per Credit:* Not specified. Dr. DeLayne Hudspeth, Associate Professor, Area Coordinator, (512) 471-5211.

University of Virgin Islands. St. Thomas, VI 00802. School offers M.A. with emphasis in Computers and Technology in Education. Master's started in 1989. In fall 1990, had 1 full-time and 0 part-time faculty member. Anticipated enrollment of 60 students. Semester credit basis. *Minimum Degree Requirements:* 36 credits (21 credits in computers and technology, 15 credits in education, 0 credits outside education); thesis optional; internship not required; practicum required. *Outside Funding for the Department:* Yes (U.S. Dept. of Educ.). *Summer Session:* 6 weeks. *Tuition Per Credit:* $82 residents; $164 nonresidents. Dr. Dennis O. Harper, Associate Professor of Computer Education, (809) 776-9200.

Virginia Polytechnic Institute and State University (Virginia Tech). Instructional Systems Development, College of Education, War Memorial Hall, Blacksburg, VA 24061. Offers M.S. in Computers in Education, Education Media, Training, Instructional Design, Learning Improvement, Learning Disabilities and Educational Psychology; and Ed.D. in Educational Computing, Instructional Design and Development, Training, Educational Media, Learning Improvement and Educational Psychology. Master's began in 1973 and doctorate in 1974. In fall, 1990, had 10 full-time and 6 part-time faculty on master's and doctoral levels; 3 male and 6 female students on master's level, and 10 males and 6 females on doctoral level. Semester credit basis. *Minimum Degree Requirements:* Master's—30 hours (6 foundations, 6 cognate, 18 professional studies); thesis, internship and practicum not required though they are often recommended. Doctorate—90 hours (12 hours research studies, 9 hours general studies, 9 hours cognate, 15 hours research, 57 hours professional studies). *Outside Funding for the Department:* Yes, from several local, state, and national sources. *Summer Session:* Two 5-week sessions. *Tuition Per Credit:* $161 Virginia residents; $194 nonresidents. Thomas M. Sherman, Professor, Instructional Systems Development, (703) 231-5598.

Western Carolina University. Cullowhee, NC 28723. Department offers M.A.Ed. in Supervision, with concentration in Educational Technology—Computers. Master's started in 1987. In fall 1989, had 25+ full-time and 0 part-time faculty members; 6 male and 7 female students. Semester credit basis. *Minimum Degree Requirements:* 41 hours (18 hours in computers, 20 hours in education, 3 hours outside education); thesis not required; internship required; practicum not required. *Outside Funding for the Department:* No. *Summer Session:* Two 5-week sessions. *Tuition Per Credit:* Residents, $71.05 per semester hour; nonresidents, $551.05 per semester hour. Dr. Don Chalker, Head, Department of Administration, Curriculum and Instruction, (704) 227-7415.

Western Washington University. Woodring College of Education, Bellingham, WA 98225. School offers M.Ed. in Computers in Education. Master's started in 1981. In fall 1989, had 2-⅓ full-time and 6 part-time faculty members; 10 male and 15 female students. Quarter credit basis. *Minimum Degree Requirements:* 52 hours (15 hours in computers, 24 hours in education, 0 hours outside education); thesis required; internship and practicum possible. *Outside Funding for the Department:* No. *Summer Session:* 9 weeks. *Tuition Per Credit:* $87 residents; $263 nonresidents (up to 10 credits). Prof. Tony Jongejan, Assistant Professor of Education, (206) 676-3381.

Widener University. Center for Education, Chester, PA 19013. School offers M.Ed. in Computer Science Education. Master's started in 1986. In fall 1989, had 1 full-time and 4 part-time faculty members; 25 male and 28 female students. Semester credit basis. *Minimum Degree Requirements:* 30 hours (18 hours in computers, 6-12 hours in education, up to 6 hours outside education); thesis not required; internship not required; practicum not required. *Outside Funding for the Department:* No. *Summer Session:* Three terms. *Tuition Per Credit:* $200 residents and nonresidents. Dr. James P. Randall, Assistant Professor of Instructional Technology, (215) 499-4497.

Wright State University. Department of Educational Technology, Vocational Education and Allied Programs, 244 Millett Hall, Dayton, OH 45435. Department offers M.E. in Computer Education, M.E. in Computer Coordinator, and M.A. in Computer Education. Master's programs started in 1985. In fall 1990, had 2-½ full-time and 2-½ part-time faculty members; 5 male and 123 female students in master's program in computer education, and 2 male and 11 female students in master's program in computer coordinator. Quarter credit basis. *Minimum Degree Requirements:* 48 hours (hours in computers, education, and outside education not specified); thesis required for M.A. degree only; internship required (for computer education); practicum required (for computer coordinator). *Outside Funding for the Department:* No (not yet). *Summer Session:* Two 5-week sessions. *Tuition Per Credit:* Residents, $84 per quarter hour to 10.5 hours, $890 for 11-18 hours; nonresidents, $151 per quarter hour to 10.5 hours, $1,598 for 11-18 hours. Dr. Bonnie K. Mathies, Chair, Department of Educational Technology, Vocational Education, and Allied Programs, (513) 873-2509.

Xavier University. Department of Mathematics and Computer Science, 3800 Victory Parkway, Cincinnati, OH 45207. Department offers M.Ed. with concentration in Computer Science. Master's started in 1981. In fall 1989, had 4 full-time faculty members in Computer Science and 24 part-time in Education; 11 male and female students. Semester credit basis. *Minimum Degree Requirements:* 30 hours (12 hours in computers, 12 hours in education, 6 hours either computers or education). *Outside Funding for the Department:* No. *Summer Session:* 6 weeks. *Tuition Per Credit:* $150 residents and nonresidents. Dr. David D. Berry, Director, Computer Science, (513) 745-3462.

Scholarships, Fellowships, and Awards

Brenda Branyan-Broadbent, Ph.D.
Associate Professor
Department of Instructional Technology
Utah State University
Logan, Utah

Lois A. Ward
Staff Assistant II
Department of Instructional Technology
Utah State University
Logan, Utah

In the instructional technology/media-related fields, various scholarships, fellowships, and awards have been established. Many of these are available to those who either are or will be pursuing advanced degrees at the master's, six-year specialist, or doctoral levels.

Because various colleges, universities, professional organizations, and governmental agencies offer scholarships, fellowships, and awards and may wish to have them included in this section, it would be greatly appreciated if those aware of such financial awards would contact either the editors or the publisher for inclusion of such entries in the next edition of *EMTY*.

We are greatly indebted to the staff members of the Association for Educational Communications and Technology (AECT) and to Dr. Donald Ely, the editor of *EMTY 1988*, for initiating this interest area.

Information is furnished in the following sequence:

- Overview of AECT and ECT Foundation Awards

- AECT Awards

- ECT Foundation Awards

AECT AND ECT
FOUNDATION AWARDS

The Association for Educational Communications and Technology recognizes and rewards the outstanding achievement of its members and associates through a program that provides for three major annual awards—Achievement, Special Service, and Distinguished Service—and through the ECT Foundation, which provides awards in the areas of leadership, scholarship, and research.

AECT encourages members and associates to apply for these awards and to disseminate information about the awards to professional colleagues. Specific information about each award is available from the AECT national office. The annual deadline for submitting award applications is November 1.

All ECT Foundation and AECT awards are presented during the AECT National Convention and INFOCOMM International Exposition.

For additional information on all awards, please contact:

AECT Awards Program
1126 Sixteenth Street NW
Washington, DC 20036

(202) 466-4780

AECT Awards

The Association for Educational Communications and Technology (AECT) provides for three annual awards:

Special Service Award: Granted to a person who has shown notable service to AECT as a whole or to one of its programs or divisions (nominee must have been a member of AECT for at least 10 years and must not be currently an AECT officer, board member or member of the Awards Committee).

Distinguished Service Award: Granted to a person who has shown outstanding leadership in advancing the theory and/or practice of educational communications and technology over a substantial period of time (nominee need not be an AECT member but must not have received this award previously).

Annual Achievement Award: Honors the individual who during the past year has made the most significant contribution to the advancement of educational communications and technology (nominee need not be a member of AECT, and the award can be given to the same person more than once).

ECT Foundation Awards

The ECT Foundation, a nonprofit organization that carries out the purposes of AECT that are charitable and educational in nature, coordinates the following awards:

AECT/SIRS Intellectual Freedom Award (in conjunction with the Social Issues Resources Services Inc.): Recognizes a media specialist at any level who has upheld the principles of intellectual freedom as set forth in AECT's publication "Media, the Learner, and Intellectual Freedom" and provides $1,000 for the individual and $1,000 for the media center of the recipient's choice (recipient must be a personal member of AECT).

AECT Annual Conference and Earl F. Strobehn Internship Award: Provides complimentary registration and housing at the annual conference plus a cash award for four full-time graduate students (applicant must be a member of AECT and enrolled in a recognized program in educational communications and technology).

Richard B. Lewis Memorial Award: Presented to the outstanding school district media utilization program along with a cash award (awarded to either a public or private school having media utilization programs in place).

AECT Leadership Development Grants: Supports innovative leadership development activities undertaken by affiliates, divisions, or regions with cash grants (special consideration will be given to proposals that demonstrate a commitment to leadership development, that propose programs unique to the applicant's organization, and that include activities of potential benefit to other AECT programs).

AECT Memorial Scholarship Award: Donations given in memory of specific past leaders of the field provide a scholarship fund that gives annual cash grants to AECT members enrolled in educational technology graduate studies (three letters of recommendation are required).

Dean and Sybil McClusky Research Award: Recognizes the year's outstanding doctoral thesis proposal that has been approved by the student's university and offers a cash reward to defray the research expenses (the winner must agree to complete the proposed study).

Carl F. & Viola V. Mahnke Film Production Award: Honors excellence in message design for film and video products created by undergraduate students who are members of AECT (products must have been completed within a two-year period prior to the competition).

Robert M. Gagné Instructional Development Research Award: Recognizes the most significant contribution by a graduate student to the body of knowledge on which instructional development is based with a plaque and a cash prize (the research must have been done in past three years while the candidate was enrolled as a graduate student).

James W. Brown Publication Award: Recognizes the outstanding publication in the field of educational technology in any media format during the past year with a cash award (excluded from consideration are doctoral, master's, or other types of dissertations prepared in fulfillment of degree program requirements).

ECTJ Young Scholar Award: Recognizes fresh, creative approach to research and theory in educational technology by a young scholar (applicant must be an individual who does not hold a doctorate degree or who has received a doctorate degree within the past three years).

Young Researcher Award: Recognizes an outstanding unpublished report of research of an experimental, descriptive, or historical nature by a researcher who has not yet attained the doctorate or is less than three years beyond the degree (jointly published papers are not accepted).

Jerry R. Coltharp Award: Recognizes innovative media management practices which enhance the provision of instructional media services or advance media applications.

DOT-AECT Crystal Award: Recognizes the most innovative and outstanding instructional telecommunications project for 1991.

AECT Special Service Award

Qualifications

- Award is granted to a person who has shown notable service to AECT. This service may be to the organization as a whole, one of its programs, or one of its divisions.
- Nominee currently must be a member of AECT and have at least 10 years of service to AECT.

Disqualifications

- Recipient may not now be serving as an elected officer of AECT nor as a member of the board of directors.
- Nominee must not be currently serving as a member of the AECT Awards Committee.

Nomination

Nominations are judged and selected on the basis of an outstanding contribution to a division, committee, commission, or program of AECT but not to an affiliate organization. Please provide as much information as you can.

- Write in one hundred words or less why you think nominee should receive this award. Include a description of nominee's contribution.
- What year did nominee join AECT?

AECT Distinguished Service Award

Qualifications

- Award is granted to a person who has shown outstanding leadership in advancing the theory and/or practice of educational communications and technology over a substantial period of time.
- The nominee need not be a member of AECT.
- Award may be given posthumously.

Disqualifications

- Nominee must not have received this award previously.
- Nominee must not be currently serving as a member of the AECT Awards Committee.

Nomination

Nominations are judged primarily on the distinction or magnitude of the nominee's leadership in advancing the field rather than the association.

Categories

- The following categories suggest areas in which the nominee may have rendered distinguished service to the field. The nominee may not be represented in these areas. Use those that apply or add others.

    - Leadership • Research/Theory • Development/Production • Writing
    - Major Contribution to Education Outside the United States

AECT Annual Achievement Award

Qualifications

- Recipient may be an individual or a group.
- The AAA honors the individual who during the past year has made the most significant contribution to the advancement of educational communications and technology.
- The nominee need not be a member of AECT.
- The contribution being honored should be publicly visible — a specific thing or event.
- It must be timely — taking place within approximately the past year.
- Award can be given to the same person more than once.

Nomination

The nature of this award precludes the use of a single checklist or set of categories for nomination. The nomination and selection are inherently subjective. You are asked simply to present a succinct argument in favor of your nominee. Your statement ought to answer the following questions:

- What is the specific achievement being honored?
- What impact has this achievement had, or is likely to have, on the field?
- How is the nominee connected with the achievement?

ECT Foundation
1992 AECT/SIRS Intellectual Freedom Award

Purpose: To recognize, annually, a media professional at any level who has upheld the principles of intellectual freedom as set forth in *Media, the Learner, and Intellectual Freedom: A Handbook*, published by AECT.

The Award: The award shall consist of:

1. a plaque and $1,000 for the winning media professional, to be presented at the AECT National Convention and INFO-COMM International Exposition;

2. a framed certificate plus $1,000 for the media center designated by the recipient;

3. the opportunity for the recipient to present a session on intellectual freedom at the AECT National Convention and COMMTEX International Exposition.

Selection: The following criteria will be used in the selection process:

1. the recipient will be a media specialist at any level.

2. the recipient will be a member of AECT.

3. the recipient shall not have received another intellectual freedom award in the same year if that award was sponsored by SIRS, Inc.

4. the recipient will meet at least one of the following criteria:
   - has developed and implemented an exemplary selection policy/challenge procedure for educational nonprint material.
   - has developed an innovative information program on intellectual freedom for nonprint media.
   - has upheld intellectual freedom principles in the face of a challenge to educational nonprint media
   - has been active in the establishment and/or continuation of a coalition relating to intellectual freedom.
   - has been active in the development of a legal base for the continued enjoyment of intellectual freedom.

Selection
Committee: A subcommittee of the AECT Intellectual Freedom committee is responsible for the selection of the winner.

ECT Foundation
1992 AECT National Convention—
Earl F. Strobehn Internship Program

Awards: Six students will be chosen as convention interns. The winners will receive complimentary convention registration, complimentary housing, and a $100 cash award. The interns will be expected to arrive at the convention on Thursday and to stay until Tuesday. (Applicants are encouraged to request financial support for transportation and on-site expenses from their institutions or state affiliate organizations.)

Program
Activities: Each intern will be expected to participate fully in a coordinated program of activities. These activities include private seminars with selected association and professional leaders in the field, observation of the AECT governance and program committees, and behind-the-scenes views of the convention itself. Each intern will also be responsible for specific convention-related assignments, which will require approximately 15 hours of time during the convention. A former intern, who is now a member of the AECT Leadership Development Committee, will serve as the program coordinator.

Eligibility: To qualify for consideration, an applicant must be a full-time student throughout the current academic year in a recognized graduate program in educational communications and technology, and must be a member of AECT. (Applicant may join AECT when applying for the award.)

Application
Process: To apply for the internship program, qualified graduate students must complete and return an application form and must submit two (2) letters of recommendation.

ECT Foundation
1992 Richard B. Lewis Memorial Award

Award: $500, provided by the Richard B. Lewis Memorial Fund for "Outstanding School District Media Utilization," is awarded to the winner.

Selection
Process: The winner will be selected by a unified committee appointed from the divisions of Educational Media Management (DEMM) and School Media Specialists (DSMS) of the Association for Educational Communications and Technology, and the National Association of Regional Media Centers (NARMC).

Selection
Criteria: • Evidence of strong media utilization as gathered from:

1. special utilization studies conducted by or for the school district;

2. specific instances of good utilization as described in writing by school district or other personnel.

• Evidence of having provided in the school district budget means of implementing good utilization programs in its schools and of the degree to which AECT/ALA media standards are met for services, equipment, and personnel.

• Assessment of applicant's statements as to how the $500 (if awarded) would be spent, such as for:

1. attending national, regional, or state conferences or workshops related to media utilization;

2. selecting media specialist(s) to attend advanced training programs;

3. buying software or hardware needed to improve media utilization programs;

4. other purposes (indicating especially creative approaches).

• Recognition by an AECT state, regional, or national affiliate organization or representative, or from a National Association of Regional Media Centers state or regional representative:

1. through prior recognition or awards;

2. through a recommendation

Eligibility: All school districts, public and private, having media utilization programs in place, and conforming to the above criteria, are eligible.

Other: The winning district will receive a plaque as part of this award.

ECT Foundation
1992 Leadership Development Grants

Grants:	Grants of up to $250 are provided by the ECT Foundation and administered by the AECT Leadership Development Committee. The grants are awarded to assist AECT affiliates, AECT divisions, and AECT regional organizations to undertake leadership development activities that will improve participants' skills as leaders in the professional organization or in educational technology.
Selection:	Grant awards will be recommended by the Leadership Committee's Subcommittee on Leadership Development Grants.
Criteria for Selection:	All AECT state affiliates, divisions, and regional organizations are eligible for these competitive grants. An application from a previous grant recipient will not be considered unless a summary report has been submitted to the Leadership Development Committee and the AECT national office. Organizations that have not received a grant in the past are particularly invited to apply. Funds must be intended for some unique aspect or function not previously undertaken. Proposals that demonstrate a commitment to leadership development, that propose programs that are unique to the applicant's organization, and that include activities or products of potential benefit to other AECT programs will be given special consideration.
Awards:	The awards will be presented during the AECT National Convention and INFOCOMM International Exposition.

ECT Foundation
1992 AECT Memorial Scholarships

Awards: One scholarship of $750 and one scholarship of $500 are awarded to graduate students in educational communications/technology to carry out a research project in the field. The scholarships may be used to assist the recipients to further their education in a summer session or academic year of graduate study at any accredited college or university in the United States or Canada. Programs of study may be at the master's or doctoral level.

Eligibility: All recipients must be members of AECT and accepted in or enrolled in a graduate-level degree program as outlined above.

Selection
Criteria: Selections will be based on the following:

1. scholarship;

2. experience related to the field of educational media, communications, or technology, such as employment, field experience, course work, assistantships, publications, etc.;

3. service to the field through AECT activities and membership in other related professional organizations;

4. three letters of recommendation from persons familiar with the candidate's professional qualifications and leadership potential;

5. the candidate's own knowledge of key issues and opportunities facing the educational communications/technology field today, with respect to the candidate's own goals.

ECT Foundation
1992 Dean and Sybil McClusky
Research Award

Award: $500 will be awarded for the best submitted doctoral research proposal in educational technology, as selected by a jury of researchers from AECT's Research and Theory Division.

Guidelines
for Preparing
and Submitting
Papers: Submitted proposals may follow acceptable formats of individual schools but must include at least:

1. The definition of the problem including a statement of significance.

2. A review of pertinent literature.

3. Research hypothesis to be examined.

4. Research design and procedures including statistical techniques.

Applicants are encouraged to review pages 157-61 of Stephen Isaac and William B. Michaels, *Handbook in Research and Evaluation*, Robert R. Knapp, San Diego, CA, 1971.

Eligibility: Applicants must be presently enrolled in a doctoral program in educational technology and have obtained committee acceptance of their proposal. The winner will be expected to sign a statement that the proposed doctoral study will be completed in accordance with the sponsoring university's graduate school policies (including any time limitations) or be required to return the funds received.

ECT Foundation
1992 Carl F. and Viola V. Mahnke
Film Production Award

Award:
$500 will be awarded to honor a film or video product that demonstrates excellence in message design and production for educational purposes. In addition, certificates of merit will be awarded to entries with outstanding qualities worthy of recognition. In the event that no entry demonstrates excellence, in the opinion of the judges, no award will be given.

Eligibility:
Eligibility is limited to film and video products that are educational in nature and produced by undergraduate or graduate students. The winners must be members of AECT. Only entries completed within a two-year period prior to the competition will qualify.

Formats:
All entries must be either on film or videotape. Film entries are limited to 16mm. Video entries can either be ½-inch VHS or ¾-inch U-matic.

Judging:
All entries will be judged during the AECT National Convention by a panel of judges from the AECT Media Design and Production Division.

Entry Fee:
Entrants must include an entry fee of $10 per program, made payable to MDPD-AECT. For programs consisting of more than one film or videocassette, each must be submitted separately. An entry form must be completed for each entry. The entry form may be duplicated if necessary.

ECT Foundation
1992 Robert M. Gagné Award for Graduate Student
Research in Instructional Technology

Purpose: To provide recognition and financial assistance for outstanding research by a graduate student in the field of instructional development.

Description: The Robert M. Gagne Award Fund is coordinated by the ECT Foundation, a nonprofit organization sponsored and controlled by the Association for Educational Communications and Technology (AECT). The Division of Instructional Development will solicit nominations for the Gagné Award and will select the winner. The ECT Foundation is responsible for the administration of the award fund and will issue the cash award to the recipient.

Award: $500 is awarded for the most significant contribution to the body of knowledge upon which instructional development is based. The Gagné Award competition is sponsored by the Association for Educational Communications and Technology (AECT) and its Division of Instructional Development. A jury of scholars will select the winning contribution. The award will be presented to the recipient during the AECT National Convention. The winner will receive the cash award and a plaque.

Eligibility: The work must have been completed after December 31, 1988, while the award candidate was enrolled as a graduate student.

Nomination
Procedure: You may nominate any individual (including yourself) for the Gagne Award.

ECT Foundation
1992 James W. Brown Publication Award

Award: $200 will be given to the author or authors of an outstanding publication in the field of educational technology.

Eligibility: Nominated items are not restricted to books or print; they may be in any media format (film, video, broadcast program, book, etc.). Any non-periodic publication in the field of educational technology is eligible if it bears a publication date of 1989 or 1990.

Guidelines
for
Nominations: Nominations are solicited from all possible sources: AECT members, media-related publishers and producers, authors themselves, the AECT nonperiodic publications committee, and others.

Criteria: Nominated publications shall be judged on the basis of:

1. Significance of the item's content for the field of media/instructional technology, as defined in the *Definition of Educational Technology*, published by AECT in 1977, or in any subset of the publication.

2. Professional quality of the item.

3. Potential impact of the item's content on the field of media/instructional technology, as defined in the *Definition of Educational Technology*.

4. Technical quality of the item.

ECT Foundation
1992 ECTJ Young Scholar Award

Award:
$250 plus a certificate suitable for framing will be presented to the winner. Additionally, the winning paper will be published in *ECTJ*, the refereed scholarly research journal published by the Association for Educational Communications and Technology (AECT).

For:
The best paper discussing a theoretical construct that could guide research in educational technology, considered worthy by a panel of judges.

Eligibility:
An individual who does not hold a doctorate degree or who received a doctorate not more than three (3) years ago as of September 1, 1991.

Guidelines
for Preparing
and Submitting
Papers:

1. Papers must deal with research and theory in educational technology and must include:

    - A problem area stated within a well-explicated theoretical construct;

    - Supporting citations and analyses of related research;

    - A concluding discussion centering on what directions future research might take, with specific regard to variables, subjects, settings, etc., and, if appropriate, suggestions concerning other theoretical constructs that should be taken into consideration;

2. The paper should not be a report of a specific study;

3. A fresh, imaginative approach — which may go beyond the data — is encouraged;

4. The paper must be an original unpublished work;

5. The paper should be a maximum of 35 double-spaced typewritten pages;

6. The paper must be submitted in publishable journal format and must conform to the *American Psychological Association Style Manual*, 3rd edition.

Selection
of
Winner:
The selection of the winning paper will be the responsibility of the editor and editorial board of *ECTJ*. Only the best paper judged worthy of the award will win. (There may not be a recipient of this award every year.)

ECT Foundation
1992 Young Research Award

Award: $500 for the best report of an experimental, descriptive, or historical study in educational technology. The Young Researcher Award competition is sponsored by the Research and Theory Division of the Association for Educational Communications and Technology (AECT). A jury of scholars will select the best contribution for presentation at the AECT National Convention and INFOCOMM International Exposition. The winner will receive the cash award plus a certificate suitable for framing.

Eligibility: Anyone who is not more than three (3) years beyond a doctorate as of December 31, 1991. A doctorate is *not* required. Jointly published papers are not acceptable.

Guidelines
for Preparing
and Submitting
Papers: Papers must report an original, unpublished research effort of experimental, descriptive, or historical nature and must include the following:

    1.   problem area stated within a well-explicated theoretical construct(s);

    2.   supporting citations and analyses of related research;

    3.   exemplary reporting of research design or procedures and full description of statistical procedures where applicable;

    4.   concluding discussion that centers on directions for future research and implications for future directions in the field.

Other: Manuscripts may be a maximum of 35 double-spaced typewritten pages. The manuscript must be submitted in publishable journal format and must conform to the *American Psychological Association Style Manual*, 3rd edition. The author's name should be included *only* on the cover sheet. All manuscripts will be coded and reviewed "blind."

ECT Foundation
1992 Jerry R. Coltharp Memorial
Innovative Media Management Award

Award:
This award is funded and coordinated by DEMM. One $400 award is presented annually, in recognition of innovative media management practices that enhance the provision of instructional media services or advance media applications.

Eligibility:
Media service programs in schools, school districts, colleges and universities, regional media centers, government/military, allied health, and business and industry are eligible for the award.

Submission:
Projects that demonstrate exemplary management practices and a potential for enhancing associated media services are to be described in an article format not to exceed 10 double-spaced typed pages. Supporting photographs and graphic materials are encouraged. Article organization may be determined by the author but must include a definition of the specific need to be addressed, a review of the management approach applied, and an evaluation of the effectiveness of the project. Project categories are unrestricted and may encompass such areas as staff development, client training, public relations, service assessment, facilities design, etc.

Selection:
Submissions are reviewed and the recipient is determined by a selection committee appointed by the president of the AECT Division of Educational Media Management.

Criteria:
Criteria for evaluating submissions are as follows:

Originality: Did the project demonstrate a unique approach to addressing specific needs?

Need: Did the need to be addressed relate to the enhancement of media services or the advancement of media utilization?

Design: Was the structure of the project appropriate to the need?

Impact: Was the project successful in meeting the defined needs?

Reporting:
Articles detailing project parameters shall be considered for publication in an AECT publication. Publication rights will be assumed by AECT.

Other:
Manuscripts may be a maximum of 35 double-spaced typewritten pages. The manuscript must be submitted in publishable journal format and must conform to the *American Psychological Association Style Manual*, 3rd edition. The author's name should be included *only* on the cover sheet. All manuscripts will be coded and reviewed "blind."

1992 DOT-AECT Crystal Award

Purpose:	To recognize the most innovative and outstanding instructional telecommunications project for 1991.
Sponsor:	The Division of Telecommunications of the Association for Educational Communications and Technology (AECT).
Eligibility:	Limited to telecommunications projects that include a video component, that are instructional in nature and are designed for any age level, and that have been completed since September 30, 1990. Awards will be presented to the producing agency.
Entry Fee:	A $25 fee must accompany each entry. Make checks payable to DOT-AECT.
Judging:	Entries will be judged by a "blue ribbon" panel chosen by the president of DOT.
Criteria:	Entries will be judged using the following criteria:

- Instructional value and relevance
- Quality of production
- Evidence of successful utilization and implementation
- Evidence of achievement of goals and objectives

Entry
Information:

The following information must be provided for each entry. Please provide the essential information only. This information may not exceed 4 pages.

1. Contact person's name, title, address, and telephone number
2. Official name of submitting agency
3. Name of individual to accept award for producing agency, if selected as winner
4. Intended audience(s)
5. Goals and objectives of project
6. Design and production process, including names of principal project staff
7. Time line for project
8. Budget and sources of funding
9. Evidence of successful utilization and implementation
10. Samples of all project components
11. Return address for all items sent.

Part Six

Mediagraphy
Print and Nonprint Resources

Introduction

Warren E. Babcock
Reference Librarian
Merrill Library
Utah State University
Logan, Utah

This current resource section of *EMTY 91* represents journal articles and other recent publications in areas that are of potential interest to professionals in the field and other individuals who are interested in educational technology. It is planned that the comprehensive list of professional publications such as that which appeared in *EMTY 88* will be revised on a three-year schedule. In the interim editions of *EMTY*, a mediagraphy of current resources will appear.

Data for entries in this section were collected by using Books in Print Plus (CD-ROM) and ERIC ONDISC and through database searches online. Generally, to be included in this mediagraphy, all publications had to have been published in 1990. There are a few entries with earlier publication dates that have been included because it was felt they would be of general interest and because they did not appear in the last edition of *EMTY*. It is anticipated that the method of organization of the citations will prove helpful to the reader.

ORDERING INFORMATION

The names of publishers or producers that are identical to the titles of the periodicals in the mediagraphy have not been repeated. Users are reminded that name and address data are provided in the "Directory of Producers, Distributors, and Publishers" appearing at the end of this section. It is suggested that users refer directly to the index in cases where names of individuals or organizations are known but specific titles are not.

OBTAINING ERIC DOCUMENTS

All entries in this section carrying "EDRS" identifying numbers (ED ...) are publications available from the Educational Resources Information Center (ERIC). Copies of most of these publications can be obtained from the ERIC Documents Reproduction Service (EDRS), 3900 Wheeler Avenue, Alexandria, VA 22304-5110. (Phone toll free: 1-800-227-3742.)

Most publications can be obtained in both paper and microfiche. Up-to-date information about costs and ordering procedures is available in the publication entitled *Resources in Education* (*RIE*), which is available in most large libraries. Also, many large libraries maintain an ERIC microfiche collection where these publications can be located and used, generally without charge.

ARRANGEMENT

The citations are classified according to major subject emphasis and are listed under a main entry. Journals, newsletters, and other periodically published items are listed alphabetically in the "Journal Articles" section.

The following is a list of major subject headings used in this mediagraphy:

- Adult Education

- Artificial Intelligence and Robotics

- CD-ROM

- Communication Systems

- Computers and Instructional Uses of Computers

- Databases, Online Searching, Networking, Telecommunications

- Distance Education

- Educational Research

- Educational Technology

- Electronic Publishing

- Information Science

- Instructional Design, Training

- Instructional Media

- Libraries, Media Centers, Technical Applications

- Microforms and Micrographics

- Videodisc Technology

Mediagraphy

ADULT EDUCATION

Reference Tools/ERIC Documents

Computer Assisted Learning in Numeracy. Freda Hollin. (ED 317 836. EDRS, 1990.) 5p. Discusses how instructors can use content-free software and teach computer skills for adults.

Older Adults: Community College Students of the 1990s. Ford M. Craig. (ED 315 106. EDRS, 1990.) 15p. Discusses the fact that with the declining pool of youth to draw from, community colleges need to be concerned with serving the needs of a burgeoning older adult population.

Books

The Adult Learner: A Neglected Species. 4th ed. Malcolm Knowles. (Gulf, 1990.) 293p., $23.95. Covers building blocks of human potential.

Lifelong Education for Adults: An International Handbook. Colin J. Titmus. (Routledge, 1990.) 590p. The first work to offer encyclopedic coverage of this field in a single volume. The handbook contains 127 articles that have been written by specialists from all parts of the world.

Journal Articles

Gayle, Margaret. "Toward the 21st Century." **Adult Learning, 1** (4), 10-14, January 1990. (EJ 400 054.) Major issues for the next decade are the aging of the population, emergence of a high-tech society, and higher skill demands of the workplace. A systems approach to strategic planning is needed to ensure that education keeps pace with the emphasis on workplace literacy and global competitiveness.

Geber, Beverly. "Goodbye Classrooms (Redux)." **Training, 27** (1), 27-32, 34-35, January 1990. (EJ 400 044.) Discusses the location of corporate training in view of modern technology. Indicates that training will be brought out of the classroom and to the work station. Describes training programs offered at several large corporations.

Howie, Sherry Hill. "Adult Literacy in a Multiliterate Society." **Journal of Reading, 33** (4), 260-63, January 1990. (EJ 403 635.) The article argues that the computer has many advantages over traditional technologies in learning, thinking, and problem solving. Argues that if reading and writing are taught as thinking processes akin to problem solving, then skills and experiences acquired on the computer should transfer well, with guidance, to print literacy.

Parker, James T. "Modeling a Future for Adult Basic Education." **Adult Learning, 1** (4), 16-18, 28, January 1990. (EJ 400 055.) Discusses four trends or models for the future of ABE.

Rieber, Lloyd P., et al. "The Effects of Computer Animation on Adult Learning and Retrieval Tasks." **Journal of Computer-Based Instruction, 17** (2), 46-52, Spring 1990. This study examines the effects of different levels of visual elaborations and practice on adult application learning in a computer-based science lesson.

Rosenberg, Marc J. "Performance Technology: Working the System." **Training, 27** (2), 42-48, February 1990. (EJ 401 967.) The United States needs a skilled, productive work force. The science of human performance technology can be applied to the establishment of performance improvement systems in organizations.

Shaeffer, James M. "Preparing Faculty and Designing Courses for Delivery via Audio Teleconferencing." **Journal of Adult Education, 18** (2), Spring 1990. Discusses the process one postsecondary institution adopted for preparing faculty and designing courses for delivery via audio teleconferencing.

Stanton, Michael. "Workers Who Train Workers." **Occupational Outlook Quarterly, 33** (4), 2-11, Winter 1989-90. (EJ 404 711.) Workers in today's world need continual training to keep up with new technology and to learn new skills. This article looks at people who provide that training—how they do it, who employs them, and how they were trained themselves.

Wilson, Lois S. "An On-line Prescription for Basic Skills." **Training and Development Journal, 44** (4), 36-41, April 1990. (EJ 404 724.) The army's Job Skills Education Program is a computer-based instructional program that teaches academic skills in a job-related context. Its transferability to the civilian workplace provides another tool for enhancing workplace literacy.

ARTIFICIAL INTELLIGENCE AND ROBOTICS

Reference Tools/ERIC Documents

Artificial Intelligence Abstracts Annual 1990. (Bowker A&I, 1991.) Provides a timely review of developments in the field of artificial intelligence.

Artificial Intelligence, Expert Systems, Natural Language Interfaces, Knowledge Engineering and the Librarian. Jim Davies. 1987. (ED 318 428. EDRS, 1990.) 13p. Paper presented at the First Pacific Conference on New Information Technology for Library and Information Professionals (Bangkok, Thailand, June 16-17, 1987).

Concise International Encyclopedia of Robotics: Applications and Automation. Richard C. Dorf and Shimony Nof, editors. (John Wiley & Sons, 1990.) 1,190p., $99.95. Designed as a ready-reference guide for scientists, engineers, and technologists seeking answers on subjects in the fields of robotics and automation.

Pedagogical Strategies for Human and Computer Tutoring. Brian J. Reiser. 1989. (ED 316 185. EDRS, 1990.) 34p. Paper presented at the annual meeting of the American Educational Research Association (San Francisco, California, March 30-April 2, 1989).

Books

Artificial Experts: Social Knowledge and Intelligent Machines. Harry M. Collings. (MIT, 1990.) 250p., $19.95. Explains what computers can't do but also studies the ordinary and extraordinary things that they can do.

Artificial Intelligence: Concepts and Applications. A. R. Mirzai, editor. (MIT, 1990.) 320p., $39.95. Explores both the principles underlying basic AI research and their application in practice.

Artificial Intelligence and Learning Environments. William Clancey and E. Soloway, editors. (MIT, 1990.) 150p., $17.50.

Artificial Intelligence and the Future of Testing. Roy Freedle. (Educational Testing Service, 1990.) 344p., $39.95. This volume consists of a series of essays, most of which were written by experts who took part in a conference conducted by the Educational Testing Service to explore how current fields of artificial intelligence might contribute to ETS's plans to automate one or more of its testing activities.

Artificial Intelligence, IV: Methodology, Systems, Applications. P. Jorrand and V. Sgurev, editors. (MIT, 1990.) 434p., $95. Contains the proceedings of the Fourth International Conference on Artificial Intelligence, Methodology, Systems Application (AIMSA '90) (Albena, Bulgaria, September 19-22, 1990).

Foundations of Robotics: Analysis and Control. Tsuneo Yoshikawa. (MIT, 1990.) 300p., $40. Presents the fundamental concepts and methodologies for analysis, design, and control of robot manipulators.

Intelligent Tutoring Systems: Evolutions in Design. Hugh L. Burns et al. (Lawrence Erlbaum, 1990.) 312p., $46. Contains a collection of essays on issues related to the evolutionary design and the practical future of intelligent tutoring systems.

Journal Articles

Elsom-Cook, Mark T., et al. "ECAL: Bridging the Gap between CAL and Intelligent Tutoring Systems." **Computers and Education, 15** (1-3), 69-81, 1990. (EJ 407 230.) Describes ECAL (extended computer-assisted learning), which was designed to incorporate artificial intelligence to extend traditional CAL tools.

Kirkpatrick, Susan N., and Barbara Biglan. "AI in the Elementary, Middle, and Secondary Classroom." **Computing Teacher, 17** (5), 14-19, February 1990. (EJ 405 719.) Describes activities that present concepts and applications of artificial intelligence (AI) for elementary and secondary school students. The use of Logo with elementary students is discussed.

Perez, Ray S., and Robert J. Seidel. "Using Artificial Intelligence in Education: Computer-Based Tools for Instructional Development." **Educational Technology, 30** (3), 51-58, March 1990. (EJ 407 308.) Discussion of the use of artificial intelligence in computer-based instruction focuses on training development for the U.S. Army. Topics discussed include the Systems Approach to Training (SAT), knowledge acquisition, domain expertise, intelligent computer-assisted instruction, software tools and decision aids, and expert systems.

Young, Robert J. "Artificial Intelligence and School Library Media Centers." **School Library Media Quarterly, 18** (3), 150-57, Spring 1990. (EJ 410 586.) Discusses developments in artificial intelligence in terms of their impact on school library media centers and the role of media specialists.

CD-ROM

Reference Tools/ERIC Documents

CD-ROM Directory 1990. 4th ed. Joanne Mitchell and Adam Daum, editors. (Omnigraphics, 1990.) 450p., $80. A comprehensive guide to CD-ROM products, drives, and companies. Contains information on approximately 750 companies and 820 products from the United States, United Kingdom, Europe, Scandinavia, Australia, Japan, and others.

CD-ROM in Print: 1990. Norman Desmarals, editor. (Meckler, 1990.) 232p., $49.50. A comprehensive, current listing of CD-ROM products, providers, and distributors. Also eight indexes of acronyms, data providers, CD-ROM products, CD-ROM drives, software, software producers, player types, and subject titles.

CD-ROM Market Place: An International Guide, 1990 Edition. (Meckler, 1990.) 150p., $30. Offering detailed information on approximately 800 organizations worldwide.

An Examination of the Role of Reference Librarians in the Light of New Technology. Mona Y. Kratzert. (ED 316 259. EDRS, 1989.) 8p. Paper presented at the California Library Association Meeting (Oakland, California, November 11-14, 1989). Discusses a three-part CD-ROM master plan at California State University (Fullerton).

Microsoft CD-ROM Yearbook 1989-1990. Microsoft Press Staff. (Microsoft, 1989.) 960p., $79.95. A dynamic sourcebook of facts, statistics, forecasts, articles, reviews, profiles, and analyses of the CD-ROM industry and its products.

Books

Case Studies of Optical Storage Applications. Judith Paris Roth, editor. (Meckler, 1990.) 125p., $45. Chapters include "Imaging Technology and the Law Environment" and "Implementing a FileNet Workflo System for Personnel Records Management."

CD-ROM in the Library: Today and Tomorrow. Mary Kay Dugann et al., editors. (G. K. Hall, 1990.) 130p., $22.50. Presents the proceedings of the conference "CD-ROM in the Library: Today and Tomorrow" held at the University of California at Berkeley in the autumn of 1990.

Converting Information for WORM Optical Storage: A Case Study Approach. Judith Paris Roth. (Meckler, 1990.) 225p., $49.50. Educates the potential end-user of WORM optical storage about converting information stored in digital and analog formats to WORM optical storage.

Guide to Electronic Encyclopedia. (Grolier Electronic, 1990.) $49. Through the activities set forth in the guide, students learn how to use the CD-ROM encyclopedia to narrow or expand research topics, and in general, how to find information on any topic in the encyclopedia.

Interactive Optical Technologies in Education and Training: Markets and Trends. Sandra Helsel. (Meckler, 1990.) 165p., $39.50. Describes the current use of interactive optical technologies in the major education and training markets. Also analyzes the trends that will affect the future use of interactive optical media.

Mass Storage Technologies. Sanjay Ranade. (Meckler, 1990.) 175p., $49.50. The first book to address the mass storage applications of helical scan tape, digital audio tape, and other developing optical formats.

Microsoft 1990 CD-ROM Conference and Exposition Videotape. Marty Perlmutter. (Microsoft, 1990.) VHS videotape. 60 minutes. $95. A VHS videotape from the Fifth International CD-ROM Conference and Expo in San Francisco, California. Covers industry announcements, interviews, exhibit hall vendors, and show analysis.

Optical Publishing Industry Assessment 1990. (Optical Publishing Association, 1990.) 120p., $450. The third annual report card on the state of the CD-ROM publishing industry.

Optical Storage Jukebox Technology: A Systems Integrator's Perspective. Sanjay Ranade. (Meckler, 1990.) 275p., $49.50. The first book to address the 5.25-, 8-, and 12-inch write-once and rewritable optical storage jukeboxes currently on the market.

Optical Storage Technology: A State of the Art Review. William Saffady. (Meckler, 1990.) 215p., $49.50. Written for those responsible for the evaluation, planning, and implementation of optical information systems for data and document storage.

Rewritable Optical Storage Technology. Judith Paris Roth. (Meckler, 1990.) 150p., $45. Overview of the rewritable optical storage technology: drives, media, and systems.

The Second Generation of CD-ROM. (Information Industry Association, 1990.) $55.95. Outlines what corporations should know about CD-ROM.

Journals

Baumbach, Donna. "CD-ROM: Information at Your Fingertips!" **School Library Media Quarterly, 18** (3), 142-49, Spring 1990. (EJ 410 585.) Briefly describes CD-ROM technology and discusses the possible impact of this technology on school library media centers.

Bayard-White, Claire, editor. "Multimedia Conference on Interactive CD: London, England, June 18-19, 1990." **The Videodisc Monitor,** July-August 1990, 32. Provides a summary of the conference.

Belanger, Anne-Marie, and Sandra D. Hoffman. "Factors Related to Frequency of Use of CD-ROM: A Study of ERIC in an Academic Library." **College and Research Libraries, 51** (2), 153-62, March 1990. (EJ 410 636.) Describes a study that investigated factors associated with frequency of use of ERIC CD-ROM in an academic library, including gender, age, level of familiarity with computers, and level of study.

Dickinson, Gail. "Choosing a CD-ROM Encyclopedia: How to Critically Evaluate the Product." **Library Software Review, 9** (5), September-October 1990. Provides criteria for the critical evaluation of CD-ROM encyclopedias.

Hoekema, Jim. "Getting Sensible about CD-I and DVI." **The Videodisc Monitor,** November 1990, 24. Discusses the fact that CD-I and DVI have a lot in common and that other new technologies will come along as well to muddy the waters even further.

Melin, Nancy. "CD-ROM Roundup." **Library Journal, 115** (2), 45-50, February 1, 1990. (EJ 407 242.) Describes new CD-ROM products, services, software and data enhancements, and products with unique or interesting features.

Reeve, Vici, and April Rivers. "Fifth International CD-ROM Conference and Exposition: San Francisco CA, February 27-March 1 1990." **The Videodisc Monitor,** May 1990, 12. Provides a summary of the conference.

Zink, Steven D. "Planning for the Perils of CD-ROM." **Library Journal, 115** (2), 51-55, February 1, 1990. (EJ 407 243.) Argues that because of its meteoric entrance into the library marketplace, too few institutions have reviewed the implications of CD-ROM before making their purchases.

COMMUNICATION SYSTEMS

Reference Tools/ERIC Documents

National Directory of Bulletin Systems 1990. Patrick R. Dewey. (Meckler, 1990.) 114p., $39.95. A comprehensive directory of international bulletin boards available.

TVOntario and the School System. A Report Based on Case Studies in Nine School Boards. Donna Sharon et al. (ED 317 221. EDRS, 1990.) Through a series of case studies, this report examines the varied connections between selected Ontario schools and the TVOntario programs and services designed to support teaching and learning.

Books

The Complete Handbook of Personal Computer Communications. 3d ed. Alfred Glossbrenner. (St. Martin's, 1990.) 405p., $18.95. Covers every kind of communication that can be done with a computer, from online shopping to scholarly research.

Integrating Telecommunications into Education. Nancy Roberts et al. (Prentice-Hall, 1990.) 224p., $30.60. This is a complete manual guiding students through the entire process of establishing telecommunications in either a classroom or home. Includes classroom applications in several disciplines, as well as practical information for working with school administrators.

Interactive Television. Diana Gagnon. (Arlen Communications, 1990.) $495. This comprehensive study probes the operations of more than two dozen companies that are developing programs and technology for interactive TV.

Journals

Ely, Donald P. "Protocols and Processes for Promoting Interactive Cross-Cultural Media Transfer." **Educational Media International, 26** (1), 7-12, March 1989. (EJ 394 021.) Discusses interaction and the need for considering cultural dimensions when translating instructional materials between nations. A taxonomy of educational objectives for interaction is introduced and Stolovitch's procedures for learning verification and revision LVRO are discussed.

Graves, Bill. "Classroom Tune In." **School Administrator, 47** (3), 8-11, 14-16, March 1990. (EJ 403 830.) As television programs and networks proliferate, many districts and education groups are drafting guidelines to help teachers choose high-quality, curriculum-related programs.

Hackman, Michael Zane, and Kim B. Walker. "Instructional Communication in the Televised Classroom: The Effects of System Design and Teacher Immediacy on Student Learning and Satisfaction." **Communication Education, 39** (3), 196-206, July 1990. This study was designed to investigate the effects of conveyance system design and social presence, in the form of teacher immediacy behavior, on perceived student learning and satisfaction in the televised classroom.

Kaplan, George. "TV's Version of Education (and What to Do about It)." **Phi Delta Kappan, 71** (5), K1-K12, January 1990. (EJ 400 587.) While television's potential as the nation's "great educator" is expanding, messages about schooling come across as colorless and forgettable. Cable television could make the difference.

Kubey, Robert, and Reed Larsen. "The Use and Experience of the New Video Media among Children and Young Adolescents." **Communication Research, 17** (1), 107-30, February 1990. (EJ 406 646.) Examines the use and experience of music videos, video games, and videocassettes among children and young adolescents.

Lunde, Ken R. "Using Electronic Mail as a Medium for Foreign Language Study and Instruction." **CALICO Journal, 7** (3), 68-78, March 1990. (EJ 407 119.) The Japanese character set is used to describe electronic mail utilization in sending and receiving foreign character sets. Because electronic mail is fast, inexpensive, storable, and printable, it can accelerate the traditional letter-writing process, as well as act as a medium of instruction in correspondence courses and sending other computerized information.

Rickelman, Robert J., and William A. Henk. "Telecommunications in the Reading Classroom (Reading Technology)." **Reading Teacher, 43** (6), 418-19, February 1990. (EJ 405 106.) Discusses the three required components for telecommunications: a modem, software, and a computer. Reviews the advantages of CompuServe.

Rudinow, Joel. "Channel One Whittles Away at Education." **Educational Leadership, 47** (4), 70-73, December-January 1989/1990. (EJ 400 506.) Whittle Communications's vaunted Channel One, a news and information station for high school audiences, is long on MTV-style flash and short on true educational value. The best defense against commercially sponsored television in the schools is organized, informed, and sustained resistance by educators, especially classroom teachers.

Rukeyser, William S. "No Hidden Agenda: A Response to Rudinow." **Educational Leadership, 47** (4), 74-75, December-January 1989/1990. (EJ 400 507.) Refutes Joel Rudinow's critique of the Whittle Educational Network, especially his remarks concerning Channel One's availability, teacher viewing discretion, and commercials.

Wartella, Ellen, et al. "Television and Beyond: Children's Video Media in One Community." **Communication Research, 17** (1), 45-64, February 1990. (EJ 406 643.) Surveys children's access to media sources and assesses their diversity of content. Suggests broadcasting and videocassettes offer little diversity in children's content, whereas cable enhances programming choices.

COMPUTERS AND INSTRUCTIONAL USES OF COMPUTERS

Reference Tools/ERIC Documents

The Annual Guide to Highest-Rated Educational Software, 1991 Edition. Pre-School-Grade 12. (R. R. Bowker, 1990.) 130p., $26.95. Identifies more than 375 programs, from among 8,000 programs evaluated, that have received high grades in the past 12 months from 32 respected evaluation services.

Directory of Educational Objectives and Networkable Software. (IBM, 1990.) $10.75. Helps educators match their curriculum objectives with available courseware. Lists networkable courseware from IBM and other vendors.

Making Informed Decisions: Management Issues Influencing Computers in the Classroom. James Strickland. (ED 316 866. EDRS, 1990.) 15p. Paper presented at the annual spring conference of the National Council of Teachers of English (Colorado Springs, Colorado, March 8-10, 1990).

Teaching and Learning Mathematics in the 1990s: 1990 Yearbook. Thomas J. Cooney et al. (ED 317 412. EDRS, 1990.) 256p. This yearbook includes 28 articles related to teachers and students of mathematics education and their changing roles.

Writing with a Microcomputer in Grade One: A Study in Collaboration. Sydney Butler et al. (ED 314 763. EDRS, 1990.) 23p. A case study explores the composing processes of two first-grade students to determine the role of the computer as a learning tool in the first grade classroom.

Books

AppleWorks for Educators: A Beginning and Intermediate Workbook. Linda Rathje. (ISTE, 1990.) 265p., $26.95. Covers version 3.0 and helps the educator quickly master the most recent enhancements.

Beginning to Read: Thinking and Learning about Print. Marilyn Jager Adams. (MIT, 1990.) 504p., $29.95. A review of phonics and early reading instruction from the Center for the Study of Reading, a group sponsored by the Office of Educational Research and Improvement.

The Best of Research Windows: Trends and Issues in Educational Computing. Betty Collis. (ISTE, 1990.) 94p., $12.95. Based on four years of reviewing research for her popular column in *The Computing Teacher*, Betty Collis pulls it all together. Identifies key trends and issues relevant for all computer-using educators.

Computer-Assisted Instruction: A Synthesis of Theory, Practice, and Technology. Esther R. Steinberg. (Lawrence Erlbaum, 1990.) 300p., $45. This volume, the second of a two-volume series, presents a theoretical framework and background for designing computer-assisted instruction (CAI).

Computers in Education. Reza Azarmsa. (Educational Technology, 1990.) $19.95. A textbook for introductory college courses and for in-service classes for teachers. Covers the full range of current applications of computers in schooling.

Computers, Thinking, and Social Studies. Gene E. Rooze and Terry Northup. (Libraries Unlimited, 1989.) 258p., $27.50. Discussion of newly emerging applications of the computer for the classroom, such as CAI, databases, telecommunications, word processing, and desktop publishing.

Educational Computing: Principles and Applications. Resa Azarmsa. (Educational Technology, 1990.) $19.95. Provides a comprehensive view of educational computing and discusses basic information related to computer literacy.

Evaluating Computer Integration in the Elementary School: A Step by Step Guide. Richard Mowe. (ISTE, 1990.) 71p., $15. A guidebook to help elementary teachers, computer coordinators, and principals integrate computers into their curriculum.

Strategies for Effective Instruction. (Business Videoworks, 1990.) A series of four videotapes. The tapes were produced in league with the National Staff Development Council.

Teaching with Computers: A New Menu for the '90's. Mary Jo Langhorne et al. (Oryx Press, 1989.) 224p., $25. Provides an overview of the educational computing field and offers guidelines for planning and for decision making associated with major computer-related issues.

Young Children and Computers. Charles Hohmann. (High/Scope, 1990.) 112p., $15. A guide to selecting hardware and software appropriate for use with three- to five-year-olds.

Journals

Brittain, David. "A Model State for Technology." **School Administrator. Special Issue: Computer Technology Report, 1990**, 31, 1990. (EJ 403 773.) Florida Department of Education promotes computer use in schools through various programs. Florida business and industry allocates efforts and resources to support education.

Brooks, Susan. "Is Your Computer Working Hard, or Hardly Working?" **Instructor, 100** (3), 45-51, October 1990. If you're not getting the most from your classroom computers, maybe you'd better develop a plan. This article will show you how.

Burns, M. Susan, et al. "A Computer in My Room." **Young Children, 45** (2), 62-67, January 1990. (EJ 402 925.) Answers early childhood teachers' questions concerning the addition of a computer to the classroom setting.

Frisse, Mark E. "The Case for Hypermedia." **Academic Medicine, 65** (1), 17-19, January 1990. (EJ 402 646.) Hypermedia technology represents a new and extremely significant paradigm for the future of computer use.

Hawkridge, David. "Who Needs Computers in Schools, and Why?" **Computers and Education, 15** (1-3), 1-6, 1990. (EJ 407 227.) Discusses several rationales for the use of computers in elementary and secondary schools and describes differences in policies and needs in developing and industrial countries.

Kull, Judith A., and Joyce Carter. "Wrapping in the First Grade Classroom." **Computing Teacher, 17** (4), 12-13, 52, December-January 1989/1990. (EJ 405 602.) Describes an action research study that observed the use of Logo by first grade children in public schools.

Malaney, Gary D., and Quint Thurman. "Key Factors in the Use and Frequency of Use of Microcomputers by College Students." **Journal of Educational Technology Systems, 18** (2), 151-60, 1989-1990. (EJ 405 695.) Describes study that was conducted at the University of Massachusetts at Amherst to examine variables that determine which undergraduates use microcomputers and how often they use them.

McGinnis, Tommye Sue. "Computer Simulations on a No-Frills Budget." **Vocational Education Journal, 65** (3), 31-32, 40, April 1990. (EJ 404 761.) Describes a cost-effective way to create an effective simulation for students that teaches them how personal computers are used in the workplace.

Ross, David. "Computer Managed Learning for Technology Programs." **Technology Teacher, 49** (6), 33-34, March 1990. (EJ 404 688.) Discusses computer-managed learning (CML), which uses a microcomputer to present educational material to students.

Stone, Antonia. "How to Make All Children 'Techno-Able.'" **School Administrator, Special Issue: Computer Technology Report**, 28-29, 1990. (EJ 403 771.) The issue of equitable access regarding technology has three components: (1) access, (2) countering "techno-phobia," and (3) creating the "techno-able."

Symington, Lois. "Pre-Computer Skills for Young Children." **Exceptional Parent, 20** (1), 36, 38, January-February 1990. (EJ 405 314.) This article outlines a series of skills young children with disabilities need to effectively use computers later in life and provides exercises to promote these skills.

Watson, Deryn M. "The Classroom vs. the Computer Room." **Computers and Education, 15** (1-3), 33-37, 1990. (EJ 407 229.) Discussion of the use of microcomputers in secondary schools in the United Kingdom focuses on classroom use versus separate computer laboratories.

DATABASES, ONLINE SEARCHING, NETWORKING, TELECOMMUNICATIONS

Reference Tools/ERIC Documents

Computer-Readable Databases. 1990. 6th ed. Kathleen Young Marcaccio and Martha E. Williams, editors. 1,350p., $165. (Gale Research, 1990.) Contains descriptions of more than 5,000 publicly available databases including online and transactional databases, CD-ROM databases, electronic bulletin boards, offline files available for batch processing, and databases on magnetic tape and diskette.

Encyclopedia of Telecommunications. Vol. 1. Fritze E. Froehlich. (Marcel Dekker, 1990.) 553p., $160. When completed, this basic reference set will include eight volumes.

Books

Democratizing Information: Online Databases and the Rise of End-User Searching. Bryan Pfaffenbaerger. (ALA, 1989.) 208p., $32.50. Explores two issues of vital importance: the potential of online database technology for making information widely available and the social and economic significance of end-user searching.

Online 89 Information: 13th International Online Meeting. Proceedings. (Learned Information, 1989.) 610p., $90. Meeting was held December 12-14, 1989, in London, England. Contains more than 57 papers.

Online Searching: A Primer. 3d ed. Carol H. Fenichel and Thomas H. Hogan. (Learned Information, 1989.) $16.95. Provides an overview of the online industry and goes on to explain the basics of searching techniques.

Planning for Telecommunications: A School Leader's Primer. Karen Kitchen. (National School Boards Association, 1989.) Written for administrators, this book will help school library media specialists understand the issues relating to technology and provide needed information for decision making.

Telecommunications: Make the Connection. Chris Clark et al. (ISTE, 1990.) $10. Details what telecommunications is, how to apply it in your classroom, what hardware and software are needed, and what services are available.

Telecommunications for Learning. Educational Technology Magazine Staff, editors. (Educational Technology, 1990.) 175p., $27.95. Comprises 40 articles dealing with the broad usage of telecommunications technologies in education and training.

Journals

Deming, Mary P., and Maria Valeri-Gold. "Databases: A Hidden Treasure for Language-Arts Instruction (Computers in the Classroom)." **English Journal, 79** (2), 69-70, February 1990. (EJ 406 662.) Discusses how computerized databases can be used successfully in the language arts classroom.

Eddison, Betty. "Teaching Information Professionals about Database Design." **Database, 13** (1), 33-37. February 1990. (EJ 405 724.) Discusses the need for information science schools to prepare graduates for computer use and database design and reports the findings of a survey of schools that examined the extent to which such courses are taught and the content of those courses.

Friedman, Charles P., et al. "Computer Databases as an Educational Tool in the Basic Sciences." **Academic Medicine, 65** (1), 15-16, January 1990. (EJ 402 645.) The University of North Carolina School of Medicine developed a computer database, INQUIRER, containing scientific information in bacteriology, and then integrated the database into routine educational activities for first-year medical students in their microbiology course.

Riggs, Howard N. "Computer Data Base Activities in Upper Elementary School Social Studies: A Stimulus for Curriculum Integration." **History and Social Science Teacher, 25** (3), 145-50, Spring 1990. (EJ 407 754.) Maintains that the use of a microcomputer database is useful for developing integrative learning activities with social studies as the core. Defines a database and recommends ways to help children create and use one, giving an example of a database project.

DISTANCE EDUCATION

Reference Tools/ERIC Documents

Distance Education: Selected References. Kenda C. Wise. (Maxwell Air Force Base, 1990.) 15p. A special bibliography that contains some excellent references on distance education. This volume is contained in volume 292 of the Air University Library.

Educational Broadcasting and Distance Education as a Strategy for Revitalizing Education of the Disadvantaged. Motilal Sharma. (ED 317 837. EDRS, 1990.) Paper presented at the Symposium on Educational Broadcasting for More Effective Distance Education in the 1990s: Strategies and Approaches (Manila, Philippines, March 28-30, 1990).

The Effects of Distance Learning: A Summary of Literature. M. G. Moore and M. M. Thompson. (American Center for the Study of Distance Education, 1990.) Consists of an annotated bibliography of literature concerning the effectiveness of distance education. Reviews research of the 1980s.

Teletraining Directory. 1990 Edition. (Virginia A. Ostendorf, 1990.) 375p., $100. Lists more than 100 vendors, 274 user organizations, and 212 individual instructors.

Books

Contemporary Issues in American Distance Education. Michael G. Moore. (Pergamon, 1990.) 380p. Attempts to draw an overall picture of the rapid growth and achievements in the field of American distance education and the problems and issues that confront it.

Critical Reflections on Distance Learning. Terry Evans and Daryl Nation, editors. (Falmer, 1989.) 272p., $55. Provides a range of practical evaluative descriptions, which are themselves subjected to an evaluative scrutiny.

Distance Education Systems. Sergio Elliot. (UNIPUB, 1990.) 80p., $9. Economic and Social Development Paper No. 67.

Teleclass Teaching: A Resource Guide. 2d ed. Thomas E. Cyrs and Frank A. Smith. (New Mexico State University, 1990.) $38. A comprehensive text on how to teach on television.

Journals

Beaudoin, Michael. "The Instructor's Changing Role in Distance Education." **American Journal of Distance Education, 4** (2), 21-29, 1990. With the likelihood of significant increases in distance learning, enrollments within the next decade will have a profound impact on faculty members' instructional roles.

Hanson, Gordon. "Distance Education and Educational Needs: A Model for Assessment." **Media and Methods, 27** (1), 14-19, September/October 1990. Discusses how education can be transported into the classroom via satellite, cable, and broadcast technologies.

Latham, S., et al. "Mitchell College/IBM Distance Learning Project. **Research in Distance Education, 2** (1), 7-14, January 1990. (EJ 401 877.) At Mitchell College of Advanced Education (Australia), 15 students took a course in methods and statistics in social sciences and 15 took a course in computing using Pascal on an interactive, microcomputer-based distance education system. Results are covered in the paper.

O'Malley, Claire E., and Eileen Scanlon. "Computer-Supported Collaborative Learning: Problem Solving and Distance Education." **Computers and Education, 15** (1-3), 127-36, 1990. (EJ 407 233.) Discusses cooperative problem solving among open university physics and math students and describes three studies that investigated how to design effective computer-based support for collaborative learning in distance education.

Rawson, James H. "Simulation at a Distance Using Computer Conferencing." **Educational & Training Technology International, 27** (3), 284-92, August 1990. Computer-based conferencing, a type of computer-mediated communication, can provide geographically dispersed students the educational opportunity equivalent to that offered in the traditional classroom environment.

Wagner, Ellen D. "Looking at Distance Education through an Educational Technologist's Eyes." **American Journal of Distance Education, 4** (1), 53-68, 1990. Addresses the relationship that exists between the fields of distance education and educational technology, a discipline focused on performance.

Warriner-Burke, Helen P. "Distance Learning: What We Don't Know Can Hurt Us." **Foreign Language Annals, 23** (2), 129-33, April 1990. (EJ 407 113.) Raises a series of questions concerning the use of distance learning in second-language instruction, including (1) why use distance learning, (2) what are the limitations to distance learning, and (3) what does research say about the use of distance learning in the second-language classroom?

EDUCATIONAL RESEARCH

Reference Tools/ERIC Documents

The Importance of Computer Programming Skills to Educational Researchers. Stephen Lawson. (ED 317 569. EDRS, 1990.) 24p. A paper presented at the annual meeting of the Southwest Educational Research Association (Austin, Texas, January 25-27, 1990).

The International Encyclopedia of Curriculum. Arieh Lewry, editor. (Pergamon, 1990.) 800p., $115. Provides a systematic review of curriculum-related knowledge worldwide. Contains more than 280 articles on a wide range of curriculum topics.

The International Encyclopedia of Education, Supplementary Volume Two. Torsten Husen and T. Neville Postlethwaite, editors. (Pergamon, 1990.) 670p., $225. Contains 170 new and important articles on educational policy, process, and practice throughout the world.

The International Encyclopedia of Educational Evaluation. Herbert J. Walberg and Geneva D. Haeretel, editors. (Pergamon, 1990.) 650p., $110. Provides a current and comprehensive treatment of evaluation theories and practices in education. Contains more than 150 articles written by international authorities in educational evaluation.

Books

Handbook of Educational Ideas and Practices. Noel Entwistle, editor. (Routledge, 1990.) 1,140p., $89.95. This comprehensive, international handbook includes 101 chapters divided into four large sections.

Informal Reasoning & Education. James F. Voss et al. (Lawrence Erlbaum, 1990.) 500p. Focuses specifically on the question of how logic occurs in school activities and how students acquire such reasoning skills.

Research Methods in Education. 3d ed. Louis Cohen and Lawrence Manion. (Routledge, 1990.) 432p., $27.50. Written to cover the whole range of methods currently employed by educational researchers.

Restructuring America's Schools. Anne Lewis. (AASA, 1990.) $15.95. Takes a hard, objective look at restructuring.

Systems Design of Education. A Journal to Create the Future. Bela H. Banathy. (Educational Technology, 1990.) $29.95. Groundbreaking work describing how to create schools for the future. The emphasis is on systemic change rather than surface-level restructuring.

Journals

Bowers, Dennis, and Chia Tsai. "HyperCard in Educational Research: An Introduction and Case Study." **Educational Technology, 30** (2), 19-24, February 1990. (EJ 407 276.) Describes the HyperCard program and explains HyperTalk, the programming language it uses.

Peper, John B. "Exciting Dynamics Occur When Education Is a Leading Edge Industry." **School Administrator. Special Issue: Computer Technology Report**, 23-24, 1990. (EJ 403 769.) Jefferson County (Colorado) schools have used computers in instructional programs for 25 years, but with limited student access until the district purchased its first lab.

Peterson, Kenneth D. "DOSSIER: A Computer System Simulation of Professional Judgments on Schoolteacher Promotion." **Journal of Educational Research, 83** (3), 134-39. (EJ 406 324.) In a simulation study, 12 teachers submitted performance dossiers that were judged by 26 human experts and by a computer expert system. Both the judges and the expert system made promotion decisions and ranked the dossiers by quality. The expert system showed high levels of agreement with the human judges.

EDUCATIONAL TECHNOLOGY

Reference Tools/ERIC Documents

Directory of Expert Systems Tools. Anne Morris and Anne Reed, editors. (Learned Information, 1989.) 150p., $76.50. Comprehensive, up-to-date, and state-of-the-art surveys of expert system shells, AI tool kits, and machine learning systems available.

Educational Media and Technology Yearbook 1990. Brenda Branyan-Broadbent and R. Kent Wood, editors. (Libraries Unlimited, 1990.) 403p., $50. *EMTY 90* continues to provide broad coverage of new developments in educational media, technology, and communications.

Evaluation and Educational Technology: A Selected Bibliography. Robert D. Tennyson and Ronald O. Anderson. (Educational Technology, 1990.) 65p., $14.95. Areas of the field covered include methodology, evaluation methods and models, measurement application, evaluation of computer-based software and programs, evaluation of curricular programs, and evaluation of instructional materials.

Visual Literacy: A Selected Bibliography. Rebecca Clemente and Roy M. Bohlin. (Educational Technology, 1990.) $14.95. Some of the areas covered include aesthetic education, general visual literacy, television viewing, visual aids, and visual stimuli.

Books

Educational Technology: A Planning and Resource Guide Supporting Curriculum. James E. Eisele and Mary Ellin Eisele. (Garland, 1990.) 288p., $40. This guide offers the educator practical guidance in the classroom and other educational applications of computer, videodisc, and telecommunications technology.

Educational Technology: Challenging Issues. M. Mukhopadhyay, editor. (Sterling, 1990.) 225p. Includes bibliographies and index.

Educational Technology: Old Wine in New Bottles. (Videocassette, 80 minutes.) Sharon Rogers et al. (Capitol Television, 1990.) Address delivered on March 8, 1990, at the Information Options for the 90's technology fair.

Formative Evaluation for Educational Technologies. Barbara N. Flagg. (Lawrence Erlbaum, 1990.) 272p., $34.50. The book is divided into three major sections: concepts, practice, and methods. Provides a description of formative evaluations of a variety of electronic media.

Instructional Technology. Gary Anglin. (Libraries Unlimited, 1990.) 300p., $35. Presents a comprehensive view of the field—a state-of-the-art overview of education technology today.

Paradigms Regained: The Use of Illuminative, Semeiotic, and Post-Modern Criticism as Modes of Inquiry in Educational Technology. Denis Hlynka and John C. Belland, editors. (Educational Technology, 1990.) 525p., $39.95. Provides those in the fields of education technology and mass communications an opportunity to explore criticism as an alternative paradigm for studying media/technology in education.

12th Annual Proceedings of Selected Research Paper Presentations at the 1990 AECT Annual Convention. (AECT, RTD, 1990.) 700p., $35. Contains more than 50 research papers written by leaders in the field.

Journals

Cook, E. K. "The Use of Macintosh Authoring Languages in Effective Computer-Assisted Instruction." **Journal of Educational Technology Systems, 18** (2), 109-22, 1989-1990. (EJ 405 693.) This survey of authoring languages that are used in computer-assisted instruction (CAI) highlights recent developments in Macintosh authoring languages and discusses their use in courseware development.

Dede, Christopher. "What Will the Future Hold for Schools and Technology?" **School Administrator. Special Issue: Computer Technology Report**, 39-40, 1990. (EJ 403 778.) Education will experience future transformations in the face of changing societal and workplace needs. The technology-intensive paradigm for education will completely reshape today's classrooms and schools.

Fawson, E. Curtis, and Don C. Smellie. "Technology Transfer: A Model for Public Education." **Educational Technology, 30** (4), 19-25, April 1990. Discusses the proper use of technology in the classroom and how this enables the learner to take an active role.

Main, Robert G., and Lily Roberts. "Educational Technology in the California Public Schools: A Statewide Survey." **Educational Technology, 30** (12), 7-19, December 1990. The results of the study are now online in the CTP Training Resource in Education (TRIE) database and provide empirical evidence to assist the California Department of Education and the state legislature in policy formation and decision making regarding program support and budget actions.

Vasilakis, John E. "Are Your Schools Ready for the 21st Century?" **School Business Affairs, 56** (1), 26-29, January 1990. (EJ 402 307.) Although changes in instructional technology and population growth are the usual reasons school districts approach master planning as a tool for identifying and managing these changes, environmental concerns play a role. A dozen tips for developing a master plan are provided.

ELECTRONIC PUBLISHING

Reference Tools/ERIC Documents

The Electronic Journal: Promises and Predicaments. Technical Report No. 3. Michael Ehringhaus. (ED 316 732. EDRS, 1990.) 29p. *New Horizons in Adult Education* is an electronic journal started in the fall of 1987 by the Syracuse University Kellogg Project. In the Spring of 1989, the project surveyed readers of New Horizons to find out how they were reacting to the journal and its methods of transmission.

Books

Desktop Publishing for Librarians. Walt Crawford. (G. K. Hall, 1990.) 403p., $38.50. Uses actual library publications to illustrate the appropriate uses for a desktop system, the principles involved in creating desktop documents, and the mechanics of layout and design.

The Electronic Text: Learning to Write, Read, and Reason with Computers. William V. Costanzo. (Educational Technology, 1989.) 301p., $32.95. Begins with an overview of the entire range of software and then probes more deeply into the worlds of computer-managed reading, interactive fiction, word processing, writing aids, programming, natural language processing, and artificial intelligence.

The Presentation Design Book: Projecting a Good Image with Your Desktop Computer. Margaret Y. Rabb, editor. (Ventana Press, 1990.) 240p., $24.95. Designed to be used with any combination of software and hardware, the book teaches basic techniques for producing attractive, persuasive slides, overheads, handouts, and screen shows.

Text Displays: Analysis and Systematic Design. George L. Gropper. (Educational Technology, 1990.) $37.95. Describes a detailed text display model, setting forth principles of how text displays work and what makes them effective.

Journals

Glushko, Robert J. "Designing a Hypertext Electronic Encyclopedia." **Bulletin of the American Society for Information Science, 16** (3), 14-16, 21-22. (EJ 407 190.) Identifies five design requirements for electronic encyclopedias, based on the content and structure of printed encyclopedias and the uses that people make of them.

Quinn, Judy, editor. "Visions of the '90s." **Library Journal, 115** (3), 137, 141-62, February 15, 1990. (EJ 407 289.) Five articles present the views of editors, publishers, librarians, and distributors on the future of book publishing and libraries.

Schuman, Patricia Glass. "Reclaiming Our Technological Future." **Library Journal, 115** (4), 34-38, March 1, 1990. (EJ 407 294.) Discusses the future of libraries and librarians, focusing on the effects of the information explosion and new technology. The topics considered include the information industry, electronic publishing, and the role of libraries.

Seiler, Lauren H. "The Future of the Scholarly Journal." **Modern Language Journal, 74** (1), 1-9, Spring 1990. (EJ 405 444.) Explores the impact of rapidly changing information technology on the future of scholarly journals. A discussion focuses on how such digital electronic media as word processors, fax machines, and electronic libraries could change journal format, printing medium, quality of information, centralization of journals, and costs.

INFORMATION SCIENCE

Reference Tools/ERIC Documents

Annual Review of Information Science and Technology. Vol. 25. Martha E. Williams, editor. (Learned Information, 1990.) 458p., $91. Continues to be the first port of call for those requiring up-to-date reviews on topics in information science.

Dictionary of Information Science. E. Burger. (Elsevier, 1990.) 904p., 2 vols. $202.50. Covers the general fundamentals of informatics, such as computer architecture and interactive processing. Terms are in English, German, French, and Russian.

Information Industry Directory. 1991. Bradley J. Morgan. (Gale, 1990.) 2,250p., 2 vols. $440. Offers comprehensive international coverage of computer-based information systems and services. Covers more than 4,500 information organizations, systems, and services.

Books

Education and Informatics—Worldwide: The State of the Art and Beyond. Frank Lovis, editor. (Jessica Kingsley, 1990.) 280p., $55. Looks at the current use of information technology in education and examines why the main objectives behind its introduction in this area have not been achieved.

Ideas and Information. Arno Penzias. (Touchstone/Simon and Schuster, 1990.) 224p., $8.95. Predicts that the reader will have a better understanding of the mind and technology and will be better equipped to select a suitable information strategy.

The Information Game: Ethical Issues in a Microchip World. Geoffrey Brown. (Humanities Press International, 1990.) 163p., $39.95. Introduces and explores such themes as moral neutrality, privacy rights, and ownership of intellectual property. Argues that technological determinism is false but that moral problems relative to technology arise from certain features of human nature and specific manifestations of human culture.

Information Literacies of the Twenty-first Century. Virgil Blake and Renee Tjoumas, editors. (G. K. Hall, 1990.) 544p., $29.95. Contains more than 40 papers addressing literacy in America. All were delivered at "Information Literacies of the Twenty-first Century," a national conference held in 1988 at Queens College, New York.

Information Science: The Interdisciplinary Contest. J. Michael Pemberton and Ann Prentice, editors. (Neal-Schuman, 1989.) 189p., $39.50. Includes papers presented at the annual conference of the Association for Library and Information Science Education held in January 1987.

Managing Information and Technology. (Learned Information, 1989.) 268p., $32. Contains the proceedings of the fifty-second annual meeting of the American Society for Information Science. Consists of 32 papers that were presented at the conference.

Megatrends 2000: Ten New Directions for the 1990s. J. Naisbitt and P. Aburdene. (William Morrow, 1990.) 384p., $21.95. This work picks up from the original approach of collecting and integrating massive amounts of data to develop likely global possibilities. The authors are not fainthearted in their conclusions.

Journals

Moursund, David. "Education for the Information Age." **School Administrator. Special Issue: Computer Technology Report**, 5-9, 1990. (EJ 403 764.) Three key questions are raised by the introduction of computers in education: (1) what constitutes a good education, (2) what should students now learn differently, and (3) how does technology help students. Answers are provided to these important questions.

Ross, Shirley L. "Information Skills in the Information Laboratory." **School Library Media Activities Monthly, 6** (7), 31-33, March 1990. (EJ 407 239.) Describes a process approach to library media skills instruction that would focus on the development of students' critical thinking skills and give them the ability to examine and utilize information.

Sankar, Chetan S. "A Framework to Integrate Applications, Management, and Movement of Information." **Information Management Review, 5** (3), 55-57, Winter 1990. (EJ 405 781.) Argues that organizations need to integrate information systems, database management systems, and telecommunications in order to effectively manage and move information.

Schaaf, Robert W. "Information Policies of International Organizations." **Government Publications Review, 17** (1), 49-61, January-February 1990. (EJ 407 249.) Examines the factors affecting the flow of information from international organizations to users in libraries.

INSTRUCTIONAL DESIGN, TRAINING

Reference Tools/ERIC Documents

Emerging Technologies and Instruction: Hypertext, Hypermedia, and Interactive Multimedia. William D. Milheim, editor. (Educational Technology, 1990.) $14.95. A selected bibliography.

What Cognitive Science May Learn from Instructional Design: A Case Study in Introductory Computer Programming. Jeroen J. G. Van Merrienboer. (ED 318 764. EDRS, 1990.) 12p. Paper presented at the annual meeting of the American Educational Research Association (Boston, Massachusetts, April 16-20, 1990).

Books

A Conversation on Instructional Design. M. David Merrill and Robert M. Gagne. (Utah State University, 1990.) Four VHS videocassettes (219 minutes). Discussions cover component display theory, component design theory, and other principles of instruction theory.

Grouprograms and Instruction: Applying Programmed Instruction Techniques to Group and Team Processes. N. R. Machiraju. (Educational Technology, 1990.) A three-cassette audiotape series. These six discussions focus on a new way of conducting group instruction, modeled on essential elements of the programmed instruction but allowing for divergent thinking and individualistic behavior within a group setting.

Human-Computer Interaction: A Design Guide. Mark K. Jones. (Educational Technology, 1990.) 160p., $21.95. This book can help professionals design and implement computing applications that are easy to learn and exciting to use.

Individualized Learning Using Instructional Modules. Richard W. Burns and Joe Lars Klingstedt. (Educational Technology, 1990.) A three-cassette audiotape series. These six lectures and discussions are designed for teachers and instructional developers who wish to learn how to go about designing individualized instructional modules.

Instructional Design: Principles and Applications. 2d ed. Leslie J. Briggs et al., editors. (Educational Technology, 1990.) 562p., $37.95. One of the most important books in the field of instructional design has been updated to reflect recent trends and developments in research and practice.

Research on Instruction: Design and Effects. S. Dijkstra et al. (Educational Technology, 1990.) $39.95. Provides a discussion of the progress and advances in the development of instructional design rules and the assessment of their usefulness.

The Systematic Design of Instruction. 3d ed. Walter Dick and Lou Carey. (HarperCollins, 1990.) 351p. The third edition has expanded the treatment of nearly every topic, especially goal analysis, instructional analysis, media selection, instructional strategies, and fomative evaluation.

Journals

Gagne, Robert M., and M. David Merrill. "Integrative Goals for Instructional Design." **Educational Technology Research and Development, 38** (1), 22-30, 1990. Affirm a need to identify learning goals that require an integration of multiple objectives.

Jonassen, David H. "Functions, Applications, and Design Guidelines for Multiple Window Environments." **Computers in Human Behavior, 5** (3), 185-94, 1989. (EJ 401 023.) Defines the functions of windows that are used as visual display techniques in computer software systems, reviews research on the effectiveness of window environments, discusses knowledge structures, and presents principles for designing windowed environments based on research findings and individual differences and screen design research.

Jonassen, David H. "Mapping the Structure of Research and Theory in Instructional Systems Technology." **Educational Technology, 29** (5), 7-10, May 1990. (EJ 395 528.) Discusses the field of instructional systems technology (IST) and the definition of its subject matter domain, describes cognitive mapping and semantic relatedness, and reports results of a study that generated a cognitive map to define the structure of research and theory in IST.

Jonassen, David H. "Performance Analysis." **Performance and Instruction, 28** (4), 15-23, April 1989. (EJ 394 034.) Discussion of the performance analysis process focuses on its use in traditional educational settings to prepare students as designers and trainers in a variety of settings.

Merrill, M. David, et al. "ID2 and Constructivist Theory." **Educational Technology, 30** (12), 52-54, December 1990. This is a response to an article by Kember and Murphy in the August 1990 issue of *Educational Technology*.

Merrill, M. David, et al. "Limitations of First Generation Instructional Design." **Educational Technology, 30** (1), 7-11, January 1990. (EJ 405 756.) Discusses the theories of instructional design methodologies and describes limitations for developing instruction for interactive, technology-based delivery systems.

Merrill, M. David, et al. "Second Generation Instructional Design (ID2)." **Educational Technology, 30** (2), 7-14, February 1990. (EJ 407 275.) Discusses the need for improved methodologies and tools to guide the design and development of interactive technology-based instructional material.

Merrill, M. David, et al. "The Second Generation Instructional Design Research Program." **Educational Technology, 30** (3), March 1990. (EJ 407 307.) Discusses a research program at Utah State University that is developing an advanced instructional design theory to help produce an integrated computer-based system.

Wilson, Brent G., and David H. Jonassen. "Hypertext and Instructional Design: Some Preliminary Guidelines." **Performance Improvement Quarterly, 2** (3), 34-49, 1989. (EJ 404 232.) Discusses the use of hypertext as an instructional tool and compares hypertext instruction with traditional instructional formats.

INSTRUCTIONAL MEDIA

Reference Tools/ERIC Documents

Audio Video Market Place, 1990. (R. R. Bowker, 1990.) 1,146p., $85. A comprehensive directory of audiovisual equipment and services for business, education, government, and the library world. Updated annually.

Directory of Instructional Programs, 1990/91. (Brown Publishing Network, 1990.) Set of seven directories, $89.95. Provides a listing of each publisher's customer service office and/or regional sales office for fast contact.

Educational Film and Video Locator. 4th ed. (R. R. Bowker, 1990.) 3,361p., 2 vols. $166.25. Brings together 51,900 selected educational films and videos, about 9,400 new to this edition, along with 13,000 additional media library holdings, providing users with a greater choice of rental sources.

The Educational Software Locator. 1989-1990. (The Educational Software Center, 1989.) Lists more than 11,800 software titles by publishers within subject area.

The Equipment Directory of Audio-Visual, Computer, and Video Products. 1990-91 Edition. (International Communications Industries Association, 1990.) 606p., $35. Features the latest technology in audiovisual, video, and computer-based equipment.

Guide to Free Computer Materials. 1990-91. 8th ed. Kathleen S. Nehmer, editor. (Educators Progress Service, 1990.) 431p., $36.95. A special section listing more than 2,000 shareware titles for Apple, Commodore, IBM, and Macintosh.

International Directory of Interactive Multimedia Producers. 1989 Edition. (Multimedia Computing, 1989.) 190p., $32. A directory of 350 companies and individuals in America, Europe, Japan, and elsewhere that specialize in the production of interactive presentations. Descriptions of specialties, experience, and contact information are included.

Only the Best. The Annual Guide to Highest-Rated Educational Software. 1991 Edition. Shirley Boes Neill and George W. Neill. (R. R. Bowker, 1990.) 144p., $29.95. Lists the best software available for preschool to grade 12. Provides detailed product descriptions and review information.

Software Resource Guide. Carol Truett. (Libraries Unlimited, 1990.) $28.50. Includes a full chapter on educational software and another on machine-specific software. Included in each chapter are listings of books, journals, and newsletters that publish information about microcomputer software.

Books

Cognition, Education, and Multimedia: Exploring Ideas in High Technology. Don Nix and Rand Spiro, editors. (Lawrence Erlbaum, 1990.) 214p. Focuses primarily on how people with ideas about education may actually get a computer to work for them with a minimal amount of difficulty.

Complete Audio-Visual Guide for Teachers & Media Specialists. Jacquelyn Peake and Carol Ann Tarter Peterson. (Parker Publishing, 1989.) 193p. A comprehensive compendium to effective usage of audiovisual techniques and procedures that add the excitement of sight and sound to elementary and secondary classroom presentations.

Cooperative Learning & Educational Media: Collaborating with Technology and Each Other. Dennis Adams et al. (Educational Technology, 1990.) 197p., $32.95. Designed to be a guide through the ideas, issues, trends, and possibilities for linking cooperative learning to educational technology.

Learning with Interactive Multimedia. Sueann Ambron and Kristina Hooper. (Microsoft, 1990.) 383p., $22.95. This collection of 20 articles compiled by Apple Computer Inc. explores the wide-ranging innovation of multimedia.

Managing Interactive Video/Multimedia Projects. Robert E. Bergman and Thomas V. Moore. (Educational Technology, 1990.) 215p., $39.95. Provides the necessary background for working with everyone involved in the project and helping them to work effectively with each other.

Media and You: An Elementary Media Literacy Curriculum. Donna Lloyd-Kolkin and Kathleen R. Tyner. (Educational Technology, 1991.) $29.95. A comprehensive curriculum guide for teachers and supervisors in elementary schools, this book is designed to provide students with the skills and knowledge they need in today's media-rich environment.

Micro Multimedia. John Gale. (Future Systems, 1990.) 220p., $1,490. This report describes the relevant markets for multimedia and provides industry statistics from 28 sources.

Planning, Producing, and Using Instructional Media. 6th ed. Jerrold E. Kemp and Don C. Smellie. (HarperCollins, 1989.) 395p., $43.50. Covers planning and producing instructional media.

Teaching the Media. Len Master. (Routledge, 1990.) 362p., $15.95. Critiques the inadequacies that have characterized media teaching in its fifty-year history, offering provocative suggestions toward a program of media literacy for the late twentieth century and beyond.

Using Video: Interactive and Linear Designs. Joseph W. Arwady and Diane M. Gayeski. (Educational Technology, 1989.) 178p., $34.95. Discusses the importance of good design in its treatment of 40 techniques that are at once creative and practical.

Visuals for Information. Ruane Pettersson. (Educational Technology, 1990.) 315p., $37.95. This encyclopedic analysis of the role of visuals in the evolving world of integrated information systems opens up new areas of research and practice for scholars and information specialists alike.

Who's Teaching the Kids. Curt Dahl. (Bonneville Media Communications, 1990.) Videocassette introducing "Skills for Growing," a values-based program for children in kindergarten through fifth grade.

Journals

Joiner, Elizabeth G. "Choosing and Using Videotexts." **Foreign Language Annals, 23** (1), 53-64, February 1990. (EJ 404 006.) A form is presented for choosing and using videotexts for video-based teaching.

Squires, Nancy, and Robin Inlander. "A Freireian-Inspired Video Curriculum for At-Risk High-School Students." **English Journal, 79** (2), 49-56, February 1990. (EJ 406 658.) Describes a video/language arts curriculum for at-risk students that is based on Paulo Freire's *Education for Critical Consciousness*.

LIBRARIES, MEDIA CENTERS, TECHNICAL APPLICATION

Reference Tools/ERIC Documents

Library and Information Science Annual (LISCA). Bohdan S. Wynar et al. (Libraries Unlimited, 1990.) 286p., $37.50. A comprehensive review source in library science, with thought-provoking essays on the state of the profession.

The School Librarian's Sourcebook. Claire Rudin. (R. R. Bowker, 1990.) 504p., $34.95. Highlights more than 270 books that meet the varied needs of school library media specialists.

School Library Media Annual, 1990. Jane Bandy Smith, editor. (Libraries Unlimited, 1990.) 384p., $29.50. Contains sections on the best books and software, state and national awards, research findings and projects in progress, and trends in automation.

Books

Cooperative Learning Activities in the Library Media Center. Lesley S. J. Farmer. (Libraries Unlimited, 1991.) 175p., $23.50. Provides middle school and senior high faculty with strategies to implement cooperative learning activities that will help students assimilate information skills and content knowledge concurrently, while sharpening critical thinking skills.

The Librarian, the Scholar, and the Future of the Research Library. Eldred Smith. (Greenwood Publishing, 1990.) 119p., $35. This work represents the first analytical discussion of the role of the research librarian and the scholar in the future.

Microcomputer Facilities in Schools. Leonard J. Espinosa. (Libraries Unlimited, 1990.) 140p., $23.50. Describes computer use in several model floor plans, taking into account traffic patterns, visual supervision, basic electricity requirements, and display and instruction needs.

Microcomputer Software Sources: A Guide for Buyers, Librarians, Programmers, Business People, and Educators. Carol Truett. (Libraries Unlimited, 1990.) 193p., $28.50. This work should serve as the most authoritative and comprehensive guide to microcomputer software sources available today.

Public Access CD-ROMs in Libraries: Case Studies. Linda Stewart et al. (Meckler, 1990.) 325p., $39.50. Presents more than 20 case studies from public, academic, school, and special libraries that have installed CD-ROM workstations in public access areas.

The Research of School Library Media Centers. Blanche Woolls, editor. (Libraries Unlimited, 1990.) 300p., $35. Contains papers presented at the Treasure Mountain Research Retreat (Park City, Utah, October 17-18, 1989).

Journals

Lora, Pat. "Getting Ready for the 21st Century. Media Moves into the Library Main-stream." **Wilson Library Bulletin, 64** (8), 30-33, April 1990. (EJ 407 329.) Describes the growing demand for video materials in public libraries and argues that libraries should develop policies for videos that are comparable to policies for print materials.

Mathews, Virginia H., et al. "Kids Need Libraries: School and Public Libraries Preparing the Youth of Today for the World of Tomorrow." **School Library Journal, 36** (4), 33-37, April 1990. (EJ 407 325.) Reviews issues identified by the White House Conference on Library and Information Services that related to the needs of youth and offers specific suggestions for ways in which libraries can meet those needs.

MICROFORMS AND MICROGRAPHICS

Reference Tools/ERIC Documents

Guide to Microforms in Print: 1990 Supplement. (Meckler, 1990.) A cumulative annual listing of microform titles comprising books, journals, newspapers, government documents, archival material, and collections that are currently available from micropublishing organizations throughout the world.

Microform Market Place, 1990/1991. (K. G. Saur Verlag, 1990.) 250p., $45. A comprehensive international directory to microform publishers that provides users with easier access to this specialized group of publishers.

Books

Preservation Microfilming: Planning & Production. Association for Library Collections & Technology Services. (ALA, 1989.) $12. Compiled from papers from the RTSD Preservation Microfilming Institute (New Haven, Connecticut, April 21-23, 1988).

Journals

Breuer, James E. "From Technology to Function. How an Imaging Association Is Coping with a Changing Environment." **Microform Review, 19** (3), 139-41, Summer 1990. Discusses how the Association for Information Image Management (AIIM) is dealing with technical changes in its field and how its members are responding to an evolving industry.

Hazen, Dan C. "Preservation in Poverty and Plenty: Policy Issues for the 1990s." **Journal of Academic Librarianship, 15** (6), 344-51. (EJ 405 784.) Discusses the growing emphasis on preservation in academic libraries and examines the assumptions underlying the prevalent approach of one-time reformatting using microforms.

Nicely, Chris. "Pricing and Micropublishing." **Microform Review, 19** (1), 17-19, Winter 1990. Contains a discussion of pricing issues with the ALA Micropublishing Committee.

Saffady, William. "An Introduction Microfacsimile: Concepts, Technology, and History." **Micrographics and Optical Storage Equipment Review, 14**, 1989. Microfacsimile — variously termed microimage transmission, video transmission of microimage, or video-micrographics — is a technology that scans microfilm images for transmission to remote workstations.

VIDEODISC TECHNOLOGY

Reference Tools/ERIC Documents

The Complete Interactive Video Courseware Directory. 1990 Edition. (Convergent Technologies Associates, 1990.) 440p., $70. Contains information on more than 360 interactive video courses.

Interactive Video Industry Directory. 1989-1990. (Video Industry Association, 1990.) 160p., $26.95. Lists the leading corporate developers and vendors of interactive multimedia for business, education, and government.

The New Video Encyclopedia. Larry Langman and Joseph Molinari. (Garland, 1990.) 328p., $59.95. Defines more than 1,500 terms related to videocassette recorders, video cameras, videodisc players, projection TV systems, satellite TV, and conventional TV sets.

Videodisc Compendium for Education and Training. (Emerging Technology Consultants, 1990.) $30. Features more than 1,000 videodiscs, related software, and CD titles in more than 40 subject areas for K-12, higher education, and adult training groups.

Books

Creating a Slice of Life: Producing a Generic Videodisc for Medical Education. A 90-minute videocassette reviewing the design and production process of this generic disc project—a visual database of 26,000 medical images from 25 institutions, produced by the University of Utah.

The Feasibility of Low-Cost Videodisc Repurposing. Scott Sayre and Rae Montgomery. (Telecommunications Development Center, University of Minnesota, 1990.) The latest title in a monograph series on telecommunication development. The report is available at no cost.

The Interactive Marketing Report. (ItMk, 1990.) 250p., $265. Completely covers this booming industry. Contains more than 100 tables and graphs plus six appendixes.

Interactive Optical Technologies in Educating and Training: Markets and Trends. Sandra Kay Helsel. (Meckler, 1990.) $39.50. Describes the current use of interactive optical technologies in the major education and training markets and then analyzes the trends that will affect the future use of interactive optical media.

Interactive Video Archive. Vol. 3. (AECT, 1990.) $45. Videocassette providing an overview of interactive video programs selected from the special interactive video showcase presentations held at the 1989 Association for Educational Communications and Technology's annual convention.

Journals

Bolton, J. P. R., et al. "The Water Videodisc: A Problem-Solving Environment." **Computers and Education, 15** (1-3), 165-72. (EJ 407 234.) Describes the development and evaluation of an interactive videodisc designed for open university students in a physics course that explores the physical properties of water.

Cohen, Kathleen. "So You Want to Make a Videodisc!" **Educational Technology, 30** (6), 35-38, June 1990. Describes how a professor of art history decided to make a videodisc and how he accomplished it.

Hudson, Brian. "Interactive Video in the Mathematics Classroom." **Mathematics in School, 19** (1), 4-7, January 1990. (EJ 407 677.) Describes the use of interactive video material for teaching mathematics using the doomsday system developed in England.

Pollak, Richard, and Rubyanna Pollak. "Laserdisc Technology Emerges into the 1990s." **Media and Methods, 27** (2), 18-19, November/December 1990. Provides an update to the world of videodisc technology.

Rubin, Joan, et al. "Survey of Interactive Language Discs." **CALICO Journal, 7** (3), 31-47, 50-56. (EJ 407 117.) A compilation of videodisc materials ready for use in language teaching and learning.

Whiteley, Jerry, and Joseph Roberts. "Josef Albers' 'Interaction Color': From Print to Interactive Multimedia." **Academic Computing, 4** (4), 6-11, January 1990. (EJ 407 245.) Describes the development of interactive multimedia courseware based on Josef Alber's book *Interaction of Color*.

Directory of Producers, Distributors, and Publishers

This directory provides, in one alphabetical listing, the names and addresses of producers, distributors, and publishers whose media-related products are mentioned in the Mediagraphy.

This arrangement saves space that would otherwise be required for duplications of addresses. At the same time, a useful directory is provided for quick reference by those requiring address information.

The directory itself is arranged alphabetically by principal name. Foreign and U.S. entries are interfiled.

Users of this list are reminded that addresses of this type change often. Accuracy of addresses was carefully checked — addresses are believed to be correct as of 1 January 1991.

Ablex Publishing Corp.
355 Chestnut Street
Norwood, NJ 07648

Acropolis Books, Ltd.
1250-22 Roger Bacon Drive
Reston, VA 22090

Addison-Wesley Publishing Co., Inc.
Route 128
Reading, MA 01867

Allyn & Bacon, Inc.
Subsidiary of Simon & Schuster
160 Gould Street
Needham Heights, MA 02194-2310

**American Association of School
Administrators (AASA)**
1801 North Moore Street
Arlington, VA 22209

**American Educational Research
Association**
1230 17th Street, NW
Washington, DC 20036

**American Center for the Study of
Distance Education**
Pennsylvania State University
University Park, PA 16803

American Library Association
50 East Huron Street
Chicago, IL 60611-2729

APT Books, Inc.
141 East 44 Street
Suite 511
New York, NY 10017

Arlen Communications, Inc.
7315 Wisconsin Avenue
Suite 600 East
Bethesda, MD 20814

**Association for Educational Communica-
tions and Technology**
Research and Theory Division
1025 Vermont Avenue
Suite 820
Washington, DC 20005

Bonneville Media Communications
179 Social Hall
Salt Lake City, UT 84111-1542

Brookline Books
P.O. Box 1046
Cambridge, MA 02238

Brown Publishing Network, Inc.
555 Washington Street
P.O. Box 82-738
Wellesley, MA 02181

Budgetbytes, Inc.
P.O. Box 2248
Topeka, KS 66609

Business Videoworks
A Division of Training Media, Inc.
601 Wythe Street 300
Alexandria, VA 22314

Cambridge University Press
40 West 20th Street
New York, NY 10011

Capitol Television Inc.
1909 Lyttonville Road
Silver Springs, MD 20910

Convergent Technologies Associates
97 Devonshire Drive
New Hyde Park, NY 11040-3635

**Educational Technology Publications,
Inc.**
720 Palisade Avenue
Englewood Cliffs, NJ 07632

Educational Testing Service
Publications Division
Rosedale Road
Princeton, NJ 08541

Educators Progress Service, Inc.
Department AZD
214 Center Street
Randolph, WI 53956

Elsevier Science Publishing Co., Inc.
A Subsidiary of Elsevier NDU NV
655 Avenue of the Americas
New York, NY 10010

Emerging Technology Consultants, Inc.
P.O. Box 12444
St. Paul, MN 55112

EPIE Institute
P.O. Box 839
Water Mill, NY 11976

Facts on File
Subsidiary of Commerce Clearing House
460 Park Avenue South
New York, NY 10016

The Falmer Press
see **Taylor & Francis Inc.**

Future Systems, Inc.
see **Multimedia Videodisc Monitor**

G. K. Hall
A Division of Macmillan
70 Lincoln Street
Boston, MA 02111

Gale Research, Inc.
Subsidiary of International Thomson
Publishing, Inc.
835 Penobscot Building
Detroit, MI 48226-4094

Garland Publishing
136 Madison Avenue
New York, NY 10016

Greenwood Publishing
8780 West Golf Road
Des Plaines, IL 60016

Grolier Electronic Publishing
Sherman Turnpike
Danbury, CT 06816

Gulf Publishing Co.
Book Division
Box 2608
Houston, TX 77252-2608

Harper & Row Publishers, Inc.
see **HarperCollins Publishers**

HarperCollins Publishers
10 East 53rd Street
New York, NY 10022

High/Scope Press
A Division of High/Scope Educational
Research Foundation
600 North River Street
Ypsilanti, MI 48198

Humanities Press International
171 First Avenue
Atlantic Highlands, NJ 07716-1289

IBM Corp.
Information Systems Group
National Accounts Division
1133 Westchester Avenue
White Plains, NY 10604

IEEE Computer Society Press
A Subsidiary of IEEE Computer Society
1730 Massachusetts Avenue, NW
Washington, DC 20036-1903

Information Industry Association
Suite 800
555 New Jersey Avenue, NW
Washington, DC 20001

Instrument Society of America
P.O. Box 12277
67 Alexander Drive
Research Triangle Park, NC 27709

**International Communications Industries
Association (ICIA)**
3150 Spring Street
Fairfax, VA 22031-2399

**International Society for Technology
in Education (ISTE)**
1787 Agate Street
Eugene, OR 97403-9905

ItMk
see **Multimedia & Videodisc Monitor**

Jessica Kingsley Publishers (UK)
see **UNIPUB**

John Wiley and Sons, Inc.
605 Third Avenue
New York, NY 10158

Jossey-Bass, Inc., Publishers
Subsidiary of Maxwell Communications
  Corp.
350 Sansome Street
San Francisco, CA 94104-9825

Kendall/Hunt Publishing Co.
Subsidiary of William C. Brown Co.,
  Publishers
2460 Kerper Blvd.
Dubuque, IA 52001

K. G. Saur Verlag
Post Fach 71 10 09
8000 Munich 71
Germany

Knowledge Industry Publications
Subsidiary of Knowledge Sciences Inc.
701 Westchester Avenue
White Plains, NY 10604

Langley Books, Inc.
6609 Rosecroft Plain
Falls Church, VA 22043-1828

Lawrence Erlbaum Associates, Inc.
365 Broadway
Hillsdale, NJ 07642

Learned Information, Inc.
143 Old Marlton Pike
Medford, NJ 08055

Libraries Unlimited, Inc.
P.O. Box 3988
Englewood, CO 80155-3988

Longman Publishing Group
A Division of Addison-Wesley
  Publishing Co.
Longman Building
95 Church Street
White Plains, NY 10601

Macmillan Publishing Co., Inc.
866 Third Avenue
New York, NY 10022

Marcel Dekker, Inc.
270 Madison Avenue
New York, NY 10016

Maxwell Air Force Base
Montgomery, AL 36112-5564

Meckler Corporation
11 Ferry Lane West
Westport, CT 06880

Merrill Publishing Company
A Division of Macmillan/McGraw-Hill
  School Publishing Co.
936 Eastwind Drive
Westerville, OH 43801

Microsoft Press
A Division of Microsoft Corp.
One Microsoft Way
Redmond, WA 98052-6399

MIT Press
55 Hayward Street
Cambridge, MA 02142

Multimedia & Videodisc Monitor
P.O. Box 26
Falls Church, VA 22040

Multimedia Computing Corp.
see **Multimedia & Videodisc Monitor**

National Interactive Video Center
24 Stephenson Way
London NW1 2HD
England

National School Boards Association
1680 Duke Street
Alexandria, VA 22314

Neal-Schuman Publishers, Inc.
23 Leonard Street
New York, NY 10013

New Mexico State University
Las Cruces, NM 88003

Nichols Publishing Co.
1 Harts Lane
Suite 1
East Brunswick, NJ 08816

Omnigraphics, Inc.
Penobscot Building
Detroit, MI 48226

Optical Publishing Association
1880 Mackenzie Drive
Suite 111
Columbus, OH 43220

Orange County Department of Education
200 Kalmus Drive
Costa Mesa, CA 92626

Oryx Press
4041 North Central
Suite 700
Phoenix, AZ 85012-3397

Oxford University Press, Inc.
200 Madison Avenue
New York, NY 10016

Parker Publishing Co.
see **Prentice Hall**

Pergamon Press, Inc.
Subsidiary of Maxwell Communications
    Corp.
Maxwell House
Fairview Park
Elmsford, NY 10523

Praeger Publishers
One Madison Avenue
New York, NY 10010

Prentice Hall
A Division of Simon & Schuster
Route 9W
Englewood Cliffs, NJ 07632

R. R. Bowker
A Division of Reed Publishing USA
245 West 17th Street
New York, NY 10011

Routledge, Chapman, and Hall, Inc.
Subsidiary of International Thomson
    Organization (ITO)
29 East 35th Street
New York, NY 10001-2291

Scott, Foresman
Subsidiary of HarperCollins Publishers
1900 East Lake Avenue
Glenview, IL 60025

St. Martin's Press
Subsidiary of Macmillan Publishers
    Ltd. (UK)
175 Fifth Avenue
New York, NY 10010

Sterling Publishing Co., Inc.
387 Park Avenue South
5th Floor
New York, NY 10016-8810

Stewart, Tabori & Chang, Publishers
Subsidiary of Brant Publications, Inc.
575 Broadway
New York, NY 10003

Taylor & Francis
79 Madison Avenue
New York, NY 10016

Touchstone Books
Subsidiary of Simon & Schuster
The Simon & Schuster Building
1230 Avenue of the Americas
New York, NY 10020

UNIPUB
Division of Kraus Organizations, Ltd.
4611-F Assembly Drive
Lanham, MD 20706-4391

University of Minnesota
Telecommunications Development Center
TDC 43 Classroom Office Building
1994 Buford Avenue
St. Paul, MN 55108

University of Oklahoma
Oklahoma Center for Continuing Profes-
    sional & Higher Education
Norman, OK 73019

Utah State University
Department of Instructional Technology
Logan, UT 84322-2830

Ventana Press
P.O. Box 2468
Chapel Hill, NC 27515

Video Industry Association
see **Multimedia & Videodisc Monitor**

Virginia A. Ostendorf, Inc.
P.O. Box 2896
Littleton, CO 80161-2896

William Morrow & Co.
Subsidiary of the Hearst Corporation
105 Madison Avenue
New York, NY 10016

Index

This index gives page locations of names of associations and organizations, authors, titles, and subjects. In addition, acronyms for all organizations and associations are cross-referenced to the full name. Please note that a classified list of U.S. organizations and associations appears on pages 175 to 180.

Association for the Development of Computer-
Based Instructional Systems, 20
Association of American Colleges, 192
Association of American Publishers, 193
Association of Audio-Visual Technicians, 193
Association of College and Research Libraries,
813
Association of Independent Video and Film-
makers and the Foundation for Inde-
pendent Video and Film, 193
Association of Indiana Media Educators, 168
Association of Specialized and Cooperative
Library Agencies, 183
Association of Systematics Collections, 193
Association of Teacher Educators, 193
ASTD. *See* American Society for Training
and Development
ASTS. *See* Arts and Sciences Teleconferencing
Service
ASWLC. *See* American Shortwave Listeners'
Club
ATE. *See* Association of Teacher Educators
Auburn University, 251
Audio Video Market Place, 1990, 336
Audio Visual Education Association of
California, 164
Audio-Visual Center, 167, 168
Audiovisual Committee (of the Public Library
Association), 183
Audio-Visual Instruction Directors of Indiana,
168
Audiovisual organizations, 193, 203, 210, 216
Audiovisual suppliers, 194
Authors' League of America, Inc., 193
Automobiles, and railroads, 9
AVEAC. *See* Audio Visual Education Asso-
ciation of California
AVID. *See* Audio-Visual Instruction Directors
of Indiana
Awards. *See* Scholarships, fellowships, and
awards
AWRT. *See* American Women in Radio and
Television
Azarmsa, Reza, 324

Banathy, Bela H., 329
Barry University, 256
Baumbach, Donna, 321
Bayard-White, Claire, 321
Beaudoin, Michael, 328
Beecher, Henry Ward, 8
Beginning to Read, 324
Behavioral sciences, organizations, 217
Belanger, Anne-Marie, 321
Bell, Terrel H., 6
Belland, John C., 331
Bergman, Robert E., 337
Bergwall Productions Inc., 194
Best of Research Windows, 324
Biglan, Barbara, 319

Bilingual education, organizations, 211
Biological collections, organizations, 193
Biomedical communications, organizations, 207
Blake, Virgil, 333
Blanchard, James, 113
Boards of education, organizations, 210
Bohlin, Roy M., 330
Boise State University, 258
Bolton, J. P. R., 340
Books in Print Plus, 315
Booksellers, organizations, 181
Boston College, 263
Boston University, 238, 263
Bowers, Dennis, 329
Bowsher, Jack, 6
Branyan-Broadbent, Brenda, 330
Breuer, James E., 339
Bridgewater State College, 263
Briggs, Leslie J., 334
Brigham Young University, 246, 275
Brittain, David, 325
Broadcasting. *See also* Radio; Television
organizations, 209, 210, 212, 213, 217,
218, 225
Brooks, Susan, 325
Brown, Geoffrey, 333
Brown, James W., 164
James W. Brown Publication Award,
297, 308
Buffalo State College, 279
BUGGY, 37
Burger, E., 333
Burns, Hugh L., 319
Burns, M. Susan, 325
Burns, Richard W., 334
Business communications, organizations, 204
Butler, Sydney, 324

CAB. *See* Canadian Association of Broad-
casters
Cable television. *See also* Television
organizations, 211, 220
CAI. *See* Computer-assisted instruction
California, 79-83
California, University of, at Berkeley, 231, 254
California, University of, at Los Angeles,
231, 254
California, University of, at Santa Barbara,
254
California State University—Chico, 252-53
California State University—Dominguez
Hills, 253
California State University—Los Angeles, 253
California State University—Northridge, 253
California State University—San Bernardino,
253
California Technology Project, 81
Canadian Association of Broadcasters, 225
Canadian Book Publishers' Council, 225
Canadian Broadcasting Corporation, 225